D1526937

THE DOSTOEVSKY ARCHIVE

Fyodor Mikhailovich Dostoevsky. An insignificant appear-
ance; the hair and the beard are reddish, the face skinny, thin,
with big bones; a mole on the right cheek. The eyes have a
grim expression; sometimes you see in his eyes suspiciousness
and distrust, but mostly thoughtfulness and sadness...

(E.N. OPOCHININ,
"Talking to Dostoevsky,
or My Notes in St. Petersburg,
1879–1881")

THE DOSTOEVSKY ARCHIVE

Firsthand Accounts of the Novelist
from Contemporaries' Memoirs
and Rare Periodicals

Most Translated into English for the First Time

---

with a Detailed Lifetime Chronology

and Annotated Bibliography

by PETER SEKIRIN

with an introduction by IGOR VOLGIN

McFarland & Company, Inc., Publishers
Jefferson, North Carolina, and London

Frontispiece: An 1880s portrait by N. Gusev, from a famous 1880 photograph by Panov

British Library Cataloguing-in-Publication data are available

Library of Congress Cataloguing-in-Publication Data

The Dostoevsky archive : firsthand accounts of the novelist from
  contemporaries' memoirs and rare periodicals, most translated
  into English for the first time, with a detailed lifetime
  chronology and annotated bibliography / [compiled] by Peter
  Sekirin ; with an introduction by Igor Volgin.
      p.   cm.
  Includes bibliographical references and index.
  ISBN 0-7864-0264-4 (library binding :
    50# and 70# alkaline papers) ∞
  1. Dostoyevsky, Fyodor, 1821–1881—Biography.
  2. Dostoyevsky, Fyodor, 1821–1881—Chronology.   3. Authors,
  Russian—19th century—Biography.   I. Sekirin, Peter.
  PG3328.D6425   1997
  891.73'3—dc21
  [B]   96-29656
                                                              CIP

Manufactured in the United States of America

McFarland & Company, Inc., Publishers
  Box 611, Jefferson, North Carolina 28640

"Verily, verily, I say unto you, except a corn of wheat fall into the ground and die, it abideth alone: but if it die, it bringeth forth much fruit."

John 12:24

Dostoevsky selected this verse as the epigraph for The Brothers Karamazov. *It also appears on his tombstone in St. Petersburg.*

ACKNOWLEDGMENTS

I would like to express my deepest and most sincere gratitude to the following people:

Professor Kenneth Lantz, Professor Ralph Bogert, Professor Christopher Barnes, Professor Ralph Lindheim, Professor Sergei Ponomareff and other professors and students from the Slavic Department at the University of Toronto who read portions of my manuscript and advised me at different stages of my work.

Professor Mario Valdez for his advice regarding the structure of the manuscript and the selection of a proper publisher, and for his encouraging remarks.

The Faculty of Arts and Sciences of the University of Toronto, headed by Dean Don Cohen, for supporting me with several grants and fellowships from 1992 to 1995.

Professor R. Johnson from the Center for Russian and East-European Studies at the University of Toronto, for assisting me with travel grants to the Library of Congress in Washington, D.C., in 1993.

Carol Peaker, who made a major contribution to the editing of the manuscript at the final stage. Our cooperation was very fruitful. It was due to her enthusiasm and dedication that the project was completed in time.

Robert Reid, Peter Gorelik, Lillias Allward and Brett Smith, who helped with editing and proofreading the manuscript and arranging copyright permissions.

Jim Temerty and Louise Temerty for assistance in legal matters and financial support of my research.

My colleagues in Russia, in particular Mrs. V. Akopjanova, director of the Dostoevsky Museum in Moscow, and the staff of the museum. Also the Archives of Literature and the Museum of Literature, both of which provided photographs.

The staff of the Manuscript Department of the Lenin State Library in Moscow, particularly including librarian Liudmila Riazanova, and the librarians from the Interlibrary Loan Department of the John Robarts Library in Toronto: Candy Cheung, Jane Lynch and Shamin Allani.

Oxford University Press, Alfred A. Knopf, and Farrar Straus & Giroux for their permissions to quote Dostoevsky translations.

My parents for their wisdom, patience and support.

CONTENTS

6. Three Love Stories in the 1860s, in Russia and Abroad.

*Between pages 178 and 179 are 16 pages of plates
containing 29 photographs and illustrations.*

7. Socialists Become "the Demons." *The Citizen, A Writer's Diary, The Idiot,* and *The Brothers Karamazov.* Friendship with the Royal Family.

PREFACE

The life story of Fyodor Dostoevsky is so unusual and impressive, so filled with exciting events, unbelievable coincidences and dramatic situations, that it could constitute a plot for one of his own novels. Years of poverty were followed by the overwhelming success of his first novel; his participation in the anti-government conspiracy and secret socialist circle led to years in Siberian prisons; yet by the end of his life he had acquired an enduring reputation as a prophet and one of the best Russian writers, and had developed a close personal friendship with the royal family. One of Dostoevsky's biographers, H. Troyat, wrote that "Dostoevsky arranged his life in the style of his novels and made his own story the most captivating of them all. Its truth seems more incredible than the most fantastic legend" (Troyat 1946: 5).*

The list of writings about Dostoevsky numbers in the thousands and is the subject of several existing volumes (A. Dostoevskaya 1906, Dolinin 1964, Leatherbarrow 1990; see also *The Dostoevsky Studies* Journal). When I started my work on this book, I first set out to determine what firsthand material was contained in the numerous Dostoevsky biographies; the next task was to see what new facts about Dostoevsky could be discovered, and where the materials containing this information could be found.

All of the major Dostoevsky biographies, of which there have been at least twelve in the last seventy years, are good in their own way, each highlighting particular aspects of Dostoevsky's life and work. Among the most outstanding recent works are those by R. Belknap (1990), J. Frank (1976; 1983; 1986; 1995; Vols. 1–4), R.L. Jackson (1984, 1993), K. Lantz (1993-94), and V. Terras (1984). To create a valuable supplement to these and other works, I tried to assemble in one volume as many primary sources as possible, concentrating on firsthand material from Dostoevsky's own time, both from the archival collections and from the memoirs of Dostoevsky's contemporaries.

The first substantial bibliographies on Dostoevsky were compiled in the 1920s. Those of L. Grossman (1924: 104–109) and A. Dolinin (Vol. 2, 1922: 1–122) were a starting point for my research, listing several hundred articles including materials from rare Russian periodicals of the time period 1880–1924. Of special interest were listings of reminiscences of Dostoevsky's friends,

---

Full citations of sources mentioned in the Preface are located under the heading "Works Cited" on pages 5–6. Further information on sources may be found in Igor Volgin's "History of the Dostoevsky Archives in Russia" (pp. 33–41) and in the Annotated Bibliography (pp. 347–362). The latter concentrates primarily on rare Russian-language sources.

relatives and associates. This list was supplemented by a 1964 article by S. Belov dedicated to the updating of the same material with new discoveries.

Most of the sources listed in these bibliographies were difficult to access even in Russia. For example, the issues of the provincial periodical *Sibirskie Ogni* (*The Siberian Lights*, 1880–1915) which contain rare information about the Siberian period of Dostoevsky's life were missing from major Russian libraries, as were issues of *Odesskaya Pravda* and several other old Russian periodicals. The explanation was simple: they contained text about Dostoevsky's movement from socialism to monarchism, and, naturally, this version of his biography had not coincided with the Soviet Union's official party line. Similarly absent were other people's writings on the same topic; e.g., the memoirs of Prince Meshchersky, a right-wing conservative and a close friend of the writer who called Dostoevsky "the most passionate monarchist in Russia." The fact that much of the material on Dostoevsky was inaccessible to the public was acknowledged by other scholars; for example, speaking of the periodicals from Dostoevsky's time, Professor K. Lantz stressed that "Many of the nineteenth century Russian newspapers ... are not available in North America and are difficult to access even in the Soviet Union" (Lantz 1993: 1379).

Most of this material was stored during the Soviet period in the so-called "special funds" of such major libraries as the Lenin State Library in Moscow and Saltykov Public Library in St. Petersburg, among others. Special permission from the authorities was required to access these funds, and, as a rule, the material obtained there was not allowed to be published. The situation changed with the democratic reforms that began in the late 1980s, and most of the "special funds" were opened to the public. In several years of research from 1989 to 1995, I managed to find most of the documentary sources that I sought; they constitute some two-thirds of the present book. This material was collected from the "special funds" recently opened to the public, as well as from the rare and ephemeral periodicals published in Russian provincial towns (Simbirsk, Odessa, Tver, etc.) from 1880 to 1935.

Some 30 percent of the entries came from writings by Dostoevsky's contemporaries which have been collected in the Russian book *Dostoevsky in the Memoirs of His Contemporaries* (*Dostoevsky v vospominaniiakh sovremennikov*). This publication had three successful editions in Russia during the last eighty years, each under a different editor: V. Cheshikhin-Vetrinsky (1912), A. Dolinin (1964), and Tiun'kin (1990). Each of these editions included about forty memoirs written by the writer's contemporaries relating to different periods of Dostoevsky's life, but most of these reminiscences were cut severely by Soviet censors. For example, several key pages from the memoirs of Dostoevsky's brother Andrei (one of the major sources of information on the writer's childhood) were cut out even in the 1990 edition. The missing text concerns, in particular, the description of Dostoevsky's ancestors on his father's side connected with the old Russian nobility; the story of the wealthy Kumanin family on his mother's side; and the story of the admission of the Dostoevsky brothers, Fyodor and Andrei, to the Engineering Academy in St. Petersburg after they were recommended by a distant relative. The memoirs of Dostoevsky's daughter, Liubov, were published in Russia in 1924, also cut by about 30 percent; missing were her comments about Dostoevsky's friendship with the royal family and his life as an important social and political figure during the last years of his life. (The complete version of these memoirs was published recently in 1993 in Russia by Andreev and Sons Publisher.) These examples of cuts made by the Soviet censorship in the memoirs of Dostoevsky's contemporaries are only representative. In all cases, I consulted the original publications of the period 1880–1917, and included the relevant censored material in *The Dostoevsky Archive*. This is the first English publication of all of these writings. I did all the translations, however about four appeared previously in English. These were some of the memoirs of his wife and daughter.

Besides the memoirs of Dostoevsky's contemporaries, other important sources of firsthand material were several collections of archival documents published in the 1920s and early 1930s by Dostoevsky's leading Russian biographers: L. Grossman (1923, 1934, 1962) and S. Dolinin (1922). For example, Leonid Grossman created several monographs which could be used as guides and supplementary sources to the firsthand archival material on Dostoevsky. His major work, *Dostoevsky* (1962), was a popular entry in the series *Literary Biographies of Famous People* and was translated into several European languages. It is based on two rare scholarly publications by the same author which laid the foundation of Dostoevsky studies in Russia: *Seminars on Dostoevsky* (1923) and *Chronology of Dostoevsky's Life and Works* (1934). The former work included the catalogue of Dostoevsky's library, occasional notes on Dostoevsky's works, and a bibliography of memoirs of his contemporaries; the latter presented a detailed biography of Dostoevsky's life based on the archival materials available at the time, with numerous references to such firsthand documents as letters, police reports, rare memoirs, etc. Unfortunately, in many cases, Grossman did not indicate the exact source or location of the archival material. Sometimes he relied on references in sources which were not verified with the original documents.

From the 1930s to the 1950s, under the Stalin regime, publications about Dostoevsky were not welcomed by Russian officials, and indeed Dostoevsky's name was not mentioned in school curricula because of the party officials' hostility toward his political views and his strong criticism of nihilism, socialism, and communism. During this period, most of Dostoevsky's works were banned from publication.

A major event of the 1970s and 1980s was the publication of Dostoevsky's *Complete Works in 30 Volumes* by the Institute of Russian Literature of the Russian Academy of Sciences, St. Petersburg Branch, under the editorship of V. Bazhanov and G. Friedlender. These volumes included all available material written by Dostoevsky, with references to the archival funds where they were held. Three periodical publications prepared by the same academic group presented some additional material; the *Literary Heritage* series (volumes 77, 83 and 86); *Dostoevsky: Materials and Research* (ed. G. Friedlender); and *The Chronology of Dostoevsky's Life* (eds. I. Iakubovich, T. Ornatskaya; volume 1 appeared in 1993, volume 2 appeared in 1994 and volume 3 is forthcoming in 1996–97).

Three volumes of the *Literary Heritage* series (vols. 77, 83 and 86) were dedicated to new findings of Dostoevsky's notes, early versions of some of his novels, and correspondence with close friends and associates. *Dostoevsky: Materials and Research* (vols. 1–7, 1974–1987) included information about the new archival discoveries of Dostoevsky's letters, draft notes and other biographical material accompanied by the studies on his life and works by Russian and Western scholars. *The Chronology of Dostoevsky's Life* (1993–) presents an updated and more detailed version of L. Grossman's *Chronology* (1934). The editors created "a thoroughly double-checked and chronologically arranged collection of the firsthand material on the writer's biography" with the purpose of presenting "the all-embracing picture of the unique image of Dostoevsky as a writer, a journalist, a literary critic, an editor, a publisher, a social figure and a person" (Iakubovich 1993: 7–8). This publication included references to many firsthand archival sources, as well as to other rare publications containing firsthand material published during the writer's lifetime.

A valuable archival bibliography of the archival locations of all numerous Dostoevsky's works was created in 1957 by V. Nechaeva, who thoroughly studied all major archival depositories and libraries in Moscow and St. Petersburg available at the time. A good supplement to this work is Igor Volgin's "History of the Dostoevsky Archive in Russia," which follows this Preface. Volgin details discoveries made from 1957 to 1996, effectively updating Nechaeva's work to the present time. Volgin briefly summarizes the recent discoveries of Dostoevsky's manuscripts, journalistic writings and correspondence, and comments on his own discoveries in the archives of the Russian royal family and the Russian military and in some private collections.

Most of the archival material in the territory of Russia that is described by Nechaeva and Volgin is distributed among three major depositories: the Russian National Library (RNB), Department of Manuscripts, File 93; the Institute of Russian Literature (IRLI), the Pushkin House, File 100; and the Central State Archive of Literature and Art, GRALI, File 112. Some additional documents were scattered in other archives: Dostoevsky's military career is reflected in his military record available at the Archive of the Soviet Army; the ten-year Siberian period of his life is represented in the regional archives of the Siberian cities of Omsk, Tobolsk and Akmolinsk; and the history of the secret police surveillance over Dostoevsky is available at the Tver and St. Petersburg city archives. A substantial part of this material, however, was difficult to access during the Soviet period. To obtain permission to work in these archives, one had to go through an application procedure which lasted several months, and even after all permissions were obtained, it was impossible to get access to some of the funds. The situation began to change with the democratic reforms of the late 1980s, and the disintegration of the former USSR and weakening of the Communist Party further democratized access to the Russian archives. The criteria for classified documents and the censorship priorities were changed, and most of the archives were opened to the public. The archival material included in the introductory parts of each of the present book's chapters was obtained from the archives and library depositories in Russia between 1989 and 1995.

This does not mean, however, that this material was completely unknown to Dostoevsky scholars before. Most of it was either published in special archival periodicals or in special publications with small circulation (e.g., newsletters of the archives). But it was not available for the Western scholarly community or for the wide audience in Russia, and one of the major tasks of this book is to make it accessible to the reading public.

The major portion of this book consists of rare firsthand accounts which have gone unmentioned by most of Dostoevsky's biographers and which give valuable insight into the writer's life and work. Some of the highlights are:
• three early stories of Dostoevsky's epilepsy (S. Ianovsky, A. Shile, I. Izmailov);
• five contradictory versions of Dostoevsky's arrest and near execution presented by witnesses (A. Miliukov, O. Miller, A. Pinchuk, A. Pleshcheev and I. Vuich);
• the previously unknown story of Dostoevsky's love affair in Siberia (N. Feoktistov);
• revelatory memoirs about his service in the army (A. Skandin, N. Iakovlev, A. Ivanov);
• comments on Dostoevsky's support of Russian women writers (L. Simonova, V. Pribytkova, A. Toliverova);
• rare stories of the circumstances of Dostoevsky's frequent meetings with other writers (V. Korolenko, I. Iasinsky, V. Peretz, E. Garshin);
• remarks on Dostoevsky's strong and repeated criticism of nihilism, terrorism and socialism (V. Meshchersky, N. Bunaikov, O. Miller);
• accounts of Dostoevsky's overwhelming recognition at home and abroad, first as a popular jounalist and a social activist in the Russian conservative and pro-monarchist Slavophile movement, and then as one of the world's great novelists, and the account of his impressive funeral (P. Tchaikovsky, I. Pavlov, V. Davydov, A. Moshin, Count De Vollan, M. De Vogue).

None of these works mostly published in the nineteenth century have ever been mentioned after 1917. All of the translations are mine, with the sole exception of passages from the novels.

I have not uncovered new Dostoevsky letters or draft notes of the writer's novels on the back of a theater program, as did I. Volgin and S.M. Poshemanskaya in the late 1980s. My task was more modest: to put together, for the first time, the most important and revelatory archival materials pertaining to the major periods of Dostoevsky's life which were scattered in different depositories and obscure publications, and to illustrate Dostoevsky's biography almost exclusively with firsthand materials from Dostoevsky's lifetime, as no other Dostoevsky biography has done. The result is the most detailed one-volume collection of archival materials and firsthand memoirs of Dostoevsky's contemporaries available in English or Russian at present. This collection of documents is followed by a detailed chronology of Dostoevsky's life, a dictionary of persons mentioned in the various writings, and an annotated bibliography of major works on Dostoevsky based on the firsthand material.

Works Cited

Belknap, R. *The Genesis of "The Brothers Karamazov."* Evanston, Illinois, 1990.

Belov, S. "Bibliography guide," in *Dostoevsky in the Memoirs of His Contemporaries*, Vol. 2. Moscow, 1964, pp. 478–488.

Dolinin, A. *Dostoevsky: Articles and Materials (Dostoevsky: Stat'i i materialy)*, vols. 1–2. Moscow, 1922.

Dostoevskaya, A. *Bibliographic Guide ... of Dostoevsky (Bibliograficheskii ukazatel... Dostoevskogo)*. St. Petersburg, 1906.

Dostoevskaya, L. *Dostoevsky in the Reminiscences of His Daughter (Dostoevsky v izobrazhenii svoei docheri)*. Moscow, 1922.

Dostoevsky, Complete Works in 30 Volumes (eds. V. Bazhanov, G. Friedlender, et al.). Leningrad, 1978–1984.

Dostoevsky in the Memoirs of His Contemporaries (F.M. Dostoevsky v vospominaniiakh sovremennikov), vols. 1–2. Moscow, 1912, 1964, 1990. [Three editions, with different editors: A Cheshikhin-Vetrinsky (1912), A. Dolinin (1964) and J. Tiun'kin (1990).]

Frank, J. *Dostoevsky*. Vols. 1–4. Princeton, 1976–95.

Grossman, L. *The Chronology of F.M. Dostoevsky's Life and Works (Zhizn' i trudy F.M. Dostoevskogo)*. Moscow: Academia, 1934.

Grossman, L. *Dostoevsky: A Biography*. Moscow, 1962.

Grossman, L. *Seminars on Dostoevsky*. Moscow, 1923.

Iakubovich, I.D., ed. *The Chronology of Dostoevsky's Life and Works*, vol. 1. St. Petersburg, 1993.

Jackson, R.L. *Dialogues with Dostoevsky*. Stanford, 1993.

Jackson, R.L. *Dostoevsky: New Perspectives*. Englewood Cliffs, N.J., 1984.

Lantz, K. "Translator's Commentary," in *F.M. Dostoevsky, "A Writer's Diary,"* vols. 1–2. Evanston, Illinois, 1993-94.

Leatherbarrow, W. *F.M. Dostoevsky: A Reference Guide*. Boston, 1990.

Nechaeva, V. *The Description of Dostoevsky's Manuscripts (Opisanie rukopisei Dostoevskogo)*. Moscow, 1957.

Terras, V. *F.M. Dostoevsky: Life, Work and Criticism*. Fredericton, New Brunswick, 1984.

Troyat, H. *A Firebrand*. London, Toronto, 1946.

INTRODUCTION

History of the Dostoevsky Archive in Russia

(by Igor Volgin)

Fyodor Dostoevsky's creative output as a writer is conveniently divided into two periods: the time before his marriage to Anna Snitkina in 1867 and the period after this date until his death in 1881. A number of factors—the catastrophe of 1849, Dostoevsky's arrest and incarceration in a Siberian prison, his consequent service in the army, frequent moves from one place to another, and his lack of comfort in family life—interfered with the saving of manuscript texts relating to the early period of Dostoevsky's life. Major documentary material from this period was saved mostly in the archives of the family members (the families of the Karepins, the Ivanovs, A.M. and M.M. Dostoevsky), friends and literary associates (N.A. Nekrasov, A.A. Kraevsky, A.E. Vrangel, C.C. Velikhanov, M.N. Katkov, A.P. Miliukov, I. Polonsky, I.S. Turgenev, N.N. Strakhov, A.N. Ostrovsky, A.P. Suslova, A.V. Korvin-Krukovskaya) and others. Virtually no manuscripts of his fiction before 1948 have survived; some of them, of course, were seized by the Third Section of the Russian Secret Police, never to reappear.

Dostoevsky's participation in the Petrashevsky case and his behavior during this investigation of the case were reflected in the records of the Ministry of the Interior, the Third Section of the Police, Military Tribunal Commission and General Auditor. The Archive of the Ministry of Defense has an official letter of request written by Dostoevsky in 1858 and addressed to the emperor in which he asked the Tsar for permission to be dismissed from the army, and there are several other similar documents that still exist.

There are no surviving documentary materials or correspondence of any kind, nor any fictional writings of Dostoevsky, relating to his incarceration from 1850 to 1854. (There are, however, some official documents and a few memoirs.) The only manuscript source for this period is the so-called *Siberian Notebook*.

The years of 1854–1867 were a less stormy period for Dostoevsky, but his manuscripts were still not collected systematically. Dostoevsky did not have time to take care of this issue. It seemed that he followed the lines written by Pasternak many years later: "You should not create your archive; you should not worry much about manuscripts." Systematic collection of Dostoevsky's archive was started by his second wife, Anna Grigorievna Snitkina. She contributed much to the creation of the archive, but at the same time she destroyed some materials. For example, she applied some censorship and destroyed the letters of M.D. Isaeva (his first wife) as well as the letters by P.A. Isaev (his stepson), A.P. Suslova (his lover), and others.

Other manuscripts were also destroyed during this period. For example, when Dostoevsky received a secret warning about his search and possible arrest on the border after his return from abroad in 1871, he "cleared up" his archive created during several years of his trips outside of Russia. Anna Snitkina remembered, "Two days before our departure, Fyodor Mikhailovich invited me to his room and gave me several thick piles of large sheets of paper covered with his handwriting and asked me to burn everything." Naturally she did not want to destroy the papers. "But Fyodor Mikhailovich reminded me that at the border he should be searched, the papers taken from him, and that this material would disappear as all his papers had disappeared during his arrest in 1849." She had no choice. "We made a fire in a fireplace and burned all the papers. The manuscripts of the novels *The Idiot* and *The Eternal Husband* were destroyed.... I managed to save only his notebooks."

From her husband's death in 1881 until her own in 1918, Anna Grigorievna led an active effort to create an archive of all documentary material which had any connection with the life and works of Dostoevsky. It was during this time that a considerable part of this material was concentrated in the "Dostoevsky Room" created in the Moscow Historical Museum, with Anna Grigorievna in charge.

The period from the death of Anna Grigorievna in 1918 to the publication of *The Description of Dostoevsky's Manuscripts* by V.S. Nechaeva in 1957 was the next phase of the Dostoevsky archive's history. Some of the documents disappeared during the Civil War without any traces. Among them were many unique materials including the final manuscript of *The Brothers Karamazov*, which had belonged to Anna Grigorievna. Many personal collections containing original manuscripts or other documents connected with Dostoevsky were either scattered, destroyed, or moved abroad. Nevertheless, newly found sources continued to be published until the mid–1930s, when the scholarly study of Dostoevsky was effectively squelched for ideological reasons.

The publication of the so-called "Stavrogin's Confession" in 1926, a previously unpublished chapter "At Tikhon's" from *The Demons*, was a sensational event. This chapter was found in a box in the Central Archive opened in 1922. The so-called "version of a maiden" was supported by this discovery. "Stavrogin's sin" (the rape of a teenage girl) came to be attributed to Dostoevsky himself, a slander which was denied in my book *To Be Born in Russia. Dostoevsky and His Contemporaries* (1991: 128–136, 180–184; also see

Zakharov 1978). The preparatory materials and drafts to the novels *Crime and Punishment, The Idiot, The Devils* (excerpts) and *The Brothers Karamazov* (excerpts) appeared in print. The publication of Dostoevsky's letters started in 1923 and continued through the decades, with huge intervals between the third and fourth volumes, and with considerable cuts in the last volume.

A unique and comprehensive work, *The Description of Dostoevsky's Manuscripts*, was published by V.S. Nechaeva (1957). Many documents were published and briefly described in this fundamental work which is of great importance even today. It presented a huge amount of material, including all of Dostoevsky's manuscripts known at the time of publication, all official documents connected with the writer, and all correspondence to and from Dostoevsky that had been discovered at the time. This unclassified catalogue is the most important guidebook for all scholars who want to study the manuscripts of the author of *The Brothers Karamazov*.

The fate of Dostoevsky's manuscripts is different from, for example, that of the manuscripts by Alexander Pushkin or Leo Tolstoy, which were concentrated exclusively in one place (the Pushkin House in St. Petersburg and the Tolstoy Museum of Moscow). There is no one central Dostoevsky archive; instead, documentary materials are concentrated in three major archival depositories: the Russian National Library, or RNB (formerly GBL, the Lenin State Library), Department of Manuscripts, File 93; the Institute of Russian Literature Archive (IRLI), the Pushkin House, File 100; and the Central State Archive of Literature and Art, or RGALI (formerly TSGALI), File 112. Most of Dostoevsky's surviving manuscripts, correspondence, notebooks, business papers, and other original materials are located in these places.

Additionally, some original documents connected with Dostoevsky are available in the Russian State Archive of Military History (RGVIA), including, among other items, his testimony during the trial of 1849. A considerable amount of material connected with the Petrashevsky case is located at the State Archive of Russian Federation, or GARF (formerly TSGAOR—Central State Archive of the October Revolution). Letters from Dostoevsky to Alexander III, the Grand Dukes, and the famous lawyer A.F. Koni, as well as some other materials, are located here as well. The Central State Theatre Bakhrushin Museum has letters from Dostoevsky to the playwright A.N. Ostrovsky and to the actor V.V. Samoilov; the State Historical Museum has letters to E.F. Junge; the Central Museum of Literature has letters to A.M. Alexandrov and A.F. Blagonravov, and several books signed by Dostoevsky. The State Archive of St. Petersburg Region has the metrical church book of St. Vladimir's Church with an inscription about the death of the retired Junior Lieutenant Dostoevsky on 28 January 1881.

There is a relatively small amount of documentary material connected with Dostoevsky in other Russian provincial archives. For example, in the Tver Region Archive there is a file from the office of the Governor of Tver about the secret police surveillance of Dostoevsky in 1859. A similar case was started in 1875 in the office of the Governor of Novgorod, and the file on it is available at the Novgorod Region Archive. A local branch of the Tomsk Region Archive in Tobolsk has police material about the transportation of Dostoevsky to the place of his incarceration in January 1850. In the Akmolinsk Regional Literary Memorial Dostoevsky Museum in Kazakhstan there is an official letter written by Dostoevsky to Belikhov, the commander of his battalion, dated 27 July 1857. In Georgia's Tbilisi Archive, there is a file of the criminal case concerning the theft of the archive of Anna Dostoevskaya in 1918, with a description of the items from this stolen archive and quotes from some of the manuscripts.

There are reasons to believe that not all existing archival material related to Dostoevsky has yet been discovered. According to the proverb created by Voland (a character from the novel *Master and Margarita* by Mikhail Bulgakov), "the manuscripts do not burn." Therefore, we may expect more discoveries in this field in the future, perhaps including both large manuscripts of Dostoevsky's literary works and more correspondence relating to different periods of his life. For example, a manuscript of his memoirs about Belinsky was lost during his own lifetime and has never been found. So-called "indirect sources" include numerous documents and memoirs from Dostoevsky's lifetime in which his name is mentioned; such material is regularly added to the Dostoevsky archives. (Very interesting information was discovered in the archives of the Tsar's family, and is described below.)

Below I will try to define and categorize the archival sources which have become available to scholars since the publication of Nechaeva's *The Description of Dostoevsky's Manuscripts* in 1957. This overview is the first of its kind since that time, and it cannot be perfectly complete. Nevertheless, I hope that it can give a general idea about the character, direction and intensity of the archival work which was done by Russian scholars studying the life and works of Dostoevsky. First, a brief review of the major Russian publications (1957–95) which describe new archival material connected with Dostoevsky will be presented. Then the archival discoveries will be classified according to their genre, and brief annotations of the major later discoveries will be given. In conclusion, a general bibliography of the major archival publications will be presented.

A Review of Publications About New Archival Material, 1957–1995

Academic Periodicals

Three issues of the *Literary Heritage (Literaturnoe Nasledstvo)* series were completely dedicated to Dostoevsky: volumes 77, 83 and 86. Volume 77 (1965) was called *Dostoevsky's Work at the Novel "The Raw Youth"* and was edited by I.S. Silberstein and L.M. Rosenblum. Dostoevsky's manuscripts presented in this volume were published in English translation in *The Notebooks of a Raw Youth* by Fyodor Dostoevsky, Chicago: The University of Chicago Press, 1989. A.S. Dolinin, one of the first scholars who studied Dostoevsky's works, collected and made detailed comments on the writer's drafts and notebooks for this novel.

In 1971 the same editors published volume 83 of this series under the title *Unpublished Dostoevsky: Notebooks and Drafts for 1860–81*. This volume presented a huge number of formerly unknown texts, including a detailed inside view of the working laboratory of Dostoevsky-the-journalist, drafts of *A Writer's Diary*, and many business documents such as publishers' bills, addresses and other items in Dostoevsky's handwriting. These two volumes of the *Literary Heritage* series together contained more than 1200 pages of previously unknown texts.

In 1973, volume 86 of the *Literary Heritage* series, *F.M. Dostoevsky: New Research and Materials*, was published. This volume had drafts of *Oppressed and Humiliated* (prior to this no manuscripts of this novel were known) which were discovered on the back side of an invitation ticket of 1860; the articles of the *Time* journal which were banned by censors; previously unpublished fragments of *A Writer's Diary*; newly discovered or previously lost letters by Dostoevsky; shorthand notes from Anna Dostoevskaya's diary written in 1867 which were read by C.M. Poshemanskaya; previously unknown memoirs about Dostoevsky by J.B. and A.A. Von Bretzel, A.E. Riesenkampf, P.G. Kuznetsov, I.F. Tiumenev; notes by N.N. Strakhov; and other items of interest. Importantly, this volume included excerpts from the diaries and correspondence of more than 150 contemporaries. The new materials presented a detailed picture of Dostoevsky's presence in the public life of the day. All of the texts of Dostoevsky which were included in different volumes of the *Literary Heritage* series were later presented in the *Complete Works in 30 Volumes* published by the Academy of Sciences, with some more precise definitions, new text presentations, more detailed commentaries, and other improvements.

Several volumes of the *Literary Monuments* series have included detailed commentaries on Dostoevsky's manuscripts. The publication of *Crime and Punishment*, illustrated by E. Neisvestny, became a big event of 1970. This edition included complete versions of the three notebooks of drafts for the novel. It differed from the publication of editor I.I. Glivenko's *The Central Archive, From the Dostoevsky Archive, Crime and Punishment. Unpublished Materials* (*Tsentrarkhiv. Iz arkhiva Dostoevskogo*) (Moscow and Leningrad: GIHL, 1932), in which the text was presented mechanically page after page. In the new edition the text was restored both chronologically and semantically. The same publication presented all the surviving manuscript fragments of separate chapters and episodes for the first time.

In 1975, the correspondence between F.M. Dostoevsky and his wife Anna was published in the *Literary Monuments* series. It consisted of 164 letters by Dostoevsky, all of which had been previously published, and 75 letters by A.G. Dostoevskaya, almost all of which were being published for the first time. Several letters were omitted from this edition, however, and some fragments of included letters were cut by Anna Grigorievna herself, "taking into account personal and family considerations," as editors wrote.

Finally, in 1993 a complete edition of Anna Dostoevskaya's diary for 1867 was published for the first time in the same *Literary Monuments* series. This was the final version of the deciphered notebooks of Dostoevsky's second wife, and it included everyday shorthand notes which she made during the couple's trips to Germany and Switzerland. The diary was put into readable form by C.M. Pomeshanskaya, a stenographer from St. Petersburg who managed to decode Anna's idiosyncratic secret system of shorthand. Pomeshanskaya compared the text of previously published notebooks by Anna Dostoevskaya with the shorthand original which was available and was then able to decipher the rest of the shorthand records.

The complete publication of Anna Dostoevskaya's diaries was of great importance. Although they covered only a four-year span, this was the only chronicle of its kind which revealed Dostoevsky's life from the inside, family viewpoint. These notes were sincere, simple and unedited (remember that they belonged to a twenty-year-old woman), which makes them even more precious. This diary is interesting to compare with the one of Anna's notebooks which she edited herself much later, and which was also included in the 1993 volume.

The shorthand originals of the notebooks are located in the Russian National Library, and the version of one of these notebooks which Anna Dostoevskaya edited and prepared for publication by herself is located in the RGALI Archive.

Specialized Publications of Dostoevsky's Materials

The *Complete Works in 30 Volumes* was prepared by the Research Group of the Academy of sciences in IRLI (the Pushkin House). This is the most complete and accurate collection of the texts written by Dostoevsky. The texts were checked against original manuscripts to the extent possible.

The results of the latest archival discoveries were published in the series *Dostoevsky, Materials and Discoveries* (*Dostoevsky. Materialy i issledovaniia*) by the same Academic Research Group. Eleven issues appeared in print, starting in 1974. In addition to this, I have to mention the series *Dostoevsky and His Time* (*Dostoevsky i sovremmenost*) published since 1989 in Novgorod, as well as a series of collective monographs *Dostoevsky and the World*

Culture (Dostoevsky i mirovaia kultura) published in Moscow and St. Petersburg.

In 1993, the Dostoevsky Research Group of the Academy of Sciences in IRLI published the first of three planned volumes in the series *The Chronicle of Dostoevsky's Life and Works, 1821–1881*. The first volume has numerous references to the archival sources.

Other Continuing Publications

The Central State Archive of Literature and Art (RGALI, formerly TSGALI) published seven monographs in the series *Meetings with the Past (Vstrechi s proshlym)* between 1970 and 1990. Besides this publication, the series *Days of the Present Life. From the Chronicle of TSGALI (Dni nashei zhizni. Iz khroniki TSGALI)* has presented new archival discoveries and archival additions, including those concerning Dostoevsky (the personal archive of J.G. Oksman in the 1978 issue, no. 3, among others). Formerly unknown letters by Dostoevsky (1970, no. 1) and memoirs of E.N. Opochinin (1990, no. 7) were published in the series *Meetings with the Past*. The second issue of this series (1973) included an article "The Dostoevsky Archive" by J.A. Krasovsky dedicated to the history of the famous bank deposit box with the archival material of Anna Dostoevskaya, as well as some other new additions to the archive.

The IRLI (Institute of Russian Literature Archive) has a similar publication, a periodical titled *The Annual Proceedings of the Manuscript Department of the Pushkin House (Ezhegodnik rukopisnogo otdela Pushkinskogo Doma)*. Among the most interesting publications on Dostoevsky are a series of articles dedicated to the materials from the A.N. Maikov archive (1974–77); the materials from the same archival collection were described in the fourth issue of *Dostoevsky Materials and Discoveries* (1980). *The Reviews of the Archival Material of the 18th–20th Centuries (Obzory arkhivnykh materialov XVIII–XX vv)* present the new material which is added to the manuscript collection of IRLI with a listing of the incoming materials. Among the new archival material on Dostoevsky are Anna Dostoevskaya's letter from the personal collection of L.J. Gurevich and Andrei Dostoevsky's letter from the personal collection of V.M. Sayanov (1976, 1978).

Publications of RNB (Russian National Library) on this topic are less extensive. One should mention an article by S.V. Belov with the review of the memoirs by Dostoevsky's contemporaries, including unpublished memoirs. This article by S.V. Belov, among other works on Dostoevsky, was published in *The Proceedings of the Manuscript Department of GBL* (1963, no. 26).

The 1990s are characterized by an outburst of archival publications of different kinds. Several new periodicals have been founded (or moved to

Russia from abroad) which specialize in making different archival documents of the nineteenth and twentieth centuries available to the public. A historical almanac *The Past (Minuvshee)* was published by the Athenaeum Publishing House in Paris; its first twelve issues were reprinted in Russia in 1990–92, and starting in 1992 (no. 13), this periodical was published together by publishing houses Athenaeum and Phoenix in Moscow and St. Petersburg. At present, these two publishing houses, together with the Bibliographical Institute in St. Petersburg, publish several historical-biographical periodicals, among them *Faces*, *The Nevsky Archive* and *In Memoriam*. The following documents were published in Phoenix-Athenaeum almanacs: a letter by A.U. Poretsky from the personal collection of P.S. Diakonov mentioning Dostoevsky (*Faces*, no. 4); correspondence between Anna Dostoevskaya and V.V. Rozanov and letters to her from D.S. Merezhkovsky and S.N. Bulgakov (*The Past*, no. 9).

Archival documents about Dostoevsky are published in specialized academic periodicals, including literary journals (*Voprosy literatury*, *Russkaia Literatura*, *Izvestiia RAN*), journals on the archival studies (*Sovetskie arkhivy*, *Russkii arkhiv*), and bibliographical journals (*Kniga*, *Materialy i issledovaniia*, *Almanakh bibliofila*). Such materials appear more seldom in the literary art journals (*Novy Mir*, *Oktiabr'* et al.). Among the most sensational material of the recent past are publications in *The Literary Newspaper* (*Literaturnaia gazeta*, Bursov 1970, Lanskoi 1971a, Fedorov 1971, 1975) dedicated to the discovery of the criminal police file found in a regional archive and investigating the murder of Dostoevsky's father, new discoveries of manuscripts, etc.

New Archival Publications of Dostoevsky's Manuscripts

1. Literary Works

Recent discoveries of Dostoevsky's manuscript variants and drafts have been published in the following sources:
- *Notes from the House of Dead* (1860) in the *Complete Works* (Vol. 4);
- *Oppressed and Humiliated* (1861) in Kogan (1973);
- *The Gambler* (1866) in the *Complete Works* (Vol. 5);
- *Crime and Punishment* (1866) in the *Complete Works* (Vol. 7) and in Belov and Tunimanov (1970);
- *The Eternal Husband* (1870) in the *Complete Works* (Vol. 9);
- *The Demons* (1871) in the *Complete Works* (Vols. 11, 12);
- *The Raw Youth* (1875) in the *Complete Works* (Vols. 16, 17), Bursov (1970) and *Literary Inheritance* (Vol. 77);
- *The Brothers Karamazov* (1879) in the *Complete Works* (Vol. 15), Konshina (1973) and Ornatskaya (1983).

The discovery of a previously unknown draft version of *The Brothers Karamazov* has become a sensation. V.M. Fedorova discovered in the Dostoevsky File in the Manuscript Department of the Russian National Library twenty-eight pages in large format with shorthand notes by Anna Dostoevskaya. This shorthand record was read and interpreted by S.M. Poshemanskaya, who has already deciphered Anna Dostoevskaya's diary for 1867 and Dostoevsky's autobiography which he dictated to his wife in 1881; these materials were published in *Dostoevsky. Materials and Discoveries* (Kiiko and Poshemanskaya 1978).

Drafts and plans for unwritten or incomplete works of the 1860s and 1870s are numerous. Novels include *The Pawn-Broker* (*Rostovshchik*, *Complete Works*, Vol. 5); *Kartusov* (drafts and plans from 1870 to 1872 appear in *Complete Works*, Vol. 12); *Dreamer* ("Mechtatel"—see Friedlender 1964; more complete version in Rosenblum 1971a; the most complete material in *Complete Works*, Vol. 17); "Drama. In Tobolsk..." the first line of Dostoevsky's written work; *History of Karl Ivanovich* (*Complete Works*, Vol. 17). There are also humorous verses, parodies and epigrams of the 1860s and 1870s, including "The Jumping Lady..." and the final version of the pamphlet in verse "The fight between nihilism and honesty (Officer and nihilism)" *Complete Works*, Vol. 17). A shorthand record of several humorous poems by Dostoevsky was read and published by S.M. Poshemanskaya. Anna Dostoevskaya wrote these poems on several spare sheets of paper at the end of her diary in 1867 (Poshemanskaya and Zhitomirskaya 1973).

2. Notebooks and Sketchbooks

This material was published for the first time in a relatively complete form in *The Literary Heritage*, volume 83. The complete version was published in the *Complete Works*, not as arranged by Dostoevsky. Instead the material was arranged according to topic: drafts and preparatory material for different literary works (*Complete Works*, Vols. 1–17); literary criticism and journalism (*Complete Works*, vols. 18–27); and some separate casual works, mots, expressions, business and personal papers (*Complete Works*, Vol. 27).

Dostoevsky's working drafts and notebooks relating to the Siberian period occupy a very special place in his literary oeuvre. *The Siberian Notebook* was published in the fourth volume of *Complete Works*, and a separate annotated edition was prepared by Vladimirtsev and Ornatskaya (1985).

3. Journalism

Recent discoveries of Dostoevsky's manuscript variants and drafts have been published in the following sources:

• *Time* (1861–63): an article "Books and Education" in *Complete Works* (Vol. 19);

• *Epoch* (1864–65): articles "A necessary statement" and "Mr. Shedrin, or a Split of the Nihilists" in *Complete Works* (Vol. 20) and an article "About the Play of Mr. Vasiliev" in Belov (1973a);

• *Citizen* (1973): "Vlas," "Dreams," "Small Pictures," "Half a Letter by an Unknown Person," "A Contemporary Lie," "A Clown," "About One Dramatic Event," and "Foreign News" in *Complete Works* (Vol. 21);

• *A Writer's Diary* (1876): drafts in Volgin (1970, 1973b) and Pomerantz (1973); drafts, preparatory material and manuscript for printing in *Complete Works*, (Vols. 22–24); drafts and the final original manuscript of *The Meek One* in *Complete Works* (Vol. 24);

• *A Writer's Diary* (1877): in Pomerantz (1973), *Complete Works* (Vols. 25–26), Volgin (1973b);

• *A Writer's Diary* (1880): in Ivanio (1973), *Complete Works* (Vol. 26);

• *A Writer's Diary* (1881): *Complete Works* (Vol. 27) and Rosenblum (1971);

The history of censorship of *A Writer's Diary* was presented by the present author in 1970, and in the same article several new archival discoveries were published: previously unknown letters from censor N.R. Ratynsky to F. Dostoevsky; fragments of the journal previously banned for publication, etc. Additionally, I discovered rather lengthy texts originally assigned for *A Writer's Diary* but ultimately dropped from the final version by Dostoevsky himself for reasons that I analyzed in another article (1973b). His action revealed a certain "inner lack of freedom," for at the time of publication, he was cautious to defend his attitude against accusations from both the progressive and liberal press. Dostoevsky repeatedly displayed his concern about the arrogant mockery with which his prophecies about human development were met.

After excerpting passages from the book of predictions by Johann of Lichtenberg, Dostoevsky wrote that the quotes were given to him "by one of our young scholars" and that this "strange document ... was found by this scholar in London, in the Royal library." I determined that the anonymous "young scholar" was Vladimir Sergeevich Soloviev, a person with whom Dostoevsky had discussed his article about the prophecies which was not included in the final text of *A Writer's Diary*.

Some other fragments that I discovered and presented for publication were dedicated to the relationships between the people and intelligentsia. Another was Dostoevsky's analysis of the eighth part of *Anna Karenina*, which represents his most detailed analysis of any work by Leo Tolstoy. There is no doubt that these excerpts were cut out of the final version of the text out of consideration for journalistic decorum and tact. Some other previously unpublished fragments deal with different questions of the public life.

The number of texts which were dropped from the final version of *A*

Writer's Diary is rather large. Numerous recent publications give readers an opportunity to understand the reasons why Dostoevsky made the selection of a certain journalistic piece for publication.

4. Letters

In 1959 the last volume of four volumes of Dostoevsky's letters was published. This edition was started by Dolinin in 1928, but due to ideological reasons, the process of publication lasted thirty years. For the same reasons, a considerable amount of correspondence was omitted from the fourth volume.

Between 1985 and 1990 all Dostoevsky's existing letters were published in volumes 28–30 of the *Complete Works*; among them were 925 letters to private persons, 42 official letters and 15 collective letters. Another 379 lost letters were briefly mentioned in this publication. The letters were checked against the originals as closely as possible. Many of them were published for the first time.

Personal correspondence. Between the two previously mentioned editions of Dostoevsky's letters, a considerable number of the newly discovered letters by Dostoevsky were published in the *Literary Heritage* series, volume 86, among them letters to S.M. Loboda (from the collection of the writer K.A. Fedin); a letter to the Grand Prince Konstantin Konstantinovich (future poet Konstantin); a letter to the uncle of the last Russian tsar; two brief notes to M.A. Alexandrov, a publishing house worker (these letters were found by the researcher G.F. Kogan in the archive of V.J. Bogucharsky, the editor of the periodical *The Past* published at the beginning of the twentieth century); and also a shorthand record of the last letter to E.H. Heiden which Dostoevsky dictated to his wife Anna Grigorievna before his death. The latter was deciphered by S.M. Poshemanskaya (Silberstein 1973).

In the book *The Last Year of Dostoevsky* (Volgin 1986, 1990, 1991a: 197, 513) I tried to determine with greater accuracy the date of the so-called "night letter" from Dostoevsky to Anna Grigorievna in 1880. The letter read, "Deary Any, Could you please send this registered letter to Liuibimov today, without any delay. You know what it is about. Yours, F. Dostoevsky. 29, 3¾ A.M., 1880." The addressee herself dated this letter 29 January 1880 by mistake. This date was used in *The Description of Dostoevsky's Manuscripts* by Nechaeva (1957: 180). At the same time A.S. Dolinin dates this letter 29 March 1880. I proved that this date was 29 April 1880. This date, however, was not used in the *Complete Works* edition. Besides this, I corrected the slip of pen made in a letter from Dostoevsky to Anna Dostoevskaya dated 26 May 1880 (Volgin 1991: 514).

The first issue of the *Meeting with the Past* series published by the RGALI

Archive started with the publication of an unknown letter from Dostoevsky to N.F. Jushkov, which arrived at the archive together with the Rabinovich collection in 1965 (Krasovsky 1970). The letter from Dostoevsky to Strakhov was presented to the Dostoevsky Museum in Moscow by collector I.A. Polonsky (Kogan 1973a). Among the other publications of the previously unknown letters by Dostoevsky are his letters to V.M. Kachenovsky (Kapeliush 1971) and a letter to N.A. Liubimov, Liubimov's own archive (Bitiugova, Iakubovich 1990), etc.

During my work on Dostoevsky's biography, I discovered previously unknown letters. For example, S.P. Ianovsky stressed in his letter the complicated relationship which existed in the fall of 1848 between Dostoevsky, Speshnev and other members of the secret Petrashevsky society. According to Ianovsky, 500 roubles of silver which Dostoevsky borrowed from Speshnev tormented the debtor. The author of the memoirs stressed that Dostoevsky could not return his debt. I think that there was another circumstance involved, namely, "the secret seven." It was a risky enterprise by Speshnev to create a group for setting up a secret publishing house (Volgin 1994: 78–86). Dostoevsky said, "He would not take the money back...." At present the fact of this fatal debt can be proved by the existing documents. Recently, among the archival documents which were confiscated by the police from Speshnev during his arrest (File 71, dated 21 May 1849), I discovered the following note: "A letter by Dostoevsky: he asks me for some money. He reminds me of the literary meetings at Kraevsky" (Volgin 1994: 78; *Complete Works*, Vol. 30, part 2: 27; GARF Archive 109–1849–214–30). This note suggests that the circumstances for returning the money were mentioned in the letter. The only sources of income for the author of *Netochka Nezvanova* (Dostoevsky's last novel written before his exile to Siberia), were his publications in *The Fatherland Notes*.

I found indications of unknown letters by Dostoevsky in the archival fund of Duchess A.E. Komarovskaya. A day or two before Dostoevsky's death, on 26/27 January 1881, the Grand Prince Dmitry Konstantinovich, the brother of Grand Prince Konstantin, wrote to Duchess Anna Egorovna, "I am very grateful to you for your very kind invitation. It seems to me that I will definitely be available at the time and I will visit you for sure. Dostoevsky's response was charming. Most sincerely yours, Dmitry."

What kind of "charming response" was meant by Prince Dmitry Konstantinovich? This letter is missing from the *Complete Works*. Moreover, no other sources indicate the existence of such a letter. As we can see from these documents, however, Dostoevsky's response to Komarovskaya definitely existed. It was in answer to our invitation to visit the Marble Palace on 28 January 1881.

On 30 January 1881, A.E. Komarovskaya wrote to the Grand Prince Konstantin Konstantinovich, who was abroad at the time: "Your Majesty, I write to you because I cannot stop thinking about you when we mourn about our great loss. Due to your assistance, I had a chance to know Dostoevsky better. His death greatly impressed us, especially because his illness lasted only for three days. When I asked him to visit me on the next Sunday, he told me that he 'would be busy with his manuscript, but on Wednesday, the 29th, he hoped to be free' and that he would visit me on that day." Therefore, another letter by Dostoevsky must have existed. This was obviously the penultimate letter written before his death. The very last letter was addressed to Liubimov and was written on 26 January 1881 late at night, but it was dated 25 January 1881. Anna Dostoevskaya even gives a quote from this letter in her memoirs (Volgin 1992, 12: 156–157).

The Official Letters. In *The Last Year of Dostoevsky*, I present several different versions of the letter written to the Tsar on behalf of the Slavic Charity Committee in 1880, the letter in which Dostoevsky formulated the most important issues of his political program, including a greater respect from the Supreme Power—the emperor—to the people, and, in connection with this, more freedom for the people.

Some other documents were published in the same book, among them notes which were made on the letter to the Tsar by Minister of the Interior L.S. Markov—which Dostoevsky took into consideration—as well as an archival remark by Anna Dostoevskaya about "a strange response" in the letter written to Alexander II (Volgin 1991: 112–115). In the book *The Metamorphoses of Power*, I analyzed the diaries of the Grand Prince Konstantin Konstantinovich and discovered that Dostoevsky, while working at this letter to the Tsar, already knew about the future shift in government policy from political terror to a dialogue with the people. At the time, his very brave slogan about the trust of the government and about the people's freedoms was addressed to the Tsar and, moreover, to the future government (Volgin 1992, 12: 122).

Obviously, the discoveries of correspondence constitute a major part of archival discoveries of the recent years. At present, there is information about 379 lost letters by Dostoevsky, and this could be a good direction for future discoveries.

5. Inscriptions in Books and on Photographs

Dostoevsky's inscriptions in books and on photographs comprise a large group of manuscripts which have been neglected for a long time, and which came into focus of scholars only recently. For example, before 1957 only two inscriptions were published, and at present 42 inscriptions are known. There were several important reasons for this. First, some of these inscriptions belonged to private collectors: two of them were in the collection of J. Valter, and three existed in the collections of V. Lidin, M. Saparov and S. Koganer. Secondly, other inscriptions were found in different museum funds after the death of their owners, several private collections having been presented to the museums (for example, *Books and Manuscripts from the M. Leeman Collection*, Moscow, 1989), News about such findings is usually announced in periodicals (*Literary Russia*, 1988, 18.03., no. 11; *Smena* 17, October 1971: 243). Many of Dostoevsky's inscriptions—among them gifts from the private collections—are usually kept on display on the shelves of the Dostoevsky Museums: five exhibits exist in the Dostoevsky Museum in Moscow and three in the St. Petersburg Museum (*Complete Works*, Vol. 30, part 32). A signed book which was presented to S.V. Karchevskaya, who later became the wife of Ivan Pavlov, the great Russian physiologist and a Nobel prize winner, is kept in the Pavlov Memorial Museum in St. Petersburg.

V.S. Nechaeva (1957) tried to locate all such documents. Some detailed descriptions were given in various sources. In *Dostoevsky. Materials and Discoveries* vol. 6 (Ornatskaya 1985), information about 35 inscriptions was presented. In the *Complete Works* (Vol. 30, part 2) 41 inscriptions were described. The forty-second inscription was published in *Dostoevsky Materials and Discoveries* volume 11 (Iakubovich 1994). About half of the known inscriptions were reprinted in *The Literary Heritage*, volume 15 (one inscription), volumns 53–54 (one inscription), volume 83 (ten inscriptions), and volume 86 (ten inscriptions). There is no doubt that in the future more new findings of this part of the manuscript heritage of Dostoevsky will be made.

Several inscriptions are kept abroad. For example, a copy of *Notes from the House of Dead* presented to A. Herzen is now kept in the collection of the University of Geneva (*Complete Works*, Vol. 30, part 2: 97). Someone "borrowed" this copy and failed to return it to Herzen. In January 1863 Herzen advised his friends to translate this book into English and wrote, "I have this book and I will try to find it,—someone has borrowed it from me" (A. Herzen, *Works*, Vol. 27, part 2: 415). In Oakland, California, where Herzen's great-granddaughter lives, scholars from Moscow have found a small photograph with the inscription: "To Alexander Ivanovich Herzen, in the memory of our meeting in London from F. Dostoevsky on 8 July/20 July 1862" (Zelvakova 1992: 62). This discovery proves the existence of a previously unknown third meeting between Herzen and Dostoevsky in London in the summer of 1862. Two previous meetings are known, those which took place on 16 April 1862 and 19 July 1862.

6. Paintings

Recent publications (Likhachev 1984, Barsht 1984, 1985, 1986, 1987) suggest that Dostoevsky's sketches and drawings will be studied by scholars as items of considerable interest, as have been the sketches and watercolors of other Russian literary artists, including A. Pushkin, M. Lermontov, V. Zhukovsky, A. Block, A. Bely, M. Voloshin, A. Remizov and others.

At present the only known sketches are those that Dostoevsky did in his manuscripts during the 1860s and 1870s, as well as some drawings from his training courses at Chermak College and at the Engineering Academy in St. Petersburg. Unfortunately, Dostoevsky's drawings from this engineering and architecture courses were lost.

7. *Letters to Dostoevsky and Letters in Which Dostoevsky Is Mentioned*

Although the letters, diaries and memoirs of Dostoevsky's contemporaries present valuable new biographical material, publication of letters written to Dostoevsky or relating to Dostoevsky has only recently started. Previously, only those letters that belonged to the famous political and literary figures were published. In addition, letters which mention Dostoevsky's name also are of great interest. A substantial collection of such letters was published in *The Literary Heritage*, volume 86 (Lanskoi 1973). Several letters about Dostoevsky written by other people should be mentioned here. Among these are letters by A.M. Maikov (Iampolsky 1976, 1977, 1980); by E.A. and M.A. Rykhachev (Galagan 1973); from A.P. Suslova to J.D. Polonsky (Bogorad 1985); by M.M. Dostoevsky about his brother (Pistsova 1972); from S.D. Ianovsky to O.F. Miller (1970); and by I.N. Shidlovsky (Nechaeva 1979). These documents seem to be on the periphery of Dostoevsky studies. But despite their apparent secondary importance, it is striking that among this material new biographical facts have been discovered.

Among the considerable personal and literary correspondence received by Dostoevsky, several letters are of special importance, among them those by V.V. Krestovsky (Viktorovich 1991), A.N. Maikov (Ashimbaeva 1984, Iampolsky 1976), V. Soloviev (Iakubovich 1991), A.N. Pleshcheev (Pustilnik 1961), and I.S. Aksakov (Volgin 1972), as well as a considerable number of letters addressed to Dostoevsky from his readers (Volgin 1971a), especially during the time of the writing and the publication of *A Writer's Diary*. My own books have included newly discovered letters to Dostoevsky written by C. Alchevskaya, A. Arkhipova, N. Beketova, K. Galler, N. Gorelov, N. Grebtsov, A. Gusev, N. Golitsyn, I. Danilevsky, A. Deinikovsky, A. Ishimova, K. Lavrsky, O. Levin, K. Nazarieva, L. Surazevskaya (Volgin 1982); K. Islavin, V. Karepina, A. Kireev, A. Kurnosova, N. Liubimov, P. Guseva, O. Novikova, M. Polivanova, N. Liubimov, V. Putsykovich, L. Pykhacheva, V. Sinitsky, and E. Stakenshneider, as well as notes by Dostoevsky's children Fedya and Lyuba (Volgin 1986, 1990, 1991a).

Many previously unpublished letters by Dostoevsky were quoted in the volumes 28–30 of *The Complete Works*. A large number of letters written by contemporaries and mentioning Dostoevsky's name were published in *The Literary Heritage*, volume 86 (Lanskoi 1973).

In this section "The Unpublished Letters to Dostoevsky" in *Dostoevsky. Materials and Discoveries* see volumes 2, 5, and 11 (Iudina 1976; Batuto, et al. 1985; Ipatova 1994). Many important documents were published in this periodical, such as letters by A.E. Vrangel in volume 3 (Ornatskaya 1987), by P. Vainberg in volume 4 (Stepanova 1980), and by A.G. Dostoevskaya in volume 7 (Arkhipova 1987b), etc.

8. Memoirs and Diaries

A considerable number of memoirs about Dostoevsky are already available to scholars. Many of these memoirs were published in three editions of a two-volume collection *F.M. Dostoevsky in the Memoirs of His Contemporaries* (1924, 1964, 1995). A great many other memoirs, however, are scattered in rare old periodicals and are unknown to a wide scholarly audience.

Many of the memoirs were obtained from forgotten sources which were hardly accessible. Some of this material was published in *The Last Year of Dostoevsky* (Volgin 1986, 1990, 1991a) and *To Be Born in Russia* (Volgin 1991b), as well as in the collection *F.M. Dostoevsky in the Forgotten or Unknown Memoirs of His Contemporaries* (Belov 1993). In 1992 and 1993, more memoirs about Dostoevsky were published in *The Historical-Literary Memoirs* series by S.D. Below, including reminiscences of Andrei Dostoevsky about his brother, memoirs of the writer's daughter Lyubov (for the first time translated into Russian from the German edition), memoirs of A.P. Suslova and others.

Rarely discovered are the original handwritten manuscripts of the memoirs and diaries connected with Dostoevsky's life and work. Publication of such original archival texts would be greatly beneficial. Memoirs or diaries by the following persons have been published recently for the first time: P.I. Karepin, N.N. Poliansky, V.A. Sevastianova-Dostoevskaya, U.I. Fausek, N.A. Shamin, an unknown person about Dostoevsky's funeral (Belov 1993), I.L. Leontiev-Sheglov (Bitiugova 1994a), P.G. Kuznetsov (Silberstein 1973a), E.N. Opochinin (Odesskaya 1992; Bronnikova 1990), F.F. Fidler (Asadovsky 1985), S.I. Smirnova-Sazonova (Mostovskaya 1980), J.B. von Bretzel (Serebriannaia 1973); D.N. Sadovnikov (Smirnov 1972), and others.

9. Anna Grigorievna Dostoevskaya: Letters, Diaries, Memoirs

I have already mentioned the shorthand records made by Anna Dostoevskaya and read by E. Poshemanskaya (among them Dostoevsky's early versions of *A Writer's Diary* and *The Brothers Karamazov* and her own diary for 1867; about the latter, see *A Deed Worthy of Dostoevskaya Herself* by Belov; about the deciphering of Dostoevskaya's shorthand writings, see also Marr 1971, Poshemanskaya 1970). Among more recent publications are the recently read diaries of Anna Dostoevskaya for 1880 and 1881 (Belov 19881, 1993) and the note about the marriage between Dostoevsky and Anna Grigorievna (Galperina 1991).

The book *The Writer's Wife* (Belov 1986a) is dedicated to the biography of Anna Dostoevskaya. The original archival material was used widely in this book. In *The Last Year of Dostoevsky* (Volgin 1991b) I presented several findings on this topic; e.g., a new version of Dostoevsky's first meeting with Anna Grigorievna, their everyday life in the chapter "Family and Children," and some dark and formerly unknown sides of the writer's death. Unpublished versions of the manuscript of Anna Dostoevskaya's memoirs were used in the preparation of this material for publication (Volgin 1986, 1990, 1991a). Several general reviews were dedicated to Anna Dostoevskaya's personal archive (Nechaeva 1957, Krasovsky 1973, Lanskoi 1977).

The memoirs of P.G. Kuznestov, who as a boy in 1880s worked as Anna Dostoevskaya's shop assistant (Silberstein 1973a), describe her work in the bookshop "Book Trade of F. Dostoevsky" (Eisenberg 1982). Her efforts toward the creation and maintenance of the Staraya Russa Dostoevsky High School were presented in the research by Kogan (1991).

Extensive materials from Anna Dostoevsky's archive were published by Nechaeva (1957); unpublished fragments of her memoirs appeared in Belov (1971a, 1972, 1976a) and Volgin (1986, 1990, 1991a). New editions of her memoirs were supplemented and published with annotated commentaries (Belov, Tunimanov 1971, 1982, 1987). Her complete memoirs have not yet been published. Her correspondence was made public (Belov 1976b, Bedekin 1987), such as correspondence with her contemporaries, among others S.A. Tolstaya (Shifman 1983), V.V. Rozanov (Garetto, 1994), S.N. Bulgakov, D.S. Merezhkovsky, E.I. Tarle (Thaikevich 1966). A part of Anna Dostoevskaya's correspondence was published in the book *Dostoevsky in the Unpublished Correspondence of His Contemporaries* (Lanskoi 1973).

B. Biographical Materials

1. The History of the Family. Childhood Years

Recently, some new materials were published about Dostoevsky's ancestors on his father's side in the fourteenth through eighteenth centuries. The information was mostly found in the rare archival sources which are more difficult to access, among them local church periodicals of the West Russian regions, local metrical books, and church archives (Volgin 1991b, Fedorenko

1994a). Information about relatives on his mother's side appears in the sixteenth through eighteenth centuries, including the pastors and priests of the Moscow Kremlin, a poet from the eighteenth century, several mayors of Moscow at the beginning of the nineteenth century, and others (Fedorov 1976, 1980).

Several important events from Dostoevsky's childhood received new explanations. S.V. Belov has discovered testimonies by Z.A. Trubetskaya who reproduced a story about a young girl, a partner in Fyodor's childhood games, who was brutally raped by a drunk and died in front of Dostoevsky's father who was the doctor of the Marinsky Hospital for the Poor. These memoirs (see Zakharov 1978) explain the complicated origin of this topic which recurs throughout *The Demons*. I have suggested (Volgin 1991b) a documentary explanation and interpretation of this event in different works by Dostoevsky.

The relationship between the Dostoevskys and the Kumanin family during Fyodor's childhood and the influence of these relationships on his works *A Little Hero* and *Idiot*, as well as on his stay in the Chermak College, were studied in writings by G.A. Fedorov (1973, 1976, 1991) on the basis of the archival documents. The same author has published fragments of the record of the criminal investigation into the death of Dostoevsky's father, which is available in its entirety in the local criminal archives. From the material of the official investigation it becomes clear "the secret councillor M. Dostoevsky ... died as a result of an accident, and there were no doubts or suspicions in his violent death."

Almost completely convinced by these official formulations, G. Fyodorov nevertheless supports the "mistake version," or "family version," of the violent death caused by serf peasants. Fyodor Dostoevsky, as well as all other members of the Dostoevsky family, had no doubts about the violent death of Mikhail Andreevich. However, most of the Dostoevsky experts agree that before making any final conclusions, all the documents have to be studied in a much more detailed way. Until such a serious, scrupulous study is performed, we cannot make any final judgments about this discovery.

The complete text of these criminal files has not yet been published. Therefore, in the book *To Be Born in Russia* (Volgin 1991b) the tentative, preliminary official version is presented with a grain of salt. This version proposes that natural causes were responsible for the death of Dostoevsky's father. Even using the excerpts from the case alone, by which G. Fedorov tried to deny the "family version," we can see convincing evidence that a violent murder took place. In my work (Volgin 1991a), I tried to bring together and critically analyze all documentary material available on this case.

The early period of Dostoevsky's life, 1821–1849, was studied in the fundamental monograph *The Early Dostoevsky* by V. Nechaeva (1979). It was primarily based on the study of the original archival sources.

Other publications that include material from the family archives include the works about the Kumanins' inheritance (Iakubovich 1987); about the album of the writer's niece (Ornatskaya and Tunimanov 1988); about the material of the E.A. Ivanov's archive (Semenishnikova 1971); memoirs of V.A. Sevastianova-Dostoevskaya (Belov 1993); and correspondence of E.A. and M.A. Rykachevs (Galagan 1973). There were many publications dedicated to the archival material about M.M. Dostoevsky, the writer's brother: in particular, his letters (Kupman, Konechny 1981; Pistsova 1972); biographical material about his service in the Engineering Department (Konechny 1976); materials from the criminal case of the Petrashevsky Circle (Fedorenko 1973), in which he was cleared of suspicions of treason which were not based on any serious evidence; and materials about his participation in the journals *Time* and *Epoch* (Nechaeva 1971a, 1975; Ornatskaya 1988).

2. St. Petersburg Period. Academy. Beginning of the Literary Career. The Petrashevsky Circle

Several key archival materials should be mentioned in connection with Dostoevsky's first St. Petersburg period, including documents about his studies at the Academy of Military Engineering (Iakubovich 1987a), his visits to brother Mikhail in Revel (Konechny 1983), and the reconstruction of the chronology of his life in the 1840s (Konechny 1971a, 1971b; I.D. Iakubovich *Letopis zhizni i tvorchestva Dostoevskogo [The Chronology of Dostoevsky's Life]*, Vol. 1, St. Petersburg, 1993).

Among the precious documentary material about this period of Dostoevsky's life are memoirs of A.E. Riesenkampf (Kogan 1973) and A.V. Kruzhinin (Ospovat 1983); the archival material about the Dostoevsky's work on his first novel, *The Poor People* (Iakubovich 1994b); information on the history of censorship of *The Illustrated Almanac (Complete Works*, Vol. 2); and material about Dostoevsky's participation in the Beketov literary circle (Poddubnaya 1974).

Documentary publications about Dostoevsky's membership in the Petrashevsky Circle give us a chance to cast a new glance at this important page in the writer's spiritual biography. Several fundamental works were dedicated to this question: a revised and enlarged edition of the monograph *Dostoevsky and the Petrashevsky Case* which is based on the criminal police files in the RGVIA and GARF archives (Belchikov 1971); the works of A.F. Vozny (1976, 1985) which are dedicated to the role of the secret police in the Petrashevsky case; the biography of N.A. Mordvinov, one of Dostoevsky's friends in the Speshnev "Secret Seven" circle (Porokh 1971); and the publication of the handwritten translation of Lamannet, one of the spiritual tutors of Russian utopian socialists, which was confiscated during the investigation (Nikitina 1973). A.L. Ospovat published for the first time the testimonies made by Dostoevsky during the interrogations which were found in the criminal files of N.A. Mordvinov and V.R. Zotov (*Complete Works*, Vol. 18). Above, I have already commented briefly on the criminal case of the writer's brother Mikhail (Fedorenko 1973).

Only a few of the newly discovered archival materials relating to Dostoevsky's participation in the Petrashevsky case were included in the book *The Metamorphoses of Power* (Volgin 1994) and in *Complete Works* (Vol. 30, part 2: 27). The second volume of my documentary biography of Dostoevsky, *The Political Process*, is completely dedicated to this topic, and is forthcoming in Russia.

3. Siberia: 1850–54. Omsk, Semipalatinsk, Kuznetsk

The Siberian period of Dostoevsky's life is widely described in the recent publications. First of all, I have to mention the works of M.M. Gromyko which were based on the previously unknown material from RNB and IRLI archives, the archive of the Geographical Society of Russia, and the regional archives in Tomsk, Omsk, Tumen and Tobolsk (Gromyko 1983, 1985).

The works of the local Siberian scholars include important information from the local archives and collections from Omsk, Semipalatinsk and Kuznetsk (Weinerman 1985, 1991; Leifer 1975, 1982; Diakov 1987; Gabdullina 1983, 1985; Grishaev 1985; Levchenko 1974; Lushnikov 1971; Kushnikova 1990, 1992; Shadrina 1993). The publication of the criminal case of Dmyitry Ilinsky is very important for the understanding of the history of *The Brothers Karamazov*, for this man was the namesake and one of the prototypes of Dmitry Karamazov (Iakubovich 1976). Materials of RGVIA and GARF archives are dedicated to Dostoevsky's friends and inmates in prison (who were also used in creation of his prototypes), I.D. Iakubovich and B.F. Fedorenko (*Complete Works* Vol. 4, 28, part 1). The Semipalatinsk period was reflected in letters in the 1860s from A.E. Vrangel to F. Dostoevsky (Ornatskaya 1973a).

Important information about Dostoevsky's life in Kuznetsk can be found in the letters of his wife, Anna Grigorievna (Bedekin 1987). New information about M.D. Isaeva, his first wife, is presented in the works of Ivanova (1991).

4. Dostoevsky in the 1860s

The archival documents relating to the history of the Dostoevsky's editorial work in the periodicals *Time* and *Epoch* were studied by the scholars in a very thorough manner. Two monographs by V.S. Nechaeva were dedicated to this topic (1972, 1975; see also Nechaeva 1971). A series of publications is dedicated to the editorial group and literary circle around the two Dostoevsky brothers (Ornatskaya 1988). The series includes works dedicated to individual members of the group, including P.V. Bykov (Elson 1987) and K.I. Nemshevich (Rak 1988a); to the history of censorship of these journals (Nechaeva 1971a, 1975; Rosenblum 1973), to literary acquaintances V. Krestovsky (Viktorovich 1991) and A.U. Poretsky (Viktorovich 1994); and to his relationships with the Literary Fund (Zaborova 1975) and the Society of Writers and Scholars in Need (Ornatskaya 1987). Recently, a detailed correspondence of poet A.N. Maikov was published, and a large part of it is connected with Dostoevsky (Iampolsky 1976, 1980; Bitiugova 1994b: Ashimbaeva 1984).

Several publications are dedicated to Dostoevsky's personal and family life. The memoirs of N. Poliansky describe Dostoevsky's stay at the family of the Ivanovs, his relatives in Moscow (Belov 1993). The complicated relationship between Dostoevsky and Polina Suslova is reflected in her letters to J. Polonsky (Bogorad 1985). The newly found archival material about Suslova was collected in a recently published book, *Dostoevsky's Lover* (Saraskina 1994), and included forty letters from Suslova to E.V. Salias de Turnemir, a woman writer who wrote under the pen name E. Tur; her twenty response letters; letters from the philosopher V. Rosanov, Suslova's husband; letters by E.P. Ivanov, Suslova's relative and a literary artist; unknown archival photographs; and various other items.

5. Dostoevsky in the 1870s

Materials of the RGVIA Archive were published recently. They shed new light on Dostoevsky's editorial work at *The Citizen* (Fedorenko 1994b) and on the events surrounding the attempt to close the journal (Viktorovich 1987). Materials about Dostoevsky's three-day arrest as the editor of this journal were included in the memoirs of P.I. Karepin (Belov 1983, 1993). A number of special publications are dedicated to Dostoevsky's editorial work at the section of poetry in *The Citizen* (Belov 1985) and to his relationship to two members of his editorial staff: R.R. Strandman (Bitiugova 1983) and D.D. Kishensky (Arkhipova 1976).

I would like to mention a series of my own works connected with *A Writer's Diary*. All these works were based on the archival material and were dedicated to the history of censorship of this periodical, its relationship with different circles of the Russian society; its editorial archive, etc. (Volgin 1970, 1971a, b, 1972, 1973, 1974a, b, 1975, 1976a, b, 1978, 1980a, 1982). After I had analyzed the statistics of the subscription and the bookkeeping records of this publication, I found out the general number and the social standing of its readers, the character of distribution of *A Writer's Diary* in different regions of Russia, and other statistics connected with subscriptions to the journal. I tried to prove that Dostoevsky's journal (written by one person, Fyodor

Dostoevsky) was created and existed in a new, personalized genre which was characterized by a close relationship with the reading audience. This made a great influence on the development of Russian literature.

At present we are not surprised by the vast amount of correspondence which, for example, was received by Leo Tolstoy during the last twenty years of his life, in 1890–1910. But in the 1870s, there was not a single Russian writer who was in the center of Russian social life. A direct contact between the writer and the reading audience was more the exception than the rule.

C.D. Alchevskaya wrote to the author of *A Writer's Diary*, "We, people from the province think that every writer is something mythological, unaccessible, prodigious and unusual. We can read his works, and that is all. We cannot see him, we cannot hear him speaking, we cannot write to him. What would happen with the writer when readers from the province would start attacking him with their letters?" (Volgin 1982: 41). *A Writer's Diary* created an important historical precedent. Dostoevsky stood at the beginning of a new Russian tradition. As founder of *A Writer's Diary* he was not merely an author, but an important social figure as well.

In analyzing the editorial archives of *A Writer's Diary* I came to the following conclusion: the ordinary readers of this periodical written by Dostoevsky felt the richness and diversity of different points of view united by some hidden denominator which defined the unity of publication and brought it out of the traditional limitations of the journalistic genre (Volgin 1982).

Relationships between Dostoevsky and *The Fatherland Notes*, a publication to which Dostoevsky felt an obvious sympathy, were an object of a special publication (see Arkhipova 1987a; also *Literary Heritage*, Vol. 77, edited by N. Nekrasov, which is completely dedicated to Dostoevsky's work at his novel *The Raw Youth*, and its publication in *The Fatherland Notes*). Documents about the secret police surveillance of Dostoevsky are available among the materials of the Novgorod Regional Archive, as well as among the materials of the GARF Archive, that is, the documents of the Third Section of Police (Kogan 1973). Analyses of these documents are found in Volgin 1986, 1990, and 1991a.

Based on forgotten or hardly accessible documents, mostly from the archives, I have reconstructed the details of the Pushkin Festival of 1880 and studied the hidden motivation of Dostoevsky's speech about Pushkin (Volgin 1980a, 1986, 1990, 1991a). Among the recently published materials about the Pushkin Festival the memoirs of N.A. Shamin (Belov 1993) are also noteworthy.

The archival materials about Dostoevsky's acquaintances in his last years are dedicated to the following people: K.K. Sluchevsky (Mazur 1978), I.L. Leontiev-Sheglov (Bitiugova 1994a), J.P. Polonsky (Smirnov 1972), V. Soloviev (Iakubovich 1991), S.I. Smirnova-Sazonova (Mostovskaya 1980), and J.B. von Bretzel (Serebriannaia 1973). Remembrances of V. Sevastianova-

Dostoevskaya and P.G. Kuznestov tell about the writer's family life (Belov 1993, Silberstein 1973a) and the correspondence of his contemporaries (Lanskoi 1973); these issues are reflected in the newly discovered correspondence between Dostoevsky and his friends (Volgin 1986, 1990, 1991a, 1993, 1994a, b). These documents combine to present a detailed portrait of the writer during the last years of his life.

6. Dostoevsky and the Royal Family

"Dostoevsky and the royal family" remains an unexplored topic. Here we have, so to speak, the eternal collision between "the poet and the king." This opposition is even more important to Russia, where both sides of this opposition possessed an exceptional power.

Not many works are dedicated to this topic, but one of note is the article "Dostoevsky and the Governmental Circles of the 1870s" by L. Grossman (*The Literary Heritage*, Vol. 15, 1934). Several more recent publications have studied the same issue; among them were rather extensive chapters from the books *The Last Year of Dostoevsky* and *To Be Born in Russia* (Volgin 1986, 1991a, b); the last chapter of the monograph *The Metamorphoses of Power* (Volgin 1994b) and the book *In Front of the Speechless Generations: Dostoevsky and the End of the Russian Royal House* (Volgin 1993, 1994a, 1995). Some new archival publications on the same topic were presented in volume 83 of *Literary Heritage*. Among these documents we find letters from Dostoevsky to the Grand Prince Konstantin Konstantinovich, the diaries of the Grand Prince (Silberstein 1973b), the memoirs of P.G. Kuznetsov about Dostoevsky's visits to the Winter Palace (Silberstein 1973a), and a letter from Anna Dostoevskaya to her brother Nikolai in which she comments on the evening her husband spent with the Grand Prince Sergei Nikolaevich (Lanskoi 1973). Recently, the publications on this topic were supplemented by a new version of the recorded memoirs of M.A. Ivanova, Dostoevsky's niece (Belov 1993). There exists another version of Ivanova's reminiscences published in the book *Dostoevsky in the Memoirs of His Contemporaries* in 1990.

In my book *The Metamorphoses of Power* (Volgin 1994b), as well as in an ongoing periodical publication "In Front of the Speechless Generations..." (Volgin 1993, 1994a, 1995), the history of the relationships between Dostoevsky and the members of the Russian royal family is studied for the first time. Among the members of the royal dynasty who knew Dostoevsky were Nikolai I; Alexander II; Grand Prince Alexander and the future tsar, Alexander III; Queen of Hellas, Olga Konstantinovna, other grand princes and grand princesses including Maria Fedorovna, the future Queen Maria; Princess of the House of Oldenburg, etc. I worked with materials which had never been studied before, principally including the archives of Alexander I and Alexander II (Files 678 and 677 of GARF Archive) and those of the Grand Princes Sergei and Pavel Alexandrovich, Konstantin and Dmitry Konstanti-novich, and Hoff-Meister Duchess A.E. Komarovskaya (Files 641, 648, 660, 765, 703 in the same archive). Upon studying these sources it was possible to reconstruct the complicated and dramatic history of Dostoevsky's presence in the life of the imperial family.

Several unique documents were published for the first time. These included fragments of the correspondence between the great princes Sergei and Konstantin and of their diaries, notes about Dostoevsky in the diaries of Alexander I and Alexander II, letters from the Grand Prince Dmitry and Duchess A. Komarovskaya about Dostoevsky's death and funeral, and many more similar items.

The study of the archives of the Tsar's family enables us to inquire about the degree of Dostoevsky's influence on the perceptions, attitudes and behav-ior of the members of the Russian royal family. On the other hand, there was a very clear desire of the Russian government to make Dostoevsky its ally, in order to capitalize on his huge popularity in the country at the time.

Before Dostoevsky was personally acquainted with the Grand Prince Konstantin, he was well known to the royal family. Dostoevsky's name was found in the Prince's diary describing his sin in New York when Konstantin visited a public house for the first time in his life: "I remembered Raskol-nikov from Dostoevsky's novel who was very decisive to commit a crime, and I tried to compare him with me, but there was a great difference between us. He wanted to make great deeds for humanity, and I simply wanted to sat-isfy my lust. To put it briefly, I tried to fight with my intentions, but they did not disappear" (Volgin 1994a: 218). And in the same diary, later on the same day: "Well, I have betrayed my belief…. I was in full consciousness all the time, as if I were Raskolnikov when he committed his crime" *Ibid.*, p. 21).

When I compared the notes from the diary of the Grand Prince Sergei Alexandrovich with Dostoevsky's first visits to the Winter Palace (where he was invited to have educational discussions with the Tsar's children), I came to an interesting conclusion. The personal invitation addressed to Dostoev-sky was personally signed by Alexander II and was passed to him, most prob-ably, at the same time when the secret scandal in the royal family burst out. Shortly before Dostoevsky's invitation as a tutor of the royal children, the Grand Prince Sergei Alexandrovich was suspected by his father, Alexander II, of homosexual desires; the accusation greatly influenced his future per-sonal and political image.

Dostoevsky's name was not mentioned in the diaries of Alexander II and Alexander III. But in these documents some additional information about the most important events from his life was discovered. The execution of the members of the Petrashevsky Circle was described in the diary of Alexander II for 1849 when he was the grand prince. Dostoevsky's contacts with the grand prince and the queen during the last years of his life were mentioned in the diary of (the future tsar) Alexander III for 1880. In the notebooks and correspondence of the royal family and their nearest circles, there were repeated reminiscences about the so-called "literary family readings" of Dostoevsky's works, as well as about discussions of these works. These were frequent events in the royal circles. I have also analyzed different versions of the legend about the personal friendship between Dostoevsky and Alexander II.

7. Dostoevsky's Death and Funeral

During recent years, several important sources relating to these events were published: namely, the correspondence of M.A. and E.A. Rykachevs (Galagan 1973); the memoirs of an unknown witness (Kuzmina 1971); the memoirs of J.B. von Bretzel (Serebriannaia 1973); the memoirs of J.I. Fausek and some unknown person (Belov 1993); and fragments of the I.F. Tiumenev's daybook (Foniakova 1973). In *The Last Year of Dostoevsky* (Volgin 1986, 1990, 1991a), I have published materials from the Anna Dostoevskaya Archive relating to the funeral: the undertaker's bill; a letter from the church warden, etc.

In the files of the Police Department (GARF Archive, File 112, vol. 1, p. 504), I discovered documents which shed additional light on the tragedy which happened at the end of January 1881 in the house at 5/2 Kuznechny Street where Dostoevsky lived. Events around this time included a police search of the apartment of Barannikov, a close neighbor of Dostoevsky in the same building who was at the same time a terrorist, a participant in the assassination attempt on the Tsar and a member of the executive committee of the terrorist organization "People's Will"; and the arrest of N.A. Kholodkevich, another member of the same terrorist organization who came to visit Barannikov after he got into a police trap. I tried to construct a coherent account based on newly discovered warrants for arrest, search warrants, records of interrogations, police correspondence, court records and other documents. I tried to create a version according to which Dostoevsky's last apartment, certainly without his knowledge, was used as a cover by the terrorist organization in the bloody game played by People's Will with the Russian government which led to the assassination of the Tsar one month after Dostoevsky's death, on 1 March 1881. It is obvious that several members of the assassination conspiracy were among the key figures in the game, among them A. Korba, a terrorist and a close personal friend of Dostoevsky.

If we compare in time the events at the Barannikov apartment with Dostoevsky's death, we can see that Dostoevsky's bleedings, which caused his death, coincided in time with the police search and the arrest at the next-door apartment. Thus we cannot rule out the possibility that these events caused the death agony of Dostoevsky, or at least greatly influenced the out-come of his disease.

Finally, several works have been dedicated to the history of conflict between Dostoevsky and government censors (Volgin 1970; Ornatskaya and Stepanova 1973).

In conclusion of this review of the archival publications of 1957–1995, I would like to stress that the latest findings in this field suggest a contribu-tion of interesting and unusual archival discoveries, despite the obvious wan-ing of undiscovered material. Therefore, it is too early to speak about the exhausted archives, especially if we consider not only "literary" but also official, business, family and other documents. The documentary material published during this period can be considered as a serious foundation for the future study of Dostoevsky's biography, as well as for the "biography" of all Russian society of the nineteenth century.

Abbreviations of Archives, Libraries and Museums

GARF the State Archive of Russian Federation (formerly TSGAOR—Central Sate
    Archive of the October Revolution)
GIM the State Historical Museum
IRLI the Institute of Russian Literature, the Pushkin House in St. Petersburg
RGALI (formerly TSGALI) the Central State Archive of Literature and Art
RGVIA the Russian State Archive of Military History
RNB (formerly GBL) the Lenin State Library
TSML the Central Museum of Literature

Selected Bibliography of Archival Publications, 1957–1995

Abbreviations of Periodicals

AB *Almanakh Bibliofila (Almanac of Bibliophile)*
DMI *Dostoevsky. Metrialy i issledovania (Dostoevsky. Materials and Discoveries)*
DS *Dostoevsky i sovremennost (Dostoevsky Today)*
DV *Dostoevsky i ego vremia (Dostoevsky and His Time)*
ERO.PD *Ezhegodnik rukopisnogo otdela Pushkinskogo Doma (The Annual Book of the
    Manuscript Department of Pushkin House,* Institute of Russian Literature)
IAN *Izvestiia Akademii Nauk SSSR. Seria literatury i iazyka (The Proceedings of the
    Academy of Sciences of the USSR. Series: Language and Literature)*
Kniga Kniga. Issledovania i materialy (Books, Discoveries and Materials)
*Letopis Letopis zhizni i tvorchestva Dostoevskogo (The Chronicle of Dostoevsky's Life and
    Works)*
LG *Literaturnaia Gazeta (Literary Newspaper)*
LN *Literaturnoe Nasledstvo (Literary Inheritance)*

NM *Novy Mir* (*The New World*)
PK NO *Pamiatniki kultury. Novye otkrytia* (*The Monuments of Culture. New Discoveries*)
PSS *F. Dostoevsky. Polnoe sobranie sochinenii* (*F. Dostoevsky. The Complete Works*)
RL *Russkaia Literatura* (*Russian Literature*)
SA *Sovetskie Arkhivy* (*Soviet Archives*)
VL *Voprosy Literatury* (*Issues of Literature*)
VP *Vstrechi s Proshlym* (*Meetings with the Past*)

Multiple works by the same author are arranged chronologically.

Arenin, E. "An Outstanding Stenographer Finds New Materials About Dostoevsky" *Izvestiia*, 3 June (1959).
_____. "Dostoevsky's Manuscript" (*Aftograf Dostoevskogo*). *Smena*, 17 October (1971): 243.
Arkhipova, A.V. "Dostoevsky and Kishensky." DMI 2 (1976).
_____. "Dostoevsky and *The Fatherland Notes* in 1867." DMI 7 (1987a).
_____. "Unpublished Letters from Anna Dostoevskaya to Dostoevsky" (*Neizvestnye pis'ma A.G. Dostoevskoi k Dostoevskomu*). *Ibid.*, (1987b).
_____ and Ipatova, S.A. "Unpublished Letters Addressed to Dostoevsky. From the Dostoevsky Archive" (*Neizdannye pis'ma k Dostoevskomy. Iz arkhiva Dostoevskogo*). DMI 11 (1994).
Asadovsky, K.M. "Dostoevsky and His Contemporaries, According to F. Fidler's Diary" (*Dostoevsky glazami sovremennikov: po materialam dnevnika F. Fidlera*). NM 8 (1985).
Ashimbaeva, N.T. "A.I. Maikov. Letters to Dostoevsky" (*A.I. Maikov. Pis'ma k F. Dostoevskomy*). PK NO (1982).
Barsht, K.A. "Gothic Architecture of Dostoevsky" (*Gotika Dostoevskogo*). *Neva* 10 (1984).
_____. *Fyodor Dostoevsky. Texts and Drawings.* Leningrad, 1985.
_____. "Two Drawings by Dostoevsky" (*Dva risunka Dostoevskogo*). RL, 3 (1985).
_____. "Graphical Sketches by Dostoevsky and Literary-Graphical Art." *Russian Literature and Art Abroad* (*Grafika v chernovikakh Dostoevskogo i slovensno-graficheskie vidy tvorchestva. Russkaia literatura i zarubezhnoe iskusstvo*). Leningrad, 1986.
_____ ,et al. "Unpublished letters to Dostoevsky" (*Neizdannye pis'ma k Dostoevbskomu*). DMI 5 (1985).
Bedekin, P.V. "Unknown Materials About Dostoevsky's Stay in Kuznetsk" (*Neizvestnye materialy o prebyvanii Dostoevskogo v Kuznetske*). DMI 7 (1987).
Belchikov, N.F. *Dostoevsky in the Petrashevsky Process* (*Dostoevsky u protsesse Petrashevtsev*). Moscow, 1971.
Belov, S.V. "Dostoevsky in the Memoirs of His Contemporaries. A Bibliography" (*Dostoevsky v vospominaniiakh sovremennikov*). *The Manuscript Department of the Lenin State Library* 26 (1963).
_____. *F.M. Dostoevsky in the Memoirs of His Contemporaries* (*F.M. Dostoevsky v vospominaniakh sovremennikov*), vols. 1–2, Moscow, 1964.
_____. "Dostoevsky in the Memoirs of His Contemporaries. A Bibliography" (*Dostoevsky v vospominaniakh sovremennikov. Bibliografia*), in *Problems of Genre in the History of Russian Literature.* Leningrad, 1969.
_____. "A.G. Dostoevskaya. Unpublished Excerpts and Variants" (*Neopublikovannye otryvki i varianty*). *Dalnii vostok*, 11; *Knizhnaia torgovlia*, no. 10; *Vechernii Leningrad*, 11 November, no. 267; *Nedelia*, 13–19 September, no. 38.

_____. "From Dostoevskaya's Memoirs" (*Iz vospominanii Dostoevskoi*). *Kniga* 23 (1973).

_____. "A Lost Book Review by Dostoevsky" (*Zabytaia retsenziia Dostoevskogo*). LN 83 (1973).

_____. "From Anna Dostoevskaya's Correspondence with Her Husband" (*Iz peripiski Dostoevskoy s muzhem*). *Baikal* 5 (1975).

_____. "From the Memoirs of Anna Dostoevskaya" (*Iz vospominanii A. Dostoevskoi*). *Kniga* 32 (1976a).

_____. "Dostoevskaya's Correspondence with Her Contemporaries" (*Perepiska A.S. Dostoevskoi s sovremennikami*). *Baikal* 5 (1976b).

_____. "Search for Dostoevsky's Materials" (*Poiski materialov o Dostoevskom*). AB 10 (1981).

_____. "Dostoevsky's Second Arrest. Newly Discovered Memoirs" (*Vtoroi arest Dostoevskogo. Neizvestnye vospominaniia*). *Russkii arkhiv* 3 (1983).

_____. "Around Dostoevsky" (*Vokrug Dostoevskogo*). NM 1 (1985).

_____. *The Writer's Wife: The Last Love of Dostoevsky* (*Zhena pisatelia: posledniaia liubov Dostoebuskogo*). Moscow, 1986a.

_____. *Romantics of the Book Discovery* (*Romantika knizhnykh poiskov*). Moscow, 1986b.

_____. "'I love you...' F. Dostoevsky in the Unpublished Notebook of Anna Dostoevskaya" (*"Ja tebia liubliu..." F. Dostoevskii v neizdasnnoi zapisnoi knizhke A. Dostoevskoi*). *Volga* 9 (1988).

_____. "Dostoevsky in the Previously Unpublished Correspondence" (*Dostoevsky v neizdannoi perepiske*). *Sever* 11 (1991).

_____. "The Unknown Dostoevsky" (*Neizvestnyi Dostoevskii*). *Slovo* 11 (1992).

_____. *Dostoevsky in the Forgotten and Unpublished Memoirs of His Contemporaries* (*Dostoevskii v zabytykh i neizvestnykh vospominaniiakh sovremennikov*). St. Petersburg, 1993.

_____ and Tunimanov, V.A. *F. Dostoevsky. Crime and Punishment. A Commentary* (*Prestuplenie i nakazanie*). Moscow, 1970.

_____ and _____. *A.G. Dostoevskaya. Memoirs* (*Vospominaniia*). Moscow, 1971.

_____ and _____. *F.M. Dostoevsky. A.G. Dostoevskaya. Correspondence*. Moscow, 1976.

_____ and _____. *A.G. Dostoevskaya. Memoirs* (*Vospominaniia*), 2nd ed. Moscow, 1982.

_____ and _____. *A.G. Dostoevskaya. Memoirs* (*Vospominaniia*), 3rd ed. Moscow, 1987.

Bitiugova, I. A. "An Unpublished Letter by Dostoevsky" (*Neopublikovannoe pis'mo F.M. Dostoevskogo*). PL 4 (1961).

_____. "I.A. Dostoevsky and R.R. Strandman." DMI 5 (1983).

_____. "Dostoevsky as Editor of Poems Published in *The Citizen*" (*Dostoievsky-redaktor stikhotvorenii v "Grazhdabnine"*). DMI 6 (1985).

_____. "Correspondence Between Dostoevsky and Maikov. Unknown autographs of some poems" (*K perepiske Dostoevskogo s Maikovym. Neizvestnye aftorgafy stikhotvorenii*). DMI 9 (1994a).

_____. "The Chronology of Dostoevsky's Life and Work" (*Letopis zhizni i tvorchestva Dostoevskogo: 1866–1870*). *Letopis* 2 (1994b).

_____ and Iakubovich, I.D. "An Unknown Letter from Dostoevsky to Liuibimov Dedicated to *The Brothers Karamazov*" (*Neizvestnoe pis'mo Dostoevskogo k N.A. Liuibimovu, bosviashennoe Bratiam Karvazovym*). RL 1 (1990).

_____ and Leontiev, I. "Sheglov and Dostoevsky." DMI 11 (1994).

Blum, A.V. "F.M. Dostoevsky and the 'Pedagogical' Censorship" (*Dostoevsky i "pedagogicheskaia" tsenzura*). SA 5 (1971).

Bogorad, G.L. "Two Letters from Suslova to I.P. Polonsky" (*Dva pis'ma Suslovoi k I.P. Polonskomu*). DMI 6 (1985).

Bogorad, V.E. "Polemics with Dostoevsky: Articles Prohibited for Publication by the Censor" *Literary Heritage*. Moscow: Nauka (Academy Press), 1959, vol. 67.

Borodin, A.A. "File from the Archive, About a Black File 'Documents and Official Papers Connected with Dostoevsky's Résumé,' Found in Moscow by G. Kogan. The Original of the Diploma of the Member of the Russian Academy of Sciences, Issued to Dostoevsky." *Izvestiia* 1 September (1976).

Borshevsky S.S., et al. "Notebooks and Sketchbooks by Dostoevsky" (*Zapisnye knizhki i tetradi Dostoevskogo*). LN 83 (1971).

Bronnikova, V.V. "Memoirs of E.N. Opochinin" (*Vospominaniia E.N. Opochinina*). VP 7 (1990).

Bursov, B.I. "Unknown Dostoevsky" (*Dostoevsky neizvestny*). LG, 23 September (1970):39.

Desiatkina, L.P. and Friedlender, G.M. "Dostoevsky's Library. New Findings" (*Biblioteka Dostoevskogo. Novye materialy*). DMI 4 (1980).

Diakov, V.A. "Dostoevsky in Prison. New Sources," in *Political Prisoners in Siberia in the 19th Century* (*Katorzhnye gody Dostoevskogo. Po novym istochnikam. Politichaskaia ssylka v Sibiri XIX*). Novosibirsk, 1987.

Dolinin, A.S. *F.M. Dostoevsky. Letters* (*Pis'ma*), Vol. 4. Moscow–St. Petersburg, 1959.

_____. *The Last Novels by Dostoevsky: History of Creation of "The Raw Youth" and "The Brothers Karamazov."* Moscow, 1963.

Duganov, R.V. *Drawings by Russian Writers*. Moscow: Sovetskaia Russiia, 1988, pp. 152–156.67.

Eisenberg, T.D. "Unpublished documents of 'The Dostoevsky Book Trade Company'" (*Neopublikovannye dokumenty "Knizhnoi torgovli Dostoevskogo"*). *Kniga* 45 (1982).

Eisner, A. "From the Memoirs About Dostoevsky" (*Iz vospominanii o Dostoevskom*). *Znamia* 11 (1991).

Elson, M.D. "P. Bykov and *Time* Journal" (*P. Bykov i zhurnal "Vremia"*). DMI 7 (1987).

Fedorenko, B.V. "Criminal Case of Dostoevsky, the Member of the Petrashevsky Circle" (*Sledstvennoe delo Dostoevskogo-petrashevtsa*). DMI 1 (1973).

_____. "New Discoveries About Dostoevsky," in *New Aspects of Dostoevsky Studies* (*Iz razyskanii o Dostoevskom. Novye aspekty v izuchenii Dostoevskogo*). Petrozavodsk, 1994a.

_____. "To the History of Periodical *The Citizen*" (*K istorii gazety-zhurnala "Grazhdanin"*). DMI 11 (1994b).

Fedorov, G.A. "The Dostoevsky's Moscow" (*Moskva Dostoevskogo*). LG 20 (1971).

_____. "Chermak's College in 1834–37. New Discoveries" (*Pansion Chermaka v 1834–37gg. Po novym istochnikam*). DMI 1 (1973).

_____. "Fantasies and the Logic of the Facts" (*Domysly i logika faktov*). LG 18 June (1975).

_____. "Stories About the Dostoevsky Family in Moscow" (*Iz razyskanii o moskovskoi rodne F.M. Dostoevskogo*). DMI 2 (1976).

_____. "Father and Son, the Kotelnytskys" (*Otets i syn Kotelnitskie*). PK NO (1979).

Foniakova, N.N. "The Landlord. The Father Was Killed... The Story of One's Life" (*Pomeshik. Otsa ubili ... istoriia odnoi sudby*). NM 10 (1988).

Friedlender, G.M. *Dostoevsky's Realism*. Moscow, 1964.

_____. "New Materials from Manuscript Heritage" (*Novye materialy iz rukopisnogo naslediia*). LN 83 (1971).

_____. "A Letter to Y. Volfram" (*Pis'mo k J. Volframu*). DMI 5 (1983).

Gabdullina, V.I. "Dostoevsky's Prototypes from Semipalatinsk," in *Literature and*

Folklore of Kazakstan. (*Semipalatinskie prototipy F.M. Dostoevskogo. Literaura i folklor Kazakhstana*) Karaganda, 1983.

_____. "Siberian Impressions of Dostoevsky and 'A Writer's Diary'," in *The Future of the Siberian Literature* (*Sibirskie vpechatleniia F. Dostoevskogo i "Dnevnik pisatelia." Tendentsii razvitiia russkoi literatury v Sibiri*). Novosibirsk, 1985.

Galagan, G.J. "The Death and the Funeral of Dostoevsky" (*Konchina i pokhorony Dostoevskogo*). DMI 1 (1973).

Galperina, R.G. "About a Record in a Metrical Book" (*Ob odnoi zapisi v metricheskoi knige*). DS 2 (1991).

Garetto, E. "From the Anna Dostoevskaya Archive. Letters by D. Merezhkovsky, S. Bulgakov, V. Riazanov" (*Iz arkhiva A.G. Dostoevskoi. Pis'ma D. Merezhkovskogo, S. Bulgakova, V. Riazanova*). Minuvshee 9 (1994).

Gomon, M.L. "Dostoevsky's Friend from Biruchevsky," from *The Belgorod Literary Journal* (*Biruchevsky drug Dostoevskogo. Belgorodshina literaturnaia*). Voronezh 1 (1979).

Grishaev, V.F. "About Dostoevsky's Stay in the Altai" (*K prebyvaniju Dostoevskogo na Altae*). DMI 6 (1985).

Gromyko, M.M. "F.M. Dostoevsky and the Family of the Decembrist I. Annenkov," in *Political Prisoners and Exiles in the 18th–19th Centuries* (*Dostoevsky i semia dekabrista I. Annenkova. Poiticheskie ssylnye v Sibiri XVIII–XXvv*). Novosibirsk, 1983.

_____. *Siberian Friends of Dostoevsky* (*Sibirskie znakomye i druzia Dostoevskogo*). Novosibirsk, 1985.

Iakubovich, I.D. "*The Brothers Karamazov* and the Police File of D.I. Illinsky" ("*Bratia Karamazovy*" *i sledstvennoe delo D.I. Ilinskogo*). IO (1976).

_____. "Unknown Book Review About the Novel *My Uncle's Dream*" (*Neizvestny otzyv o povesti "Diadushkin Son"*). IO (1983).

_____. "Dostoevsky at the Engineering Academy" (*Dostoevsky v glavnom inzhenernom uchilishe*). DMI 7 (1987a).

_____. "Unknown Business Papers by Dostoevsky" (*Nezvestnye delovye bumagi Dostoevskogo*). DMI 7 (1987b).

_____. "Letters from V. Solovyov to Dostoevsky" (*Pis'ma V. Solovyova k Dostoevskomu*). Nashe nasledie 6 (1991).

_____. "The Chronology of Dostoevsky's Life and Works" (*Letopis zhizni i tvorchestva F.M. Dostoevskogo, 1821–1864*). Letopis, 1993.

_____. "Addendum to the List Called 'The Book Autographs of 1847–81'" (*Dopolnenie k spisku "Darstvennye nadpisi" na knigakh 1847–81 godov*). DMI 11 (1994a).

_____. "Dostoevsky's Work at His Novel *The Poor People*" (*Dostoevsky v rabote nad romanom "Bednye Liudi"*). DMI 9 (1994b).

Iampolsky, I.G. "From the A.N. Maikov Archive" (*Iz arkhiva A.N. Maikova*). EPO PD (1976).

_____. "Unpublished Letters from A. Maikov to F. Dostoevsky" (*Neizdannye pis'ma A.N. Maikova o Dostoevskom*). DMI 4 (1980).

Iudina, I.M., et al. "Unpublished Letters to Dostoevsky" (*Neizdannye pis'ma k Dostoevskomu*). DMI 2 (1976).

Ivanio, I.V. "Draft Variants of the Pushkin Speech" (*Chernovye nabroski k rechi o Pushkine*). LN 86 (1973).

Ivanova, L.I. "New Information About Dostoevsky's First Wife" (*Novye svedeniia o pervoi zhene Dostoevskogo*). CA 6 (1991).

Kapeliush, B.I. "An Unpublished Letter from Dostoevsky to V.M. Kachanovsky" (*Neizdannoe pis'mo Dostoevskogo k V.M. Kachanovskomu*). DV (1979).

Kiiko, E.I. "The Chronicle of Dostoevsky's Life and Works" (*Letopis zhizni i tvorchestva F.M. Dostoevskogo*). *Letopis* 2 (1994).

_____ and Poshemanskaia, S.M. "A Previously Unknown Text of *The Brothers Karamazov Novel*" (*Neizvestny istochnik teksta romana "Bratia Karamazovy"*). DMI 3 (1978).

Kogan, G.F. "New Discoveries on Dostoevsky" (*Razyskaniia o Dostoevskom*). LN 86 (1973a).

_____. "A Riesenkampf. Memoirs About F.M. Dostoevsky" (*Vospominaiia o Fyodore Mikhailoviche Dostoevskom*). LN 86 (1973b).

_____. "A Draft Variant of the Novel *Oppressed and Humiliated*" (*Chernovoi nabrosok k romanu "Unizhennye i oskorblennye"*). LN 86 (1973c).

_____. "An Unpublished Letter to N.N. Strakhov (*Neopublikovannoe pis'mo k N.N. Strakhovu*). DMI 4 (1980).

_____. "About the History of the Evening Parties in St. Petersburg" (*Iz istorii peterburgskikh vecherov*). DS 2 (1991).

_____. "An Important Page in the Study of Dostoevsky's Works" (*Vazhnaia stranitsa v issledovanii tvorchestva Dostoevskogo*) in *The Old Times of Kuznetsk* (*Kuznetskaia starina*), vol. 1 (1993).

Konechny, A.M. "Dostoevsky in Revel" (*Dostoevsky v Revele*). VL 5 (1971a).

_____. "Dostoevsky in the 1840s" (*Dostoevsky v 1840-e gody*). DV (1971b).

_____. "Dostoevsky's Trips to Revel" (*Poezdki Dostoevskogo v Revel*). AB 15 (1983).

Konshina, E.N. "Notes to *The Brothers Karamazov* and *A Writer's Diary*." LN 86 (1973).

Krasovsky, J.A. "Dostoevsky's Correspondent from Kazan" (*Kazansky korrespondent Dostoevskogo*). VP 1 (1970).

_____. "The Dostoevsky Archive" (*Arkhiv Dostoevskogo*). VP 2 (1973).

Kupman, K.A. and Konechny, A.M. "Letters from Mikhail Dostoevsky to His Father" (*Pis'ma Mikhaila Dostoevskaoa k otsu*). PK NO (1980–81).

Kushnikova, M.M. "Dostoevsky's Days in Kuznetsk" (*Kuznetskie dni F.M. Dostoevskogo*). Kemerovo, 1990.

_____. "Dostoevsky's Stay in Kuznetsk" (*Kuznetsky period F. Dostoevskogo*). Povince 4 (1992).

Kuzmina, L.I. "St. Petersburg Never Saw Anything Like This. About Dostoevsky's Funeral" (*Peterburg ne videl nichego podobnogo*). DV (1971).

Lanskoi, L.R. "A Good and Encouraging Word" (*Dobroe i obodriajushee slovo*). LG 33 (1971a).

_____. "Lost Letters by Dostoevsky" (*Utrachennye pis'ma Dostoevskogo*). VL 11 (1971b).

_____. "Dostoevsky in the Unpublished Correspondence by His Contemporaries" (*Dostoevsky v neizdannoi perepiske sovremennikov*). LN 86 (1973).

_____. "Collection of Anna Dostopevskaya's Manuscripts" (*Kollekstii aftografov A.G. Dostoevskoi*). PK NO (1977).

Lebedev, V.K. "An Excerpt from *The Brothers Karamazov* and the Story of Its Censorship" (*Otryvok iz romana "Bratia Karamazovy" pered sudom tsensury*). RL 2 (1970).

Leifer, A. "It's Always with Me" (*Vsegda so mnoi*). Sibirskie ogni 7 (1975).

_____. "A Real Treasure. New Materials About Dostoevsky" (*Istinnoe bogatstvo. Novye materialy o Dostoevskom*). Sibirskie ogni 1 (1982).

Levchenko, N.I. "A Circle of Dostoevsky's Friends in Semipalatinsk" (*Krug znakomykh Dostoevskogo v Semipalatinske*). DMI 11 (1974).

Likhachev, D.S. "Gothical Windows: Drawings by Dostoevsky" (*Gotichestkie okna Dostoevskogo*) in *Literature—Reality—Literature*. Moscow, 1984.

Liubimov, L. "Abroad [Na Tchuzhbine]. Memoirs About Dostoevsky and D. Liubi-mov During the Creation of *The Brothers Karamazov.*" *Novii Mir* 2 (1957): 177–206.

Lushnikov, A. "Dostoevsky in the Altai Region" (*Distoevsky na Altae*). *Altai* 4 (1971).

Mar, N. "How Dostoevskaya's Notebooks Were Read" (*Kak byli rashifrovany zapis-nye knizhki Dostoevskoi*). LG, 17 November (1971):47.

Mazur, T.P. "Dostoevsky and Sluchevsky." DMI 3 (1978).

Mostovskaya, N.I. "Dostoevsky in the Notebooks by S. Smirnova-Sazonova" (*Dos-toievsky v zapisnykh knizhkakh S. Smirnovoi-Sazonovoi*). DMI 4 (1980).

Nechaeva, V.S. "From the Archives of the *Time* Journal" (*Iz arkhiva zhurnala "Vremia"*). DV (1971a).

_____. "From the Archives of the *Epoch* Journal" (*Iz arkhiva zhurnala "Epokha"*). DV (1971b).

_____. *Journal* Time *by F. and M. Dostoevsky* (*Zhurnal F. i M. Dostoevskikh "Vremia," 1861–1863*). Moscow, 1975.

_____. *Journal* Epoch *by F. and M. Dostoevsky* (*Zhurnal F. i M. Dostoevskikh "Epokha"*). Moscow, 1975.

_____. *Dostoevsky in His Early Years, 1821–1849* (*Rannii Dostoevsky*). Moscow, 1979.

_____ ,et al. *The Description of Dostoevsky's Manuscripts* (*Opisanie rukopisei Dosto-evskogo*). Moscow, 1957.

Nikitina, F.G. "Petrashevsky and Lamennet." DMI 3 (1978).

Odesskaya, M.E. Opochinin. "F. Dostoevsky: My Memoirs and Notes" (*F. Dostoev-sky: Moi vospominaniia i zametki*). NM 8 (1992).

Ornatskaya, T.I. "Letters from Vrangel to Dostoevsky" (*Pis'ma A. Vrangela k Dos-toevskomu*). DMI 3 (1983a).

_____. "*The Brothers Karamazov.* Drafts and Variants" (*"Bratia Karamazovy." Cher-novye nabroski*). DMI 5 (1983b).

_____. "Lines Written by Dostoevsky's Hand" (*Rukoyu Dostoevskogo*). DMI 6 (1985).

_____. "Dostoevsky's Activity in the Society Supporting the Literary Artists and Scholars in Need" (*Deiatelnost Dostoevskogo v Obshestve dlia posobiia nuzhda-jushimsia literatoram i uchenym*). DMI 7 (1987).

_____. "Editorial-Literary Circle of the Dostoevskys, 1865–71" (*Redaktsionny liter-aturny kruzhok Dostoevskikh, 1865–71*). DMI 8 (1988).

_____. "The Chronicle of Dostoevsky's Life and Work" (*Letopis zhizni i tvorchestva Dostoevskogo: 1865–71*). *Letopis* 2 (1994).

_____ and Stepanova, G.V. "Dostoevsky's Novels and the Theater Censorship" (*Romany Dostoevskogo i dramaticheskaia tsensura*) DMI 1 (1973).

_____ and Tunimanov, V.A. "The Album of Dostoevsky's Niece." (*Albom plemian-nitsy F. Dostoevskogo*). *The Leningrad Panorama* 2 (1988).

Ospovat, A.L. "Druzhnin About Young Dostoevsky" (*Druzhinin o molodom Dostoev-skom*). DMI 5 (1983).

Pistsova, A.Z. "Unknown Letters by M.M. Dostoevsky About His Brother" (*Neizvest-nye pis'ma M.M. Dostoevskogo o brate*). *The Proceedings of the St. Petersburg Uni-versity, Series of Literature and Linguistics* 2 (1972).

Poddubnaia, R.N. "The Beketov Circle and the Artistic Search of Dostoevsky" (*Kruzhok Beketovykh v ideinykh iskaniiakh Dostoevskogo. Voprosy russkoi literatury*). *Russian Literature* 2 (1974).

Pomerantz, S.G. "From the Manuscript of *A Writer's Diary*" (*Iz rukopisi "Dnevnika Pisatelia"*). LN 86 (1973).

Porokh, I.V. *History Reflected in a Man* (*Istoriia v cheloveke*). Saratov, 1971.

Poshemanskaya, S.M. "You Are the Most Interesting Woman for Me" (*Dia menia— samaia interesnaia*). *Smena*, 27 December (1970):302.

_____ and Zhitomirskaya, S.M. "The Deciphered Notebook of Anna Dostoevskaya" (*Rashifrovanny dnevnik A. Dostoevskoi*). LN 86 (1973).

Pustilnik, L.S. "Letters from A. Pleshcheev to F. Dostoevsky" (*Pis'ma A. Pleshcheeva k F. Dostoevskomu*). *Literary Archive* 6 (1961).

Rak, V.D. "K.I. Nemshevich, a Staff Member of the *Epoch* Journal" (*K.I. Nemshevich—sotyrudnik "Epokhi"*). DMI 8 (1988a).

_____. "Finding a More Precise Date in the Diaries of 1875–76" (*Utochnenie odnoi zapisi v tetradi 1875–76gg*). DMI 8 (1988b).

Reinus, L.M. "About the Prototype of Grushenka in *The Brothers Karamazov*" (*O prototipe Grushenki iz "Bratiev Karamazovykh"*). PL 4 (1967).

_____. *Dostoevsky in Staraya Russa* (*Dostoevsky v Staroi Russe*). Leningrad, 1971.

_____. "About the House Described in *The Brothers Karamazov*" (*O realiakh doma Karamazovykh*). DMI 6 (1985a).

_____. *Three Addresses of Dostoevsky* (*Tri adresa Dostoevskogo*). Leningrad, 1985b.

_____. "About the landscape of Skotoprigonievsk" (*O peizazhe Skotoprigonievska*). DMI 9 (1991).

Rosenblum, L.M. "Dostoevsky's Unfulfilled Plan" (*Neosushestvelenny zamysel Dostoevskogo*). IAN, XXX, 5 (1971a).

_____. "Drafts and Notebooks by Dostoevsky" (*Tvorcheskie dnevniki Dostoevskogo*). LN 83 (1971b).

_____. "The Fires in St. Petersburg in 1862 and F. Dostoevsky" (*Peterburgskie pozhary 1862 g. i Dostoevsky*). LN 86 (1973).

Saraskina, L.I. *Dostoevsky's Lover* (*Vozliublennaia Dostoevskogo*). Moscow, 1994.

Semenishnikova, L.L. "From the Personal Archive of E.A. Ivanova" (*Iz lichnogo arkhiva E.A. Ivanovoi*). DS 2 (1991).

Serebriannaia, N.Z. "J.B. Von Bretzel About Dostoevsky." LN 86 (1973).

Shadrina, A. "About Dostoevsky's Friends in Kuznetsk. The Father Evgeny" (*Iz kuznetskogo okruzheniia Dostoevskogo. Otets Evgeni.*) *Razyskania.* (*Discoveries*) Kemerovo, 1993.

Shifman, A. "From the Correspondence Between S.A. Tolstaya and A.G. Dostoevskaya" (*Iz perepiski S.A. Tolstoi i A.G. Dostoevskoi*). *Neva* 2 (1983).

Silberstein, I.S. "My Work with Dostoevsky: 1879–81" (*Na sluzhbe u Dostoevskogo 1879–81 gg*). LN 86 (1973a).

_____. "New Discoveries: Letters Written by Dostoevsky" (*Novonaidennye i zabytye pis'ma Dostoevskogo*). LN 86 (1973b).

Smirnov, V.B. "Dostoevsky at the Polonsky House on Fridays" (*Dostoevsky na piatnitsakh u Y. Polonskogo*). In *Issues of Soviet and Russian Literature* (*Problemy istorii russkoi i sovetskoi literatury*). Ufa, 1972.

Stepanova, G.V. "Letters from Veinberg to Dostoevsky" (*Pis'ma O. Veinberga k Dostoevskomu*). DMI 4 (1980).

Tchaikevich, E.I. "Tarle About Dostoevsky." SA 6 (1966).

Tikhomirov, V.N. "About Some Unknown Facts from the Dostoevsky Biography" (*Ob odnom belom piatne v biografii Dostoevskogo*). RL 2 (1986).

Veinerman, V.S. "Dostoevsky's Friends in Omsk" (*Omsoe okruzhenie Dostoevskogo*). DMI 6 (1985).

Veinerman, V.S. *Dostoevsky and Omsk*. Omsk, 1991.

Viktorovich, V.A. "Dostoevsky and V. Krestovsky." DMI 9 (1991).

_____. "An Unknown Literary Artist. Dostoevsky's Friends" (*Literator-nivedimka. Sputniki Dostoevskogo*). *Litsa* (1994a):4.

_____. "The Chronicle of Dostoevsky's Life and Works" (*Letopis zhizni i tvorchestva Dostoevskogo, 1983–1874*). *Letopis* (1994b):2.

Vladimirtsev, V.P., and Ornatskaia, T.I. *F. Dostoevsky. My Prison Notebook. The Siberian Notebook* (*F. Dostoevsky. Moia tetradka katorzhnaia. Sibirskaia tetrad'*). Krasnoiarsk, 1985.

Vodovazsky, V. "Paintings and Drawings by Dostoevsky." *Izvestiia*, 17 February (1979).

Volgin, I.L. "Dostoevsky and the Censorship of the Tsar. To the History of the Creation of *A Writer's Diary*" (*Dostoevsky i tsarskaia tsenzura. K istorii sozdaniia "Dnevnika pisatelia"*). PL 4 (1970).

_____. "Letters from the Readers to F.M. Dostoevsky" (*Pis'ma chtatelei k F.M. Dostoevskomu*). VL 9 (1971a).

_____. "The Moral Questions of Dostoevsky's Journalism. The Eastern Question in *A Writer's Diary*" (*Nravstvennye problemy publististiki Dostoevskogo. Vostochny voprios v "Dnevnike pisatelia"*). IAN, XXX, 4 (1971b).

_____. "Letters from I. Aksakov to F. Dostoevsky." IAN, XXXI, 4 (1972).

_____. "Fragments from *A Writer's Diary*" (*Fragmenty "Dnevnika pisatelia"*). LN 86 (1973).

_____. *Dostoevsky's "A Writer's Diary." The History of Creation* (*"Dnevnik pistaelia" Dostoevskogo. Istoriia izdania*). Moscow, 1974a.

_____. "The Editorial Archive of *A Writer's Diary*" (*Redaktsionnii arkhiv "Dnevnika pisatelia"*). PL 1 (1974b).

_____. *An Unfinished Dialogue"* (*Nezavershenny dialog*). VL 4 (1975).

_____. "An Obvious Proof. Dostoevsky and the Second Revolutionary Situation in Russia" (*Dokazatelstvo ot protivnogo. Dostoevsky i vtoraia revlutsionnaia sitautsiia v Rossii*). VL 9 (1976a).

_____. "Dostoevsky and Russian Society" (*Dostoevsky i russkoe obshestvo*). RL 3 (1976b).

_____. "*A Writer's Diary:* It's Text and Context" (*"Dnevnik pistatelia": Tekst i kontekst*). DMI 3 (1978).

_____. "Dostoevsky and the Governmental Policy in Education" (*Dostoevsky i pravitelstvennaia politika v oblastu prosvesheniia*). DMI 4 (1980a).

_____. "Dostoevsky's Inheritance" (*Zaveshchanie Dostoevskogo*). VL 6 (1980b).

_____. "The Last Year of Dostoevsky" (*Poslednii god Dostoevskogo*). NM 10 (1981).

_____. *Dostoevsky as a Journalist* (*Dostoevsky—zhurnalist*). Moscow, 1982.

_____. "The Last Year of Dostoevsky" (*Poslednii god Dostoevskogo*). *Druzhba Narodov* 1 (1984).

_____. "The Last Year of Dostoevsky" (*Poslednii god Dostoevskogo*). *Druzhba Narodov* 4–7 (1985).

_____. *The Last Year of Dostoevsky* (*Poslednii god Dostoevskogo*). Moscow, 1986.

_____. "To Be Born in Russia. Dostoevsky and His Contemporaries" (*Roditsia v Rossii. Dostoevsky i sovremenniki*). *Oktyabr'*, 3–5 (1989).

_____. *The Last Year of Dostoevsky. Historical Notes* (*Poslednii god Dostoevskogo. Istoricheskie zapiski*), 2nd ed. Moscow, 1990.

_____. *The Last Year of Distoevsky. Historical Notes* (*Poslednii god Dostoevskogo. Istoricheskie zapiski*), 3rd ed. Moscow, 1991a.

_____. *To Be Born in Russia. Dostoevsky and His Contemporaries* (*Roditsia v Rossii. Dostoevsky i sovremenniki*). Moscow, 1991b.

_____. "In Front of the Silent Generations. Dostoevsky and the End of the Russian Royal House" (*V vidu bezmolvnogo potomstva. Dostoevsky i gibel' russkogo imperatorskogo doma*). *Oktyabr'*, 11–12 (1993).

_____. *The Metamorphoses of Power. The Assassinations of the Russian Royal Family in the 18th–19th Centuries* (*Metamorphosy vlasti. Pokusheniia na rossijsky tron v 18–19 vv*). Moscow, 1994.

_____ and Rabinovich, V.L. "Dostoevsky and Mendeleev. A Dialogue on Anti-Spiritualism" (*Dostoievsky i Mendeleev. Antispiritichesky dialog*). *Voprosy filosofii* 11 (1971).
_____ and _____. "F. Dostoevsky's Notes About Mendeleev" (*Zametki F. Dostoevskogo o D.I. Mendeleeve*). In *Mendeleev in the Memoirs of His Contemporaries* (*D. Mendeleev v vospominaniiakh sovremennikov*). Moscow, 1973.
Vozny, A.F. *Political Police and the Petrashevsky Circle* (*Politseisky sysk i kruzhok petrashevtsev*). Kiev, 1976.
_____. *The Petrashevsky Circle and the Secret Police of the Tsar* (*Petrashevtsy i tsraskaia tainaia politsiia*). Kiev, 1985.
Zaborova, R.B. *Doestoevsky's Manuscripts.* (*Rukopisi Dostoevskogo*). Leningrad, 1973.
_____. "F.M. Dostoevsky and the Literary Fund. From the Archival Documents" (*Dostoevsky i literaturny fond. Po arkhivnym dokumentam*). RL 3 (1975).
Zakharov, V.N. *The Dostoevsky Studies* (*Problemy izuchenia Dostoevskogo*). Petrozavodsk, 1978.
Zhavoronkov, A.Z. "Police Case About the Secret Police Surveillance Over Dostoevsky in Staraya Russa in 1872–1876" (*Politicheskoe delo o sekretnom nadzore za Dostoevskim v Staroi Russe, 1872–1876*). IAN, XXIV, 4 (1965).
_____ and Belov, S.V. "Police Case About the Retired Lieutenant F. Dostoevsky" (*Delo ob otstavnom podporuchike F. Dostoevskom*). RL 4 (1963).
Zhitomirskaya, S.V. *A.G. Dostoevskaia. The Diary for 1867* (*A.G. Dostoevskaya. Dnevnik 1867 goda*). Moscow, 1993.

Works Describing the Archival Funds Connected with Dostoevsky

Belov, S.V. "F.M. Dostoevsky in the Memoirs of His Contemporaries. A Bibliography." In *Problems of Genre in the History of Russian Literature*. Moscow, 1969.
A Catalogue for the Personal Funds of the Manuscripts of the State Museum of History. Moscow, 1967.
The Central Archive of the Literature and Art of the USSR. A Guide. Moscow. Vol. 2 (1963), vol. 3 (1968), vol. 4 (1975).
The Central State Archive in Kiev. A Guide. Kiev, 1958.
The Description of the Manuscripts and the Visual Materials of the Pushkin House. Vol. 5: *I.A. Goncharov and F.M. Dostoevsky*. Moscow-Leningrad, 1959. (New Discoveries are published in ERO PD).
Krasovsky, Y.A. "The Dostoevsky Archive" (In *Russian State Literature Archive*). VP 2 (1973).
Mylnikov, A.S. *The Manuscript Funds of the Leningrad Libraries*. Leningrad, 1970.
Nechaeva, V.S. *The Description of F.M. Dostoevsky's Manuscripts*. Moscow, 1967.
Zaborova, R.B. *Dostoevsky's Manuscripts. A Catalogue*. Leningrad, 1963.

PART I

Dostoevsky's Biography in Documents and Memoirs of His Contemporaries

Chapter 1. Childhood in Moscow, 1821–1837.
The Raped Girl.
Shelter for the Poor.

"The Stretensk Parish of Moscow, in St. Peter and Paul's Church, at the shelter for the poor, on the 30th day of October 1821, an infant was born, to the family of a doctor, Mikhail Andreevich Dostoevsky; the child was called Fyodor.... He was baptized on the fourth day of November."

(from the church metrical book)

F YODOR MIKHAILOVICH DOSTOEVSKY was born at the Moscow Marinskaja Shelter for the Poor into the family of a doctor. He was the second child in what would become a family of eight children: Mikhail, Fyodor, Andrei, Nikolai, Liubov, Vera, Alexandra and Varvara. Fyodor Dostoevsky was most probably named after Fyodor Nechaev, his grandfather (the father of his mother), who was also his godfather.

His father, Mikhail Dostoevsky (1789–1839), was a doctor at the shelter. An affectionate father and fond of his family, he also possessed a difficult character; Dostoevsky's accounts of him were few and contradictory. He was born in the village of Voitovich in the Podolsk Region; at the age of fourteen he began studying at a religious school; in 1805 he entered the Academy of Medical Surgeons. In 1812–1813 he participated in the Russian war against Napoleon. After 1819 he worked as a surgeon in Moscow. On January 14, 1820, he married Maria Nechaeva, the daughter of a rich Moscow merchant and a distant relative of the very rich Kumanin merchant family.

In October 1820, Mikhail, their first son and Fyodor's only elder brother, was born. In 1823, the painter Popov, brother-in-law of Maria Dostoevskaya, made portraits of Fyodor's parents. Fyodor's younger brother Andrei recalled that "Our parents were very religious people, especially our mother. Every Sunday and on every religious holiday we went to the church … we had a big, beautiful hospital church…" (Andrei Dostoevsky, *Memoirs*, p. 49).

Indeed, one of Fyodor Dostoevsky's earliest memories was a visit to this church. As his wife Anna Dostoevskaya wrote, "Fyodor Mikhailovich remembered back to the age of two, when his mother gave him sacred wine in the village church and he saw a pigeon flying from one window of the church to another" (L. Grossman, *Seminars on Dostoevsky*, p. 66).

Dostoevsky remembered his childhood years: "I came from a religious Russian family. … I remember the love of my parents. In our family we were familiar with the New Testament from early childhood. By the age of ten, I already knew all the major episodes of Russian history from Karamzin's book which my father used to read aloud to us in the evenings" (*A Writer's Diary*, 1873). S. Ianovsky, one of his early biographers, recalled that "By Dostoevsky's accounts, the atmosphere of his childhood was hard and joyless. He had a great deal of admiration for his mother, his sisters and his brother Mikhail, but he did not like to talk about his father and asked me not to question him" (L. Grossman, *Dostoevsky*, Vol. 1, p. 25).

In 1831 the Dostoevsky family bought Darovoe, a small estate south of Moscow where they spent each summer. These summer retreats were among Fyodor Dostoevsky's cherished memories, and he often referred to this period of his life in his numerous fictional works, his letters and *A Writer's Diary*. "I have liked nothing in my life more than the forest with its mushrooms and wild berries," he wrote in *A Writer's Diary* (February 1876). "I write these lines now and feel the smell of the birch-trees: these things remain with you for the rest of your life...." He recalled becoming acquainted with Russian peasants during these summers: "When I was a child, the peasant named Marei caressed my head and touched my cheek with his hand. I forgot this, but I did not forget it completely, and remembered it in prison. Such childhood memories were what made my survival in prison possible" ("From the Notebooks, 1875–76," *Literary Heritage*, Vol. 83, p. 401).

In the summer of 1830, a neighborhood girl and playmate of Dostoevsky's was raped and subsequently died. An excerpt from the memoirs of Zinaida Trubetskaya, an acquaintance of Dostoevsky reveals the impact it had on the young Fyodor:

> Dostoevsky said to me that to take somebody's life is a terrible sin, but to take away one's faith in the beauty of life, is an even more terrible crime. And Dostoevsky told me that when he was a child ... and lived at the hospital for the poor, where his father was a doctor, he used to play with the daughter of a cook or a horse groom. She was a slim, beautiful girl, nine years old.... A drunken scoundrel raped this girl, and she died from bleeding. Dostoevsky remembered how he was sent to fetch his father, the doctor. When he came, it was too late. This terrible memory haunted him throughout his life, and this most terrible sin he assigned to Stavrogin in *The Demons* [*Journal of Russian Literature*, 1973, no. 3, p. 117].

The crime committed by Stavrogin was omitted, according to the decision of the publisher and censor, from the first edition of *The Demons*. The following passage was substituted:

> I kissed her hand again and took her on my knee. I kissed her face and legs.... The little girl flung her arms around my neck and suddenly began to kiss me passionately. Her face expressed perfect ecstasy. ... When all was over, she was confused.... About eleven o'clock the doorkeeper's little daughter came from the landlady at Gorochovaya Street with a message to me that Matryosha had hanged herself.

Dostoevsky referred to this topic several times in his notes:

> He liked to torture and, because of this, he raped a child... [*Complete Works*, "Notes to *The Demons*," Vol. 11, p. 274].

> Something terrible and unforgettable happened to him in childhood, and his epileptic illness was a result of this [*The New Times*, February 1, 1881].

> Boulevard. A girl. My first personal abuse, a horse, an officer, a raped child. ["Notes to *Crime and Punishment*," *Complete Works*, Vol. 7, p. 138].

It is likely that this incident precipitated the stories about sexually abused children which later appeared in many of his works. In 1863 his friend Nikolai Strakhov, a literary critic, sent a letter to Leo Tolstoy in which he accused Dostoevsky of sexually abusing a young girl. This letter was published after Dostoevsky's death, and his widow indignantly rejected the accusation.

In April of 1832, a fire destroyed the village where the Dostoevskys spent their summers. Maria Dostoevskaya moved to the village with her three eldest sons to supervise the rebuilding of the peasants' houses. The following year, Fyodor and his elder brother Mikhail entered the Chermak Private High School in Moscow. Fyodor suffered a great deal after the death of his mother in 1837, which very nearly coincided with the death of Pushkin, his favorite writer and poet. In 1837 his father resigned and moved to live with his four younger children at Darovoe, his country estate. In May 1837, Fyodor went to St. Petersburg and entered the St. Petersburg Military Engineering Academy.

The following bits of biographical narrative by Orest Miller are taken from a unique publication, the first biography of Dostoevsky, published in 1883. Andrei Dostoevsky's *Memoirs* (1930) are practically the only firsthand source on the early period of Dostoevsky's life.

Orest Miller: About F.M. Dostoevsky

(From Orest Miller, *Biographiia, pis'ma i zametki iz zapisnoi knizhki Dostoevskogo* [*Biography, Letters and Notes from the Dostoevsky Notebooks*]. St. Petersburg, 1883, pp. 2–74.)

Dostoevsky left us some materials for his biography (though he did not make any autobiographical notes). This material exists in the following sources:

1. In the data dictated by Dostoevsky to Anna Grigorievna [his wife] several years before his death;

2. In his memoirs, mostly about his younger years, scattered throughout *A Writer's Diary*;

3. In the many facts about his life in Siberia which he systematically described in *Notes from the House of the Dead*;

4. In subjective passages scattered throughout his novels (mostly in *White Nights, Oppressed and Humiliated, Crime and Punishment, The Idiot*);

5. In his letters.

One of the first remembrances of Fyodor Mikhailovich was when his nurse, brought him, at the age of three, to the guests....

Fyodor Mikhailovich often reminisced in his *Diary* (July–August 1877) about his life in the countryside and its impact on his works. During his journey across Russia at the time of writing his *Diary* (1877), he made a detour, about 150 versts* around Moscow, to the village which

---

An old Russian measurement (singular: versta) equivalent to 1.06 kilometers.

had previously belonged to his parents, and which later, at the time of this visit, belonged to members of his family. He remembered that this village "had made a great impact on my whole life" and that "everything there was filled with great remembrances."

In these places, where he spent his childhood, he met simple [lower class] people; he wrote in *A Writer's Diary* that he remembered one such simple peasant, a man called Marei, many years later, in Siberia, during his stay in prison....

Another vivid example of the life among the simple people for the nine-year-old Fyodor Mikhailovich was his nurse, Alyona Frolovna.... She was really an outstanding person. For example, during the Enlightenment Week [a religious holiday], the Dostoevskys received the news that their estate had been destroyed in a fire. Alyona Frolovna, an Old Believer, knelt and started to pray. She, who had tried to save every penny from her salary, suddenly whispered to the mother of the children she took care of: "Well, if you need money, take mine, I do not need much."

... The father left his two sons in St. Petersburg, in the Kostomarov school.... In his first letter from St. Petersburg to his father, Dostoevsky remembers discussing questions about religion, literature and the arts with a newly found friend, Shidlovsky....

When Dostoevsky's father sent his sons to the Engineering Academy, he counted on the support of the General-Lieutenant Krivoshein, who was their distant relative and who occupied a senior position at the inspector's department. However, the father's plans were thwarted after Dr. Volkenau, the chief doctor of the Academy, examined both brothers and discovered that the healthy-looking elder brother [Mikhail] had tuberculosis, and the weaker younger brother [Fyodor] who had been disposed to illness, was quite healthy.

In 1838, Mikhail Mikhailovich was not accepted to the Academy, and had to move to Revel. Fyodor Mikhailovich entered the Academy, and had to suddenly say good-bye to his brother....

The Engineering Academy, a military school, was not a very attractive place for those young men who dreamt about poetry. It was a school of mathematics, blue-printing, and military drills—inspections, parades and other exercises. When Dostoevsky's father sent his children to this school, he hoped that it would lead to profitable careers, because he himself had a very modest income. We must remember that the Academy was different from most of the other military schools of the time.

A historical sketch written in the *Anniversary Book* published for the fiftieth anniversary of the Academy stated that, among other things, the founder of the school, the Grand Russian Prince Nikolai Pavlovich, invited professor Arseniev, a famous mathematician, to fill a teaching position. The anniversary reference book recalls: "The educational process in the Academy ... was much more important than in any other military school. In the Engineering Academy you could not meet a cadet who did not study the sciences. No one was solely interested in military training."

The students who entered this college were not children; they were teenagers, not younger than fourteen years old; and they were accepted only after they passed the entrance exam. To be enrolled, an applicant had to demonstrate a good degree of knowledge in several basic subjects....

Dostoevsky did not like the curriculum; neither did he like the camp life in the summer.... In a letter to his father he asks his father to send some money.... In a letter to his brother about what he was reading, Dostoevsky does not mention George Sand, but he does write about her in *A Writer's Diary* (June 1876): "I think that I was 16 years old (in 1838) when I read her [George Sand's] novel. I became feverish, and could not sleep all night." From this we can see that Dostoevsky was completely immersed in reading literature....

In November 1838, Fyodor Mikhailovich was visited by Aleksandr Egorovich Riesenkampf. He had come to St. Petersburg from Revel, where he had made friends with Mikhail Mikhailovich [the elder brother] who asked him to pass a letter to Fyodor Mikhailovich. Riesenkampf was entering the Academy of Medical Surgeons. He remembers his first meeting with Fyodor Dostoevsky:

> Here, in the visitor's room, in the South Wing of the Engineering Academy, we spent several wonderful hours. He recited several poems, with his usual passion: "Egyptian Nights" by Pushkin, "Baron Shmagolm" by Zhukovsky and some others, and he told me about his first literary work. He was disappointed that, according to the strict rules of the Academy, he was not allowed to go outside. This, however, did not stop me from visiting him every Sunday morning; besides, every Friday we met at the De-Ron Swedish gym, which was situated in one of the houses adjoining the Academy.

Here is Riesenkampf's description of Fyodor Mikhailovich at the time:

> He was rather plump, with fair blond hair, a round form, round face, and a slightly turned-up nose. His fair brown hair was cut short; his grey eyes were rather deeply set; he had a big forehead and thin eyebrows. His cheeks were pale, and the skin on his face had an unhealthy green pallor. He had big lips. He was much more agile and hot-tempered than his elder brother. He loved poetry with a passion, though he wrote only prose; probably because he did not have enough patience to work with the form of his writing.... He was always composing new thoughts in his head, like drops of water in the ocean. He could recite literary works in a wonderful manner, better than any actor....

At the end of 1840, Fyodor Mikhailovich met his brother [Mikhail] who, according to Riesenkampf's memoirs, came to St. Petersburg to take examinations to obtain the rank of lieutenant. In January 1841, he became an officer, and then stayed in St. Petersburg until 17 February. Before he left, he organized a party for his friends. Fyodor Mikhailovich was there, at the party, and read the first two plays he had written, namely, *Mary Stuart* and *Boris Godunov* [now lost], which, supposedly, were influenced by Schiller and Pushkin. According to Riesenkampf, Fyodor Mikhailovich continued to work on these pieces in 1842, because he was greatly influenced by the theater, in particular by the German tragic actress Lily Lueve, performing as Mary Stuart. Dostoevsky, researching historical material, wanted to develop this tragic scene in his own vision....

Saveliev recalled that, "among the unpleasant and confusing things which happened to Dostoevsky, was his meeting with the Great Prince Mikhail Pavlovich" (A.I. Saveliev, "Vospominanila o Dostoevskom" ["Memoirs About Dostoevsky"] *Russkaia Starina* [The Russian Past], 1918, 1–2). Dmitry Grigorovich transcribed this story from Dostoevsky's own words. When he was sent to deliver a message to the Grand Prince, he forgot to address him formally as "Your Royal Majesty," and simply said "Dear Sir." "Why do they send such fools for errands?" remarked the Prince.

Only Dostoevsky, Grigorovich and Trutovsky, among the cadets of the Academy, did not follow a military career. All other cadets became army officers; for example, Radetsky, one of their schoolmates, became a General, a Russian national hero, after the Russo-Turkish war on the Balkans....

Dostoevsky included some autobiographical pages in *Notes from the Underground*: "his first wish after graduation was to quit the military career for which he was trained, and to burn all the bridges behind him...."

As Riesenkampf recollects, after all his salaries and wages, Dostoevsky received about 5,000 roubles per year. But Fyodor Mikhailovich was a very unpractical man, and most of the time he was penniless. Right after graduation he rented a huge luxurious apartment on Vladimirskaya Street, in the Prianishnikov House, for 1,200 roubles. There was no furniture in this apartment, except for an old sofa, a writing table and several chairs. The reason Dostoevsky liked it there was because he was fond of the landlord, a soft and polite man who loved the arts and who never bothered Dostoevsky with such things as reminders to pay the rent, etc. ... He also liked his servant, Semyon, with his simple-looking face. When he was told that this servant was stealing small amounts of money from him, Dostoevsky replied: "Let him do so, I won't become a bankrupt." The real truth was, he really did become a bankrupt, and incurred more and more debts. Soon he was compelled to use his literary gift to make some money. ...

On 12 August 1843, after finishing the full course of the officer's class at the Academy, Dostoevsky started his career as a military engineer at the blueprint section of the Engineering Department in St. Petersburg. Soon the conflict between an engineer and a writer became obvious.

The first year after graduation, Fyodor Mikhailovich did not write many letters to his brother [or a diary], and Dr. Riesenkampf's precious memoirs can fill this gap. Aleksandr Egorovich Riesenkampf visited Revel in July 1842 and there met Mikhail Mikhailovich. After his return to St. Petersburg in the fall, Riesenkampf started to visit Dostoevsky more often, one of the reasons being that he knew about Dostoevsky's financial need from Mikhail Mikhailovich, his elder brother. It turned out that only one study room was heated in Dostoevsky's apartment. Fyodor Mikhailovich was forced to save money by sacrificing his comfort, after he had spent all his money on the Alexandrovsky Theatre, then very popular (in 1841 and in early 1842). He loved the ballet performances and, besides, he attended concerts featuring such virtuoso musicians as Ole Bull and Liszt.

... After going to the officer's classes in the morning, he sat for long hours in his study, busy with a literary work. It was in these early mornings that he became tormented by a dry cough and a hoarse voice, and his face acquired a grey color, along with some other unhealthy symptoms, such as swelling. He tried to hide his condition from the others. This required the help of his friend, Dr. Riesenkampf, who prescribed some medicine to cure his cough and to limit his smoking of the terrible Zhukov tobacco.

Dmitry Vasilievich Grigorovich, whose character was in many respects opposite to Dostoevsky's, was one of the few friends who visited him on a regular basis. Riesenkampf remembers Grigorovich as "a smart, nice-looking, beautiful and optimistic young man, the son of a wealthy cavalry colonel and an aristocratic French lady." He was very popular among women, a member of the high society of St. Petersburg, and, strangely enough, he became a friend of Dostoevsky, who was a reserved person and lived a lonely life in his isolated apartment.

There was a common feature which united them: a passion for literature. Grigorovich, as Riesenkampf remembers, translated into Russian some French plays about Chinese life. Dostoevsky, at the time, quit working on *Mary Stuart* and started another piece, *Boris Godunov*, which he also did not finish. Besides this, Fyodor Mikhailovich's imagination was busy with many ideas for future stories and novels. Among the Russian writers, he loved Gogol most of all, and he could recite by heart numerous pages from Gogol's *The Dead Souls*. Among the French writers, he loved, most of all, Balzac, George Sand and Victor Hugo....

In November 1842, Fyodor Mikhailovich received news from Revel that Mikhail's son had been born. Fyodor Mikhailovich was appointed the godfather of this child, and displayed unusual generosity and interest.... He was introduced to the Revel society [which was largely Baltic and German] and was disappointed: "all the sense of caste, all the snobbism, all the intolerance" made a bad impression on Dostoevsky. This attitude [toward the Germans] remained with Dostoevsky for the rest of his life. Riesenkampf wrote: "I tried to convince Fyodor Mikhailovich that it was only the local atmosphere.... Even with his broad general outlook, he acquired, after this, a prejudiced attitude towards everything that was German."

During this time Mikhail Mikhailovich, with the help of his wife, supplied his brother with a full set of underwear and upper dress which was inexpensive in Revel. He knew that Fyodor Mikhailovich was not a practical man, and he asked Riesenkampf to share a rented apartment with Fyodor Mikhailovich and to influence Dostoevsky with all the German precision. When Riesenkampf returned to St. Petersburg, he did as he was instructed. He found Fyodor Mikhailovich eating only bread and milk obtained on credit from the nearest grocery shop. Riesenkampf remembered: "Fyodor Mikhailovich was the type of man who is in need all the time, but is surrounded by people who live well. His servants stole his money all the time, but he was always very kind and generous to them, and he never questioned them, being careless about this things of this sort."

Dostoevsky shared an apartment with the doctor.... Every one of the doctor's new visitors became a dear guest for Fyodor Mikhailovich as well. He said: "I started to write about the poor people in the capital, and I want to know them better...."

Dostoevsky was very short of money, and this lasted for almost two months. Suddenly, in November, the doctor saw him pacing across the room, with a self-assured look, with pride. It turned out that he had received about 100 roubles from Moscow. Riesenkampf writes: "The other day he again came to my room, but this time with a reserved, quiet step, and asked me to lend him five roubles. It turned out that most of the sum was spent paying for previous debts. The remaining money was all but lost yesterday at billiards, and the last small portion was simply stolen by his partner in the game."

They had visitors [mostly Dr. Riesenkampf's patients, representatives of the lowest classes of the Russian capital], among them Mr. Keller, a poor German in a shabby frock.... Fyodor Mikhailovich was known for his hospitality, and Mr. Keller soon visited several times a day for tea, lunch and supper. Fyodor Mikhailovich patiently listened to the stories from the life of the poorest classes, sometimes jotting them down on paper. Later Riesenkampf found out that some of this material was used in the novels *Poor People*, *The Double*, *Netochka Nezvanova*, etc.

In December 1843, Fyodor Mikhailovich was again in great financial

need. He had to borrow money.... On 1 February 1844, Fyodor Mikhailovich received 1,000 roubles from Moscow [sent by his relatives], but by
the evening he had only 100 roubles left. He had bad luck that day. He
went for dinner at the Dominica Restaurant and was asked to play a game
of billiards....

The next day he was once again without a cent, and had to borrow
money again and again, sometimes with huge interest rates, just to buy
sugar, tea, etc. In March, Dr. Riesenkampf had to leave St. Petersburg,
so he did not succeed in teaching Dostoevsky such German features as
precision, thrift and particularity. From February to September Dostoevsky wrote several letters to his brother. On 24 March 1854, he wrote
about *Poor People* that "the novel was finished in November, but in
December I decided to change everything...." We find out about the further fate of *Poor People* from *A Writer's Diary* (1877) and in the *Memoirs*
by Grigorovich.

In Dostoevsky's letters of this period, we find reference to the Maikov
family, with whom Dostoevsky developed a close friendship and later
corresponded regularly. As S.D. Ianovsky remembers:

> At the Maikov parties there were gatherings of gifted, artistic young peo-
> ple.... Here, at these parties, Fyodor Mikhailovich analyzed the literary char-
> acters of Gogol and Turgenev with his detailed precision, and later explained
> his character Mr. Prokharchin, who was not understood by most of his read-
> ers. All the listeners understood not only the whole idea, but all the small
> details of the literary character....

Andrei Dostoevsky: The Dostoevsky Brothers in Their Childhood

(From A.M. Dostoevsky, *Vospominaniia* [*Memoirs*]. Leningrad:
Izdatelstvo pisatelei v Leningrade, 1930.)

We were all born in the three-storied right wing of the Moscow Mariinskaya Shelter; all, except for Mikhail, the eldest brother, who was born
in the Military Hospital when our father worked there, ... our brother
Fyodor, who was born in the left wing of Moscow Mariinskaya Shelter,
and our sister Alexandra, who was born in our village Darovoe in Tula
region Kashirsk county....

As I mentioned before, the apartment where our family lived was
situated in the right wing of the shelter, on the ground floor. If we compare it to contemporary apartments of people who work for the government, I have to note that before they had much smaller living spaces.

You can see for yourself; my father, a man with a family of four to five children, and a captain at the time, only had a two-bedroom apartment plus a corridor and a kitchen.

Now I will write about my childhood. As I remember my childhood days, from a very young age, the following people were my family: my father, my mother, the eldest brother Mikhail, brother Fyodor, sister Varya and me. I was the last in the series of, so to speak, elder children. There were younger children who were born after me: sister Verochka [or Vera], brother Nicolai and sister Sasha [or Alexandra], but they were quite young at the time so they did not participate in our activities and games; they lived their own lives. The four of us (elder children) were together all the time and engaged in pretty much the same games and activities. I remember well being of three to five years of age. At the time my brother Mikhail was eight, Fyodor was seven and sister Varya about five years old.

My sister was, at the time, the only girl in the family, and she spent most of her time with our mother, sitting in the living room. We two boys didn't have separate bedrooms, and we spent all our time together in the hall.

I mention this in order to show that I witnessed the childhood of my two elder brothers until they started to attend the Chermak school. I was involved in all their activities and all their conversations; they were never embarrassed by my presence and only in some cases did they ask me to leave them alone and call me by my nickname, which meant "a small tail." There was a one-year age difference between the two elder brothers; they lived together and were close friends. This friendship continued through all their lives until the eldest brother died. However, in spite of all this friendship they had completely different characters. Mikhail, the eldest brother, was much less smart, quick and hot tempered in conversation than my brother Fyodor, who was always "a real ball of fire," as our parents called him.

You could never call my father "a gloomy, nervous and suspicious man," as Orest Miller called him in *The Biography of Dostoevsky....* Though our father had some faults, he was neither gloomy nor suspicious. On the contrary, he was always friendly, even joyful, with the family.

Those people who read our mother's letters will find ... that she had an outstanding personality. You should be an outstanding person, when you could write in such a good, I would say, poetic language ... and my mother was a woman from a modest merchant family who received a complete education in the 1820s.

In the end [of this chapter] ... I would like to mention the attitude of my brother Fyodor Mikhailovich towards our parents. It was the end of the 1870s. I was in St. Petersburg and I started talking to him [to

Fyodor Dostoevsky] about things that had passed a long time ago and about our father. My brother became interested in this subject at once, he grabbed me by the arm a little above the elbow (it was his favorite habit when he talked privately) and ... said, "Well, you know, my brother, they were outstanding people ... and we will never be such family men, ... such fathers ... No, my brother, we can't be like that!"

Chapter 2. Studies in the St. Petersburg Military Engineering Academy. Father's Death. First Literary Success.

"Not guilty! I'm guilty of other blood, of another old man's blood, but not of my father's. And I weep for it! I killed the old man, killed him and struck him down ... But who killed my father, who killed him? Who could have killed him if not me? It's a wonder, an absurdity, an impossibility...!"

(*The Brothers Karamazov*)

"News about a new genius, Mr. Dostoevsky, is circulating across St. Petersburg. We do not know whether it is his real name or a pen-name. The reading audience is praising his new novel, *Poor People*. I have read this novel and said: 'Poor Russian readers!' However, Mr. Dostoevsky is a man of some talent and, if he finds his way in literature, he will be able to write something decent."

(*The Northern Bee*, February 1, 1848, no. 27)

A T THE AGE OF SEVENTEEN, in 1838, Fyodor Dostoevsky entered the St. Petersburg Military Engineering Academy. This is how young Dostoevsky described his usual day: "From early morning we were fully occupied attending lectures and sitting in classes. We practiced marching, had fencing, dancing and singing lessons ... stood on guard ... every moment was filled with activities" (*Complete Works*, Vol. 28, part 1, p. 46). Fyodor was not suited to a military career, as he complained in a letter to his father written July 5, 1838. He described the tedium of military exercises: "We were exhausted after the inspection of five parades by the Grand Duke and the Tsar ... at one of the parades the whole royal family and one hundred forty thousand military men were present" (*Complete Works*, Vol. 28, part 1, p. 48). In a letter dated October 30–31, 1938, Fyodor informed his father and his brother of his failure at school: "I am not transferring to the next year! Oh my God! One year wasted! ... One of the algebra teachers to whom I was rude during the year, reminded me of this during the examination" (*Complete Works*, Vol. 28, part 1, pp. 52–53).

These difficult times were softened by the presence of real friends, among them the student Shidlovsky, Doctor Aleksandr Riesenkampf, the painter Konstantin Trutovsky and the officer A. Saveliev. In 1838 he told Riesenkampf about his first literary activity. According to Grigorovich, Dostoevsky created a literary circle in the Academy which included Alexei Beketov, N. Vitkovsky, Ivan Berezhetsky, and himself. In his spare time, Dostoevsky discussed literary topics with these few friends at the Academy, "speaking about Homer, Shakespeare, Schiller, Hoffman." An exploration into the world of literature was one of the major occupations of Fyodor's young mind, as he wrote on August 9, 1838: "I have read the complete works of Hoffman ... Almost all the works of Balzac, ... Goethe, ... and Victor Hugo" (*Complete Works*, Vol. 28, part 1, p. 51).

In a letter to his brother, dated August 16, 1839, Dostoevsky made some brief but very important remarks which became the motto for his whole life and revealed much about his psychological makeup: "I am confident in myself. Man is a mystery. And this mystery should be solved!" (*Complete Works*, Vol. 28, part 1, p. 63). It is difficult to believe that these words were written by a teenaged youth.

In his youth, Dostoevsky experienced his first serious epileptic fit. Sigmund Freud, in his famous article on Dostoevsky, attributes the cause of the fit to his father's death. Mikhail Andreevich died in 1839, the year after Fyodor began his studies at the Engineering Academy. There are at least three contradictory explanations of Dostoevsky's father's death: he was killed by his village serfs; he died from alcoholism stemming from the despair into which he sank after his wife's death; he died from a heart attack [probably after receiving the news that his son Fyodor had not passed the examinations at the Academy]. G.A. Fyodorov studied the materials concerning Mikhail

Andreevich Dostoevsky's death in the Archives of the Tula and Kashira Local Courts. According to the archival documents, there were no contradictions in the different materials supporting the official version of his death. On June 16, 1839, a letter was sent from the Kashira Local Court to the Governor-General about the cause of Mikhail Dostoevsky's death; it stated that: "Mikhail Dostoevsky died recently, and according to the police investigation there were no traces of a violent cause of his death" (G.A. Fyodorov, "Domysly i logika faktov" ["The Rumors and the Logic of the Facts"], *Literaturnaia Gazeta*, June 19, 1975, no. 25).

Patricide is a major theme in *The Brothers Karamazov*, in which three sons are indirectly guilty of the death of their father. The actual crime is committed by the fourth, illegitimate, son, who commits suicide; the falsely accused Dmitry receives a prison sentence. The death of his father is one of the most mysterious incidents in Dostoevsky's life.

While Dostoevsky was devastated by his father's death, he was also very much concerned with the fate of his younger brothers and sisters. He wrote on August 16, 1939, "My dear brother, I shed many tears after the death of father, but my personal state is even worse now. When I think not of myself but of my family ... are there any people more unhappy than our brothers and sisters?" (*Complete Works*, Vol. 28, part 1, p. 62). After Dostoevsky's father's death, his mother's relatives, the Kumanins who had no family, took care of the children. In 1841 Dostoevsky passed a major examination and was allowed to live outside the Academy residence, in a rented apartment. In 1843 he graduated from the Academy and began his service at St. Petersburg's Engineering Department.

Dostoevsky's resignation from the civil service in 1844 was one of the most extreme steps he made in his life. The young writer had not yet published his prose and lacked the money to support himself, but he nonetheless made a resolute decision to resign in order to dedicate all his time to writing, his favorite activity. He wrote to his brother Mikhail on September 30, 1844, "I have resigned because I swear I could not serve any more. I will find my bread elsewhere. I will work hard.... Right now I do not have a penny to my name and my resignation is on October 14th" (*Complete Works*, Vol. 28, part 1, p. 100).

During this period, from early 1844 to May 1845, Dostoevsky wrote his first novel, *Poor People*. He did not tell anybody about his work when it was in progress. It took the young writer several months to rewrite his first novel repeatedly, trying to reach perfection in his style. Almost half a year after the first version was finished, he informed his brother on March 23, 1845, that "I finished the novel in November, then rewrote it in December, and again in February–March. I am seriously satisfied with my novel. It is a serious and elegant work..." (*Complete Works*, Vol. 28, part 1, p. 107). His friend Dmitry Grigorovich took the manuscript of *Poor People* to publisher Nikolai Nekrasov and they read the novel all night long. The next day, the manuscript was forwarded to Vissarion Belinsky, a leading literary critic, who accepted it as a work of a genius, describing Dostoevsky as "a new Gogol." *Poor People* was published by Nekrasov in his *St. Petersburg Collection* in 1846. The book edition followed in 1847, and enjoyed great success. Dostoevsky combined the tradition of Gogol with a psychological analysis of people of the lowest classes living in St. Petersburg.

All major literary critics included the new novel in their book reviews, including Apollon Grigoriev, who wrote: "Dostoevsky starts to play in our literature the same role which Hoffman played in German literature.... He became so deeply immersed in the life of civil servants that the dull and uninteresting everyday life became for him a nightmare close to madness" (*The Finnish Herald*, April 30, 1847, sec. 5, pp. 29–30).

Dostoevsky was introduced to the St. Petersburg literary circles, including the leading literary artists and critics, and to high society. "Well, brother," he wrote in a letter, "my glory will never be as big as it is now ... people respect me, they are curious about me, ... I have met many new well respected people..." (*Complete Works*, Vol. 28, part 1, p. 115).

The memoirs of those "well-respected people" whom Dostoevsky met at this important period of his life constitute the remaining part of this chapter. Dmitry Grigorovich, a close personal friend, relates the story about the publication of *Poor People*, Dostoevsky's first novel. Konstantin Trutovsky reveals some additional facts about Dostoevsky's early interest in literature. Stepan Ianovsky provides a doctor's account of Dostoevsky's first epileptic seizure. And finally, Pavel Annenkov and Vladimir Sollogub comment on Dostoevsky's huge popularity in St. Petersburg after the publication of his first novel.

Andrei Dostoevsky: The Father's Death. Fyodor Dostoevsky in the Forties

(From A.M. Dostoevsky, *Vospominaniia* [*Memoirs*]. Leningrad: Izdatelstvo pisatelei v Leningrade, 1930.)

I would like to relate all the details I know concerning my father's death.... Here, I am going to describe the last years of my father's life in the country, and the reason for his death, or, to be precise, for his murder....

After a very difficult and busy career of twenty-five years, my father found himself immured in two or three rooms of his small village house, without any society around him.... He was not an old man, being only around forty-six or forty-seven years of age, when he became a widower. My nurse, Alyona Frolovna, told me that at first [after the death of his wife, my mother], he used to talk loudly to himself. He imagined that he was speaking to his deceased wife and he would reply to himself in her usual phrases.... He was in a state bordering on madness, especially when one considers that he was completely alone. Furthermore, he started to drink alcohol. He became intimate with a servant woman, Catherine, who worked at our house in Moscow. At his age, in his situation, who could have blamed him for this?...

He remained alone through a long autumn and a long winter. He became even more attached to liquor, and drunkenness became his habitual condition. Then spring came, but it did not bring any good. Let us remember here the anguish which my father felt, and which he expressed in his letter to Fyodor, dated May 27, 1839, several days before his death [ten days, to be more exact]. From this letter we can see that he was in a desperate situation.

At that time, beyond Cheremoshnia village, on the edge of the fields, a group of about ten to fifteen peasants were working. My father shouted at these peasants for some reason. He was a hot-tempered man, and it seemed that he lost control for a moment when he saw some of the peasants. One of the serfs, the boldest, rudely answered my father's tirades, and then became afraid of the possible consequences...

"Men, let's get him," he cried, and with these words, all the peasants, about fifteen in number, leaped upon Father and easily finished him off.

The so-called "local police detachment" arrived to investigate the scene of the murder. Their main concern was to find out how much money the peasants could pay to have the crime concealed. I do not know what the exact amount involved was, and where the peasants managed to find a large enough sum of money, but I do know that the police were satisfied. The corpse was sent for an autopsy and its finding and the police findings reported that my father had died of a heart attack. He was buried in the Monogarov village churchyard.

Less than a week after the death and funeral of my father, my grandmother, Olga Jakovlevna, came to the village to take care of his orphaned children.... The Khotiaintsev family, both the husband and the wife, did not hide from her the real cause of my father's death, but they advised her and his other relatives not to start a new investigation. There were several reasons for this:

1. No one could restore my father to his children;

2. It was difficult to expose the fraud of the local police, and a second autopsy could produce the same results;

3. Even if the case could be investigated properly, and all the details revealed, this would mean the complete bankruptcy of the estate, for the

whole adult male population of the estate at Cheremoshnia village might
be sent to prison.

These were the considerations whereby my father's murder remained
concealed and those guilty of the crime were not punished. My elder brothers probably knew the truth about our father's death, but they kept silent....*

... As soon as my family in Moscow found out about my entering the
Academy of Civil Engineers, my uncle, Alexander Kumanin, sent me
100 roubles in cash, as he said, "to buy me a pie." This money was not
sent directly to me, but to Ivan Grigorievich Krivopishin, and I received
a letter about this from Moscow, and he, in his turn, passed the money
over to me through Fyodor Karlovich Pritvitz, the director of the school.

Naturally, I did not conceal all this from my brother Fyodor, who was
constantly short of money, and who sent me numerous messages [in
which he asked me to lend him some].

I have all these notes and messages, and I treasure them as well as
everything else which my brother left behind. Here are some of the notes
which I received from him.

The first message is dated 1842:

> Dear brother, If you received the money, please send me about five roubles
> or at least one rouble. For three days or so, I have had no wood for the fireplace,
> and I do not have a cent. Later this week, I will borrow some more money, two
> hundred roubles, and I will repay my debt to you. If you did not receive any
> money, please write to Krivopishin. Egor [F.Dostoevsky's servant] will take the
> message to him. And I will send you your money at once. Dostoevsky.

The second letter is dated early 1843:

> Brother, did you get anything from Pritvitz? If so, please send me some of it.
> I have nothing. Well, please write to tell me when are you going to visit me, and
> if you do not send the money now, please bring it with you later. For God's sake,
> please. Please go to Pritvitz's apartment. Your brother, Fyodor Dostoevsky.

The third letter is also dated 1843:

> You wrote to me that you cannot get the money before "Maslenitsa" [Russian
> folk festival in winter]. So, I decided, together with this letter, I would enclose
> another letter in which I ask you to lend me fifty roubles. I will return this money
> to you, on my word of honor. I know that you do not need money now, and, please
> believe me, I am in great need. Please help me. Yours, Fyodor Dostoevsky.

I include and put here these notes from my brother Fyodor for only
one reason: to show that my brother Fyodor was in grave financial straits.
The year 1844-45 was a successful one for me. I passed my examinations

*The relatives decided to send me [Andrei Dostoevsky] to St. Petersburg Military Academy where Fyo-
dor studied. Some pages from his memoirs—for example, pp. 136 and 139—were not included in the
1990 edition of "The Memoirs," probably because of Soviet censorship.

and advanced to the Third Grade.... This year brought some changes for our family as well. My brother, Fyodor, resigned and devoted himself to literature. When I found out about it, I wondered how he could possibly live without an income, without any regular means of support, or a salary....

My brother, Fyodor Mikhailovich, was engaged in literary activity, and his first literary work, *Poor People*, was published in 1846.

This work was first published in *The St. Petersburg Collection* edited by N. Nekrasov, and it placed Dostoevsky among our outstanding artists, and people began to talk about him. Belinsky glorified him. As a result of this, his financial situation improved, but he quickly spent a great deal of money and was once again in financial need....

In 1848 ... my brother Mikhail finally moved to St. Petersburg with his family.... My brother lived in decent apartments on the Nevsky Prospect, and I, together with my other brother, Fyodor, made it a rule to visit our elder brother for lunch (because he was a family man) every weekend and on every holiday. We would arrive without any preliminary arrangements. We followed this custom until the end of 1849....

My two brothers, Mikhail and Fyodor, rented a house in Pargolovo [a suburb of St. Petersburg], where they lived for the whole summer. They lived there without fear of contracting cholera, because we had an epidemic in St. Petersburg.... During my visit to Pargolovo, the first case of cholera was registered. A sick person was overcome by the disease in the street, and my brother, Fyodor [who was passing by], rushed over to him to render emergency medical assistance: to administer medicine and massage.

Dmitry Grigorovich: The Literary Memoirs. *Poor People*, Dostoevsky in the Forties

(From D.V. Grigorovich, *Literaturnye Vospominaniia* [*Literary Memoirs*]. Moscow: Goslitizdat, 1961, pp. 46–49, 86–93.)

The first year in the Military School was extremely difficult for me. Even now, after a period of almost fifty years, I remember it with an unpleasant feeling; this was due to the strict discipline set up by the leaders among the school cadets; constant military drills, marching; it was not only the difficult curriculum, but also the constant life together with your schoolmates, with whom you had to live, to study and to sleep in the same rooms, twenty-four hours a day....

Once, and it was Sunday, I left school to visit Mr. M. Kostomarov, my former teacher. I returned the next morning, when the cadets were not in their studies…. There were about five freshmen, new boys who had just entered the school. I was surrounded by them at once, being the object of their curiosity. I could tell them about the life at the school which they were planning to enter the next spring.

Among the other young men, I noticed a fellow of about seventeen years old, of average height, rather strongly built, blonde, with a very unhealthy pale face. This young man was Fyodor Mikhailovich Dostoevsky, who arrived from Moscow together with Mikhail Mikhailovich, his elder brother. His brother was not going to enter the military school, but instead entered the military service, became an officer and was directed to Revel. After several years he returned, resigned, opened a tobacco factory and did some translations from Goethe. He wrote a comedy *The Old and the Young*, and became the editor of the journal *Epoch* after his brother returned from exile.

We became good friends, Dostoevsky and I, almost from the first day he entered the school. Almost half a century has passed since then, but I remember that time very well. I did not like anyone, and was not attached to anyone among the friends of my youth, except for Dostoevsky. It seemed that he responded to me with the same feeling, in spite of his natural features of reservation and intolerance towards others. He was, however, happy to meet a friend among this new group of people who were often hostile towards newcomers.

Even at that time, Fyodor Mikhailovich displayed some lack of sociability. He did not take part in our games. Most of the time he sat in a quiet place reading a book…. He found such a quiet corner which soon became his favorite place. It was a deep corner in the fourth room, a place opposite a window facing the Fontanka River. In the cadet's spare time you could always find him there, always reading a book.

I was not a very sociable young man, but at the same time I was a simple and easily influenced person. Therefore, I was not simply attached to Dostoevsky, but I was completely subject to his influence. I have to say that it was very useful for me, because Dostoevsky was more developed in every respect. He read a lot, and it amazed me. He told me about the works of writers I had never even heard of. Before I met him, I, like most of our schoolmates, read only textbooks for our special courses. This could be explained not only by the fact that we were not allowed to bring other books inside the school, but also by the general indifference towards literature there.

Among our cadets there was only one person, Dostoevsky, who responded to Pushkin's death in 1837. He had read Pushkin's works in the Chermak School in Moscow…. I met other people who graduated from the Chermak Private School where Dostoevsky studied. All of them received a wonderful educational background in literature and read many books.

The first fiction books in Russian which I read were recommended to me by Dostoevsky. They were *Cat Meow* by Hoffman and *The Confession of a British Opium Smoker* by Maturen. At the time, Dostoevsky especially appreciated the latter, a rather gloomy book. *Astrologer* by W. Scott and *The Pioneers* by James Fenimore Cooper made me addicted to literature. When I read about the parting [of major characters] ... on the shores of Lake Ontario in *The Pioneers*, I cried out; I tried to conceal the tears rolling down my face so that my friends would not start laughing at me. As concerned literature, Dostoevsky influenced not only me, but three other schoolmates: Beketov, Vitkovsky and Berezhetsky. We therefore created a literary circle which was separate from the other cadets, and we spent most of our spare time together....

Dostoevsky was, as far as I remember, not very good in his studies; he forced himself to finish his courses and to go from one year to the next. He even failed his examinations one year, and had to stay another year in the same grade. So much was he shaken by his failure that he fell ill, and was forced to spend some time in the hospital....

Around that time there appeared in the book stores many foreign books published in the "Physiology" series. Every book described some particular aspect of Parisian life.... The first book in this series was a Paris edition, *French People as Described by Themselves*. There were the followers of these writings in Russia ... Nekrasov, whose practical mind was always on the alert, had the idea of publishing something of this sort in Russia; he founded a series of books "Physiology of St. Petersburg." These books included everyday scenes from the street life of St. Petersburg. Nekrasov asked me to write one of the sketches for the first volume....

I was planning to describe the life of street organ-grinders, and so I started to write with passion.... At the time, I occasionally met with Dostoevsky who had just graduated from the Academy and had changed his military uniform to the costume of a civil servant. When I saw him I embraced him and told him how happy I was to see him. Dostoevsky was also happy to see me, though I noticed that he was a bit too reserved. With all his warm and passionate heart, even at school in our small and almost childish circle, he was always a concentrated and reserved person and disliked the open expression of one's emotions.

When I met him by chance that day, my joy was so great that I did not feel offended by his outer coldness. I told him at once about my new literary acquaintances and my efforts, and I asked him to visit the place where he had lived so that I could read my work to him. He gladly agreed. He seemed to be satisfied with my sketch, though he did not give too much of an appraisal....

During that time I met with Dostoevsky more and more often. It ended in an agreement to share the same apartment with our expenses in separate accounts. Every month my mother sent me 50 roubles from Moscow. Dostoevsky received almost the same amount of money. It was more than enough for two young men, though we usually spent our money too quickly, in the first two weeks. The last two weeks of the month we ate only bread and drank coffee at the nearest Frederick's grocery store.

We lived in a house situated on the corner of Vladimirskaya Street and Grafsky Street. Dostoevsky occupied the back room, I occupied the room closest to the entrance door. We did not have servants, so we prepared our own *samovar* [a big teapot] and did our own shopping.

When I started sharing the same apartment with Dostoevsky, he had just finished translating *Eugenia Grande*, a novel by Balzac. Balzac was our favorite writer, I say "our favorite" because we both liked to read him and we considered him to be much better that other French writers. I do not know what Dostoevsky thought about this later, but I still agree with this opinion and I read Balzac again and again. I cannot remember who helped publish Dostoevsky's translation of *Eugenia Grande* in *The Library for Reading*, but I remember that when we received the first copy of the book, Dostoevsky was upset. There was a reason for this: the text of the original was cut almost by one third. They said it was a regular habit of Senkovsky, the editor of *The Library for Reading*, who did the same thing with the original works of other authors. Young and beginning authors did not object to this and kept silent because they were happy to see their works and their names published....

Dostoevsky, by the way, continued to work. He sat at the writing table the whole day through and part of the night. He did not tell me a word about what he was writing and he answered my questions in an unwilling and brief manner.

I knew his habit of concealing things and I stopped asking questions. I only saw numerous sheets of paper covered with Dostoevsky's peculiar handwriting. The letters came out from his feather, like the beads of a necklace, sometimes appearing as if they were printed. Later I saw such handwriting only once, from Dumas-the-Father. When Dostoevsky stopped writing, he would pick up a book and start reading.... Hours of hard work and sitting at home badly influenced his health and developed his illness, which had first appeared during his younger years when he was studying at the Academy, [and now] got progressively worse. He had fits of illness several times, when we were out walking. Once, when we were walking along Troitsky Street, we met a funeral procession.

Dostoevsky quickly turned aside; he wanted to return home, but, as soon as he walked several steps, he had a strong attack of the illness. It was so strong that I had to ask passers-by to take him to the nearest drugstore, and we could hardly revive him. Usually, after such fits, he experienced a depression which lasted for two or three days.

One morning (it was in the summer) Dostoevsky called me into his room and when I entered, I saw him sitting on the sofa which served him as a bed. In front of him, on a small writing table, there was a rather thick pile of regular postal paper of the large format. Some edges of the sheets of paper were folded, and the pages were covered with his handwriting. "Please, Grigorovich, sit down. I made the copy of this just yesterday, and I want to read it to you. Sit down, please, and do not interrupt me," he said very enthusiastically.

The work which he read to me almost without interruption was his novel which was soon published under the title *Poor People*.

I had always a high opinion of Dostoevsky. He read much, he knew literature, he had his own opinions, and he was a serious character, which impressed me greatly. I often thought of how this could happen, that I had already published several literary pieces and thought of myself as a literary artist, but Dostoevsky, with all his qualities, had done very little in this sphere.

But from the first pages of *Poor People* I understood that Dostoevsky wrote much better than I did and, as I continued listening, this impression grew. I admired him so much that I wanted to embrace him several times and I was stopped only by his unwillingness to make noisy and open displays of emotion. I could not, however, sit quietly, and interrupted him from time to time with exclamations of admiration.

The result of this reading is more or less known to the public. Dostoevsky himself described the story of how I took the manuscript of *Poor People* from him, almost by force, and then took it to Nekrasov. He saved some details, though (Dostoevsky was a humble person), as to how the reading at Nekrasov took place. I was reading the novel. On the last page, when Devushkin, an old man, says goodbye to Varen'ka, I lost control over myself and started to cry. I cast a secret glance at Nekrasov; tears were rolling down his cheeks as well.

I started to convince him with passion that it was not necessary to postpone a good thing, and that we must go to Dostoevsky at once, in spite of the late hour (it was about four in the morning), and to tell him about his success and to make an agreement about the publication of his novel.

Nekrasov, who was very excited as well, agreed and dressed quickly and we set off to see Dostoevsky.

I must admit, I made a spontaneous decision. I knew the character

of my friend very well, his loneliness and his excitability, and I would
have done better to tell him what had happened in a reserved way the
following day, not to wake him up in the middle of the night to disturb
him with all this unexpected joy and to bring an unknown man at night
to our home! I was, however, very excited then; maybe a more reserved
person would have behaved in a more logical way.

Dostoevsky opened the door when we knocked. He became embarrassed when he saw an unfamiliar person with me. After Nekrasov told
him everything, Dostoevsky turned white as a sheet and was unable to
utter a single word for the longest time. When Nekrasov went away I
was afraid that Dostoevsky would start scolding me for all the excitement. But this did not happen; he only shut the door of his room. As I
was lying in my bed, I could hear his footsteps in his room which indicated his excitement.

After he met Nekrasov and then, through him, got acquainted with
Belinsky who had also read the manuscript of *Poor People*, Dostoevsky
changed a lot. During the publishing of *Poor People* he was in a state of
extreme nervous excitement. Due to his reserved character, he did not
tell me how he met Nekrasov and what had happened between them
later. On a few occasions I heard some rumors that he had asked that
Poor People be published in special fonts and that a special ornament be
made as a decoration for each page. I was not present at the conversation and I do not know whether this was true or not. Even if something
like this did happen, the whole story must have been exaggerated.

I can say with confidence that the success of *Poor People*, as well as
the admiration of Belinsky, definitely had a negative influence on Dostoevsky. Before, he loved to have a rather lonely introspective life and
to meet occasionally with several friends who did not share his interest
in literature. Could such a person, even with his intellect, stay in a normal condition when as great a literary critic as Belinsky bowed in front
of him and told him that he was the new genius of Russian literature?
Soon after *Poor People* Dostoevsky wrote *Mr. Prokharchin*....

Belinsky's praise would not produce such a great impression on Dostoevsky, but the unexpected change of opinion about Dostoevsky made
by the same Belinsky and his circle affected the young writer greatly.
After the admiration of Belinsky ... Dostoevsky completely changed his
attitude to Belinsky and his associates. Here is what Belinsky wrote to
Annenkov after the break-up with Dostoevsky: "I do not remember
whether I wrote to you that Dostoevsky has written a novel, *The Landlady*; it is terrible nonsense. He wanted to unite Marlinsky and Hoffman
in it, with some Gogol. He has written something else as well, but every
new work becomes worse than the previous one. The readers in the
province do not like him, and in the capital there are bad reviews even

about *Poor People*; I feel terrible at the thought of reading it again. Well, my friend, we made a big mistake with Dostoevsky when we called him 'a genius!'"

And this was written by Belinsky, an honest man who was sometimes inclined to exaggerate. But these lines were written very sincerely, like everything else he wrote. Belinsky did not feel shy about expressing his opinion about Dostoevsky, and his friends in his circle joined him.

The sudden shift from adoration and descriptive terms like "genius" for the author of *Poor People* to statements on the opposite extreme describing a talentless writer could have ruined an even less selfish and sensitive man than Dostoevsky. He started avoiding people from the Belinsky circle and kept his feelings into himself, becoming more and more irritable. Once, when Dostoevsky met Turgenev who belonged to the circle, he could not restrain his feelings and released all his indignation, saying that he was not afraid of them and that he, after some time, would mix them all in the mud. I did not remember exactly what the pretext was for such a scene, but it seemed to me that they were talking about Gogol....

Anyway, it was completely Dostoevsky's fault. Turgenev had a very mild and kind character, one that could even be reproached for being too soft. There was a complete break between Dostoevsky and the Belinsky circle and he did not visit them any more. They started to make jokes and write epigrams about him accusing him of being too selfish and of being jealous of Gogol, for whom he must have had the deepest respect, since on every page of *Poor People* you could see Gogol's influence.... I do not remember the reason, but once there was a heated discussion between me and Dostoevsky. As a result we decided to live separately. We moved to different apartments, quite peacefully, without a quarrel. After that we often visited Beketov and greeted each other as good friends....

Konstantin Trutovsky: Memoirs About Dostoevsky

(From K.A. Trutovsky, "Vospominaniia o Dostoevskom" ["Memoirs About Dostoevsky"], *Russkoe obozreniie* [*The Russian Review*] 1 [1893]: 212–217.)

In 1839, at the age of thirteen, I entered the Military Engineering Academy ... in the fourth junior class. Fyodor Mikhailovich studied in the second class....

I drew better than the others and therefore was in a privileged position. I made drawings at the request of the senior students, as well as ornaments for architectural projects, blueprints of some projects or simply sketches. Students from the senior, so-called "officer" classes brought me such projects, and I made drawings, decorations and ornaments for the buildings.

Once Fyodor Mikhailovich asked me to perform such a service for him and when I did what he requested, Fyodor Mikhailovich became a friend of mine. He defended me from the rude behavior of some of the senior students.

At the time, Fyodor Mikhailovich was a very skinny young man. He had pale grey skin on his face, thin fair hair and his eyes were deeply set, always piercing you with their glance.

Fyodor Mikhailovich was the least suitable person for a military life in the entire school. His movements were somewhat jerky and rough. His uniform never suited him well and his military cap, belts and gear always seemed to be in some kind of disorder and appeared to be a burden to him. His behavior was different from that of his friends. He was always concentrating, spending his spare time walking back and forth somewhere in the distance, oblivious to what was going on around him.

He was always kind and tender, but rarely was he really on close terms with anyone. There were only two people with whom he had lengthy conversations concerning different questions. They were cadets named Berezhetsky and Beketov. Dostoevsky's isolation from the other schoolmates caused some teasing from their side, and he received the nickname Fotii [the name of a Russian monk who lived in isolation]. But Fyodor Mikhailovich did not pay much attention to the ridicule of his schoolmates. In spite of this mockery, Fyodor Mikhailovich was treated with respect. The younger ones always felt the intellectual and spiritual superiority of their schoolmate and kidded him only occasionally.

When Fyodor Mikhailovich finished the senior academic course he entered his new position at the Engineering Department in St. Petersburg. There he lived on the corner of Vladimirskaya and Grafsky streets.

Once Fyodor Mikhailovich met me accidentally in the street and he started to ask me questions as to what I was doing and what books I was reading. He said that he knew I was a talented young man and he advised me to study more seriously. He suggested that I read more books, especially works by great writers, and he invited me to visit him some weekend.

I decided to take advantage of this invitation and I visited Fyodor Mikhailovich the following Sunday. His second floor apartment had four rooms: a large living room, a small hall and two bedrooms. Fyodor Mikhailovich occupied one of the rooms; the other rooms had no furniture. In a small, narrow room where he lived, worked and slept, there was a writing table, a sofa which also served as a bed, and several chairs. Books and sheets of paper covered with his handwriting were scattered all over the room: on the table, on the chairs and on the floor.

Fyodor Mikhailovich gave me a friendly welcome and started to ask me questions about my studies. For a long time he spoke about literature and the arts and told me which books I should read, lending some of them to me. Most clearly I remember his words about Gogol. He simply "opened my eyes" with respect to this writer and explained to me the depth and the meaning of his works. Students of the military school, I among them, were not prepared to have an understanding of Gogol. This is easy to explain, for our Russian teacher, Mr. Plaksin, used to say that Gogol was a poor writer and that his works were not gifted and dirty.

But at that time Gogol already had become an important writer and the youth had discovered an alternative reality. Even professors from the old school could not distract our attention from Gogol. Everyone read *Evenings at the Dikan'ka Village*. We were young, however, and, of course, the features we liked most of all in Gogol's works were his lyrics and his humor.

Then Fyodor Mikhailovich suggested that I read other Russian and foreign writers, among them Shakespeare. I followed his advice to improve my French: I read more in French and did some translations. To put it briefly, Fyodor Mikhailovich gave a push to my spiritual development, guiding my reading and studies.

In 1843, at the age of seventeen, I finished the main course at the Engineering School and entered the academic classes. At this time I lived with a friend of mine, Beszus, and Fyodor Mikhailovich visited us on occasion. At this time he had finished his novel *Poor People*, but he had not spoken to anyone about it. People found out about the novel after it was already published.

In 1844, I was eighteen years old and, as is often the case at this age, I was in love and constantly wrote letters and poems to my beloved. With the sincerity of a young man, I confided to Fyodor Mikhailovich all the secrets of my love story. I described the object of my adoration with all the passion of a young man, the way she moved and talked.... The name of this young woman was Anna L'vovna and at home they called her Netochka. Fyodor Mikhailovich liked the name so much, he titled his new novel *Netochka Nezvanova*.

I completed the full course of the Engineering Academy in 1845 and, in spite of my rather young years (I was nineteen), I was left in the Academy as the instructor of drawing and architecture. The heads of the Academy gave me an opportunity to study at the Academy of Arts at the same time....

Before 1849 I met Fyodor Mikhailovich only occasionally, since most of the time I was busy with my artistic studies. When I visited him at his home I sometimes met other people, among them Filippov, Petrashevsky and others who were later sentenced together with him.

Certainly I did not have the slightest idea about their plans, because Fyodor Mikhailovich was not going to share these things with such a young man as I was at that time. It happened once in 1849 that Fyodor Mikhailovich lived for several days in my apartment. During this time he asked me, every time he went to bed, not to bury him for at least three days if he fell into a lethargic sleep. The thought of having a lethargic sleep was always scaring him.

At the end of 1849 Fyodor Mikhailovich told me that there was a group of people who gathered at his place on Fridays to read literary works written for people, that is, for the middle class people and for the workers who were present, and he asked me to join this group.

I do not remember exactly why, but I could not attend those meetings and I did not have any idea as to what was going on there. However, I was a curious young man (they say that curiosity killed the cat), and I decided to go there once, to finally attend one of these gatherings.

Suddenly, however, a very special event changed my entire life. I received news of my mother's death. I arranged for several days off and immediately went to our estate in the Kharkov region. After I arrived at our village, and after my visit to Kharkov, I received my inheritance.

At the same time, I received the frightening news from St. Petersburg that the entire group had been arrested on the same Friday that I had planned to attend.

In 1862, when I lived in St. Petersburg, Fyodor Mikhailovich returned from his exile. I felt very happy when I saw him entering my apartment. He was free at last. He told me what he had experienced during these years. Is spite of all these troubles, he looked healthier than before, and he told me that his fits of epilepsy were now less frequent.

He had completely changed his views on many things.... But, unfortunately, this was practically our last meeting. The circumstances of life separated us. I saw him briefly and for the last time, in Moscow, during the unveiling of the Pushkin monument (in 1880).

Stepan Ianovsky: First Accounts of a Doctor About Dostoevsky's Epilepsy

(From S.D. Ianovsky, "Bolezn' Dostoevskogo" ["Dostoevsky's Illness"] *Novoe Vremia* [*New Times*] 24 February 1881: 17930.)

During the second year of my friendship with Fyodor Mikhailovich, I lived in Pavlovsk and he lived in Pargolovo [two suburbs of St. Petersburg]. I had to visit St. Petersburg three times a week for business purposes so I agreed to meet with Fyodor Mikhailovich in my apartment from 3 to 6 P.M.

After having my usual dinner I felt some unexplained excitement and around four o'clock, instead of going home as usual, along Morskaya Street and Obukhovsky Prospect to the Tsar Village Railway, I went the other way, turning left to the Hay Market Square. I did this instinctively, being driven by some strange force.

As soon as I approached the Hay Market Square, I saw Fyodor Mikhailovich. He was bareheaded, his coat was unbuttoned, and his tie was loosened. Some officer in a military uniform was supporting him by the elbow. Fyodor Mikhailovich saw me and yelled at the top of his voice: "...Here is the man who will save me!" ... Every time Fyodor Mikhailovich remembered the incident, he repeated: "Well, after this, you have to believe in fate...." He wanted to tell this story in one of the issues of *A Writer's Diary*, but he was critical of my Spiritualism at the time and therefore he choose not to.

Pavel Annenkov: Dostoevsky's First Literary Success

(From P. Annenkov, *Literaturnye vospominaniia* [*Literary Memoirs*]. Moscow: Goslitizdat, 1960.)

When I visited Belinsky one day, I saw that he was very excited. As soon as he noticed me, he screamed, "Come here, I will tell you the news...." He greeted me and continued, "I have been reading this manuscript for the past two days. This is a new talent.... This novel reveals such mysteries and such characters in Russian life as never discussed before. You see, this is the first social novel to appear in Russia, and it is written by a great artist who does not know how good he really is.

"It is a great drama, with great characters! Oh yes, I forgot to tell you that the artist's name is Dostoevsky, and samples of his work are in my hands."

Belinsky thereupon started to read those pieces which impressed him most of all, emphasizing some parts of the text by his intonation. Such was his reaction to the appearance of our new novelist. This was only the beginning. Belinsky wanted to do with this young writer what he had done before with other writers, for example with Koltsov and

Nekrasov: to strengthen his talent, ... to give him, so to speak, nerves and muscles. But here our critic had to face a stubborn rejection....

Belinsky was wrong. He had met a writer who was already formed, not a novice in need of instruction to perfect his writing. This new writer already had his own style and working habits, although this was his first literary creation. Dostoevsky listened to the advice of the critic with a calm but unreceptive manner. The sudden success which his work had obtained, created in the writer a great degree of self-respect and a high opinion of his own work....

When he submitted his first novel for publication in the forthcoming literary almanac, he asked the publisher to embellish his work with a special ornament in the margins in order to distinguish it from that of the others.

Later, Dostoevsky became a great, prodigious writer, as we all know ... and although for a long time their views and outlook continued to be quite similar, it was not long before he distanced himself from Belinsky.

Count Vladimir Sollogub: First Meeting with Dostoevsky

(From V. Sollogub, "Vospominaniia" ["Memoirs"], *Istorichesky Vestnik* [*The History Herald*] 6 [1886]: 561–562.)

Once I dragged Dostoevsky to my home. Here is the story of how I got acquainted with him.

In 1845 or 1846 I read *Poor People* in one of our monthly periodicals. I admired the novel, for it was written with force and simplicity by a great talent. As soon as I read it I went to the publisher of the journal— it seems to me that it was Andrei Alexandrovich Kraevsky—since I wanted to find out about the author. The publisher told me about Dostoevsky and gave me his address. I immediately paid him a call and found him in a small apartment, I believe it was on one of the streets in St. Petersburg, in the Pesky district.

He was a young man who looked pale and unhealthy. He had a rather shabby old coat, with very short sleeves that did not suit him.

He became confused when I introduced myself. I expressed my admiration of how profoundly astonished and impressed I was by his novel. It was so different from other works written at the time. He looked embarrassed and offered me a seat, the only armchair present in the room.

I sat down and we started our conversation. Chatting is my weak point so, to tell you the truth, it was I who spoke most of the time. Dostoevsky looked shy and avoided answering my questions directly. I noticed that he was a quiet, reserved and rather selfish person, but also a very talented and pleasant one. I sat talking to him for about twenty minutes, and then invited him for dinner at my home.

Dostoevsky became simply scared. "No, Count, excuse me," he said embarrassedly, rubbing his hands, "but I never have been in high society, and I cannot make such a decision...." "But who said anything about the high society, dear Fyodor Mikhailovich?" I replied. "We, my wife and I, really belong to it, we go there, but we do not let it into our house!"

Dostoevsky laughed, but remained stiff, and two months later he decided to show up at my "zoo." But then came the year of 1848, the year he was involved in the Petrashevsky case, and was sent to prison in Siberia.

Chapter 3. Socialist Circle, Arrest and Investigation, 1846–1849.

"Fyodor Dostoevsky, twenty-seven years old, by the decision of the General-in-Charge of the Military Court, for criminal conspiracy, for the distribution of a private letter filled with abusive remarks regarding the Orthodox Church and the Government, and for planning to set up an underground publishing house, in which to print anti-Government propaganda, is sentenced to death by firing squad."

(From the court verdict of the military tribunal)

"Starting from unlimited freedom, I arrive at unlimited despotism. I am a scoundrel, of course, and not a Socialist.... We will proclaim destruction.... Russia will be overwhelmed with darkness, the earth will weep for its old gods..."

(From *The Demons* by F. Dostoevsky)

D OSTOEVSKY BECAME FAMOUS ALMOST OVERNIGHT after finish-
ing *Poor People*, his first novel, a love story of the lower classes. After
Poor People, Dostoevsky wrote several smaller novels and short stories, including *The Double* and *The Landlady*, among others. These works met with sharp
criticism from major literary critics, most notably including Vissarion Belinsky.

Disappointed in the literary circles, at the age of twenty-five Dostoevsky started to attend the secret meetings of a revolutionary socialist circle
which discussed the freedom of the press, the liberation of serfs and the theories of French socialists. The organization was investigated by officials and
on April 22, 1849, the chief of the St. Petersburg Secret Police issued an
order to a group of police officers:

> To: Major Tchudinov
> Head of Secret Police,
> St. Petersburg
>   According to the supreme order of the Tsar, I command you to arrest
> the resigned Junior-Lieutenant and literary artist, Fyodor Mikhailovich
> Dostoevsky, at four o'clock in the morning ... to put a seal on all his
> papers, manuscripts and books and to dispatch instantly all these mate-
> rials, together with Dostoevsky, to the Third Section of the Royal Police
> of His Majesty.... If Dostoevsky claims that certain documents and
> books belong to other people, ignore these statements and seal these
> items as well.
> Count General Orlov
> Head
> Third Section of [Secret] Police
> [Archives, Third Section of Police, File 13; L. Grossman *Zhizn' i trudy
> F.M. Dostoevskogo* (*The Chronology of F.M. Dostoevsky's Life and Works*).
> Moscow: Academia, 1935, p. 55].

Fyodor Dostoevsky was arrested on April 23, 1849, together with 34
other members* of the Petrashevsky socialist circle. The were moved to a
special prison in St. Peter and Paul Fortress, a place for the most dangerous
state criminals. Some documents from the time give interesting detail about
the Fortress Prison.

> From: Count A. Orlov
> Director
> Third Section of Police
>
> To: I.A. Nabokov
> Director, Prison at
> St. Peter and Paul Fortress
>   Report: About sending to the Fortress 36 people of different ranks
> who were arrested by the Third Section of Police. A list of their names
> is enclosed. All convicts will be sent in separate carts, accompanied by
> a police officer, one after another [Archives, Third Section of Police,
> File 13].

Several people were arrested by mistake and later released.

Dostoevsky was moved from the headquarters of the Third Section of Police to the St. Peter and Paul Fortress Prison at 11:25 P.M. on the same day, April 23, 1849, and General Nabokov reported about this in his reply letter to Count Orlov: "There are 34 people in St. Peter and Paul Fortress, and 13 people in single cells. F. Dostoevsky was in cell No. 9..." (*Archives*, CGIA, File 1280-128, no. 156).

A fellow prisoner in the single cell of St. Peter and Paul Fortress, Nikolai Akhsharumov, remembered his arrest and incarceration as follows:

> The thick door opened in front of me, and I found myself in a very small and dark room. I felt the smell of stale air. There was a bed at the wall covered with a grey cloth, there was a stool and a box. I was ordered to take off all my clothes and to put on a thick prison robe and a pair of very thick stockings. I also had boots and a gown from the same grey cloth. All my belongings and my dress were taken from me.... The room itself was not more than three by two meters, with a very high ceiling.... The windows were barred by thick iron rods and the door was covered with iron [*The History Herald*, 11 (1901): 155–156].

Some archival documents describe the belongings of the prisoners. Dostoevsky's effects were listed as follows: "From cell no. 9: Mr. Dostoevsky, resigned Junior-Lieutenant: 60 kopecks of money, a winter coat, a shirt, a vest, underwear, boots, stockings, a scarf, a handkerchief and a comb" (*Archives*, CGIA, File 1280-128, no. 156).

Dostoevsky was interrogated by the Special Committee investigating the activity of the secret revolutionary circle. At first he refused to admit that the meetings at the socialist circle were of a criminal nature. According to his early statements, they were literary evenings, where young people discussed books about socialism. These meetings were "more a gathering of friends than a political society." Later on, during consecutive interrogations, Dostoevsky admitted that they were "involved in discussing socialist theories, ... in a conspiracy to create a secret socialist publishing house, ... to organize a rebellion and to free serfs" (L. Grossman *Zhisn' i trudy Dostoevskogo*, 1935, p. 59).

The investigation lasted several months. The Investigatory Committee prepared a special report for the Minister of Defense about the Petrashevsky case. It stated: "This group of people had meetings at which the government was criticized, but they were neither united in their views ... nor in any agreement regarding their actions.... Therefore, this group of people cannot be called a secret organized society" (*Russikie Zapiski* [*Russian Notes*] 11 [1916]: 26).

On September 26, a dissatisfied Nikolai I appointed another investigatory committee, which he named the Military Court Committee and put it under the leadership of Count General V.E. Perovsky. The new military tribunal condemned Dostoevsky to death on November 13, 1849. The court verdict was very cruel:

This case was started April 29, 1849, by the Investigation Commission. The court hearing began September 30, and ended November 16. The case was transferred to the Auditor's Department November 13.

Military Court found the convict, Fyodor Dostoevsky, guilty of the following charges: in March, this year, he received from Moscow a copy of the criminal letter by the literary artist Belinsky; he read this letter at different meetings and gave it to Mombelli to make copies....

Fyodor Dostoevsky, twenty-seven years old, by the decision of the General-in-Charge of the Military Court, for criminal conspiracy, for the distribution of a private letter filled with abusive remarks regarding the Orthodox Church and the Government, and for planning to set up an underground publishing house, in which to print anti-Government propaganda, is sentenced to death by firing squad.

This verdict of the military tribunal was quickly reviewed by the General Auditor's Commission. On November 19, an important memo was issued by the General Auditor concerning this case. It recommended that "Ex-Engineer Lieutenant Dostoevsky, for the distribution of Belinsky's letter ... should be removed of his civil rights and sent to a maximum security prison for eight years" (P. Shchegolev, *Petrashevtsy [The Petrashevsky Case]*. Moscow, 1928, Vol. 3, pp. 208, 335).

On the margins of this document the Tsar made a note in his own handwriting, changing the sentence from eight to four years in a maximum security prison, to be followed by army service in Siberia. This was the Tsar's final verdict for Dostoevsky: "Four years, and then, a private in the army."

The letter from Belinsky to Gogol was among the prosecution's major pieces of evidence in the Dostoevsky case. Here is an excerpt from this document, which the Russian government considered so dangerous that Dostoevsky had to spend ten years in Siberia after reading it among a circle of friends:

> Russia produces a terrible impression.... This is a country where people sell other people ... where there is no guarantee for the individual, for honor, for private property. There is no police order, but there exists a huge network of different types of thieves and robbers instead. The most urgent questions of national importance for Russia at present are: the abolition of serfdom; the abolition of physical punishment; and the activation of those laws which already exist... Russia is sleeping in apathy! [See L. Grossman, *Dostoevsky*, Moscow, 1962, pp. 131–132.]

Apollon Maikov, one of Dostoevsky's close friends, described the writer's involvement with the Petrashevsky secret socialist circle:

> One day, somewhere in January of 1849, Dostoevsky came to me and asked me if he could spend the night at my house ... he told me that some of the Petrashevsky people had decided to establish a publishing house ... to publish literature, etc. I tried to prove [to them] that they could ruin themselves. ... And I remember how Dostoevsky, sitting in front of his friends, looking like a dying Socrates, with his unbuttoned shirt, made a wonderful speech about our holy duty to stay with our fatherland, etc.

Later, I found out that the parts for the printing press were made in different districts of the city, after blueprints made by Mr. Filippov, and that the equipment had been brought to the apartment of one of their members, and was assembled there a day or two before their arrest... ["Letter from Maikov to Viskobatov," 1885].

Dostoevsky described the outset of his trip to Siberia in a letter to his brother Mikhail, dated February 22, 1854:

At 12 p.m. sharp, that is, exactly on Christmas, I put my chains on my legs for the first time, they weighed about ten pounds, and it was very uncomfortable to walk with them. They put us into open sleighs, separately; everyone was accompanied by a police officer, and in a caravan of four sledges, with the postal officer in front, we departed from St. Petersburg. I had a heavy feeling in my heart [*Complete Works*, Vol. 28, part 1, pp. 167–174].

On December 24 at 9 P.M., General Nabokov, the director of the St. Peter and Paul Fortress Prison, wrote to the Tsar, "I have the honor to inform Your Majesty that the criminals Sergei Durov, Fyodor Dostoevsky and Ivan Iastrzhembsky were sent to Tobolsk on 24 December 1849 with the lieutenant Prokofiev and three other police officers" (Archives, Third Section of Police, 1849, File 13).

On January 11, 1850, an order was issued by the Governor-General of Western Siberia about the transfer of Dostoevsky from Tobolsk, a large Siberian city, to a maximum security prison in the remote town of Omsk. It read, "Send him in the strictest way, with hands and feet cuffed" (*Rabochii put'* [*Worker's Way*], 1926, no. 34).

On January 20, Dostoevsky and Sergei Durov were moved from Tobolsk Fortress to Omsk Prison (Archives, CVIGA, File 395/285, no. 81, p. 213), where they were incarcerated for four years. During the years of his incarceration in Siberia, Dostoevsky completely altered his views: he referred to his former socialist friends as "the demons" and became a passionate monarchist, an attitude which he would support for the rest of his life.

Avdotia Panaeva: The Beginning of Dostoevsky's Literary Career

(From A. Panaeva [Golovachova], *Vospominaniia* [*Memoirs*]. Moscow: Goslitizdat, 1956, pp. 143–146, 175, 177–178.)

In his literary memoirs Panaev wrote about the effect produced by Dostoevsky's *Poor People*, so I am not going to write about this here.

When Dostoevsky visited us for the first time, he came with Nekrasov and Grigorovich, who had just started his literary career. You could tell immediately that Dostoevsky was an extremely nervous and easily irritated young man. He was thin, short and blonde; his face had an unhealthy pallor; his small grey eyes moved nervously from one object to another, and his pale lips trembled nervously.

Almost all of the people present at the party knew him, but he, nevertheless, looked confused and did not get involved in the general conversation. Everyone wanted to talk to him, to help him overcome his shyness and to show him that he was a member of our circle. Eventually his shyness disappeared; he even showed some joy and initiated discussions, but it seemed that he contradicted the others only out of stubbornness....

He was a young, nervous man who often could not control himself and openly displayed his exaggerated high self-regard as an author.

Being a very sensitive man, he could not hide his feelings of pride and of being a very special person among other young literary artists whose first attempts at literary careers were more modest. But he was also embarrassed by his own very successful first steps as a writer.

When young literary artists appeared in our circle, one had to be gentle with them, but it seemed that Dostoevsky, on the contrary, did everything to produce a negative effect, and indeed, on purpose. When he showed them that his talent was much greater than theirs, he spoke in an irritating and snobbish tone.

So they started to criticize him and to mock him with nasty jokes. Turgenev was an expert at such things. He usually engaged Dostoevsky in a discussion and then made him completely excited and irritated. Dostoevsky would lose control and make completely ridiculous assertions while defending absurd views on different subjects. Turgenev, who waited for such moments, picked up on these statements and mocked at Dostoevsky even more. Dostoevsky became terribly suspicious because one of his friends [most probably Grigorovich] used to tell him everything which was said about him and about *Poor People* at our meetings [when he was not present]. They said that Dostoevsky's friend told him everything, all about "who told what to whom" just for the sake of art. Dostoevsky suspected us all to be jealous of his talent and he tried to find hidden meanings in every word, in every innocent phrase. He said that people wanted to make his literary work look less important....

When they told Belinsky what Dostoevsky thought of himself, he just shrugged his shoulders: "It's a pity, because Dostoevsky definitely has a talent. But if he, instead of developing his talent, thinks of himself as if he were a genius, he will not move any further. He must be treated medically, because all this is caused by his shattered nerves. He probably suffered previously in his life...."

Once Turgenev told us a story about a man from the province who imagined himself to be a genius, skillfully depicting the humorous features of this person. Dostoevsky was present. He became completely pale, trembled all over and then ran away without listening to the end of Turgenev's story. I said, addressing the audience, "Why do you all torment Dostoevsky like this?" But Turgenev was in a good mood. He quickly changed the subject, involving others in some conversation, and nobody paid any attention to the early departure of Dostoevsky. Turgenev started to create humorous poems about Devushkin, the hero of *Poor People*, as if it were this character himself who wrote poems about Dostoevsky. In this poem he was grateful that Dostoevsky made him famous all over Russia. He used the phrase "my dear mother" too often, just as Devushkin did.

After this evening, Dostoevsky no longer visited our house and even avoided meeting us in the streets. Once, when Panaev met him in the street and wanted to ask him why he did not attend our parties, Dostoevsky quickly ran to the other side of the street. He met only one person from our circle, Dr. Grigorovich, who told us that Dostoevsky scolded everyone in our company, that he did not want to continue his friendship with any one of us, that he was completely disappointed in us, and that we all were jealous, heartless, and cruel people.

In 1848 we lived in Pargolovo in a summer cottage. Petrashevsky also lived here, and many young people came to visit him from the city. Dostoevsky, Pleshcheev and Toll also payed him visits on occasion. Dostoevsky did not visit us, since Belinsky had offended him by publishing in *The Contemporary* an article critical of *The Double* and *Mr. Prokharchin*. When he met Nekrasov and Panaev, he looked at them proudly and mockingly, did not speak to them and refused even to greet them. They were surprised by Dostoevsky's strange quirks.

Once Dostoevsky came to the editor's office and said that he wanted to talk to Nekrasov. He was in a very excited state. I went out of Nekrasov's office and from the cafeteria heard them yelling at each other. When Dostoevsky ran out of the office into the corridor he was completely pale, and struggling to get his hands into the sleeves of his coat. Failing this he grabbed his coat from the servant who was holding it and rushed out to the staircase. When I entered Nekrasov's office, I found him also in a very heated state.

"Dostoevsky has simply gone mad," said Nekrasov in an indignant and trembling voice. "He came here and began threatening me, saying that he forbids me to publish a book review of his work in our next issue. Someone lied to him and told him that I wrote some humorous couplets about him and read them everywhere I go. He just went completely crazy."

Aleksandr Miliukov: About Dostoevsky's Involvement in the Petrashevsky Secret Socialist Circle

(From Aleksandr Petrovich Miliukov, *Literaturnye vstrechi i znakomstva* [*Literary Meetings and Friends*]. St. Petersburg: Suvorin Press, 1890, pp. 168–249.)

Dostoevsky occupies a unique place in our literature: he was not a member of any group nor did he belong to any school. Instead, he represented the entire Russian society and the interests of our people....

I knew him for more than thirty years; our friendship was interrupted only by his exile. When we met [after his return from Siberia], he gave me new details for a complete and extensive account of his life, to be written in the future.

I met Dostoevsky in the winter of 1848. ... I developed a close friendship with Dostoevsky and Mombelli, who lived in the Moscow Military Barracks and who held meetings with a circle of young people. There I also met some other people, who told me that there was a larger group in St. Petersburg whose members studied works of a political and social character. I did not wish to become closely associated with these people....

I had a mixed attitude towards the Durov Circle, which consisted, as I discovered later, of people who attended the meetings of the Petrashevsky Circle but who did not share Petrashevsky's views. They were more moderate young people....

I knew about the Petrashevsky Circle only from rumors. As for the Durov Circle, which I visited on a regular basis, I treated it as family.

I can say positively that there was nothing resembling revolutionary ideas in this group, whose gatherings had no fixed rules, no statutes, nor even anything resembling a program. In any case, it could not be called a secret society. The principal activity of the circle was reading and circulating among its members some books of current revolutionary or social interest. Several questions were discussed, among them issues which could not be aired in public. Most of all, they were interested in the problem of the abolition of serfdom, and how it could be achieved. When someone expressed doubts about the possibility of abolishing serfdom by the highest legal authority, Dostoevsky sharply contradicted this person, saying that he did not believe in any other way.

Another issue, which was often discussed in our circle, was censorship.... Our literary discussions were mostly dedicated to relevant articles in the recent periodicals....

On 23 April 1848, when I returned home from my lectures, I found Mikhail Dostoevsky, who had already been waiting for me for some time. I saw immediately that he was worried by something.

"What has happened?" I asked him.

"Don't you know?" he replied.

"About what?"

"My brother Fyodor was arrested."

"How did this come about? What are you talking about? When?"

"Tonight... They searched his apartment... Took him away... The place is sealed."

"And the others?"

"Petrashevsky and Speshnev were arrested as well... I have no accurate information about the others... Today or tomorrow they will arrest me."

"What makes you think so?"

"My brother Andrei was arrested... He does not know anything, he was not even there... He was taken by mistake, instead of me."

At once we decided to go and see who among our friends had been arrested, and to meet again that night. First of all, I went to S. Durov's apartment. It was closed and locked, and there were government seals on the door. I found the same seals at Mombelli's door in the Moscow Military Barracks, and at P. Filippov's place on Vasilevsky Island. When I asked the caretakers, they answered, "The man was arrested tonight." Mombelli's servant knew me, and he spoke to me with tears in his eyes. That night I visited Mikhail Mikhailovich Dostoevsky and we exchanged news of what we had discovered during the day. He had visited the homes of other members and discovered that most of them had been apprehended the previous night. From what we knew, we concluded that the members of the Durov Circle were not in custody and that only those who had attended the Petrashevsky Circle's meeting had been arrested....

We found out, from rumors, that about thirty people were in custody. First they were brought to the secret police headquarters, and then to the St. Peter and Paul Fortress, where they were confined in the top tier of single cells. It turned out that the authorities had been keeping an eye on the Petrashevsky Circle for a long time and that a certain young man among them had been a police agent, although he pretended to be a man with liberal ideas. He had attended their meetings, where he had incited others to speak on different radical political topics. Then he put down everything on paper and sent his reports to the police. M. Dostoevsky told me that he had long suspected this man. Soon it became known that a special commission had been created to investigate the Petrashevsky case.

Two weeks passed, and one morning I received news that M. Dostoevsky had been arrested the previous night.... As far as I know there was no serious evidence against him. Furthermore, he had been distancing himself from the circle for some time. I therefore hoped that he would not remain under arrest for very long. I was right. At the end of March 1849, my friend was released and he hurried to my home to see me....

He told me about his interrogation and the questions he was asked about Fyodor Mikhailovich. We both came to the conclusion that his brother had been accused of having freely expressed some liberal views, of criticizing several highly placed officials, and of having distributed prohibited literature, including the famous Belinsky letter.

Therefore, the charges laid against him were not very grave, but on the other hand, if the authorities wanted to take a serious view of this case, which was quite possible, then we could expect a sad ending.

The autumn passed, and the long winter began. The fate of the prisoners was decided only just before Christmas. We were all greatly surprised and alarmed by the verdict [of the military tribunal]: all those arraigned were sentenced to death by the firing squad. But, as you know, the sentence was not carried out. On the day of the execution, at the Semyonovsky Parade Ground, there occurred a mock execution, and a new sentence was announced; the lives of all were spared, but different punishments were handed out. Fyodor Mikhailovich was sentenced to maximum security prison for four years, with a consecutive term of military service as a private soldier in one of the infantry battalions stationed in Siberia.

The convicts were sent from the Fortress to Siberia in groups of two or three. As far as I can recall, on the third day after the mock execution M. Dostoevsky came to me and told me that his brother would be sent away the same night and that he would like to go and bid him farewell.

I also wanted to say goodbye to a man whom I would not be able to see again for a very long time, perhaps never. We went to the Fortress, directly to Major M. whom we knew before and from whom we hoped to obtain permission to see the prisoner. The major was a very nice man....

We were brought to a large room in the basement of the Fortress Office. It was evening, and the big room was dimly lit by a single lamp. We waited for a rather long time, while the clock in the Fortress Tower twice struck the quarter hour.

At last the door opened, we heard the clang of arms, and then we saw F. Dostoevsky and F. Durov enter the room escorted by two officers.

We exchanged a friendly, warm handshake. In spite of eight months in prison, they had not changed much. There was a serious expression on the face of one man and a friendly smile on the face of the other. They were both dressed in prison garb, including coats and winter boots, ready to travel.

The Officer of the Guard did not interfere and sat inconspicuously on a chair at the entrance to the room.

First of all, Fyodor Mikhailovich said that he was glad that his brother was not involved in this case and that he did not have to suffer. He expressed his deep interest and concern for his brother's family and children and he asked about many details of their health and life....

The elder brother had tears in his eyes, but Fyodor Mikhailovich was calm and tried to comfort him. "Stop, brother," he said. "You know me, I am not going to die. The people in prison are not animals; they are people like us and, perhaps, even better.... I know that we will see each other again, I have no doubt about it. ... Please write to me ... I will experience more and I will pick up more ideas so that I will have something to write about..."

It seemed that this man looked at his future stay in prison as if it were a pleasure trip abroad, where he was going to see the beauties of nature and the monuments of art, to meet new and attractive people, and to enjoy the freedom of travel. It seemed that he did not really think that he was going to be incarcerated in the "House of the Dead" for almost four years, always in fetters, with people who were outcasts from society because of their terrible crimes. He may have hoped, as he always did, to find some human features in these terrible criminals, these fallen creatures. He believed that under the ash there was always gleaming the light of God, even in the soul of the worst criminal and outcast. ...

We embraced and shook hands for the last time. I did not know that I would never see Durov again and that I would see Dostoevsky only eight years later....

Here is Dostoevsky's own account of his arrest, which he wrote in my daughter's album after his return from exile in 1860....

> On the 22nd or, to be more exact, on the 23rd of April 1849, at 4 a.m., I returned home from seeing Grigoriev and fell asleep. In less than an hour, as if in a dream, I saw several peculiar and suspicious people enter my room. I heard the sound of a sword hitting something in the room, as if by accident. What was that? I struggled to open my eyes, and I heard a pleasant and sympathetic voice: "Please get up!" I saw a handsome District Police Officer with delicate whiskers. It was not he who spoke, however, but a man dressed in a blue uniform with colonel's insignia.
>
> "What has happened?" I asked him, getting up from my bed.
>
> "Pursuant to the order..." I understood, at least, that they had a warrant, an order for my arrest. I noticed a soldier, also dressed in a blue uniform and standing at the door.

"Well, well, here you are," I thought. "Please let me..." I started talking.

"Please do not worry. Get dressed, we will wait," said the colonel in an even nicer voice. When I dressed myself, they asked for books. They did not find much, but made a complete mess of the table.

All my papers and letters were neatly bound with a small rope. One of the police officers wanted to show how smart he was, so he went to the fireplace and shuffled the ashes.

Another police officer, receiving an order, put a chair to the fireplace and stepped on it. He wanted to see whether anything was hidden in the wall. He fell down on the floor, making a terrible noise....

There was an old coin on the table. The police officer investigated it attentively and nodded to the colonel.

"What do you think, is it counterfeit?" I asked him.

"Well, we still have to investigate," he stammered and added it to the confiscated materials.

We went out into the fresh air. The landlady and her husband saw me off. Ivan, the husband, looked at me in a dull, official way which did not suit the event. There was a carriage waiting at the door. The soldier, I, the police officer and the colonel sat inside and we went down to the Fontanka River, across the chain bridge and along the Summer Garden.

When we arrived [at the police headquarters], I saw that there were many people inside, some of whom I recognized. All of them were silent and sleepy. One of the high-ranking officers conducted the reception of the newcomers. Men in blue uniforms were constantly coming in, bringing with them new victims...

We surrounded the high-ranking officer, who held a list of names. In front of Antonelli's name it was written: "The police agent in this case."

"Well, it was Antonelli," we thought. We were put into different corners of the room, waiting for the final decision as to where we would be put. There were about seventeen people in the so-called "White Room." Leonid Vasilievich [General Dubelt, the chief of the Secret Police] entered the room. At this point I will interrupt my story. But I assure you that Leonid Vasilievich was the most pleasant man....

F. Dostoevsky. 24 May 1880.

Orest Miller: The Catastrophe

(From Orest Miller, "About F.M. Dostoevsky," in *Biographiia, pis'ma i zametki iz zapisnoi knizhki Dostoevskogo* [*Biography, Letters and Notes from Dostoevsky's Notebooks*]. St. Petersburg, 1883, pp. 75–103.)

Dostoevsky wrote in his novel *White Nights*: "there are strange corners in St. Petersburg where the dreamers live...." He remembered this period of his life later, when he depicted a new political movement in *The Demons* and in *A Writer's Diary* (1873 and 1876).

Miliukov characterized this period as "the time of the oppressed social life and public opinion in Russia." Many liberal books were illegally brought from abroad. These forbidden works were the main subject to be studied by different scholarly and literary circles.... There was a man who knew about such circles and who wanted to use them for his cause. It was Petrashevsky, a former college student who graduated from the University in 1841 and who served at the Department of Communication at the Foreign Ministry. Although he was a civil servant, he had an unusual appearance, including a beard and a huge hat. He wanted to have more and more such circles develop the propaganda and believed that it was not necessary for the people from different groups to know each other.... Mr. Petrashevsky supervised them all.

The personal memoirs of Fyodor Mikhailovich about "the stories which took place long ago" helped Dostoevsky to understand these events better. He described these events in his novel *The Demons*, and he remembered this story in his *Diary* of 1873.

In his biography dictated to Anna Grigorievna, he said: "Socialists appeared in Russia from the Petrashevsky circles. The Petrashevsky people put many seeds in the soil." ... The Petrashevsky circles were certainly dangerous for the security of the state. Dostoevsky wrote: "When we were convicted, it was the state which only defended itself." ...

In the Durov circle there were different kinds of people, some of whom were ardent, which made them dangerously bold. Petrashevsky did not appreciate this. One of the members of another circle (those of Khanykov's) said that Petrashevsky was not happy with the decision of the Durov group to install a secret publishing house to publish [revolutionary] speeches and articles to distribute among the people....

They wanted to promote the criticism of the existing regime everywhere, including schools and colleges, and to find allies in other social groups, such as serfs or religious sects....

I.M. Dubois remembers that many members of this circle thought that Dostoevsky was well suited for this type of propaganda, because he could make an overwhelming impact on the listeners. ...

Anna Grigorievna Dostoevskaya wrote down in Speshnev's memoirs that Dostoevsky disliked Petrashevsky because he was an atheist and he blasphemed the faith. Dostoevsky rarely visited the Petrashevsky Circle. Miliukov also stated that Dostoevsky did read socialist writers but he had a critical attitude toward their works.

Dostoevsky insisted that these [socialist] theories have no importance for Russia, because Russian traditional, peasant communities are stronger and have a more solid foundation than all the theoretical dreams of St. Simon and his school....

Dostoevsky had Slavophile views. Pleshcheev knew this and sent from Moscow a famous letter written from Belinsky to Gogol which was considered to be the manifesto of the Westernizers.

Dostoevsky, as other Slavophiles, liked *Correspondence* by Gogol but he did not appreciate his views on serfdom. Nevertheless, Dostoevsky read this famous Belinsky letter at the meeting of the Petrashevsky Circle and this was one of the major reasons for his conviction.

The Society of Propaganda includes the following remarks: "One of the members of the circle, I.L. Iastrzhembsky, was present at the meeting and he heard Dostoevsky speak. He was greatly astonished by Dostoevsky's wonderful voice: 'He was an expert at reading, and this was the major reason for Dostoevsky's conviction, and my incarceration, since I expressed support and sympathy for Dostoevsky's speech and nodded with my head in approval.'" ...

At the time of the trial, Dostoevsky was twenty-seven years old.

Iastrzhembsky described Dostoevsky's appearance at the time: "He was a quiet, humble, nice-looking young man, although his face looked unhealthy. He spoke very little, in a quiet voice.... We all saw in him a man who had a very sensitive nervous system and who was able to experience the most refined sensations. When you talked to him in private, you could recognize the author of *Netochka Nezvanova*."

Fyodor Mikhailovich testified that he was guilty of attending the Petrashevsky Circle for almost three years, although we knew that he did not attend its meetings very often. This means that he joined it in 1846 and he was among the first visitors of Petrashevsky, together with Pleshcheev, Kalmykov and Toll. All other members joined the circle in 1847 and in 1848....

There are no letters written by Dostoevsky from this period. Maybe they were destroyed by the police....

Meetings of the Kachkin Circle started at the end of 1848, and the Durov Circle started its activities in March 1849. Mr. Mombelli informed me that the Petrashevsky meetings were coordinated by a chairman and that it was the custom to make speeches (usually about atheism, the liberation of the peasants, etc.) which were later discussed by the group....

Most probably, it was the dinner dedicated to Fourier on the seventh of April 1849 that precipitated the demise of the circle. It was one of a number of dinners dedicated to famous people of the present or past....
On this day Dostoevsky made a speech which he ended with the following words: "We have condemned the present state of our society to death and we must fulfil this sentence." Akhsharumov made a speech at the same meeting in which he urged the destruction of private property, family, law, state, army, cities and churches.

From the police reports it was stated that Dostoevsky was accused of "attending Petrashevsky's meetings and criticizing the strict censorship of the time."

At one of the meetings, in 1849, Dostoevsky read a letter from Belinsky to Gogol, which he received from Pleshcheev in Moscow.

He also read this letter at a meeting of the Durov Circle and then gave it to Mombelli to make a copy. At the meetings of the Durov Circle, he listened to the articles being read, and became familiar with the plans to establish a secret publishing house.

Doomsday for Petrashevsky occurred on the 23rd of April when he and all the people who visited his house, thirty-four altogether, were arrested…. Out of those arrested, twenty-three were finally investigated by the police. Dostoevsky was among them….

Count Gagarin, as well as General Dubelt, made a bad impression on I. Iastrzhembsky, who left detailed memoirs about the police investigation.

As Speshnev remembered, Count Gagarin asked all suspects to make full confessions. Rostovtsev testified that Gagarin was primarily interested in those few members of the circle who studied at military schools.

Fyodor Mikhailovich remembered that General Rostovtsev asked him to tell everything he knew.

Dostoevsky did not give any direct answers. Rostovtsev addressed Dostoevsky with the following words: "I cannot believe that a man that wrote *Poor People* could have been connected with these vile people. This is impossible. You were not involved in this case and I have the authority on behalf of the Tsar to tell you that you will be granted amnesty if you disclose all the details." Dostoevsky remembered, "I kept silent." After this, General Dubelt said, with a smile, "Well, I told you so." Rostovtsev yelled, "I cannot see Dostoevsky any more," and ran out into an adjoining room….

As was mentioned before, Petrashevsky accused other members of his circle. It is written in the police report that he did so to make his own sentence less severe.

Dostoevsky testified that he was against monarchy and this coincides with Miliukov's memoirs: "He was never a socialist, though he liked to study social issues."

Fyodor Mikhailovich himself told me that he avoided giving direct answers during the oral investigation and that he didn't even want to take advantage of the amnesty promised by Rostovtsev. In any case, it seemed clear that Dostoevsky did not betray anyone. They asked for a written testimony. Dostoevsky was tired, his nervous system was exhausted and besides he was a very nervous man and he, without disclosing complicated details, started to blame only himself. Maybe he did this with the sole purpose of satisfying them so that they would leave him alone.

In *A Writer's Diary* of 1873 he clearly writes that nobody felt regret or remorse when their sentence was announced. He also remembered that his own views on these events changed later.

They were held in the fortress for eight months. Fyodor Mikhailovich was imprisoned in Alexeevsky cells, numbers seven and nine. He was prohibited from reading and writing for the first two months of his sentence and after this he was allowed to read only religious books, to write and to go out for small fifteen minute walks in the prison yard accompanied by a guard. The only means of communication with those in the neighboring cells was with a special code, knocking on the prison walls.

Iastrzhembsky was also incarcerated in the same Alexeevsky cells, and he remembered that "the living conditions were satisfactory: clean air and surroundings, and healthy food." In support of this, he remembered that though there was an epidemic of cholera in St. Petersburg, nobody among the inmates fell ill. The air was probably not very clean because all utilities were contained within each room; and it must have been damp because his hat was covered with mold by the end of his stay. The most difficult thing to deal with was solitude. As Ipollit Dubois remembered, the prison guard in the corridor, who was a private and very old fellow, felt sympathy towards them. From time to time he opened small windows in the doors of the cells and said, "You are sad! Hold on, Christ did! Why have you been put there? You are such quiet people. Before you, we had some really violent guys here."

Dostoevsky wrote several letters to his brother from prison.

The novel he refers to in these letters is *The Little Hero.* As he recollected later, in prison he was allowed to write only about very innocent things. This work was subsequently passed along by Mikhail Dostoevsky to the publisher of *The Fatherland Notes,* and it was published later in 1857 without the author's name. The plot of *The Little Hero* is really innocent, but there is one character in whom Fyodor Mikhailovich depicted an unsympathetic person from the "Society of Propaganda." He was "a European, a contemporary man full of new ideas and vanity…. He had a phrase ready for every occasion, especially many phrases which expressed sympathy for mankind."

Dostoevsky tolerated his position. This is even more striking because he, as he himself recollected or remembered, was very much concerned about his health before this catastrophe. He suspected that he had all sorts of illnesses and became genuinely ill from these thoughts. He even treated himself with primitive mustard plasters. … As Fyodor Mikhailovich testifies, he would have gone mad if not for this catastrophe which completely changed his life. He understood that there existed a great universal idea and all his personal troubles were minor in comparison with it.

Iastrzhembsky recollects that he heard from a trusted source that the first regional commission decided to set them free because of the lack of evidence. He said that this must be true because there are no traces of the decision of the commission in the police reports. The official copy of these police files was passed to me by Iastrzhembsky who found it in the garbage at the Apraskin Court.

There were no traces of the decision of this commission in the materials published abroad under the title "The Society of Propaganda." The case was passed to a general auditor. There were no legal grounds for this because the investigative commission was appointed by the Tsar himself and it was higher in rank than the general auditor. Dubois remembered that the chief of the fortress was very much surprised by this and he excitedly told the prisoners about this decision....

The general auditor's report has a note indicating the date when the police investigation took place: "The investigation case started on 29 April 1849, went to court 30 September, ended 16 November and entered the general auditor's department 13 November." Some of the suspects testified differently in order to make their comrades appear less guilty, and the general auditor also saw different degrees of guilt among the members of this society. He wrote: "Some of the suspects were more guilty than the others in the committing of these crimes, though all of them are accused of the crime against the state. According to the existing law, there is no difference between the organizers of such a crime and other members of the criminal group. Based on this, all members of the circle, except for Chernovtsov, are sentenced to death by a shooting squad."

Chernovtsov, who did not admit his guilt and whose guilt was not proven, "was left under supervision and sent to Viatka" [a remote town in Siberia].

After this statement, the general auditor "took into consideration some circumstances concerning the case, in particular: "Many of the prisoners sincerely regret their involvement in the group and they pleaded guilty and testified about many facts which could have been hidden but were revealed only due to their cooperation. Many of the convicts are rather young people and, finally, their plans were not fulfilled, due to the measures taken by the government."

Based on all this, the general auditor asked in his petition [to the Tsar], "to change the capital punishment to other terms, according to the level of guilt."

Petrashevsky, as "the organizer of the criminal group," was sentenced by the general auditor "to be deprived of all his civil rights and sent to prison for a life term of hard labor."

Nikolai Pavlovich, the Tsar, wrote on the report, "Be it like this."

Mombelli and Speshnev belonged to the second category of the convicted, and they were sentenced, respectively, to fifteen and twelve years in prison. The Tsar wrote beside the name of Speshnev, "Ten years." Student Kalmykov, for making a speech dedicated to Fourier, received ten years in prison followed by service in the army as a private.

Durov was sentenced to eight years for organizing meetings at his apartment and for his plans to make a secret publishing house. The Tsar reduced this sentence to four years.

Dostoevsky followed Durov in the list. Initially he was sentenced to eight years in prison "for his participation in the criminal plans, for distributing the Belinsky letter filled with many critical remarks against the Orthodox Church and the supreme state power, and for his plans to organize a secret publishing house to publish the anti-government literature."

The Tsar's decision [about Dostoevsky's sentence] was the same as the one concerning Durov: "Four years, followed by army service as a private."

Dostoevsky dictated in his *Biography* written abroad:

> This sentence was the first of its kind in Russia, since previously everyone who was sentenced to "katorga" [hard labor in a maximum security prison] lost their civil rights forever, even after having finished serving their prison term. Dostoevsky (as well as Durov) was sentenced to serve in the army as a private after the prison term. This meant that he regained his civil rights as a citizen. Later such cases happened many times, but then it was the first such case, and it happened due to the personal decision of Nikolai I, the Emperor, who felt compassion for Dostoevsky's young years and his talent.

The Russian Invalid (issue dated 22 December 1849) publicized the case:

> The dangerous theories which create riots throughout all of Europe and which threaten to destroy the order and the prosperity of the people, appeared in our country.... A small group of people, completely unimportant, most of them very young and with low morals, dreamt of destroying the sacred rights of religion, law and private property.... Civil servant Butashevich-Petrashevsky organized meetings at his home which consisted of young people belonging to different classes. At the end of 1848, he started to organize a secret society. The plan of the general uprising against the existing regime in our country was created.

As Fyodor Mikhailovich remembered, nobody knew the exact date of when the sentence would be announced. Early in the morning, on 22 December, they heard a commotion of many people walking in the prison corridors and they understood that something important was going to happen. The diseased Speshnev remembered with confidence that it was not at 6 A.M. but at 7 A.M. when they were taken to the carriages and brought away.

According to Fyodor Mikhailovich's words, the convicts had to dress

themselves and were then escorted by the prison guards…. The carriages
were moving for a long time. On the way Speshnev asked the soldier,
"Where are they bringing us?" and heard the answer, "I am not allowed
to tell you this." The temperature was minus forty degrees and the windows of the carriage were frozen, so they could not see the road. It
seemed to Speshnev that they crossed the Neva River and were moving
along the Liteiny Prospect. In order to make sure, he wanted to clear
the frost from the window with his fingers, but the soldier said, "Please
do not do this, otherwise I will be severely punished." After this Speshnev refused any attempts to satisfy his curiosity. As it was ordered by
the authorities before, they did not suspect the possibility of a capital
punishment. Neither did they expect that the sentence carried out by
the military tribunal and signed by the Tsar could be pronounced just
with the purpose of scaring them. All this was told by Speshnev.

At last, after they came to the end of the road which seemed endless
to them, they were brought to the Semyonovsky Parade Ground and were
lined up into columns in a certain order. Then they were brought to the
podium, as Fyodor Mikhailovich remembered, nine people on the one
side, and eleven people on the other. Speshnev said that they wanted to
greet each other and to talk, but since this was not allowed, they could
whisper with their neighbors.

N.A. Mombelli personally told me [Orest Miller] that Fyodor
Mikhailovich stood next to him and told him the plot of the novel he
wrote in the fortress. This proves that moods were mixed, different, quiet
and excited at the same time, as we know from Fyodor Mikhailovich's
works.

So they were put on the three sides of the podium while the auditor
stepped out and read the sentence. During the reading of the sentence
the sun appeared in the sky and Fyodor Mikhailovich said to Durov: "It
cannot be that we could be executed." In response, Durov indicated on
the nearby cart, on which there appeared to them to be coffins covered
with some cloth.* At this point, as Fyodor Mikhailovich remembered,
there were no doubts. For the rest of his life he remembered the sound-
ing of the words: "Sentenced to execution by firing squad." He also
remembered some minor details, such as in the description of the death
in *The Idiot*.

When the priest appeared for the confession, Fyodor Mikhailovich
started to believe that the execution would be carried out: he could not
believe that they could have invited a priest to participate in the spec-
tacle.

Kashkin recollected that the priest had no wine and bread [commu-

---

*Later it turned out that the cloth was their prison uniforms.

nion gifts]. Kashkin stood at the end of the podium, right in front of the police officer, so he bowed and asked the officer a question, whispering in French: "How can it be that we will make confession without the holy communion?" General Galakhov whispered back to him, also in French: "You will all receive an amnesty." Therefore, there was at least one person present on the podium who found out before the others that the execution would be stopped.

At the time, as Speshnev recollects, three persons were fixed with ropes to the three poles. Fyodor Mikhailovich gave their names: Petrashevsky, Mombelli and Grigoriev. In front of each pole there was an officer with a group of soldiers and the words of the command were pronounced.

Fyodor Mikhailovich remembered that he did not feel pity for the people he left in this world, and he had very little time to think. He felt only a kind of mystical fear and was under the impression that in about five minutes he would move to some new, unknown life....

He was shaken, but not lost. Mr. Zaguliaev, present at the square at the time, remembered that Dostoevsky was not very pale, that he quickly went to the podium, that he did not look depressed, but he did seem to be in a hurry. This scene had a different impact on his friends. We know from Speshnev's memoirs that [Nikolai] Grigoriev already had gone mad in prison. When they were fixing him with the ropes to the pole and when he heard the sound of the military command, everything was finished for him. All that was missing was the command "Fire!" and he would have been dead. At this point, according to Speshnev, someone waved with a handkerchief and the execution was stopped.

I.M. Dubois remembers that some of them were not very happy with the news about the amnesty: "Some people were disappointed."

Dostoevsky wrote in *A Writer's Diary* (1873), "The sentence was not a joke, and most of the people present were sure that they would be killed ... in ten minutes...."

This scene was later repeated in several works of Dostoevsky, such as *The Little Hero* and *Crime and Punishment*: "He had the feeling of new energy, new life; ... it was the feeling of a convict who was sentenced to death but who received an amnesty."

In *The Idiot* the religious and philosophical aspects of this scene were discussed. Dostoevsky [talking about execution] exclaimed: "No, you cannot do such a thing to a human being." In *A Writer's Diary* (1876), Dostoevsky wrote about the Kairova case: "Do you know that it was the fear of death ... Kairova ... woke up at night saying she was awakened by the razor of the killer ... it is almost the same as the expectation of death by a man tied to a pole to be executed by a firing squad, when his head is already covered with a piece of cloth."

Dostoevsky, as a psychologist, remembered more the inner side of the situation and it seemed he completely forgot about the frost ... which accompanied the event. According to Speshnev's story, in spite of the low temperature, they all had to take off their upper dress and stood on the podium in their shirts the entire time when the sentence was read. The convicts were tied to the poles until the new sentence was read. All this, according to Speshnev's memoirs, lasted more than half an hour. Dostoevsky counted twenty minutes, if we can accept this detail as autobiographical in his novel *The Idiot*. They said to each other occasionally, "Please, rub my chin" or "Rub my cheek."

After they returned to the fortress, they had a medical examination carried out by Dr. Okel, accompanied by General Nabokov, the director of the prison, who wanted to make sure that no one was affected by the cold. It was already in Tobolsk [Siberia] that Mr. Wolf, a Decembrists' doctor, discovered that Speshnev had the early symptoms of tuberculosis, but Speshnev slowly recovered after inhaling fresh air from the pine trees in the forest. They were not sent to Siberia together, but in small parties of one or two persons. Petrashevsky, directly from the place of the execution, had to put on a winter fur overcoat, and was sent immediately to Misiansk. They all went along the same road to Tobolsk, and then the groups took different routes.

Fyodor Mikhailovich moved before Christmas. He was brought up in a Christian family and he loved the Christmas holiday as a family event; it was a special day connected with other, different memories. But the authorities treated all the convicts as atheists....

Andrei Dostoevsky: My Arrest and the Investigation of the Petrashevsky Case

(From A.M. Dostoevsky, *Vospominaniia* [*Memoirs*]. Leningrad: Izdatelstvo pisatelei v Leningrade, 1930, pp. 198–239.)

> *[In this piece from his memoirs, Dostoevsky's younger brother recollects how he was arrested by mistake in the investigation of the secret revolutionary circle of Petrashevsky. The meetings of this secret society were attended by both Mikhail and Fyodor, who were arrested as well.]*

I spent the whole day, 23 April, until late at night at the Third Police Section. We were divided into groups of eight to ten people and these groups were put into different rooms. In addition we were not allowed to talk to each other. The time passed slowly. We did not know what awaited us. About midnight Count Orlov [one of the chiefs of the

Russian Secret Police] arrived. He made a short speech to the accused in every room. As far as I can remember, he said that we abused the rights and freedoms granted to all citizens, that we, by our actions, forced the Government to limit our freedom, that, after a detailed investigation, we would be put on trial, and that our final punishment would depend upon the decision of the Tsar.

... One of my neighbors, a nice-looking young man who sat on the sofa next to me, pulled a piece of paper from his pocket and wrote on it, "What is your name, and what is the reason for your arrest?" I wrote on the same scrap of paper, "My name is Dostoevsky, and I have absolutely no idea why I was arrested." I wrote the same question to him and received his reply, to the effect that his name was Danilevsky, and that he too did not know the reason for his arrest. This was Grigory Petrovich Danilevsky, who later became a famous writer and the publisher of *The Government News*....

The police officers started to call us out, one after another. Those summoned did not return. Then my turn came, and they brought me along a lengthy corridor to the office of General Dubelt.

An old and gaunt General sat in a study behind a large writing table covered with piles of papers. This was Dubelt. He peered at me attentively and asked, in a rather stern tone of voice, "Dostoevsky?"

"Yes, sir," I answered.

"Please go along with Lieutenant N." He pronounced the name, but I do not remember it now.... After we had several times passed through the different gates of the Fortress, the carriage stopped and I got out and entered the office of the Fortress Commandant, where an old General was holding a list of incoming prisoners. This was General Nabokov.

"Dostoevsky?"—the same question. "Yes, sir," answered the lieutenant who had brought me there. I was taken through an open prison yard, entered a corridor and found ourselves facing a door, which opened with a grating noise. I entered the room...

At a table sat General Nabokov; on his right was Pavel Gagarin, who later became the Chief of the Cabinet of Ministers, and the third man was L.V. Dubelt....

Count Gagarin began the interrogation: "Mr. Dostoevsky, you do not live for the first year of your life in this world, and you know that there should be a reason for curtailing a man's freedom. Do you know why your freedom is curtailed? ... We know everything."

I replied, "You told me that I didn't live in the world for one year, but you are mistaken. I live as a free and independent person for only a few months, for less than a year. Before June of last year I studied in the confines of a military school. I was a student. You can make inquiries from the Director of the Engineering School where I studied. I am sure you will be given good references about me because my name was engraved on a marble plaque at the school as the best student in our course.

"I received a Governmental Fellowship for my studies, and after school I started to work for the Government.... Can you tell me now, please, the reason of my arrest?" I spoke to him with some passion and with the confidence of innocence.

"These are all fine words, but let us speak about your actions. You see, Mr. Dostoevsky, some bad companions can bring a young man like you to bad deeds, even to crime. Please think, have you many friends, Mr. Dostoevsky?"

"My friends are limited to my schoolmaster and my colleagues at work." I gave them about ten names.

"Where did you usually spend your Fridays?"

"Friday, for me, is the same as any other day, and I did not visit anyone on a regular basis..."

"Do you know Butashevich-Petrashevsky?"

"Which Petrashevsky? No, I do not know him. But Your Excellency, what was the name of the other man?"

I was really hearing of Petrashevsky for the first time, and I did not know that he had a double surname. I thought that they were asking about two different people. My simple, naive answers indicated to the General that my testimony was true. Count Gagarin consulted briefly with the other people present in the room.

"Listen, Mr. Dostoevsky, do you know people with the same name as yours?"

There were no such people except for my family. My late father had repeatedly told me this. "All the people with this name are my relatives, my brothers."

"Did you say 'brothers'?"

"Yes."

"You did not tell us that on the day of your arrest you met with your brother in the Third Police Section." I saw that even the briefest of meetings was reported to the Investigating Commission.

"I did not have a chance. Our meeting lasted for only a second, and we did not exchange a single word."

"Well ... do you have other brothers, except for this one?"

"Yes, in addition to my brother Fyodor, I have two more brothers; the younger one, who is seventeen years old, has just entered the Engineering College where I studied, and there is also my eldest brother, Mikhail Mikhailovich..."

"What is the profession of your eldest brother, and where does he live?"

"He is a retired military engineer and he lives in St. Petersburg."

"What does he do for a living?"

"Literature."

"Well, Mr. Dostoevsky" (there was another whispered consultation with the Chairman), "please wait in the corridor for a few minutes."

The rest of the day I spent waiting. I was completely confident in my innocence, but I had a troubled heart when I learned that two of my elder brothers had something to do with this business, about which I had no idea.

In the evening, at 11 P.M., I was called out again. It was May 3rd, a Thursday. I entered the familiar hall and Count Gagarin told me: "We made inquiries and all your testimony turned out to be true. Your arrest occurred due to a judicial error, which often happens when there is such a huge case under official investigation." ...

My detention lasted for two more days, that is, until Friday, May 6th. On the previous day, around noon, the duty officer told me that there were instructions to set me free.

"Can I be let go at once?" I asked him.

"No, you will not be released today, but tomorrow morning."

"Why tomorrow? It is so easy to do it today... I will go and ask the General about my release.... Why these obstacles?"

"It is all very simple. They want you to avoid meeting with those people in town with whom you should not associate." I understood that they did not want me to meet with my brother Mikhail.

On the night of 5-6 May, my brother Mikhail was arrested, and in the morning, on 6 May, I was released....

Time passed and I visited Emilia Fyodorovna, my sister-in-law, several times and tried to comfort her. One day she received some good news about my brother and her husband, Mikhail Mikhailovich. Many high ranking officials tried to help him, to ease his lot.

In the long run, the case of Mikhail ended favorably for him. About the end of June, or even earlier, he was released from prison because there was no evidence or proof of any criminal actions on his part. It was very touching to witness his return and his meeting with his wife and children....

When I was leaving St. Petersburg [for Ekaterinograd, the new destination], I was not allowed to see my brother Fyodor or to say goodbye to him.... No decision was made concerning my brother Fyodor Mikhailovich and I was worried about what might have happened to him. At last, this state of uncertainty ended in the early part of 1850. I read of him in the newspapers—I think it was an issue of *The Northern Bee* published by F. Bulgarin, but I do not recall the date, only that we had just received it from St. Petersburg. In it a court verdict was published which stated: "F. Dostoevsky, twenty-seven years old, by the decision of the General-in-Charge of the Military Court, was sentenced to death by firing squad for criminal conspiracy, for the distribution of a private letter filled with abusive remarks regarding the Orthodox Church and the Government, and for planning to set up an underground publishing house in which to print anti–Government propaganda."

By the supreme will of the Tsar, he received a new, final sentence: he was "deprived of all civil rights and sentenced to a term of four years in a maximum security prison, to be followed by service in the army as a private." Even now, after the passage of forty-six years—after Fyodor Mikhailovich served his sentence, regained all his civil rights and made such a famous name for himself—I cannot write these words without trembling.... On that day, I read the newspaper containing the sentence again and again....

Pyotr Semenov: About Dostoevsky's Youth: "He Was Never a Revolutionary"

(From P.P. Semenov Tian-Shansky, *Detstvo i junost'* [*Childhood and Youth*]. St. Petersburg: The Author, 1917, pp. 195–214.)

During my friendship with Dostoevsky, after the arrival of my brother and uncle in St. Petersburg, the circle of our friends became much bigger....

It consisted of young intelligentsia who graduated from the university. Not only young scholars belonged to this circle, but it also included several young literary artists who were beginning their careers, among them college schoolmates of Dostoevsky, such as Saltykov (Shchedrin),* Mey, F. Dostoevsky, A. Grigoriev, A. Pleshcheev, Apollon Maikov and Valerian Maikov. We did not visit each other very often, but we had the most pleasant time every Friday, and a place for our meetings in the home of one of the schoolmates of Danilevsky, a man named Butashevich-Petrashevsky, and that of my brother.

... All these persons visited Petrashevsky mostly because he had his own house, and he could easily organize such meetings which were of interest to us, though Petrashevsky himself seemed to us a very eccentric man. I would say he was a little crazy. ... His only duty was to translate the sittings of the local courts with the participation of the foreigners, and, even more often, to make the inventory of their estates,

---

*Satirist Mikhail Saltykov wrote under the pseudonym M. Shchedrin, or M. Saltykov-Shchedrin.

mostly libraries. Petrashevsky took advantage of this position. He took from the libraries all the forbidden books and changed them with other books which were allowed to be read, and thus formed his own library of forbidden books, which he read to his friends....

He was a radical of his time, an extreme liberal, an atheist, a republican and a socialist. He was a wonderful, natural-born propagandist, a role he liked very much, as he spread his propaganda for all social groups of the society. He preached very illogical and unsystematical, strange mixtures of anti-monarchist, even revolutionary and socialist ideas, not only in the circles of the intellectual youth of the time, but even among the elected members of the city council, etc.....

On these Friday evenings, except for the lively general conversations, our young literary artists used to criticize the existing strict censorship law.... Many of us had as an ideal the goal of the liberation of the peasants from serfdom, but all these wishes looked more like unfulfilled, unrealistic, distant dreams, and were thus discussed in a very narrow circle....

N. Danilevsky read a number of papers about socialism, especially about Fourierism, a topic which greatly interested him, and he always developed his ideas in a very serious and logical manner.

Dostoevsky read pieces from his novels, *Poor People* and *Netochka Nezvanova*, and made passionate comments about the landlords who abused the rights of people during the serfdom system. We also discussed questions as to how to fight with the censorship which we all hated so much....

Petrashevsky was about twenty-seven years old at the time. Speshnev was almost of the same age, and also had outstanding abilities for which he was sentenced to capital punishment.... He had spent six years in France, where he became a typical liberal of the 1840s: the people's electorate and the liberation of serfs were his ideals.

... The most unusual in this group, and a very special, original person, was Fyodor Mikhailovich Dostoevsky, a great Russian writer-psychologist. Danilevsky and I met both Dostoevsky brothers at the time when Fyodor Mikhailovich became very famous after the publishing of his novel *Poor People*. He already had a quarrel with Belinsky and Turgenev; he quit their literary circle and started to visit more and more often the other circles, those of Petrashevsky and Durov.

During this time, Dostoevsky, as usual, was battling financial need. The success of *Poor People* brought him some material reward from the beginning, but afterwards it did him more harm than good, because it aroused in him some unfulfilled expectations and led to large financial expenses. The failure of his next works, such as *The Double*, on which he worked so much, and *The Landlady*, from which he expected so much, brought him to the conclusion that glory, as Pushkin said, is only "a bright patch on the shabby dress of a poet."

A pretty good job has already been done on Dostoevsky's biography, but I cannot agree with the two conclusions of his biographers. The first misconception is that Dostoevsky, supposedly, read a lot, but was a poorly educated person. We all—that is, all the people who knew Dostoevsky closely and personally in 1846–49—can say the contrary. He often visited us and had lengthy conversations with Danilevsky.

I can state for sure, together with O. Miller, that Dostoevsky was not only a person who read much, but he was a very well-educated person. In his childhood years, he received a wonderful early education from his well-educated father, a Moscow military doctor. Fyodor Mikhailovich knew French and German well enough to understand all the detail about everything he read in these two languages.... His father taught him Latin as well. In general, the education of Fyodor Mikhailovich was good and systematic before he, at the age of sixteen, entered a higher educational institution, the Engineering College, where he also systematically studied all the general subjects, as well as high mathematics, physics, mechanics, and technical subjects which related to engineering.

He graduated in 1843, at the age of 22. Therefore, though he had a special education, it was a systematic education at a higher institution, and, in addition to this, he read many books.

We have to admit that Dostoevsky was a very well-educated man, taking into consideration that he, starting from his childhood, had read works by all the major Russian poets and writers several times. He knew the Karamzin history almost by heart; and he also studied with great interest French and German authors—mainly his favorites, Schiller, Goethe, Victor Hugo, Lamartin, Beranger and George Sand. He also read many historical works ... as well as socialist works of Saint-Simon and Fourier.

Therefore, whatever has been said, Dostoevsky was a more educated person than many Russian authors of his time, including such people as Nekrasov, Grigorovich, Pleshcheev, and even Gogol.

Secondly, least of all could I agree with the point of view of some biographers that "Dostoevsky was a hysterical and nervous product of the city." He really was an excitable and nervous person, but he was like this from birth, and would have remained like this even if he had never left the village, where he spent the best years of his life. During those years, he was in touch with peasant life, and learned about the moral characteristics of simple Russian people. Therefore, he was different from the so-called liberal bureaucrats in the capital, that is, people who never visited the countryside in their childhood years, as well as those among the wealthy Russian nobility, such as Count Alexei Tolstoy,

Count Sollogub, and even Turgenev (although Turgenev eventually got to know village life better), who were sheltered by their parents from any contact with the peasants. It is well worth remembering the memoirs of Andrei Mikhailovich Dostoevsky about his brother, as well as the words told to me by Fyodor Mikhailovich himself that his life in the countryside had a great impact on his entire life.

We become sure that Fyodor Mikhailovich was a product of the countryside, and not of the city, if we remember his own stories about peasant Marei, his passionate stories at the meetings of the Petrashevsky Circle when he told about the acts [of abuse and violence] performed by the landlords against their serf peasants, as well as his idealistic attitude to the liberation of serf peasants, his demands to give them their land and his deep faith in the Russian people, under which he understood the peasant population of the country.

One of the major features of the highly artistic creations of Fyodor Mikhailovich Dostoevsky was his gift to describe with a great skill only those people with whom he became very close—so close, as if he lived with them "in their skin," that he got deep in their souls, suffered with their sufferings and rejoiced with their pleasures. He was like this, for example, during the years of his childhood when he brought a barrel of water to a thirsty child, or when he helped peasants in their works in the field. And at the time when he wrote his first novel, *Poor People*, he simply did not have at his hand another object than "a city proletariat of a lower class."

Dostoevsky himself was neither of the low class, nor a proletariat. He felt himself to be a nobleman even in prison, and he did not live in great need, though the kind of life he had was sometimes completely unsuitable for him; he had sometimes not the real needs but the psychological demands of his imagination, such as, for example, his request directed to his father about his camp expenses.

I lived in the same camp with him, in a cloth tent which was situated at the distance of 20 sazhens [1 sazhen = 2.13 meters] from the tent where he stayed (we were not familiar at the time). I could live without my own tea. We were given tea twice a day while in camps, in the morning and at night; and we had tea once a day when we were at the Engineering Academy. Besides, we were given college uniforms including boots. I could do without my own personal library of books as well, and even without my own chest for such books, though I read not less than Fyodor Mikhailovich Dostoevsky. My point is that his requests were not all the most necessary things, but they had only one purpose: not to lag behind his other schoolmates, those who had their own tea, boots and chests for books.

In our rather rich and aristocratic college, some of my schoolmates could spend, on the average, 300 roubles per camp period, and there were such people who spent even up to 3,000 roubles. As for myself, I received by mail 10 roubles from time to time, and I did not suffer from the lack of money.

Upon graduation from the Engineering Academy, before he resigned, Dostoevsky received a salary from his trustee, about 5,000 roubles in cash, and I, after graduation from the Academy, at the time when I was attending the University, received only 1,000 roubles per year.

It was only during the first year after he resigned (1844), and before he published *Poor People*, that Dostoevsky was in a real financial need, because at the time he had nothing except for the money made by the literary work. N. Danilevsky, who had nothing and did not have any additional income, lived with the same money made by literary work from 1841 to 1849, and he was not in financial need; though the same publisher, Kraevsky, paid a lesser amount of money for his articles than for the fiction works by Dostoevsky. However, Dostoevsky was in a relatively (in comparison to the others) permanent financial need even after 1845, that is, after he became famous. We became on rather close friendly terms with him; this was at the time when he was "expecting a material reward." He faced real financial difficulty only after he came out of prison in 1854. After he returned from his exile in 1859, Dostoevsky entered the period of his glory which he really deserved, and, though he needed money, he did not and could not belong to a proletariat.

I will write elsewhere about the influence of prison on Dostoevsky. Here I would like to stress that Dostoevsky never was a revolutionary, and could not be one; but, as a sensitive man, he was subjected to the feeling of hatred and even indignation when he saw [in prison] the violence directed at the oppressed and humiliated....

Among this group of the convicted people, there was only one man, other than Petrashevsky himself, who could be called a revolutionary; this man was Durov, who was the only person planning to achieve liberal reforms by violence....

I was simply shocked by the severe sentence carried out by the tribunal commission in December 1849. All the members of the group were to receive capital punishment and were brought on December 22, 1849, to the Semyonovsky Parade Grounds, to be executed.

I. Vuich: The Near Execution of the Members of the Petrashevsky Circle: A Witness's Report

(From I. Vuich "Dnevnik" ["Diary"]. *Poriadok* [*The Order*] 18 February 1881: 48.)

[An editorial introduction to this account read in part, "Recently an article was published containing the following phrase: 'F. Dostoevsky and A. Pleshcheev, another famous writer, were among the prisoners sentenced to death.' An eyewitness wrote us a letter."]

I would like to reveal some authentic details of the event, and I think that it is my duty to describe to you all the following circumstances, with which I am thoroughly acquainted.

The reason for this arises from the fact that, at the time, I held the rank of colonel, serving as chief of staff with the Imperial Guards Infantry Regiment. The commander of the Regiment, General S. Sumarokov (at that time he had not yet received the title of count), received an order to carry out the sentence of the military tribunal.

The original sentence of the military tribunal condemned many of the prisoners to death. But a new confirmation followed, signed by the [now deceased] Emperor, and the capital punishment was to be applied only in three instances: Petrashevsky, Mombelli and Grigoriev. We made all the necessary arrangements for the execution of the three condemned. Three wooden poles were installed near the wooden platform for the convicts, where they were to stand during the proclamation of the final sentence, and the platform for the firing squad, who had been issued all the necessary ammunition and cartridges and who were to stand in front of the prisoners.

On the assigned date, before dawn, all the involved were assembled at the Semyonovsky Parade Ground for the announcement of the sentence and the ensuing execution. The condemned criminals were brought from the prison fortress, paired up and placed into special, closed carts. When they met again on the parade square, they began to embrace each other.

It was touching to see this expression of their friendship. They demonstrated it especially to Petrashevsky, their chief, who was the reason for all their misfortunes. The convicts were led up onto a special square platform, and stood along three sides of it. One side was left unoccupied, except for a ladder that was installed, giving access to the three posts.

General Sumarokov ordered one of his officers to read out the sentence, which prescribed execution for only three persons. There was no excitement on the convicts' faces. Perhaps they already knew something about this new sentence, or perhaps they could predict the outcome, since there had been no executions in St. Petersburg for a long time.

There was a ritual of breaking a saber over the heads of those who were deprived of all their civil rights. After this ceremony, Petrashevsky,

Mombelli and Grigoriev were brought to the stakes. They were then tied
to these poles with ropes, and their eyes were bound with strips of black
cloth. The order for the firing squad rang out: "Prepare to fire!" But, at
this point, Sumarokov ordered his drummer to beat the "refuse" coun-
termanding the previous order, that is, to stop the shooting.

The cloth blindfolds were removed from the prisoners' eyes, and a
new sentence was announced: the convicts were not to be executed, and
the new sentences imposed on the rest of the prisoners were to be less
severe.

There were shouts from the crowd: "Long live the Tsar!" Many people had tears in their eyes. Before the day of the execution, all the officers
of our unit received special classified orders to visit the commanding
general at the Ministry of Defense. I personally received from the commanding general a sealed envelope to be delivered to General Sumarokov
in person. This letter contained the imperial amnesty, which was to be
proclaimed at the very last minute, when all was in readiness for the execution.

Petrashevsky, Mombelli and Grigoriev were given fur coats used by
the convicts who were to be transported during the winter, and they
were to leave instantly for Siberia on special troikas [three-horse Russian sledges], accompanied by a police escort. I remember Petrashevsky's
parting from the other prisoners ... he cast a sour glance at the police
sergeant who wanted to help him with his fur coat.... The convicts, who
had been facing death a few minutes ago, were now on their way to
Siberia.

All the details here related by me are true, and they can be corrobo-
rated by witnesses, such as Mr. Palm, our famous playwright, who
received complete amnesty from all punishment, and who stood on that
day on the left end of the platform, dressed in his uniform.... Therefore, Dostoevsky and Pleshcheev were never sentenced to death by the
late Emperor Nikolai Pavlovich.

Chapter 4. Prison, Army Service and Exile. Ten Years in Siberia: 1849–1859.

"Our prison stood on the edge of the fortress ground.... Criminals were sent to it from all parts of Russia.... One murders a sexual tyrant to save the honor of his beloved, his sister or his child. Another is a fugitive who ... commits a murder in defense of his freedom, his life, dying of hunger; and another murders little children for the pleasure of killing, of feeling their warm blood on his hands...."

(*Notes from the House of the Dead*)

D OSTOEVSKY SPENT FOUR YEARS in the Omsk maximum security prison in Siberia, where he shared a huge barracks with several hundred dangerous Russian criminals. The convicts spent most of their time engaged in physical labor, with their hands and feet heavily shackled. Dostoevsky had heavy chains on his legs, 24 hours a day, for four years. Among the prisoners Dostoevsky met serial killers, patricidal killers, professional robbers, gamblers and military criminals. The prison's "Book of Arrivals and Departures" records Dostoevsky's arrival in the entry for January 22, 1850: "Two state criminals, College Assessor Sergei Durov and Junior-Lieutenant Fyodor Dostoevsky, were delivered by the police officer. These belong to the category of the most dangerous convicts" (Archives, CGVIA, File 312/2, no. 1280, p. 2).

Dostoevsky's friends tried to help the young writer. This is clearly stated in a letter from I. Sulotsky, a local priest, written to I.V. Fonvizin:

> Dear Ivan Vikentievich: After receiving a letter from Maria Dmitrievna Frantseva, we asked several people about how to assist in easing the fate of Mr. Durov and Mr. Dostoevsky. We thought about many different possibilities, and it seems the only way to help them is through the local pastor who is allowed to enter such prisons.... Dostoevsky, on his arrival, found himself in the prison hospital and will stay there for a long period of time.... On the way to prison, his old venereal disease returned... [Archives, GBL, File 319/3/67, pp. 4–7].

On June 19, 1850, Dostoevsky's personal data were put into the *Register of State and Political Criminals* of the Omsk prison:

Fyodor Dostoevsky, 28 years

Special marks:	White skin, clear face, grey eyes, regular nose, blonde hair, small scar on the forehead over the left brow.
Body build:	Strong.
Social group:	Former Junior-Lieutenant, dismissed.
When did he start his sentence term:	January 23, 1850.
Why sentenced:	Criminal offense, distribution of printed works directed against the government.
Who made decision:	His Majesty, His personal decision with His General-Adjutant.
Type of punishment:	Deprived of all civil rights.
Behavior in prison:	Conduct is good.
Term:	Four years of hard labor in prison with consecutive service as private in the army.
Religion:	Christian Orthodox.
Height:	2 arshins, 6 vershoks.*
Family status:	Single.

Signature
Colonel De Grave
Director of the Omsk Prison

[*The History Herald* 1 (1898): 220–221]

*1 arshin = 28 inches; 1 vershok = 1¾ inches

When Dostoevsky wrote a letter to Alexander II about his resignation from the army, he referred to his first fit of epilepsy, registered in 1850 when he "cried, lost his consciousness, had convulsions all over his body, his arms, legs and his face, foam appeared from his mouth, he had difficulty breathing and a very rapid pulse. This seizure lasted for about fifteen minutes, and was followed by complete weakness and the return of his consciousness" (*Complete Works*, Vol. 28, part 1, p. 517).

The rumors which circulated claiming that his epilepsy began in prison after he was punished physically were supported neither by Dostoevsky himself nor by other people. On the contrary, according to numerous bits of documentary evidence, prison guards and officers tried to ease the conditions of Dostoevsky's stay in prison. For example, in a memo from Colonel de Grave, the director of the Omsk fortress, to General Debu, inspector of the Engineering Department in St. Petersburg, the Colonel requested an easing of the conditions of the sentences for political criminals Sergei Durov and Fyodor Dostoevsky:

> Political criminals S. Durov and F. Dostoevsky, who were in unit no. 55 in my fortress, each sentenced to four years, ... they deserve, due to their good behavior and diligent labor ... to be released from shackles ... and to be transferred to the other category of convicts, that is, regular military convicts [Archives, CGVIA, File 395/285, pp. 304–312; File 395/2, p. 1597].

This letter, unfortunately, did not receive a positive response. Dostoevsky had to finish the complete term of imprisonment, without any form of parole or improvement in his conditions.

While in prison, Dostoevsky was not allowed to write and he could read only one book, the New Testament. Anna Dostoevskaya's memoirs include the story of this book:

> The New Testament was given to Fyodor Mikhailovich in Tobolsk, on his way to prison, by the Decembrists' wives. Fyodor Mikhailovich did not part with it once during his four years in prison. He always had this book at hand, and often, when he had doubts about something, he opened the New Testament at random, and read what was on the first page [*Complete Works*, Vol. 28, part 1, p. 453].

Dostoevsky described the conditions in which he lived in a letter to his brother Mikhail:

> We lived together as if in a kind of a pile, in one big barrack. Just imagine an old shabby building which should have been demolished long ago and which was no longer functional. In the summer we had unbearable heat, in the winter—unbearable cold. The whole floor was rotten. It was covered with an inch of dirt, so you could slip on it and fall ... we slept on a wooden bed, only a straw pillow was allowed. We covered ourselves with our short winter coats, and our feet remained bare throughout the night. We trembled from the cold the whole night through [*Complete Works*, Vol. 28, part 1, p. 170].

The period of incarceration was not time completely wasted for Dostoevsky. He acquired new impressions and assimilated information for future novels:

> I brought from the prison so many stories and characters. We lived together, and it seems that I know the people well. There were so many stories told to me by tramps, robbers; the dirty side of life. It will be enough for many volumes. What wonderful people! ... This time was not lost for me. Maybe, I did not get to know Russia, but I got to know its people so well that very few know it as well as I do ... books are my life, my food and my future..." [*Complete Works*, Vol. 28, part 1, p. 170].

The most famous work Dostoevsky wrote about his life in prison was *Notes from the House of the Dead*. He characterized this novel as "the notes of an unknown man," with "characters never described before." This work was really a revelation for Russian public, the first novel about Russian prisons in Siberia.

Lev Tolstoy expressed his admiration for this work in a letter to N. Strakhov dated September 26, 1880:

> Recently I was unwell and I read *The House of the Dead*. I had forgotten much of it and I read it again. I don't know a better book in all of literature.... It is not how it is narrated, though the narration is wonderful. It is that it is sincere, natural and Christian writing. It is a good educational book as well. I enjoyed reading it yesterday, all day long, as I haven't enjoyed myself for a long time. If you see Dostoevsky, please tell him that I love him [L.Tolstoy, Perepiska L. Tolstogo i N. Strakhova (Correspondence between L. Tolstoy and N. Strakhov) St. Petersburg, 1914, Vol. 2, pp. 307–310].

Dostoevsky included in this novel many tales which had happened to him in real life. *Notes from the House of the Dead* bore witness, for the first time to the civilized world, to all the suffering of Russian prisoners in Siberia. Besides its very gloomy and sad stories, Dostoevsky included in his book stories about love and compassion:

> I was on my way home from the morning shift. I was alone, with my guard. On the road, I met a mother and a daughter, going in opposite directions; the girl was about ten years old, as beautiful as an angel. When the girl saw me, she blushed and whispered to her mother. Her mother stopped, found in her purse a quarter of a kopeck (the smallest coin in Russia), and gave it to the girl. The girl ran after me: "Here you are, poor man, take this kopeck, please, in the name of Christ." She cried to me, ran in front of me and pushed the coin in my hands. I took her kopeck, and the girl, very satisfied with herself, returned to her mother. I kept this kopeck with me for a long time.

After four years in prison, Dostoevsky served in the Russian army as a private, sergeant and a junior officer. A note in "Register of Arrivals and Departures of the Omsk Prison," made on January 23, 1854, reads, "Departed from our Fortress and transferred to the 7th Infantry Siberian Battalion, two convicts who finished serving prison terms assigned by the Imperial Order. The two prisoners are: Sergei Durov and Fyodor Dostoevsky" [*Archives*, CGVIA, File 312/2, part 1, p. 1980].

Dostoevsky served in Semipalatinsk, a city in Siberia, and described this city in a letter to his brother:

> The climate is rather healthy here. Here the Kirgiz steppe starts. The town is rather big and crowded; it is situated in the open steppe plains. The summer is long and hot. The winter is shorter than in Tobolsk or Omsk, but it is rather severe. Not a single tree around. Several versts from the town there is a forest, and it stretches for tens, maybe hundreds of versts.... Sometime later I will write you more about Semipalatinsk. It is worth it [*Complete Works*, Vol. 28, part 1, p. 166–174].

It was very difficult for Dostoevsky to live without books. As he wrote to Apollon Maikov on January 18, 1856, "I rarely read in prison; there were no books. I only had books occasionally. After I arrived in Semipalatinsk, I started reading more, but none of the books I needed right then were around.... I cannot express to you how much I suffered from not being able to write in prison. The whole time I was there, my work simmered inside of me" (*Complete Works*, Vol. 28, part 1, pp. 206–210).

Dostoevsky's friends, including Baron Aleksandr Vrangel, General Totleben and others, lobbied vigorously for his transfer from Siberia to St. Petersburg. On March 4, 1854, as a result, a report outlining Dostoevsky's good behavior was forwarded to the commanding officers from the governor of Tobolsk, a large city in the region in which Dostoevsky was serving.

On May 1, 1854, the chief of the 7th Battalion, Lieutenant-Colonel Belikhov, submitted a patriotic poem by Fyodor Dostoevsky "Written on the European Events of 1854" to General Iakovlev, the chief of staff. On June 25 of the same year, a letter from General Iakovlev, chief of staff of the headquarters of the Siberian Army, was forwarded to General Dubelt, the chief of the Royal Office in St. Petersburg: "The chief of the Seventh Siberian Infantry Battalion asks Your permission to publish in *St. Petersburg Newspaper* a patriotic poem written by former political criminal, Private Fyodor Dostoevsky..." (Archives, CGAOR, File III, p. 14).

Dostoevsky expressed his desire to be engaged in literary work in his letter to Totleben dated March 24, 1856: "I do not consider the service to be the major purpose of my life. I would like to receive permission to be published.... I think that being a writer is the most noble and useful occupation. I believe, and I am sure, that I can be useful in this activity" (*Complete Works*, Vol. 28, part 1, pp. 223–227).

It was while Dostoevsky was in the army that he married for the first time. At the age of thirty-six he married Maria Isaeva, a widow who was one of the first women he encountered after his release from prison. As an army officer, he was required to request permission from his superior, as was stated in the following letter:

From:
Colonel-Lieutenant Belikhov,

Commander, 7th Siberian Infantry Battalion,
Document 167
February 1, 1857, Semipalatinsk

Dostoevsky, a Junior Lieutenant from my battalion, proposed to Mrs. Isaeva, 29 years of age, resident of Kuznetsk, wife of the now deceased secretary, Aleksandr Isaev, and received her consent; therefore, I ask the church to arrange this marriage, in the case that there are no objections from the side of the bride. He is 34 years of age and single. Both he and his bride are Orthodox Christians; Dostoevsky attends church for confession and holy communion on a regular basis. I enclose a letter from the bride and an official certificate verifying her first husband's death. Please send me authorization of marriage, after the event. Colonel G. Belikhov

[*Sibirskaya Letopis* (*Siberian Chronicle*) 11–12 (1916): 568].

The wedding took place on February 6, 1856, in Kuznetsk, Siberia.

The following passages are excerpts from the memoirs of Pyotr Martianov, director of guards at the Omsk Prison where Dostoevsky spent four years among Russia's most dangerous criminals; N. Feoktistov, who studied Dostoevsky's love story in the army; Pyotr Semenov, a well-known geographer and discoverer who met Dostoevsky during one of his survey trips in southern Siberia; Dostoevsky's younger brother Andrei, who was the first to receive a letter from Dostoevsky after almost five years of silence; and Baron Aleksandr Vrangel, who, while serving as the military prosecutor of Semipalatinsk, became a close friend of Dostoevsky, supported him morally and financially, and wrote letters to high officials in St. Petersburg that were instrumental in obtaining Dostoevsky's release from military service.

Pyotr Martianov: Dostoevsky's Four Years in the Omsk Prison

(From P.K. Martianov, "Na perelome veka" ["At the End of the Century"] in P.K. Martianov, *Dela i liudi veka* [*Major Events and People of the Century*]. St. Petersburg, 1896, pp. 263–270, 276, 281–282.)

The city of Omsk was, at the time, the center of military and civil administration in western Siberia. It had an old fortress situated on the bend of the River Irtysh....

The most difficult part of military service for the young officers was to stand on guard, especially to guard prisoners in the fortress prison. This was the same famous prison which Dostoevsky described in *Notes from the House of the Dead.* In this prison, there were only two people from the Petrashevsky Circle, Fyodor Mikhailovich Dostoevsky and S. Durov. I do not know whether our young officers knew them in St. Petersburg, but during the incarceration of these two persons, our officers tried to support them in every way they could.

The formally brilliant young men who were members of the Petrashevsky Circle made a woeful sight. They wore the standard prisoner's uniform, which consisted of the summer wear, a grey and black cap and a coat of the same color with a yellow patch of cloth in the shape of a diamond sewn on the back. In the winter they wore gloves and a sheepskin coat with high collars to protect the ears. All year round, their feet were shackled with huge chains which made loud noises whenever they moved. The two looked the same as the rest of the prisoners. There were some features, though, which distinguished them from the general crowd of prisoners; these were traces of their upbringing and education.

Fyodor Mikhailovich Dostoevsky looked like a small but strongly built worker, with the good manners of a man who had got used to military discipline. However, accepting his difficult position was a burden for him. He was clumsy, slow in his movements and silent. His pale face looked like the face of a drunkard; it had a grey, unhealthy pallor, was covered with dark-red spots, and never carried a smile. His mouth opened only for brief and short answers connected with his work. He wore his cap low on his forehead, down to his eyebrows; his glance was gloomy, concentrated and unpleasant; he held his head down, and directed his eyes to the ground. Although they accepted him as a moral authority, most of the prisoners did not like him; they looked at him in a gloomy manner, being jealous of his superiority, and consequently avoided him. He noticed this, and he himself avoided all; and started conversations only with a select few prisoners, and only when he was experiencing very difficult or sad periods.... Dostoevsky's character, as one of our "sailors" [junior guard officers] said, was unsympathetic.

It was difficult for him to communicate with other people who expressed a humane and sympathetic attitude towards him and who wanted to be of help to him; and I do not speak only about the prisoners whom he avoided and with whom he did not have any contact. He seemed to be a wolf caught in a trap.

He was always a gloomy person who avoided people in general and preferred to remain alone in the noise of the prison room. He shared his word as if it was something too precious, only when he was obliged to do so. When the "sailors" called him into the "officers' room," he behaved in an even more reserved way, often refusing the invitation to have a seat and a small rest, and he agreed only when he felt it was a repeated request.

Naturally, he never spoke of personal matters or matters of love. He was suspicious of any expression of compassion, as if he suspected some hidden agenda which could be harmful to him. He even refused to read the books which our young officers brought to him, only twice showing interest in *David Copperfield* and *The Pickwick Papers* translated by Vedensky. He took these books with him to read when he was in the prison hospital. Dr. Troitsky attributed his loneliness and suspiciousness to the general state of poor health caused by his fits of epilepsy and his shattered nervous system; though at first glance he seemed healthy, optimistic and strong, and he went to work together with the other prisoners....

Sergei Durov, on the contrary, aroused a general response of compassion. In spite of his unhealthy and exhausted appearance, he was interested in everything, and liked to communicate with people....

The "sailors" were surprised by the fact that the two members of the Petrashevsky Circle hated each other with all their hearts, never got together, and never exchanged a single word during their stay in the Omsk Prison. When we invited them to the officers' room, they sat in opposite corners of the room with gloomy countenances and answered briefly "yes" or "no" in response to the questions of our young officers; so afterwards we decided to call them out separately.

Sergei Durov, answering our question, said that neither of them was going to speak first, because life in prison had made them enemies.

In *Notes from the House of the Dead*, Fyodor Dostoevsky wrote about almost all of the important prisoners who were incarcerated with him. He camouflaged some of them by using only their initials or first names, but he never mentioned Durov, either by his full name or his initials; never, as if such a person never existed at all in prison....

In instances when it was impossible not to talk about him [Durov], Dostoevsky only referred to him in indirect phrases, such as "we, that is, me and the other man, were scared," or "I looked at one of my friends (from nobility) as he burned his life away in prison, as if he were burning a candle from both ends...."

Dr. Troitsky, who worked as the doctor in our prison hospital, tried to help the members of the Petrashevsky Circle. Sometimes, he passed to them a word through the "sailors" that either one could go to the hospital to have some rest, so they used to stay there for several weeks. In the hospital they received better food and produce, partially from the hospital cafeteria and partially from the doctor.

Dostoevsky started to write *Notes from the House of the Dead* in the hospital, as Dr. Troitsky told one of our young officers. The doctor gave Dostoevsky permission to write. As a rule, the prisoners were not allowed to have any office appliances without the permission of the prison chiefs, and therefore, the first chapters of this novel were for a long time kept only in the prison hospital....

General Borislavsky along with his assistant, Junior Lieutenant Ivanov, tried to help the members of the Petrashevsky Circle. He allowed them to be sent to do less difficult work, except in those cases when Dostoevsky himself wanted to work with the other prisoners, especially after his arrival in prison. Among such easier jobs, both in prison and outside of it, were painting, fixing wheels, burning alabaster, cleaning the snow off the streets, etc.

Fyodor Mikhailovich was even allowed to go to the office of the local Engineering Department to write papers, though very soon, after a report written by Colonel Martin, an order was issued forbidding the political prisoners to perform office work.

One of Dr. Troitsky's associates, a junior doctor, Mikhail Krzhizhanovsky, disclosed the doctor's activities to authorities in St. Petersburg. He wrote a letter saying that the doctor showed too much compassion and rendered help to the political prisoners. A special officer was sent for an investigation of this matter.... The witnesses were interrogated, but they did not confirm the claims of Mr. Krzhizhanovsky. Political prisoners replied indirectly to all of the questions during the interrogation, which made the officer reproach them, as he felt at odds with them.

When, for example, Dostoevsky was asked whether he wrote anything in prison or in the prison hospital, he replied: "I did not write before, and I do not write, but I collect materials for my future writing...."

"And where are these materials?"

"They are in my head."

E.M. Feoktistov: Dostoevsky's Love Story in the Army

(From Evgeny Feoktistov, "Propavshie pis'ma Dostoevskogo" ["Several Lost Letters by Dostoevsky"], *Sibirskie ogni* [*The Siberian Light*] 2 [1928]: 122–125.)

Twenty years ago in Semipalatinsk, I met Elizaveta Nevrotova, a kind of silent and, it seemed, very religious spinster.... In 1909 she was in her early seventies.... Her appearance revealed that in her youth she was a very beautiful woman. She asked me, "Do you want to have a look at Fyodor Mikhailovich's handwriting?" ... She gave me a big pile of letters. On the top page I could read "My beloved Elizaveta, Yesterday I wanted to see you." I saw a date in the corner. It was 1854.... I worked at the local archive with Dostoevsky's manuscripts and knew his writing well....

Elizaveta told me that Dostoevsky had been in love with her. They met at the marketplace in 1854 when Dostoevsky was a soldier and Elizaveta sold bread in the bakery. He wrote many letters to her, and judging from this, ... we can believe her that he was in love with her. Dostoevsky met Nevrotova shortly before his meeting with Maria Isaeva, who became his wife in 1857. He met Maria in 1855. She was an educated, cultural and gifted woman and Dostoevsky forgot the beautiful but uneducated Elizaveta.... About ten years after this, in 1918, I went to Semipalatinsk (it was just after the revolution)... Dostoevsky's letters, those letters which I held in my hands ten years ago, were lost.

Pyotr Semenov: My Meeting with Dostoevsky in Siberia

(From P.P. Semenov Tian-Shansky, *Puteshestvie v Tian'-Shan'* [*Traveling to Tien-Shan*]. Moscow: Geografizdat, 1958, pp. 76–77, 134–135.)

While in Semipalatinsk, I had no other business than to pay a visit to the governor of the city, because I was recommended to him by the general governor of the province. The city and its suburbs did not arouse my interest and I decided to stay there only for twenty-four hours....

Mr. D. prepared a nice surprise for me; suddenly in his apartment he introduced me to my dear old friend Fyodor Mikhailovich Dostoevsky whom I had known in St. Petersburg. I saw that Dostoevsky was dressed in a grey soldier's overcoat. I was the first man among his old friends in St. Petersburg who saw Dostoevsky after his release from prison, "the house of the dead." Dostoevsky told me briefly what he had experienced during his exile. He told me that he looked at his position as a rather bearable or satisfactory one, due to a good attitude toward him from his direct commander, the chief of the battalion and all the rest of the administration in Semipalatinsk....

After three days' travel, I returned to Semipalatinsk where I stayed with the hospitable Mr. D. This time I stayed with him for five days and I had the pleasure of spending several whole days with Fyodor Mikhailovich Dostoevsky. Only then did I understand completely his moral and financial situation. In spite of the relative freedom he enjoyed, his situation was not happy at all. He had a bit of sunshine in his life, Maria Dmitrievna. He found a daily escape and the warmest compassion in her house and in her company.

Mrs. Isaeva was still a rather young woman, in her late twenties, and was married to a man with a good education who occupied a rather good position in Semipalatinsk. They quickly became friends with Dostoevsky, and Mr. Isaev invited him to his house with open arms. He had married his wife during his service in Astrakhan. She was born in this city and she graduated with honors from the Astrakhan Women's College. Therefore, she was the most educated and intelligent among the women of Semipalatinsk, and, irrespective of Dostoevsky's description of her, she was a good person, in the best meaning of this word.

She quickly became Dostoevsky's friend. She was not happy in her marriage. Her husband, a complete alcoholic, had rather rude instincts and could not control himself during his drinking sessions. She could not cure him and she lived with him only from the necessity of taking care of her child and protecting the child from the drunk father day after day. And then suddenly, on her horizon, a man such as Dostoevsky appeared, who had all his high moral standards and refined sensations.

It was obvious that they understood each other quickly and became friends. She felt compassion for him. She found a new life, a spiritual revival, in everyday conversations with him. And on the other hand, she was a real escape for him during his dull life in the city of Semipalatinsk which had no spiritual atmosphere at all.

During my first trip to Semipalatinsk in August 1856, Mrs. Isaeva had already left the town, and I found out about her only from Dostoevsky's stories. She moved to live in Kuznetsk, the Tomsk region, where her husband had been transferred because he was not capable of performing his duties. She started a busy correspondence with Dostoevsky which helped both of them. But all these circumstances, as well as their relationship, changed dramatically at the time of my second visit to Semipalatinsk. At that time, Mrs. Isaeva became a widow, and though she could not afford to return quickly to Semipalatinsk, Dostoevsky decided to marry her. They had only one major obstacle, namely, the absence of money; she was close to poverty at the time.

Fyodor Mikhailovich Dostoevsky certainly had his literary talent. However, she did not believe in the force of his talent ... and she called him "a man with no future".... Dostoevsky told me about his plans to marry her.

Andrei Dostoevsky: Dostoevsky's First Letters from Siberia

(From A.M. Dostoevsky, *Vospominaniia* [*Memoirs*]. Leningrad: Izdatelstvo pisatelei v Leningrade, 1930.)

... [While in Elisavetgrad], in 1854, I received letters from Moscow and St. Petersburg with some good news about my relatives....

My sister, Varvara Mikhailovna, wrote to me that my brother, Fyodor Mikhailovich, had finished serving his sentence of four years in prison, that he had begun his army service as a private in one of the Siberian infantry battalions, and that he was now allowed to correspond....

Without any delay, I wrote my first letter to my brother Fyodor Mikhailovich and sent it on 14 September.... I enclosed 10 roubles in cash, but I received his reply only the next year, 1855.... In February of 1855, we received news of the death of Nikolai I. Everyone in the city was disturbed by this sad event. Everyone thought: "What will happen? Will it bring an end to the war?" Every level of society was troubled.

I remember well that some time in early March 1855, during the Great Lent, we were seated at the table having lobster when a postman came to the door and said, "You have a registered envelope," and asked me to sign the delivery book. I looked at the huge seal and read the words on it: "The Third Section of the Police of His Majesty's Headquarters." My heart sank.... I already knew the Third Section. While I was signing for the delivery and seeing the postman off, Dominika, my wife, and her father were watching me, and they later said that I was deathly pale.... "What has happened? What is this? Who sent this letter?" they both asked me simultaneously. Without answering them, I quickly opened the envelope, and two small sheets of paper fell out of it. These were two letters from my brother, Fyodor Mikhailovich, written to me and to Dominika from Semipalatinsk. I calmed down, and then I showed the seal on the envelope to Dominika and to my father-in-law.

We understood that, although he was allowed to write letters, all letters sent by him to Russia and perhaps all letters to him passed though the Third Section where they were opened and read. I calmed down a little, and started to read the letters, which my brother wrote on 6 November 1854 and which we had received only in March! ... I was touched, and had tears in my eyes when I read those wonderful letters. I have them with me now, the paper yellowed by time. These letters were published in the *Complete Works* of F. Dostoevsky. In the meantime, rumors about the letters which I had received from the Third Section had started to circulate through the city. In order to put a stop to these rumors, I told several friends of mine the nature of the letters in the envelope.... So I told them in strictest confidence, and in a matter of days, the whole city was informed....

Aleksandr Vrangel: About Dostoevsky's Army Service and Exile in Siberia

(From A.E. Vrangel, *Vospominaniia o Dostoevskom v Sibiri* [*Memoirs About Dostoevsky in Siberia*]. St. Petersburg, 1912.)

I know many biographical facts about Fyodor Mikhailovich's life in Siberia because for many months we lived very close to each other.... I think that every small detail about our great writer is interesting....

After one year of service in the Ministry of Justice ... I chose a place to work in the most remote part of Southwestern Siberia....

Siberia was not known at that time; even educated people spoke of it as of a country of almost eternal snow, woe and sorrow; it was also a place of exile, so people called it "a big prison" and all who were sent there were considered lost to society....

I left St Petersburg in July 1854. Before my departure I met Mikhail Dostoevsky; he found out that I was going to go to Semipalatinsk where his brother Fyodor Mikhailovich was in exile. Mikhail Dostoevsky asked me to take him a letter, some underwear, books and 50 roubles. I also took a letter from Apollon Maikov to Fyodor Mikhailovich....

Five years ago I was by chance at the Semyonovsky parade ground, during the fatal moments of Fyodor Mikhailovich, and then, after five years, fate brought me close to him, this time for many years.

During his first time in prison Fyodor Mikhailovich was in need of everything. The money his brother gave him was soon gone, and every intelligent prisoner has a few small expenses....

By the way, I would like to deny several legends about Fyodor Mikhailovich during his stay in prison. I have to be honest about the fact that, in most cases, the attitude of our leaders and of all educated society towards "political prisoners" was more tolerant and humane back then. Siberia during the reign of Tsar Nikolai Pavlovich was filled with political prisoners and people in exile, both Russians and Poles. They were mostly idealists, educated, serious, and liberal people. The attitude of local authorities to Fyodor Mikhailovich was filled with special compassion. I can serve as a witness here, as Fyodor Mikhailovich told me himself that neither in prison, nor during his army service as a soldier, did anyone beat him. Nobody laid a finger on him, neither his chief, friends, inmates or soldiers, and all of the stories to the contrary which appeared in the press were mere fantasies. Once I heard such speculations that it was physical punishment which caused Fyodor Mikhailovich's epilepsy, and many people still remember this legend....

In the middle of November 1854, I went to Semipalatinsk.... On the second day of my arrival, after unpacking my suitcases, I put on a beautiful uniform created by General Gasfort, fixed my sword onto my belt and went to pay a visit to General Pyotr Mikhailovich Spiridonov, the military governor of the province.

During dinner I found out Dostoevsky's whereabouts and sent my servant to invite Dostoevsky to visit me for an evening tea. Dostoevsky lived at that time in his private and very small apartment.

Dostoevsky did not know who had invited him and why, and when he arrived he was very reserved. He had a grey soldier's overcoat on, with the red collar and red military insignia. He looked gloomy, with an unhealthy pale face covered with moles. His fair hair was cut short; in height he was a bit taller than average. He looked at me with his clever grey-blue eyes. It seemed that he wanted to look deep into my soul, to determine what kind of man I was. He told me later, confidentially, that he was very much concerned when the servant who had delivered my invitation told him that he was invited to visit a special expert on "criminal cases."

I gave him all the letters, parcels, and spoken regards and heartily and sincerely spoke to him. He quickly changed his attitude, became more joyful and seemed to trust me. He told me afterwards that when he went home that day, after visiting me, he instinctively felt that he would find in me a sincere friend....

When I read him some letters from my brother and sisters, I remember that there were tears in his eyes. During my conversation with Fyodor Mikhailovich, I had received a bunch of letters from St. Petersburg written by family and friends. I opened them quickly, started to read and burst into tears. I was an emotional young man and very much attached to my family. I felt so bad to be so far away from them. I suddenly embraced Fyodor Mikhailovich who was standing in front of me with his sad, thoughtful look. He sympathized with me, as a friend. He shook my hand warmly and we promised to see each other as often as possible.

In the spring of 1854, after serving his term in prison, Dostoevsky, as you know, was moved to Semipalatinsk, to serve as a soldier. At first he lived in the barracks with other soldiers, but soon, at the personal request of General Ivanov and others, he received permission to live separately, close to the barracks....

At first it was difficult for him to be in complete isolation. But little by little he became acquainted with some officers and civil servants, though he was far from being close to anyone. Certainly, after prison, his financial situation was difficult, but he told me that it seemed a paradox for him to have at least some limited freedom.... Several intelligent ladies in the city showed interest in his fate and tried to help him, among them Maria Dmitrievna Isaeva and the wife of officer Stepanov, the commander of his company. Mr. Stepanov was an alcoholic and had been moved from St. Petersburg because of this. Mrs. Stepanova wrote some poetry and Fyodor Mikhailovich read and corrected it. Maria Dmitrievna Isaeva, as it is known, later, after becoming a widow, married Dostoevsky....

At the time of my stay there, Semipalatinsk was half city, half village. All the houses were made of wood and most were log houses. There were about five to six thousand inhabitants in the city, including the military garrison and the Asian population.... I think that only ten to fifteen people subscribed to newspapers; at that time, people in Siberia were interested only in playing cards, drinking vodka, gossiping and their trade. This was the time of the Crimean War, but very few people took interest in it. It was too far away, it was not "Siberia's business"....

Semipalatinsk was divided into three parts by a sandy heath. In the north, there was a Cossack settlement, the most cozy, clean and beautiful part of the city.... In the southern part there was a Tatar settlement ... a real sad desert.... Between these two regions was the Russian settlement, called "the fortress".... Here Dostoevsky lived.

Fyodor Mikhailovich paid five roubles a month for his rent, food and laundry. It was poor food.... Every day he brought home his portion of cabbage soup, porridge and black bread, and if he did not eat it, then he gave it to his poor landlady.... However, he often had dinner with me, or was invited to dine with other friends. His house was situated in the dullest place. Around was an empty heath, with only sand, and not a single tree or bush.

He lived in an "isba," a Russian log house, which was crooked on one side; with time it sank farther into the earth. It had no windows on the front, as protection against bandits and thieves. The two windows in his room faced the backyard which was surrounded by a tall fence....

Dostoevsky had one room, rather big, but with a very low ceiling. It was a very dim room, and its wooden walls were covered with clay.... The room was so dark that at night I could hardly read by the light of a candle. I cannot understand how Fyodor Mikhailovich was able to write all night by such a dim light....

Every day I became closer and closer friends with Fyodor Mikhailovich. He began to visit my office at any time of the day, as soon as his soldier service and my office work afforded us the time. He often had lunch with me, but most of all he liked to visit me at night for tea—he drank lots of it, one glass after another, and smoked my tobacco....

After some time, my friendship with Dostoevsky attracted the attention of certain people [in the police]. I noticed that my letters came two to three days after the mail arrived in our town, and I noticed, by the way, that my enemies, among them corrupted civil servants, asked me sarcastic questions about Dostoevsky and expressed their surprise over the fact that I spent my time with a single soldier. Soon, even the governor himself warned me that it was dangerous for me, as a young man, to be influenced by the revolutionary ideas of Dostoevsky.

As I wrote before, P.M. Spiridonov, the military governor-general of the region, was a very kind, simple, friendly and hospitable man. I quickly became his regular guest. I had dinners at his house every second day and enjoyed his complete confidence. He met Dostoevsky occasionally, and even gave him some protection after receiving requests from Omsk. I wanted him to know and appreciate Dostoevsky better and I asked him if I could bring Dostoevsky to his home one day. He was silent for a moment and then said, "Well, all right, you can bring him, as he is, simply in his [soldier's] overcoat. Tell him that."

Soon Semipalatinsk started to love Dostoevsky, who became a regular guest at the governor's house. General Spiridonov tried to help him in every way he could, and tried to be useful. The example of the governor-general opened for Dostoevsky the doors of many other houses in Semipalatinsk society....

However, I do not remember even a single party with dancing, or a social walk-out or a picnic. Everyone lived separately; people did not communicate much. The men usually drank, ate, played, created scandals or visited rich Tatars. The women were always gossiping....

We both did not play cards and did not drink wine, except for one small glass before dinner or supper. I only saw Dostoevsky drink once, and it was connected with his duties. General K. came to Semipalatinsk to inspect our Cossack regiment. He was a well-educated, nice man, but he liked to entertain. He liked Dostoevsky at once, so he took the soldier to his house, drank alcohol with him, and then, with three bottles of real "Venue Cliquot," visited me, accompanied by his two sisters.

I will return to my description of our routine life. As soon as I became closer to Dostoevsky, our relationship was quite easy-going and my door always open to him, day and night. Often I came home after my work and found Dostoevsky. He would come before me, after military exercises or his office hours where he performed all kinds of work. He used to unbutton his soldier's overcoat with a pipe in his mouth and walk here and there across the room, talking to himself, because new ideas constantly appeared in his head. I remember him as if it were yesterday; during this time, he decided to write *My Uncle's Dream* and *The Village Stepanchikovo*. He was usually in a very joyful mood, laughed loudly and told me the adventures of the uncle, or sang songs from operas....

Fyodor Mikhailovich liked to read Gogol and Victor Hugo ... when he was in a good mood, he recited by heart. His favorite piece was *The*

Cleopatra Feast by Pushkin. His face, his eyes would shine when he read....

I must admit I did not have time for literature, I was busy with my dull science. This made Dostoevsky indignant, and he would say, "Put aside your scholarly books." When we spoke about Siberia, he ardently argued that Siberia had no future because all its rivers flow to the Arctic Ocean, and Siberia has no other connections with the sea.

Dostoevsky loved people to such an extent that it seemed he was not of this world. He found excuses for the worst sides of human nature; he explained it by bad education, influence of the environment in which a person lives as well as by human nature and temper.

"Well, my dear friend, Aleksandr Egorovich, people were created like this by God," he used to say. All unhappy, ill, and poor people could find his support. His exceptional kindness was well-known to the people who surrounded him. Everyone remembers how he supported his brother's family (he wrote about this in his letter to me), his son-in-law Pasha Isaev, and many others.

I discussed politics with him as well. He maintained a gloomy silence about his own political process, and I did not ask him questions about this. I heard from him only a few things: he did not like Petrashevsky, he did not sympathize with his plans, he thought that any political campaign in Russia was impossible at the time—it was too early—and he thought it was funny even to consider Western type constitutions in Russia, a country with the huge mass of uneducated people....

Now that I have made a rather detailed description of Fyodor Mikhailovich Dostoevsky, I want to note that I described Fyodor Mikhailovich as he was in Siberia, in the fifties. Though he was ill and not happy, he had a strong will and enthusiasm. We parted then and I do not know whether he remained like this for the rest of his life. I saw him briefly in St. Petersburg in 1873. Then I lived and was in the service abroad....

I would like to write what I know about Dostoevsky's epilepsy. God forbid, I never saw this myself, but I know that he had epileptic fits quite often; usually his landlady informed me of them instantly. After such fits he felt unwell and weak for two or three days; he could not put his thoughts together, and his head did not work. He told me that the first signs of his illness appeared in St. Petersburg, but it developed only in prison.

Our life proceeded in a routine and dull way. I visited very few people; I sat at home and spent my time reading and writing.

Fyodor Mikhailovich had more of a social life than me. He often visited the Isaev family. He would sit with them at night and had agreed to give private lessons to their only child Pasha [Paul], a smart boy eight to nine years old.

Maria Dmitrievna Isaeva was, as far as I remember, the daughter of a high school principal in Astrakhan, and she married there Mr. Isaev, a schoolteacher. I do not remember how he got to Siberia. Isaev was a sick man, ill with tuberculosis, and he drank too much alcohol. He was a quiet and calm man.

Maria Dmitrievna was in her early thirties; she was rather pretty, blonde, of average height, and very skinny; she was a passionate and refined creature. At that time she already had an unhealthy blush on her pale face and in several years she would die of tuberculosis. She read many books, knew literature, was a well-educated, inquisitive, kind and very lively and impressive person.

She had a certain interest in helping Fyodor Mikhailovich, and she tried to comfort him. I do not think that she really appreciated him; she felt pity for this poor man with a difficult fate.

It's possible that she even became attached to him, but she never was in love with him. She knew that he had epilepsy, and that he was extremely short of money; she described him as "a man without a future." Fyodor Mikhailovich, on the contrary, accepted these feelings of pity and compassion as signs of reciprocated love, and he fell in love with her with all the ardent feeling of a young man. Dostoevsky spent whole days at the Isaevs' and he tried to take me there as well, but I did not like their place because of her husband.

In early March, a court officer Akhmatov arrived from St. Petersburg after a ten days' journey and bringing news about the death of Nikolai I, the emperor. We received this news on the 12th of March. The intelligentsia of our city were stricken by the news. You must remember that most of them had been victims of the Nikolai regime. As to the people who were in exile for their political views, they were joyful. Rumors about the soft character and kindness of the new Tsar came to Siberia. We went with Fyodor Mikhailovich to the church for a religious funeral service.

Dostoevsky had some cause to hope for a change in his sentence.... In the summer, the weather in Semipalatinsk is unbearable; it is terribly suffocating, the sand is heated by the burning sun. The smallest wind raises clouds of dust and the fine sand gets into your eyes and insinuates itself everywhere. The heat is +32 degrees in the shade. I decided to go out of town in April, as soon as the trees turned green. There was only one summer cottage in Semipalatinsk which had a huge garden; it was situated behind the Cossack city, close to the military camp. It was a convenient location for Fyodor Mikhailovich and I suggested that he move there from his hut.

In early April, I went with Fyodor Mikhailovich to our cottage in "The Cossack Garden." The wooden house was a rather shabby building—

there were holes in the roof, in the floor—but it was a big house and we had a lot of space…. An old lane went through the whole garden, between the old trees…. The garden brought us many fruits and vegetables….

The estate was situated on the tall, right shore of the Irtysh River. At the river, there was a bright green meadow. There we made huts for bathing … we started bathing in May.

Together with Fyodor Mikhailovich, I worked actively in the flower garden and quickly made it look beautiful. I remember Fyodor Mikhailovich helping me water some young flowers. He worked hard, taking off his soldier's overcoat; he was in a cotton, sleeveless, rose-colored jacket that had faded from the laundry. On his neck he wore a long chain, a gift from someone, and he kept a big silver watch on it….

When I went horseback riding, I enticed Dostoevsky to ride one of my most quiet horses. It seemed that he was riding for the first time in his life, and he looked like a very funny and awkward cavalry soldier in his grey infantry overcoat. But soon he started to like it, and we took long rides on horseback, through the forest…. The steppe was so beautiful, it was all covered with flowers, and the air was filled with their smell….

Once Dostoevsky even participated in a dog hunt. It was organized by Colonel Messarosh, though Dostoevsky refused to follow the dogs. In principle, Fyodor Mikhailovich did not like hunting.

However, Dostoevsky's love for Isaeva did not cool down; he went to visit her on every occasion. Every time he came back he was in a kind of ecstasy. He admired her and he was surprised when I did not share his emotions.

Both Dostoevsky and I liked fruit and all other sweets. You could not get either of these in Semipalatinsk…. One of his favorite desserts was cedar nuts with honey.

Once Fyodor Mikhailovich came home very gloomy and upset. He told me that Isaev had received a new job as a civil servant and was being transferred to Kuznetsk, about 500 versts from Semipalatinsk. He bitterly repeated the phrase, "and she agrees, she does not object."

It was to be very soon that Isaev was to move to Kuznetsk. Dostoevsky's desperation was limitless; he was pacing across his room as if he were mad from thinking about parting with Maria Dmitrievna. It seemed to him that his life was ruined. It turned out that the Isaevs were in debt; they had to sell everything they had, and after this they did not have the money to move. I helped them and eventually they set out.

I will never forget the scene of parting. Dostoevsky was crying, sobbing loudly, like a child. Many years later he brought it up in his letters. Oh, yes, it was a very special day to remember.

I went with Fyodor Mikhailovich to see the Isaevs off. We departed late at night, a beautiful night in May. I took Dostoevsky with me, in my light open carriage. The Isaevs had also hired an open postal cart; they did not have enough money to buy a wagon. Before the departure, they visited me and we drank some champagne. I wanted to give Dostoevsky the opportunity to talk privately with Maria Dmitrievna, so I plied her husband with champagne until he became drunk. On the way, according to the Siberian custom, we had another drink; he was then completely at my disposal. I immediately took him to my carriage where he fell asleep at once and did not wake up. Fyodor Mikhailovich moved to Maria Dmitrievna's cart. The road was nice and smooth. We went through an old pine forest, surrounded by soft moonlight, the air was sweet and exciting. We went farther and farther....

But the time came to say good-bye. My doves embraced each other and swept tears from their eyes while I dragged the drunken Isaev into the cart. He snored again, probably without understanding either the time or the place. Pasha also slept. The horses moved, the cart moved, and you could already hardly see the cart in the clouds of dust.

And Dostoevsky stood, as if numb, without uttering a word, with a bent head, and with tears rolling down his cheeks. I came to him, took him by the hand, and he, as if awakening from a long sleep, without saying a word, sat with me in my carriage. We arrived home at dawn. Dostoevsky did not go to bed, he kept on pacing across the room and talking to himself. When he went to the military camp for military exercises, he was exhausted from the excitement and his sleepless night. When he returned, he lay in bed all day, neither eating nor drinking, only nervously smoking one pipe after another.

Time cures wounds and his desperation eventually started to calm down. Dostoevsky started a busy correspondence with Kuznetsk, but he was not happy with it. He felt that something was wrong....

I would like to say a few words about the dignity with which Dostoevsky behaved himself in his position. The environment in which we lived was not a very cultural one. Besides, the local chiefs behaved in a rude and snobbish way. Fyodor Mikhailovich certainly never showed any traces of being a yes-man, or flattery, or the wish to be a member of such a society. At the same time, he was very reserved and humble, as if he did not understand his outstanding talent. Due to his tactful behavior, as I said at the beginning, he enjoyed respect from all.

More news came from Kuznetsk, and each piece of news was worse than the last. M.D. Isaeva went with her husband to a remote town where she saw him drunk and ill all the time. She became bored with such a life. All her letters were filled with complaints of being lonely. She desperately wanted to talk to someone, to relieve her soul. In later letters she mentioned the name of a new friend in Kuznetsk more and more often. He was her husband's friend, a young teacher. She praised him more and more often in every letter; she praised his kindness, attachment and his refined soul. Dostoevsky was tormented by jealousy: it was painful to see his state, and it had a bad influence on his health.

Fyodor Mikhailovich mostly was in low spirits, or worked in fits of inspiration. I tried to entertain him to the best of my abilities. Yes, it was a monotonous life, without new impressions. He often had to spend days in the monotonous, routine army service which neither Fyodor Mikhailovich nor I really liked.

We used to go out for walks along the Irtysh River, take care of the flowers, swim and have our small parties on the balcony, smoking long pipes. I liked fishing and did it with passion; Dostoevsky would lie beside me on the grass, and often read aloud, the same books from our small library again and again.

There was no library in town, and most of the books I had were on geology and other natural sciences, and I knew all these books almost by heart. Dostoevsky preferred fiction, and we rushed with eagerness to every new book we received.

Our monotonous days were different when Dostoevsky had a period of inspiration. During such periods, he was in high spirits, and he passed his excitement over to me as well. It seemed for a while that our life in Semipalatinsk became better; but this good mood would disappear as fast as it came. It was enough to receive some bad news from Kuznetsk, and that was it—my Fyodor Mikhailovich faded away and looked ill.

Once I was sitting with Dostoevsky on the terrace, drinking tea and watching our female friends watering flowers. Adam [my servant] rushed to us and reported that a young woman had arrived and that she wanted to see Fyodor Mikhailovich "and the landlord."

She was let into the garden. Dostoevsky recognized her from a distance; she was the daughter of a gypsy woman who had been sentenced to prison for killing her husband from jealousy. Her name was Van'ka-Tan'ka; she herself was involved in a case of exiled Pollacks and Hungarians, and the escape of two of them from the Omsk maximum security prison in 1854.

The purpose of this escape was completely crazy: they wanted to get to the steppe, to make out a route among the dissatisfied nomad Kirgizis, to join the Khan army and to free afterwards their other inmates. It was something completely illogical and fantastic.

So, our new female guest rushed in, with a noisy and joyful air. She was a dark-skinned woman, about twenty to twenty-two years old; she had black eyes which reminded me of black-burning coal; her curly hair framed her face, she smiled all the time displaying her beautiful teeth which looked like pearls....

This meeting enticed Fyodor Mikhailovich to write a new chapter entitled "Escape" in his *Notes from the House of the Dead* (Ch. IX). As I noticed before, during some period of our life together, Fyodor Mikhailovich worked on this famous work. I was happy to see him during the minutes of his creative work, and I was the first person who listened to the notes from this outstanding work of art. Now, after many years I remember this with a special feeling. During my conversations with him, I learned many interesting, essential things.

It is interesting to note that, in spite of all the hardships and the trials that his fate served him (such as prison, exile, terrible illness and the constant need of money), Fyodor Mikhailovich's soul was filled with the most bright and the best human feelings and qualities. The absence of evil in Fyodor Mikhailovich, in spite of all this, was the thing which especially surprised me.

But let us continue with the story about our life in Semipalatinsk. One day we received the news that General Gasfort had departed from Omsk and that he was going to arrive in our city with an inspection ... we waited for him....

Not long before this, Dostoevsky had written a poem dedicated to the death of Nikolai I. I discussed this with him, and we decided to pass this poem along to the widowed Tsarina via General Gasfort. As far as I remember, this poem started with the lines:

> "Your great husband faded away
> As the dawn fades in the morning sky."

Gasfort categorically refused to help me with my deep and polite request, saying: "I will never support the former enemies of the government; but if people in St. Petersburg will remember about the case themselves, I will have nothing against it."

Here I would like to explain how, in the long run, this poem reached its destination. My purpose was to remind people about Dostoevsky, to raise some interest in him "at the top." I repeatedly wrote to my father and to other influential members of our family and asked them to pass the poem to the crowned Empress. At last, my requests were successful. His Majesty Prince P.G. Oldenburgsky agreed to pass along the poem.... The poem was received by the Empress, I know this for sure; later I received a confirmation about this from Mr. Shakhtinsky, the chief of the Third Police Section. There was also another poem by Dostoevsky, "The Dedication to the Enthronement of Alexander II." It was delivered over to Edward Ivanovich Totleben personally by me, immediately after my arrival in St. Petersburg.

Here, by the way, I would like to write several lines about the criticism directed against these poems ... as well as his article "About Russia."

In the *Efron Encyclopedic Dictionary*, for example, I recently found the following disappointing lines (Vol. IX, p. 74, col. II): "As you can see from the poor tone of his Siberian letters, and from the means by which he tried to receive his complete amnesty (patriotic poems, etc.)...."

The thing is that Dostoevsky was a patriotic person in the deepest, the best sense of this word; it was according to his essence, to his nature. He looked at Alexander II with sincere admiration (as everyone did at the time), and he saw in the Tsar the symbol of the resurrection of a new life in Russia. Was it a bad thing to admire the new monarch, who was admired by all people who loved their country? I have to mention here that Dostoevsky did not have any bad feelings toward the other Emperor, Nikolai I. Even after [being rather severely punished for] his minor political crime, as many people thought, Dostoevsky personally accepted his guilt and looked at his exile as "the act of justice," though it may seem strange to you.

Therefore, in his request addressing the Tsar there was nothing that did not coincide with Dostoevsky's own views, or which made him achieve a personal profit, even if you look at this matter from the principal, independent viewpoint. I must say also that it was cruel to criticize Dostoevsky for this, from a purely humane point of view.

Dostoevsky suffered from his illness and was afraid for his mental health and for his memory. His literary work was the most important thing in the world for him. He was in exile, and because of this, his works could not be published. He was so desperate that he even suggested that I publish his own works under my name.

Certainly, I refused this flattering suggestion. Besides, except for his glory, literature was the only source of income for him. At the time he wanted to settle his personal life, he dreamt of "eternal happiness" (as he wrote in his letters). And what about his permanent financial need? For years, he did not have the most necessary things.

He lived in permanent need of money, constantly looking for some means to survive. Was this a "low" action for a man of such intellectual and spiritual qualities as Dostoevsky? And, who knows, if Dostoevsky did not use these means (for which some critics blame him so strictly), then maybe one of the greatest Russian writers, the glory of Russia could have died, disappeared in the depths of Siberia? ...

After numerous requests from my side, supported by the military governor, I received at last permission from the battalion commander for Dostoevsky's trip to Zmeinogorsk with me. We were invited there by General Ferngross. The place was situated not very far from Kuznetsk, and Fyodor Mikhailovich dreamt of the possibility of meeting Maria Dmitrievna there. Besides, we would be pleased to visit some other educated people in Zmeinogorsk....

We stayed in Zmiev for five days; due to the existing custom, we stayed at the house of a rich merchant. We received a warm welcome from the local chiefs; we had dinners, picnics and even dancing at night.

Colonel Poletika, the manager of the local factory, had a choir and an orchestra made up of employees of the local factory. Everyone was so joyful, easy-going, polite, and Dostoevsky felt better, though M.D. Isaeva did not come to see him again (her husband felt unwell) and she even did not care to write him a letter to Zmiev....

Speaking of Zmeinogorsk, I must mention the famous Kolyvanskoe Lake, situated about 18 versts from the mines. All people who visited the city felt it as their obligation to visit the lake. The famous Baron von Humboldt was simply charmed by the beauty of the marvelous sight of nature; he said that he went around the world and did not encounter a more beautiful place.

I could not resist the temptation to go there. Fyodor Mikhailovich was unwell, he was upset again, and he stayed at home.... I have seen many mountain lakes in my life, but I cannot forget the charm which I experienced there. The Kolyvanskoe Lake is rather narrow in width, but it stretches among the high rocks and canyons for several versts. It was a very beautiful, sunny and quiet day. The surface of the lake was motionless; it looked as a mirror, and it reflected the deep blue of the cloudless sky.... It was a pity that Dostoevsky was not with me, I think that such a great-looking landscape would arouse admiration in the most indifferent person....

There was a characteristic of Dostoevsky which surprised me most of all—it was his complete indifference to the beauties of nature; such things did not concern him, they did not excite him at all. He was completely immersed in the study of man, with all his passions, strong and weak features. All other things were of minor importance for him. He, as a great anatomist, noticed and described every smallest curve of man's soul.

I and Fyodor Mikhailovich made plans for the future. We had no doubt that soon he would receive an amnesty. I had just received some good news from St. Petersburg regarding him. I was sad when I parted with Fyodor Mikhailovich, to whom I had become so much attached. Besides, I had a new love affair which occupied my heart, and tied me to the place. For the time being, we decided that I would find a new position in Barnaul. Dostoevsky also dreamt of moving there as soon as he received his freedom. He said jokingly, "I will be closer to the suffering M.D., and you will be closer to your dearest N." ...

Among the other people who visited us, there was a young Kirgiz officer, a graduate of the Omsk Cadet School, who visited us to see Dostoevsky. He was the last great-grandson of the Shah of the Middle Horde, and his name was Mukhamed Kha-Fah-Velikhanov. Dostoevsky mentioned his name in his letters to me. Mr. Velikhanov met Dostoevsky in Omsk where he visited the Ivanovs, and he liked Dostoevsky very much....

In 1865 I returned to Copenhagen after my summer vacation. There I found a desperate letter written by Dostoevsky from Wiesbaden. It turned out that he lost all his money gambling. He was in a difficult situation, with no way out, without a cent; his debtors asked money from him, and he was completely desperate about this. The new passion of Dostoevsky to gamble was a completely unexpected thing for me, because in Siberia, where card games are very popular, he never gambled. Perhaps his strong character and his shattered nerves needed some strong emotions, and he found relief playing roulette.

I could not refuse helping my friend, and I helped him with some money. I also wrote him a letter and invited him to visit me in Copenhagen. He came to me on October 1 and stayed for about a week in my home; my wife liked him very much. I discovered that he was losing weight and becoming older. We were very happy to see each other, and we remembered the time we spent together in Siberia.... As to his marriage, he wrote to me in one of his previous letters: "We were unhappy sometimes, but we did not stop loving each other; even the more unhappy we were, the more attached we became to each other...." He repeated the same in Copenhagen. I never saw any happiness in Dostoevsky's [first] marriage. All the sufferings, all the burden he put on his shoulders with the marriage, caused him to lose his inner balance. In Semipalatinsk I tried to cure Fyodor Mikhailovich from this psychosis caused by Mrs. Isaeva. But he did not even want to listen to this; for him the image of Maria Dmitrievna was painted in some rosy, fantastic colors.

By the way, during our meeting in Copenhagen, Dostoevsky expressed his views on women, and gave me a piece of good advice. When I remembered our Siberian friends, I told him about some mean and nasty Siberian women.

Fyodor Mikhailovich told me this: "We have to be grateful to a beloved woman for those hours or days of happiness and tenderness she gives us. You must not ask her to live all her life only for you and think only about you; this is pure egoism and you must get rid of this."

Dostoevsky did not look good when he visited me that time, and before, in his previous letter, he complained about him being unwell. Besides his epilepsy and hemorrhoids, he wrote that he "was burned by some fever, trembling and feeling too hot or too cold every night"; he was "losing weight terribly quickly." What health could endure this type of troubled life which Dostoevsky had at the time? He was in financial need all the time, he had the burden of his family on his shoulders, and besides, those of his brother. He was afraid to be arrested and to be put into debtor's prison. He did not have rest for twenty-four hours a day. He was visiting publishers during the day and writing his works at night. All this was reflected in Dostoevsky's health and character....

In 1873, in St. Petersburg, Dostoevsky came to see me and he returned the money he borrowed in Copenhagen in 1865. I was very happy to see him again; we met as good old friends ... but this was not my old dear Fyodor Mikhailovich from Semipalatinsk. The time and the long period of separation changed our relationship.

Besides, he seemed to be very nervous and irritated by something on that day, and he was in a hurry. He did not say a word about the past; he did not even tell me that he was married for the second time, or about how things were going. I found out from other people, quite by chance, that, thanks to his wonderful second wife, who was very attentive to him and took good care of him, he at last found peace and he did not need anything.

One could hear Dostoevsky's literary name everywhere. Soon after this I went abroad.... I was appointed to the position of a border consul in Danzig [Eastern Prussia] where I lived in the former Tsar Peter's palace. Here, in 1881, I was struck by the news about Dostoevsky's death.

All the events from the past revived in my memory, and I felt pain, I felt sorry for my old friend. Though we were separated during the last years, I kept the feeling of deep love and respect for him. My heart painfully sank at this terrible news. Russia lost one of its greatest talents.

A. Pinchuk: New Version of Dostoevsky's Arrest: A Witness Report
(From *The Kiev Newsletter* 12 [11 February 1881].)

[Accounts of Dostoevsky's arrest in 1849 were very contradictory. For example, the following report does not correspond with Dostoevsky's own version of his arrest, published in the memoirs of A. Miliukov and found on pp. 86–87 in the present volume.]

In 1849, my room was in the same corridor as Dostoevsky's room. One night, some of my friends came to my room to play cards. F.M.

did not participate in the card game because he did not like playing cards. He sat in the corner, as a lonely visitor, and about 10 P.M. he went to bed, to his room. At about two in the morning, we all heard some strange and loud noises in the corridor. Someone looked out and whispered that there were several officers of the secret police standing in the corridor. They broke somebody's door. Somebody cried. Again we heard a strange noise, as if they pulled something heavy across the floor, and we all heard many loud steps in the corridor.... In the morning, I found out that Dostoevsky had been arrested. My friend S., who was the first to leave our party the night before, told me the following news. It turned out that Dostoevsky's door was locked. The police broke in through the door. Dostoevsky smashed the window glass in his room, and stood in front of the window. He was going to jump out of his room through the window and escape, but he was stopped by the police. After a brief struggle, they brought him out of his house by force—he resisted.... In February 1850, Dostoevsky, as well as the other members of the secret socialist circle, were sentenced to death, but the Tsar changed the death penalty to a lighter sentence: several years in prison.

Aleksei Pleshcheev: "Fyodor Dostoevsky ... Is to Be Executed by a Firing Squad": A Myth or a Fact?

(From *Rumours* 50 [19 February 1881].)

> *[One of Dostoevsky's closest personal friends remembered that Dostoevsky knew about his death sentence, as well as those of the other members of the Petrashevsky Circle, and was not familiar with the new sentence until it was announced at the execution place. This contradicts the version by the Colonel Vuich, presented on pp. 106–107 in the present volume.]*

...Evidence presented by Ivan Vuich is wrong. Maybe his memory failed him, even though he was standing very close to the prisoners on the execution ground. We do not know what the expressions on the faces of the prisoners were when they heard the new sentence, but according to the documents, all the members of the Petrashevsky Circle were to be executed by a firing squad. This concerned all twenty-four people involved in the Petrashevsky case, and not only three persons named by Mr. Vuich in his memoirs.... After the new sentence was announced, they all had clean white shirts on, which are usually given to the prisoners just before the execution. Nobody knew about the new decision of the Tsar [according to which, the death penalty was changed to prison terms]. For example, one of the prisoners, Mr. Timkovsky, approached the prison priest who stood nearby in his black dress holding a cross, and wanted to confess before execution.

After the prisoners were brought back to St. Peter and Paul Fortress, they were visited by a prison doctor who checked whether the ceremony of the mock execution had produced stress which threatened the health of the prisoners.

M.D. Frantseva: Secret Meeting with Dostoevsky on His Way to a Siberian Prison
(From *The History Herald* 6 [1888]: 628–630.)

[A woman who, together with other Decembrists' wives, met Dostoevsky in Siberia, on his way to the place of his incarceration.]

We heard the news that a group of political prisoners, members of the so-called Petrashevsky Circle, were brought to Tobolsk prison. It was a group of eight people, Dostoevsky among them. We wanted to meet them on the way. It happened during an extremely cold and frosty Siberian night, with the temperatures well minus thirty below zero [Celsius]....

We heard the ringing of the bell. Then we saw a troika sledge, with a police officer and a groom in it. Then the second sledge appeared. A small caravan stopped in the middle of nowhere, on a quiet village road, as we had arranged with the police officers before. Dostoevsky and Durov jumped out of the Siberian postal sledges. The first was a thin, rather short, not very nice-looking young man; the second was about ten years older.... They both had fur prisoners' coats and fur caps on. The heavy shackles on their feet made a terrible noise every time they moved. We said good-bye to them, because we were afraid that some other travelers would meet us on the way.... I gave the police officer a letter in support of the prisoners, addressed to his superior, Mr. Pushkin, which he later delivered. They jumped back into the sledges, the groom whipped the horses, and the troika disappeared in the limitless spaces and remote landscapes.... We found our sledges and returned home, having been almost frozen to death in this terrible cold.

Boleslav Markevich: Dostoevsky's Arrival at Prison

(From *The Odessa Herald* 60 [18–30 March 1881].)

> *[One of the senior civil servants in Tobolsk, a provincial Siberian city where Dostoevsky was incarcerated.]*

We had a New Year's Eve Party in Tobolsk in 1850, at the City Hall. Governor-General Engelke was present. We had a lovely time. At one o'clock in the morning, a chief of the local police came into the hall and said something quietly to the governor. The governor was embarrassed, turned pale, and quickly left the hall. There was instantly a rumor among the people that the members of the socialist circle had been brought to the local prison. The mood changed, and all the guests went home shortly.... People who arrived on that night were put into the prison building, a huge barracks with low ceilings and terribly bad air inside. It was really a bad place to stay, and the prisoners had to live in terrible conditions. But the people who lived in Tobolsk city, especially the Decembrists, tried to help the prisoners; they sent them small personal items, underwear, etc....

Dostoevsky was a very young and small man, and he was completely calm and quiet, though all the time he had very heavy shackles on his legs and his arms.

V. Abeldiaev: The Writer Talking to the Students About Christian Values

(From V. Abeldiaev, "Pamiati Dostoevskogo" ["In Memory of Dostoevsky"], *Moskovskie Vedomosti* [*Moscow News*], 1 [29 January 1891].)

Students from the Moscow University went to St. Petersburg to see Dostoevsky, and to ask for his advice. Here is what Dostoevsky told them:

> In the most terrible periods of my life, when everybody left me, there was only one Being which supported me all the time. This Being was God. He never rejected me in His support. I feel from my own experience that there is nothing worse than atheism or the lack of faith. To all people who want to make sure that this is true, I suggest to them to go to prison. If they do not commit suicide there, then they become real believers.
>
> You can create any ideas, you can destroy any theories created by humans,

but do not touch the notion of God. He came to Earth before you, and He cannot be destroyed by you. Those who live without Him feel emptiness and darkness in their hearts, and they have nothing inside. You feel desperate and lonely, if you do not have faith…. Look around yourself—you are alone. And Jesus Christ was supported by all the heavenly forces. And what is behind you? … If you do not believe, try to behave as I suggest, start to believe without any doubts and hesitations, without any pre-conditions, and then you will understand that it will help to support any enterprise, any business you do, and any failure of yours will not seem terrible to you, and then everything will become possible for you in this life…. At present I want to express my views on faith in a novel.

A.K. Rozhnovsky: "The Dead Man": In Prison, They Called Him by a Nickname
(From *Caucasus* 40 [13 February 1882].)

[Recollections of a Polish prisoner who was incarcerated with Dostoevsky.]

Probably, you do not know a man with the nickname "a dead man." But I will tell you that was Dostoevsky's nickname…. It was a long time ago. When Dostoevsky arrived in prison, the gang, as we called it, did not like it. The criminals in prison had their own laws, and they lived according to these laws. They could even stab to death the other prisoners who violated these laws. For example, they had very strict rules concerning women, and all prisoners were supportive of each other in this respect. Each of us had his turn in the evening, when the cleaning ladies came to the laundry room, but Dostoevsky refused to go on duty, when his turn came. The next time, he took a gift from the soldier guard; it was a tobacco leaf. According to the rules of the criminal world, if somebody received tobacco as a gift, he should take half of it and divide the second half into several parts, and the other prisoners cast a lot to see who would get it. Dostoevsky refused to take it or to cast a lot. He divided the tobacco into two equal parts, and gave it to two sick prisoners. So, our local criminal chiefs of the gang were angry at him, and they decided to set him up on the next occasion…. The guard soldiers took in Dostoevsky and Golovachev only. I do not know how they were punished, but the next day we heard a rumor that Dostoevsky had died. I knew that he was not used to torture, and besides, he was an ill man…. We all were confident in his death, but we did not know the details…. About a month and a half after this execution, people forgot about Dostoevsky, but I continued thinking of him, and his image was in my memories. One day we returned to the prison barracks from work, and I heard a familiar voice, "Hello, Rozhnovsky." I looked at him—it was Dostoevsky.... It seemed to me that he was a ghost who came from the world of dead. I wanted to say, "Dostoevsky are you alive," but I could not say a word, and we embraced each other. It turned out that when Dostoevsky was brought to the prison hospital, there was a very sick person who died the day after Dostoevsky arrived at this hospital, and the prison nurse wrote in the register by mistake that it was Dostoevsky who died. When he recovered from his illness, everything cleared up, but our gang gave him the nickname "a dead man." Nobody called him by his real name afterwards.

Vladimir Iakovlev: Dostoevsky in the Army: "He Did Not Talk Much"

(From *Siberia* 80 [11 July 1897].)

Dostoevsky behaved in a very polite manner, and he took his army service very seriously. His major priority was to avoid all unpleasant surprises. He also never spoke to anyone about his criminal case—why he was sent to Siberia—or about his personal life. He was very friendly and soft with his colleagues.... About a year afterwards, Dostoevsky was promoted to the rank of sergeant, and the attitude of his superiors toward him became different. He was allowed to rent a private room outside the barracks, and he was relieved from all other routine services. When it was necessary for him to be present at the military barracks, he was sent for. He always gave some money to a soldier who brought him these messages.... Dostoevsky often recalled the day of his would-be execution. It was really a terrible story.... For all these hours he could not understand anything, and he regained consciousness only after a new sentence was announced. One day Dostoevsky showed T.N. Palshin a white shirt given to prisoners who faced capital punishment. He had received this shirt when he was on the point of being executed by a firing squad.

Evgeny Feoktistov: Several New Letters by Dostoevsky

(From E. Feoktistov, "Propavshie pis'ma Dostoevskogo" ["Several Lost Letters by Dostoevsky"], *Sibirski ogni* [*Siberian Lights*] 2 [1928]: 119–125.)

Katz, Dostoevsky's friend and military junior officer who served together with him in Semipalatinsk, remembered that it was difficult for F.M. to serve in the army. He was extremely polite and obedient to every junior officer. He was very polite, but even he could not finish his service without being beaten.... I saw this twice. Once a sergeant hit him in his head, and another time, when he was cleaning a barracks, he got a kick in his face again. It was not a big surprise for me. At present Dostoevsky is a great writer, but at the same time he was treated as a criminal, as a prisoner who did not have any rights.

I will never forget this story by Katz. You can imagine how many terrible moments the great writer had to endure during almost ten years of his incarceration and exile in Siberia.... At that time, there was a very small difference between being an army soldier or a prisoner: neither had rights....

A. Ivanov: Life in the Army Was as Bad as in Prison

(From *The Turkestan News* 12 [14 February 1893].)

[A. Ivanov was the senior officer in the Twenty-Fourth Infantry Siberian Division.]

The general was inspecting the 24th Infantry Battalion, where Dostoevsky served as a private. I knew Dostoevsky's name; I had read his novel *The Poor People*. I wanted to see this talented person, and I asked one of the officers to show me Dostoevsky. "Here he is, he is standing in this line, number seven from the right side," he told me in a whisper, so that the general could not overhear our conversation. Dostoevsky seemed to me an ill and exhausted man. His eyes were settled deep into his eye-sockets, and he gazed somewhere into the distance, lost in his dreams. He was a thin man and it seemed to me that even the soldier's rifle was too heavy for him to hold.

I felt pity for him, I wanted to talk to him and console him in his sufferings, but we had to obey the military discipline, and it was not allowed. So I felt guilty, and I promised to myself to ask his Battalion Commander not to torture him any more with military exercises, marchings, etc. At 4 P.M., a soldier told me that Private Dostoevsky wanted to see me. He came in and greeted me, slightly bowing his head. He sat down, and said, "I came to you, dear sir, with a personal request. Please forward my patriotic poem to General Gasfort, the Commander of the Army. I wrote a poem dedicated to the death of the Tsar Nikolai

Pavlovich and to the new Empress, Alexandra Fyodorovna...." I promised to help him. An hour later, we went to the governor. There were many guests there, and I had to read Dostoevsky's poem three times, because people liked it very much.

A. Skandin: Private Dostoevsky During His Routine Service in the Army

(From *The History Herald* 1 [1903]: 202–216.)

> *[Dostoevsky's army bed was next to that of N. Katz, who gave an interview to journalist A. Skandin about Dostoevsky's service in the army.]*

I remember Dostoevsky very well. He was of average height, with a shallow bosom, cleanly shaven face, his cheeks fallen. He looked older than his age. He had grey eyes, and a serious and gloomy glance. Nobody saw a smile on his face during his service in the army. Sometimes a soldier would crack a joke, and all the people in the military barracks were dying of laughter, but you could see that Dostoevsky's face remained motionless; only the ends of his lips were slightly curved.... He never wrote anything in the barracks, though soldiers had very little spare time. Most of the time in the barracks, Dostoevsky was sitting alone, lost in his dreams.... He was very diligent in his army service, and never received reprimands.... Among other duties, he had to stand on guard with a rifle at the following military objects:

1. at the windows of the local military prison;
2. at the money office of the local military unit;
3. at the windows of the gun powder deposits;
4. at the military grocery store;
5. at the entrance to the brick barracks.

Fyodor Mikhailovich was very polite, attentive and friendly to other soldiers, and he helped them as much as he could. He was very patient and obedient with other officers. He never answered the rudeness of the others. He endured patiently all the hardships of military life.

B. Gerasimov: New Facts About Dostoevsky in Semipalatinsk.

(From *The Russian Speech* 38 [22 February 1919].)

Dostoevsky arrived at Semipalatinsk on 2 March 1854, in a rank of a soldier. In January 1856, he became a sergeant, and in 1856, a junior lieutenant.... Here he wrote *The Village of Stepanchikovo* and *My Uncle's Dream*. Besides, Vrangel remembered that here Dostoevsky created several chapters for *Notes from the House of the Dead*....

Semipalatinsk in the fifties of the previous century was a big village lost in a desert sands.... There was only one brick house in the whole city, a church.... There were no street lanterns, no inns or hotels. Intellectual interests were minuscule. For 5,000–6,000 inhabitants, there were ten to fifteen families who subscribed to newspapers, and all these newspapers or magazines were loaned out to ten more families or so. The town was separated by thousands of miles from the other cultural centers.... There was only one piano in the whole town.... Material interests dominated above everything. They played cards heavily, they had huge and endless drinking parties. There were no intellectual interests whatsoever, and the people were busy with spreading gossip. The ladies were bored to death by their life. Even traveling musicians did not visit Semipalatinsk.... The life in the city was very depressing for Dostoevsky; he could not be published here. And it was very difficult for him morally. His creative aspirations could not be realized.... Semipalatinsk was boring, but F.M. Dostoevsky had to spend more than five years of his life in this town.

Boleslav Markevich: After Siberian Exile: "We Saw Nervous Convulsions on His Face..."

(From *The Odessa Herald* 32 [10–22 February 1881].)

> *[Speech about Dostoevsky made at the sitting of the Slavic Charity Society on February 8, 1881.]*

In 1859, Dostoevsky was allowed to resign and to live in Tver', and shortly afterwards, he was allowed to live in the capitals. At that time I met Dostoevsky for the only time in my lifetime. I remember when several students went to see Dostoevsky at the house of our college doctor who was his relative. The fame of Dostoevsky had not yet started; such works as *The House of the Dead* had not been published. He brought several smaller novels from Siberia, but they did not make him famous at the time. We spent a brief time with Dostoevsky, enough to have a cup of tea. He sat in an armchair in the dark corner of the room all the time.

We asked him questions about his incarceration, but he replied very briefly. His appearance is famous. He was a rather short man, skinny and pale; his eyes were very nervous. When he closed his eyes, he looked as if he were a dead man. And what was most strange about Dostoevsky were the nervous convulsions on his face. We did not know that he was an epileptic.

Chapter 5. Literary Journals
and "Innocent" Novels:
The Period of Transition

"It was indeed a fearful story.... A story of a woman.... who lay
dying for a month in a damp cellar.... It was a grim story, one of
those grim and painful stories which are so often played out
unseen, almost mysterious, under the heavy sky of Petersburg, in
the dark secret corners of the vast city, in the midst of the busy
life, of dull egoism, of clashing interests, of gloomy vice and secret
crimes in that seething hell of a senseless and abnormal life."

(Oppressed and Humiliated)

D OSTOEVSKY MADE FRIENDS with some of the influential people in Semipalatinsk, including the mayor and the military prosecutor. He wrote several poems that glorified the Russian monarch and sent these works to St. Petersburg. The Russian Tsar, Alexander II, ordered in 1859 that Dostoevsky be discharged due to illness.

The following documents shed additional light on Dostoevsky's resignation from the army and his arrival in St. Petersburg.

Dostoevsky addressed Alexander II with a very emotional letter:

> Your Majesty,
> Please allow me to come to St. Petersburg to consult with doctors who live in the capital. Please, resurrect me, allow me the possibility of improving my health, so that I can be useful to my family and maybe, to some extent, to my fatherland [*Complete Works*, Vol. 28, part 1, p. 386].

His letters to the Tsar and other officials were supported by a medical report about his health issued in 1858 by Dr. Ermakov of the Seventh Siberian Infantry Battalion:

> Dostoevsky had his first serious seizure of epilepsy in 1850.... In 1853 he had another seizure, and now he has seizures each month. His present state of health is very weak.... For several years he suffered from epilepsy, and now, as he is deteriorating from the disease, he cannot stay in the service of Your Majesty any longer [*Complete Works*, Vol. 28, part 1, p. 386].

A special Order from the Ministry of Defense was issued in 1858, stating that "Junior-Lieutenant Dostoevsky can resign, but without permission to live in Moscow, and under surveillance by the Secret Police" (*The History Herald* 1 [1903]: 224–225). The Dostoevskys moved from Siberia to Tver, and then to St. Petersburg. First, Dostoevsky was allowed to live only in Tver, a Russian provincial town between St. Petersburg and Moscow, being under police surveillance:

> Top Secret Memo no. 81
> From: Local Headquarters
> Department of Secret Police
> Tver Region
>
> > To: Count Baranov
> > Governor-General
> > The City of Tver
> > April 8, 1859
>
> The chief of the Second Section of the police informed me, in letter no. 40, dated April 3, that Fyodor Dostoevsky, Junior-Lieutenant of the 7th Siberian Infantry Battalion, formerly sentenced in connection with the Petrashevsky case, was dismissed from military service and was promoted to the next rank and consented to live in the city of Tver.
> Please inform me kindly about the time of Dostoevsky's arrival in Tver region and the place where he would live.

Colonel-Lieutenant Simanovsky
Third Department of the [Secret] Police
[State Archive of the Tver Region, File 56/6, no. 11029, p. 1].

Dostoevsky made additional efforts to receive permission to live in St. Petersburg, the center of literary life in Russia. The governor-general of Tver supported his request and on November 23, 1859, he received an important letter from the capital, written by General Dolgorukov, the head of the Secret Police:

To: General P. Baranov
The Governor-General
Tver Region
Top Secret Memo no. 2126

From: Count General Dolgorukov
Third Section of Secret Police
November 23, 1859

I received a letter from Your Honor in which you informed me that Junior-Lieutenant Fyodor Dostoevsky wrote an official request for permission to live in St. Petersburg and you, dear sir, in this letter, asked me for my support in this subject. I entered the office of the Emperor with this report and His Majesty answered this request positively, with the condition that the secret police surveillance of Dostoevsky continues.

I am informing Your Honor about this matter and consider it my obligation to add that I did not receive a personal request from Dostoevsky himself.

Sincerely,
Count General Dolgorukov
[State Archive of the Tver Region, File 56/1, no. 11029, p. 8; also GLM, File 6371/49922].

After his arrival in the capital, Dostoevsky started editing two literary journals, *Time* and *Epoch*. He wrote to his brother Mikhail on November 12, 1859: "Well, brother, we must think about something and do it seriously. We must take a risk and start some literary enterprise, for example, a journal" (*Complete Works*, Vol. 28, part 1, p. 376).

In his literary journals Dostoevsky published two novels, some short stories and many articles on literary and political topics. During the ten years he spent in Siberia, his views had changed gradually, and he now placed a new emphasis on gaining "a better understanding of the Russian soul." That was Dostoevsky's major task at the time.

His journal *Epoch* was devoted to the ideas of "the soil," a Slavophile attempt to find some common ground between Slavophiles and Westernizers. Dostoevsky wrote about this effort in articles about Russian literature (*Time*, 1861, nos. 1, 2, 7, 8, 11) and in "Winter Notes About Summer Impressions" (*Time*, 1861, nos. 2, 3), wherein he criticized the possibility of socialism in Western Europe and praised the Russian traditional peasant community.

Dostoevsky brought with him his two novels from Siberia, *The Village Stepanchikovo* and *My Uncle's Dreams*. He characterized one of these works in the following way in a letter to M.P. Fyodorov: "For fifteen years, I hadn't had the chance to read my novel, *My Uncle's Dream*. Now I find it written badly. It was my first work after prison and I wrote it in Siberia with the one purpose of again starting my literary career. At that time I was very much afraid of censorship. Therefore, I wrote a work of complete and dovelike innocence" (*Complete Works*, Vol. 29, part 1, p. 303).

Dostoevsky was nonetheless happy to tell his brother about these works in a letter written August 25, 1859: "I am sure that there are many bad and weak pages in my novel, but I swear upon my death that there are many wonderful moments in it. They came from my soul. There are also scenes of great comedy and humor" (*Complete Works*, Vol. 28, part 1, pp. 333–334).

Dostoevsky wanted his literary journals to be successful. He invited onto his staff Nikolai Nikolaevich Strakhov, a young literary critic who quickly became Dostoevsky's friend. In a letter to Strakhov on February 26, 1869, he wrote, "I always admired the clarity of your writing.... You are the only person among our literary critics who has great future" (*Complete Works*, Vol. 29, part 1, pp. 15–17). As contributors to his journals, Dostoevsky invited the best literary artists of the time, including among others poet Iakov Polonsky, playwright Aleksandr Ostrovsky and novelist Ivan Turgenev.

In June 1862, Dostoevsky made his first trip abroad, visiting Germany, France, Switzerland and Italy. Dostoevsky was critical of many aspects of West European life. For example, he wrote to Strakhov on June 26, 1862, that "Paris is the dullest city and if there was nothing really outstanding in it, I would die of boredom" (*Complete Works*, Vol. 28, part 2, p. 27).

In London, he met Aleksandr Herzen, a Russian revolutionary in exile. Herzen characterized Dostoevsky in his letter to Ogarev, written on July 17, 1862, in the following way: "Yesterday Dostoevsky visited me. He is naïve and not very easy to understand, but a very nice person. He believes in the Russian people with enthusiasm" (A. Herzen, *Pis'ma iz daleka*. [*Letters from Afar*]. Moscow: Sovremennik 1981, p. 263).

After his return home, Dostoevsky continued editing literary journals. He liked the editor's job, and combined it with creative writing. In 1864 Dostoevsky published his *Notes from the Underground* (*Epoch*, nos. 1–2), a work in which he "described a real man of the Russian majority and unveiled the crippled and tragic side of his character." Dostoevsky's advertisement for yearly subscriptions to *Epoch* for 1865 expressed his major concern at the time: "The general direction of the journal remains the same. The major purpose of our periodical will be the development of the study of our [Russian] social phenomenon from the Russian national viewpoint. We are as convinced as ever that there will be no progress in our society until we all become real Russians."

The following memoirs shed additional light on the period of transition which lasted for several years after Dostoevsky's return from Siberia. During this time, in the early 1860s, Dostoevsky edited literary journals and tried to reestablish his name in the literary world after an absence of ten years.

P. Kovalevsky witnessed the atmosphere of severe criticism existing between Dostoevsky and the editors of many other literary journals in Russia. Pyotr Boborykin, a contributor to *Time* and *Epoch*, provided detail about Dostoevsky's relationship with his editorial staff. Nikolai Strakhov was a literary critic and an active staff member in all of Dostoevsky's journals for a period of almost fifteen years. His extensive memoirs paint a detailed picture of Dostoevsky's activity as a journalist and an editor. Andrei Dostoevsky recalls his brother's explanation of the closing of his journal by the government. Maria Ivanova and Nikolai Fon-Fokht present memoirs about Dostoevsky's stay in Liublino, near Moscow, in the summer of 1866, when he wrote *Crime and Punishment*. Nikolai Chernyshevsky, a journalist and a leader of the socialist movement in Russia was visited by Dostoevsky after acts of revolutionary terror when many wooden streets of St. Petersburg were set on fire. Chernyshevsky described Dostoevsky as an almost insane man who implored him to put an end to these actions. Pyotr Veinberg, a poet and literary translator, gives a glimpse into Dostoevsky's talent as an actor in amateur drama performances which were highly popular among St. Petersburg theater enthusiasts. Evgeny Opochinin, a literary artist and a historian, provides examples of how Dostoevsky derived his plots from the notorious criminal cases of his time.

P. Kovalevsky: Why Was Dostoevsky Not Published in the Prestigious Journals?

(From P.M. Kovalevsky, *Stikhi i vospominaniia* [*Poems and Memoirs*]. St. Petersburg, 1912, pp. 275–278.)

I have never met a better editor than Nekrasov.... He never made mistakes in his choices of the manuscripts to be published. "The readers will like this!" he used to say before making a decision to publish some literary work, and, as a rule, he was right.

He was mistaken only once, though it was a big and a serious mistake. It concerned Dostoevsky's novel *Village Stepanchikovo*, which was not altogether a great work, but which Dostoevsky brought from exile. For this reason alone, it should have been published in *The Contemporary*....

Nekrasov announced his decision about this work: "Dostoevsky is finished. He cannot write anything interesting anymore."

But Nekrasov was wrong. Dostoevsky, as if he were answering him, trying to convince him of the opposite, wrote such works as *Notes from the House of the Dead* and *Crime and Punishment*. This writer was in the process of creation. This time Nekrasov's intuition failed him.

This sad event had some further sad consequences. It was not a very great loss for *The Contemporary*, which collected other masterpieces, such as works by Lev Tolstoy, Turgenev, Pisemsky, Ostrovsky.... But this made a serious change in the life of Dostoevsky, who suffered, who was exhausted by many years in prison and who was ill from epilepsy. He was very sensitive, easily hurt and enraged. For the rest of his life this writer was "cuffed" to poverty and urgent, low-paid work.... He just got rid of other [physical] handcuffs and chains....

"Well, if you think so, I will create my own journal," [he said in response to the rejection] and here Dostoevsky made a mistake.

Together with his brother, Mikhail Mikhailovich, he gathered some money and started a journal. He edited the "Letters from the Readers" section; he participated in the discussions; he was assaulted; he defended; he bit others and was bitten by the others [writers and journalists]. He put into this enterprise all the remains of his money and all his health; the same was true of his brother, who was a married man. At the end, he remained with many debts and a serious illness which he acquired in Siberia and which worsened during the years of his editorship.

He was grumpy most of the time, his enemies were laughing at him, and their laughter brought them the victory.... Even Nekrasov himself published in *The Whistle* several funny couplets laughing at the Dostoevsky's articles "The Dry Fog" and "The People from the Moon," addressing the publishers of the journal:

> When you write a small article about dry fogs,
> The wind will blow out all the money from your pockets.
> Then you lie down, and prepare to die....

Dostoevsky's journal published articles with the purpose of showing that there were no people living on the moon, but other people were laughing at him and mocking him without even reading his articles.

Poor Dostoevsky suffered from all this. He saw the face of the enemy in *The Contemporary*.... For example, the printing equipment broke down one day, just before the publishing of the next issue of the journal. Dostoevsky blamed *The Contemporary* for this. Some people tried to calm him down: "Such things can happen in every publishing house." He answered: "Yes, they happen, but not before a new issue is about to be published! And this happens just several days before the event! Before the beginning of the new year, the annual subscription campaign for the journal. Well, you tell me, this is somehow connected with *The Contemporary*! I am sure it is!"

It was really painful to see Dostoevsky during these days. I wanted to calm him down, to pity him. He looked as if he were a wild animal who got into a trap and continued to fight....

Pyotr Boborykin: My Memoirs About Journals Edited by Dostoevsky

(From P.D. Boborykin, *Za polveka. Moi vospominaniia* [*Half a Century: My Memoirs*]. Moscow: Zemlia i fabrika, 1929, pp. 212, 304–305.)

The House of the Dead was an unusual document for a Russian prison. At the time when it was published, Dostoevsky was considered almost a revolutionary, because there were so many mystical, unexplainable things in his novel. The publication of a journal changed the face of the author; he began to occupy a special place among the Slavophiles [supporters of the theory of the "fertile soil"]. F. Dostoevsky actively participated in the polemics between *The Time* and the radical journals, though he did not sign his articles....

Later on, when both *Time* and *Epoch* were closed, he started to publish *Crime and Punishment* which excited our youth so much, though we did not support his ideas....

In the long run, the author of *The Demons* made everybody become tolerant of his views, and at the end of his life he became a kind of spiritual teacher.

Nikolai Strakhov: Memories of Fyodor Mikhailovich Dostoevsky as a Journalist

(From N.N. Strakhov, "Iz vospomiananii" ["From the Memoirs"], *Semeinye Vechera* [*Family Evenings*], February 1881: 235–248.)

I feel that it is my duty to write any interesting or important facts which I remember about Fyodor Mikhailovich Dostoevsky. I was very close to him, especially when I worked in the journals where he was the editor. Therefore, I feel that I am able, and I feel an obligation, to describe his mood and his opinions during Dostoevsky's social activity of this type. We were so close that I could know his thoughts and his feelings, and I will try to put them here, on paper, in the best way I can, as I remember them and as I understand them. There is hardly anyone other than I who can tell the story of these journals, and these stories occupied an important place in the life of Fyodor Mikhailovich as an artist.... In the history of literature, he is remembered not only as an artist, the author of the novels, but also as a journalist....

The journalistic activity of Fyodor Mikhailovich is rather considerable in scope. He liked this activity very much, and the last lines written by him were the articles of the last issue of his *Diary*.

Here is the list of periodicals on which he worked as a journalist, an editor, a publicist or a literary critic:

1. *Time*, a monthly "thick" journal, edited by Fyodor Mikhailovich's brother, Mikhail Mikhailovich Dostoevsky, from January 1861 to April 1863.

2. *Epoch*, the same type of journal, issued in 1864–1865....

3. "The Citizen," a periodical which was founded in 1872 by Count V.P. Meshchersky. It was a daily newspaper. The first editor in 1872 was G.K. Gradovsky, and the editor in 1873 was Fyodor Mikhailovich. Here he started to write his articles under the title "A Writer's Diary"; this was the beginning of the new periodical.

4. *A Writer's Diary*, a monthly published in 1876–1877, with one issue in 1880 (August) and in 1881 (January, a posthumous issue).

The general spirit and direction of these journals marked a very special trend in the journalism of St. Petersburg.... The activity of Fyodor Mikhailovich was different from that of the St. Petersburg school of journalism, and he created a more serious school; it can be called the all-Russian, or national, school of journalism. I will try to speak in more detail about these proceedings....

I suggested my first big article for the first issue [of the journal *The Light*, edited by A.P. Miliukov], and with it I started my journalistic activity in St. Petersburg. I felt happy that my article was accepted for publication, and A.P. Miliukov invited me to visit his literary circle on Thursdays....

The first person in the circle was, certainly, Fyodor Mikhailovich. He was considered a great writer, but he was first not only because of this, but because of his many new, fresh thoughts and the passion with which he defended them. The circle was small, and the members were really close to each other, so there was none of the official tension which existed in many other Russian societies. At that time you could notice a special manner of Fyodor Mikhailovich's speech. He often spoke in a low voice, almost whispering. When something excited him, he started to speak with passion and raised his voice. One could say that his general mood was rather joyful; later, after experiencing all the hardships and difficulties of his life, he was not as soft as he was at that time.

I remember his appearance well, and, in spite of having a huge forehead and a beautiful head, he looked like a soldier and had the countenance of a simple person.... I saw his first wife, Maria Dmitrievna. She made a good impression on me, but she was pale and looked unhealthy....

Certainly, the outlook of this circle was directed by French literature. Political and social issues occupied the first place, and were considered to be more important than artistic interests. An artist, according to this view, had to examine society, to influence the good and bad in society and to be a teacher, a spiritual leader. ... Fyodor Mikhailovich was close to these lines, and he stuck to it to the end of his life....

So, I must add here that the reader of these notes must not think that I am trying to depict an exact portrait of the deceased writer; I refuse to do this completely. He was too close and too mysterious to me at the same time.... When I remember him, I am always surprised by the quickness of his thoughts, by the productivity of his imagination. It seemed that there was nothing fixed in him, nothing rigid. All his thoughts and feelings were constantly growing and changing. He said so many unknown things, unusual things which were different from what he had produced (said or written) before. Therefore, his literary growth in some periods cannot fit the usual form of the development of an average writer. For some time Dostoevsky would develop smoothly and steadily, then he would suddenly find some new energy, some new approach, and he would show himself from a completely new side. There were four such heights, or peaks, in his career: (1) *Poor People*; (2) *Notes from the House of the Dead*; (3) *Crime and Punishment*; (4) *A Writer's Diary*...

The New Direction: The Soil

Here, I would like to start by considering the basics, the foundations, of the journal *Time*. We must remember the period. It was 1861, and the abolition of serfdom was the major event during the previous reign, the moment of great admiration. It seemed as if a new life had started in Russia....

So new directions and literary trends appeared during these last seven years. The most recent trends then were those of *Time*, and it was founded by Fyodor Mikhailovich. He considered it to be a new direction which corresponded to the changes taking place in Russia; it was connected with the two parties, the Westernizers and the Slavophiles. He was not completely positive about this thought; he was afraid of it, and he wanted to develop it....

He thought that the previous literary movements—that is, Western-izers and Slavophiles—were exhausted and that something new was going to appear. Before, there were no parties, and literature was something homogeneous. I remember the feeling of friendship which existed between different writers then. We all supported education, freedom of expression ... we were for the most general, liberal freedoms....

Anyway, in the yearly announcement about *Time* subscriptions, it was written [by Dostoevsky] that both the Slavophiles and the Westernizers belonged to the past, and that we had to start something new....

Then there appeared a new literary party which became known in St. Petersburg literary circles as "The Soil." Fyodor Mikhailovich's favorite expressions were "we have departed from our soil" and "we must seek our soil," and he used them in his first articles.

The Dostoevsky brothers were the children of St. Petersburg literature. We must remember this when we discuss their literary preferences, literary devices and their views.... The Dostoevsky brothers made many efforts to make their journal interesting and to improve the circulation.

Illness and the Writer's Work

Fyodor Mikhailovich started to work with great energy. In the first issue he published his novel *Oppressed and Humiliated,* and he also worked in the literary criticism section, starting it with "A Series of Articles on Russian Literature. An Introduction." Besides this, he participated in the other sections of the journal, in setting up new issues and in the selection of new articles....

Fyodor Mikhailovich could not stand such hard work, and he fell ill after this third month.... In the April issue of *Time,* instead of five or six signatures, only eighteen pages of his novel were published. The editor wrote about the author's illness. This illness was a terrible fit of epilepsy, after which he remained unconscious for three days.

I remember our alarm, though his epilepsy for a long time had been general knowledge.

This was the price he had to pay for his literary work. Further on, I found out that doctors told him that he could be cured from epilepsy if he stopped writing. But this was impossible for him to do. He could not live such a life, he could not live without fulfilling his destiny, what he thought to be the main meaning of his life....

Usually, he had a fit of illness once a month, but sometimes he had fits more often, even twice a week. While living abroad, with a quieter lifestyle and in a better climate, he could go four months without any traces of his illness. He could foresee his fits, though it was not always clear. In the novel *The Idiot*, there is a detailed description of the feelings which a patient with such an illness experiences.

Once, I was one of the witnesses of such an event.... It was in 1863, just before the Bright Sunday [a Russian religious holiday]. Late at night, at 11 P.M., he visited me, and we talked. I do not remember the subject of our conversation, but I remember that it was an important philosophical issue. Fyodor Mikhailovich was very much involved in it, he was talking and walking across the room here and there, and I was sitting at the table. He was talking about something important, elevated and joyful. When I wanted to support his thought by my remark, he turned to me with an inspired face which showed that he was excited by the subject to the greatest extent. He stood for a second without movement, as if he were looking for better words to express this thought; he even opened his mouth to speak. I looked at him tense with attention, I felt that he was going to tell me something unusual, that there would be some sort of revelation, but, suddenly, I heard a senseless sound, a long howl from his mouth, and he fell on the floor unconscious, in the middle of the room. This fit of illness was not actually very strong. He trembled, his whole body beat with the convulsions, and, in the corner of his mouth, there appeared flakes of foam. In half an hour he felt better, he became conscious, and I saw him to his home. It was not very far.

Fyodor Mikhailovich told me many times that before a fit of illness he reached an elevated state.... "For several moments," he said, "I feel a happiness, which is not possible in a usual state, and usual people cannot understand it. I feel completely at harmony with myself, and with the whole world, and this feeling is so strong, and so sweet. You feel such bliss that for these several seconds you could give ten years of your life, or even your whole life."

It was clear that it was harmful for Fyodor Mikhailovich to be engaged in any activity which brought blood to his head. Certainly, mostly it was his writing. This was one of the tortures he had to suffer and which other writers suffer. The happiness of creative, artistic pleasure has another side and very few people can avoid the suffering.... If you fly very high, it hurts when you fall....

I would like to comment on his manner of writing. Fyodor Mikhailovich himself talked about this.... Usually he was in a hurry. He had to write to the deadline. He had to write quickly, and sometimes he was late.... The reason was that he lived only from the income from his literary work, and ... except for the last three or four years of his life, he was in great financial need. Consequently, he had to take money for his works in advance. He had to make promises, and he had to fulfill his obligations.... There was another thing which forced his hardships, and it was even more difficult. Fyodor Mikhailovich always postponed his work to the last day... He started to write only when there was very little time left, only when he had the amount of time which was enough to finish his piece by working hard. It was laziness, not the usual laziness, but the very special "laziness of a writer" and this I saw very clearly in Fyodor Mikhailovich. The thing was that all the time he had inner work going on. It was growing, his thoughts were developing, and it was difficult for him to interrupt this inner work and to start writing. He looked lazy, but at the same time he was working very hard. People who do not have this inner work are usually bored without some type of mechanical, outside work, the type of work you can see, and they like this mechanical work.

Fyodor Mikhailovich had so many thoughts and emotions in his head that he was never bored, and he liked this kind of work. His thoughts were boiling, they were changing, new images were developing all the time; the plots of new works and all his plans were constantly growing and developing in his imagination.

He wrote these autobiographical lines on the first pages of *The Oppressed and Humiliated*: "By the way, I always want to think my work over, to dream about it. It is more pleasant than writing it, and this happens not because I am lazy, but why?" ... He wrote late at night. Around midnight, when the whole house went to bed, he stayed alone, with his samovar, drinking not very strong, but almost cold tea, and writing until five or six o'clock in the morning. He got up around two or three o'clock in the afternoon. He received his guests, took a walk, and visited some of his friends.

You could see, looking at Fyodor Mikhailovich, that writing was a very serious and hard activity for him, especially for such a writer as he was.... Readers sometimes think that it is very easy for talented people to write, and they are misguided when they see how simple it is to follow a piece of poetry or prose. But these readers are wrong as to the estimate of the author's input....

His plans and his thoughts developed without stopping; it was a continuous process. He could have several topics developing in his head at the same time, and he wanted to finish them, to bring them to perfection, maybe in the future, when he would have more time. He was writing and writing his raw works and notes. On the one side, he had to survive on this, to find some means to live; on the other side, he had to show his voice to the reading audience and to disturb it with his thoughts....

Fyodor Mikhailovich liked journalism, and he worked in journals with the clear understanding that he sacrificed his higher art, his time and his thought. In his youth he was close to journalism, and he had this serious attachment to it to his life's end.... Literature was a sphere of work for Fyodor Mikhailovich; he had chosen it as his profession, and he was proud of this. He worked hard, and he achieved what he wanted...

Time enjoyed a very quick and definite success. I remember the important figures of the subscribers. In the first year, 1861, we had 2,300 subscribers, and Mikhail Mikhailovich said that he could balance the budget. In the second year we had 4,302 subscribers ... it was a very profitable journal starting from the second year....

The reason for *Time*'s great success was the famous name of Fyodor Mikhailovich; the story of his imprisonment was well known to everybody, and it increased his popularity. "My name is worth a million," he once said with pride in Switzerland. There was a second reason for this: a wonderful (with all its drawbacks) novel, *Oppressed and Humiliated*, a reward for the subscribers attracted by the famous name of its author. As Dobrolubov wrote, this novel was the most important event in literature in 1861....

Our conversations were endless, and they were the best conversations I had ever had in my life. He spoke in that simple, quick and understandable speech which is the beauty of the Russian language. He liked jokes, especially at the time....

The most important thing which I liked was that he had an unusual way of thinking, very quick, and he could pick up on any thought; one word or one hint was enough. This quick understanding of things was the great beauty of talking to him.... I remember these endless talks, and I am proud to have had them. The main subject was, certainly, journalistic activity, but, besides this, we talked about many other topics, sometimes philosophical. Fyodor Mikhailovich liked these conversations about the essence of things, about the limits of our knowledge. I remember he liked when I tried to connect his views with the views of famous philosophers. He would joke, "It turns out that it is difficult to create something new." And he was glad to agree with one or another famous philosopher....

He was one of the most sincere novel writers, and everything he wrote he had felt and experienced before, with great passion. Dostoevsky is among the most objective novel writers, and he created all his images according to his own life experience....

Sometimes I was afraid for his health when reading descriptions of his own dark mood or feeling. Sometimes, for example in *The Idiot*, he described the seizures of epilepsy. In fact, doctors recommend that people with epilepsy not dwell on these remembrances, because they can bring on another fit; they also should not, for example, watch some other person having a fit. But Dostoevsky did not stop at this, and he wanted to describe everything; he believed that everything he depicted must be true, and must be experienced by him. He knew that he created a reality, an objective reality, in his works.

He thought about himself as a complete realist. Crimes, suicides, inner perversions and other extremities on which many of his works are based were for him part of everyday, routine life, and he tried to describe these darkest pictures. Nobody went further than Dostoevsky in the depiction of the dark side of the human soul....

Dostoevsky showed the terrible inner wounds and he said that he could make final judgments about such things. He saw the light of God in the most fallen and perverted person; he wanted the smallest sparks of this light, and he saw the features of inner beauty in those events for which these people were despised. He excused people and he loved them, because every person has such a light given from God, though, sometimes, this light can be hidden under a terrible appearance. I can say that he wrote his works with the same light.... I can testify that he wrote his works with the blood of his heart.

Andrei Dostoevsky: A Visit to Fyodor Dostoevsky in St. Petersburg

(From A.M. Dostoevsky, *Vospominaniia* [*Memoirs*]. Leningrad: Izdatelstvo pisatelei v Leningrade, 1930, pp. 305–329.)

At the party at the Golenovskys', I met my brother, Nikolai Mikhailovich. He had already lost his job, and lived in a small wing of my sister's house.... It was very sad to see him in this state. He was still a young man, but he had fallen so low! His hands trembled, and he moved and walked like a very sick man. My poor brother, this was the result of his addiction [to alcohol]....

In the evening, around 7 P.M., we took two horse cabs, and we went to visit Emilia Fyodorovna. I introduced my wife and my family to her, and my brother soon arrived from his office at the publishing house. The last time I had seen him was more than fifteen and a half years previously, after I met him in the White Room of the Third Section of the Police.

Our meeting was very touching and friendly. My brother sat with us a little, and then went to his study where he worked for rather a long time. Late in the evening, he returned to the living room, and we spent the rest of the night together, in a very pleasant way....

New Year's Eve passed in a very lively atmosphere. My brother Fyodor was in an excellent mood, as were all the others. We returned home late, after midnight, as we usually did on New Year's Eve....

My brother Fyodor visited me once before New Year's Eve; he came to the hotel room where I was staying. I visited him on 6 January, to say goodbye, and he promised to return my visit on the evening of the same day. My wife and I wanted to bid him farewell, because we were leaving St. Petersburg on 7 January. I bought a bottle of champagne, cakes, and fruit for the evening. Incidentally, champagne was much cheaper then; I bought one bottle of Rederer for only three roubles. My brother arrived at 8 P.M. After the usual tea, we had a lengthy conversation. We had a bottle of champagne and we sat talking until three o'clock in the morning. My brother was very pleasant, and he talked to me at great length.

By the way, he told me how *Time* magazine came to be closed by the authorities. Here is his story, which I remember vividly.

In the April 1863 issue of *Time*, an article entitled "A Fatal Issue" by N. Strakhov was published. It was a patriotic article. There was no reason whatsoever why this article should have caused the journal to be suppressed, not merely for a period of time, but forever!

This article was misunderstood in Moscow. They viewed it as being too progressive and inflammatory, and all of the Moscow press, led by *The Moscow News*, considered it to be inappropriate to the political situation of the time, especially after a rebellion in Poland. All this gave the Moscow press a pretext to speak about the "pro–Polish" position of *Time*.

At the same time, Mr. Ofrosimov, the governor-general of Moscow, was involved in a busy correspondence with the Tsar. In one of his letters he, as a loyal Imperial subject, reported to the Emperor, "All Moscow is excited by the article 'A Fatal Issue,' published in *Time*, a St. Petersburg periodical."

Mr. Valuev [an Imperial minister] at the time did not suspect anything, and went to deliver a regular, routine report to Tsarskoe Selo ["Tsar's Village"], the Emperor's summer residence in the suburbs of St. Petersburg]. In the train, on his way to the Tsar, he met one of the senior Moscow officials. The Moscovite told him that all of Moscow was discussing the article "A Fatal Issue." Valuev replied that it was all nonsense, that the article was loyal to the regime, that it had been read by the censor and cleared for publication. He added that people in Moscow tend to exaggerate things, just in order to make some noise. They parted and Mr. Valuev went to his appointment with the Tsar.

After Mr. Valuev finished his report, the Emperor suddenly asked him: "What kind of article is this, 'A Fatal Issue'? All of Moscow is indignant about it!" Valuev quickly found a suitable answer: "*Time* journal is closed, Your Majesty." He was, however, very surprised that the Tsar should have heard anything about this article.

Immediately on his return to St. Petersburg, Valuev issued an order to close *Time* and he backdated this order. "He behaved not like Valuev, but like Valiaev [in Russian, "a sneak"], and we conferred this new name upon him," added Fyodor Mikhailovich.

I was parted from my brother for a very long time. I met him again only in September 1872, when I visited St. Petersburg on business. At the time, my brother was again a married man. When we parted, I gave him 16 roubles for an annual subscription to *Epoch*, but I received only two issues....

The huge estate of our aunt, Ms. Kumanina, according to the terms of her last will and testament, was divided into sums of 10–15,000 roubles, for each member of the large Dostoevsky family....

At last, I received an official letter from Veselovsky, confirming that my brother and I were both appointed trustees for the estate of A. Kumanina.... I went to Moscow and acquainted myself with the provisions of the will. All of my brothers had previously received about 20,000 roubles each, and they were excluded from the list of heirs....

Maria Ivanova: Remembrances About Dostoevsky in the Summer of 1866

(From M.A. Ivanova, *Vospominaniia* [*Memoirs*], in V. Nechaeva, "Iz literatury o Dostoevskom. Poezdka v Darovoe." ["From the Literature About Dostoevsky. A Visit to Darovoe Village,"] *Novyi Mir* [*New Times*], 14 February 1893: 12.)

F.M. Dostoevsky spent the summer of 1866 in Liublino, with the Ivanov family.... He needed complete silence for his literary work. He usually worked late at night and it was too noisy for him at the Ivanovs' summer cottage. There was either a child crying, a young person coming home late at night after a party, or people getting up early in the morning to go fishing. Therefore, Dostoevsky rented a room in an empty two-story brick house nearby. We were afraid to leave him alone during the night, because we knew about his epileptic fits. That is why the Ivanovs sent a servant to stay with him at night....

One night this servant refused to go back to Dostoevsky's room again. When the Ivanovs asked him why, he said that Dostoevsky was planning to kill someone. Throughout the night, Dostoevsky walked around the rooms of this empty house speaking loudly about the murder. (At this time Dostoevsky was writing *Crime and Punishment*.)

Dostoevsky spent days and evenings with the young people. Although

he was forty-five years old, he behaved very simply among the young people and he took an active part in many games and other forms of entertainment.

He looked younger than his age. He was always neatly dressed, usually wearing a white shirt, grey trousers and a loose blue jacket. Dostoevsky always paid great attention to his appearance. A few details upset
him; for example, his beard being too thin. His young nieces used to kid
him about this and sometimes said to him, "Hey, you little beard."

In spite of his kindness and his close friendship with children, Dostoevsky liked to notice weak or funny features or habits of other people
present and had great fun making jokes about his victims. The youth
answered him jokingly and they had a lot of fun together. The funniest
time was lunchtime. Lunch was served on a big table, about nine arshines
[1 arshine = 28 inches] long, on the Ivanovs' backyard terrace. The table
was so big that more than twenty people could sit at it at the same time.
The elder members of the Ivanov family sat on one side of the table with
Fyodor Mikhailovich; on the other side the young people sat.

Suddenly, from his end of the table, Dostoevsky addressed Nadya
Alexeeva, our young and humble friend, with the following remark:
"Nadya, aren't you ashamed that you are constantly disturbing me by
pressing your leg against mine under the table?"

Nadya blushed, she was confused, but her friend, Iulia Ivanovna, ener-
getically defended her: "You are considered to be a clever man, but you
cannot understand that Nadya's foot can't be ten arshines long and she
can't reach you under the table. This comment of yours is a sign of your
stupidity."

The elder members of the family wanted to interrupt our exchange.
They asked a question about where the whole company was going to go
after lunch, and we were all distracted from further discussion.

The best time was after supper, when we played or went out for a
walk, usually until two or three o'clock in the morning. We used to go
to Kuzminki or Tsaritsyno [two neighboring villages]. Our neighbors,
who also spent summers here in Liublino, often joined our company.

Fyodor Mikhailovich played a key role in all our games and entertainment. Sometimes he left the company in the middle of a game and
went to his cottage to write down something for his novel. In such cases
he often asked us to come and call him in ten minutes, but if someone
was sent after him, they found him so deeply immersed in his work that
he got angry at being interrupted and sent all the visitors away. After
some time he would return, joyful again and ready to continue the game.
He did not like to talk about his work.

At the Ivanovs they liked to play "the proverb game." Fyodor Mikhailovich was usually given the most difficult word puzzle. He would quickly

create a lengthy story in response, two or three pages long, and it would be impossible to make the right guess and to find out the original word. At night he used to tell us horror stories that he had just imagined, and we became scared. Once he asked us to do an experiment: to sit in front of the mirror in an empty room for about five minutes, looking at your own reflection, straight in the eye. He said that it was very difficult to do this....

Dostoevsky could easily fall in love. He liked Maria Sergeevna Ivanchina-Pisareva, a friend of Sofia Alexandrovna Ivanova. She was a quick, lively young lady. Once, when he visited the Ivanovs during Easter, he did not go to the morning church service, but stayed at home at the Inavovs'....

When Sofia Alexandrovna returned home from church, her girlfriend was laughing; she told her that Dostoevsky had just proposed to her. She was twenty years old and it was funny for her to hear this proposal from such an elderly person as she thought Dostoevsky to be. She rejected his proposal and answered him jokingly with Pushkin's verses [from "Poltava"]

> The old man's heart turned into stone with years,
> But now again it's burning with fire...

Dostoevsky had some unexplainable strange sympathies, or, on the contrary, dislikes, to the people he met. For example, he disliked one good man, Vasily Khiristoforovich Smirnov, the husband of Maria Petrovna Karepina, Dostoevsky's niece. He imagined that this man was a drunkard, and everywhere left notes such as "Smirnov was here and drank lots of vodka" [Smirnoff being the name of a Russian beverage factory and of a popular brand of Russian vodka]. Dostoevsky's behavior brought on a quarrel with the Smirnovs. Dostoevsky wanted to depict this man as Luzhin in *Crime and Punishment*. He often made mistakes in his judgments about other people, though. With special love he spoke about his brother Mikhail.

Dostoevsky told the Ivanovs about his close friendship with the royal family; it was a friendship free from the rules of etiquette. He characterized the heir and the younger generation of the royal family as rather nice but poorly educated people. He said that the Tsarina behaved as a typical female university student. Once he spoke with her for a long time, and she burst out in tears after their discussion. On another occasion, he had been so involved in the conversation that he had not noticed how, during all this time, he had been holding in his fingers one of the buttons of her dress. Dostoevsky participated as an actor in the amateur stage performances produced for the entertainment of the royal family. Once it was *Boris Godunov* [by Pushkin] and he played Pimen, the monk writer. He was in a hurry to the winter palace for the rehearsal....

Nikolai Fon-Fokht: Dostoevsky's Writing
Crime and Punishment

(From N. Fon-Fokht, "K biografii Dostoevskogo" ["Some Materials for Dostoevsky Biography"], *Istoricheskii Vestnik* [*The History Herald*] 12 [1901]: 1023–1033.)

I got to know Dostoevsky early in 1866, when I was only fifteen years old.... In the month of May, the Ivanovs moved to their summer cottage. Soon afterwards Dostoevsky arrived and rented a separate two-story brick house that was close to that of the Ivanovs. In fact, he occupied only one big room on the upper floor which served both as his sleeping room and as his study. All the other rooms were empty, so the house was completely silent. This was good for Dostoevsky who, at that time, was working on the second part of his famous novel *Crime and Punishment*.

Usually Dostoevsky got up at around nine o'clock in the morning, and, after a cup of tea or coffee, sat down to his literary work until lunchtime, that is, about three in the afternoon. He lunched at the Ivanovs, where he usually stayed until late in the evening. It would seem that Fyodor Mikhailovich wrote late at night very seldom, though he said that his best and most expressive pages were those which he wrote during the night hours. His doctors had forbidden him to write at night, because it shattered his weak nerves. It is known that Dostoevsky suffered from fits of epilepsy which he acquired during his imprisonment in Siberia....

Dostoevsky spoke quietly and slowly, he was always concentrating and you could see that he was engaged in great intellectual work. His small grey eyes almost pierced his listeners. These eyes were usually kind, but sometimes they were lit with some hidden, cold glow, especially in the moments when he spoke about things that excited him. But this expression quickly disappeared, and again his eyes looked at you quietly and kindly.

Every time he spoke, there was something mysterious in his speech; it looked as if he wanted to say something direct and straight, but then he suddenly was hiding his thoughts from other people. Sometimes he told us some fantastic stories, or created strange situations which his listeners remembered for a long time. One of A.P. Ivanov's daughters was a grown-up young lady and a good musician, but she was scared of everything. Fyodor Mikhailovich knew this, and on purpose, he told her some terrible fantastic stories after which poor Maria Alexandrovna could not fall asleep for a long time. Fyodor Mikhailovich was very much entertained by this.

He never spoke about his stay in prison or about his life in Siberia. It was something he did not like to talk about. Everybody knew this, so nobody tried to start a conversation on the subject. Only once, when we were having a cup of tea in the morning, did I hear from Fyodor Mikhailovich a brief story about the New Testament that was always on his writing table. I had been surprised to note that the leather cover pages of this old book were cut at the edges. In answer to my question about the origin of these cuts, Dostoevsky explained that as he was leaving for Siberia, his relatives blessed him and gave him this book, and inside of the leather cover there was hidden some money. The prisoners were not allowed to have money. His relatives' smart thinking helped him survive at first while in Siberian prison.

"Yes, you know," said Fyodor Mikhailovich, "money is freedom which is printed on paper...."

Dostoevsky never parted with this New Testament for the rest of his life; it was always with him, on his writing table.

Nikolai Chernyshevsky: Dostoevsky Wanted to Stop the Revolutionary Terror in Russia

(From N.G. Chernyshevsky, "Moi svidaniia s Dostoevskim" ["My Meetings with Dostoevsky"], in N.G. Chernyshevsky, *Polnoe sobranie sochinenii* [*Complete Works*], Vol. 1. Moscow: Goslitizdat, 1939, pp. 777–779.)

Several days had passed since the fire which destroyed the City Market Place [terrorist acts in St. Petersburg were actually inspired by N. Chernyshevski during May 1962]. One day my servant handed me F.M. Dostoevsky's card, saying that there was a caller who wanted to talk to me. I immediately went down to the lobby to meet the visitor.

There I saw a short man waiting for me. His face looked familiar for I had seen it before in pictures. I went to him and offered him a seat on the sofa, saying that it was a pleasure for me to meet the author of *Poor People*. After several seconds of hesitation, he explained to me, without preamble, and in a tense and businesslike manner, the purpose of his visit. He said something like, "I have come to you with a serious personal request. You are well acquainted with the people who set the Market Place on fire, and you have a certain influence over them. I beg you, please, stop them from doing anything of this sort again."

I had heard before that Dostoevsky had an unbalanced nervous system and that he could easily get out of control, coming close to madness, but I did not know that he was so ill. How could he connect these fires at the Market Place with my name? When I saw that he was on the point of a nervous breakdown, I decided that doctors would probably not recommend that he become involved in any sort of heated discussion, and, in order to calm him down, I answered: "All right, Fyodor Mikhailovich, I will do as you wish."

He grasped my hand with gratitude and shook it as strongly as he could, uttering words of admiration and thanks in a very excited voice. He said that he was very grateful to me for saving St. Petersburg from new fires which could completely destroy the city.... I asked him about his journal....

He changed the topic while answering my question, and he forgot about everything we had just discussed. I let him speak as long as he wanted, which was a long time, perhaps two hours. I barely listened to him, but I pretended that I was listening attentively. Finally, he grew tired, looked at his watch, and remembered that he had been sitting here too long. He said that he was in a hurry to read the proofs of his journal and soon afterwards left.

Pyotr Veinberg: Dostoevsky During the Day of the First Assassination Attempt on the Tsar

(From P.I. Veinberg, "4-je aprelia 1866 goda. Iz moikh vospominanii." ["The Fourth of April, 1866. From My Memoirs"] *Byloe* [*The Past*] 4 [1906]: 299–300.)

On the fourth of April 1866, I paid a brief visit to the poet Apollon Maikov. Although we held entirely different political views, I truly admired him as a great poet and as a real artist....

On the day in question, we were peacefully discussing some literary questions when Fyodor Mikhailovich Dostoevsky simply rushed into the room. He was terribly pale, his face was extremely agitated, and he was trembling as if he had a fever. "Someone shot at the Tsar!" he shouted without any greeting, his voice halting because he was out of breath and shaking with excitement. We leaped from our seats. "Has he been killed?" cried Maikov in a wild, inhuman voice, which I remember very well. "No, he has been saved ... All is well now ... But they shot, they shot ... shot," and, repeating this word, Dostoevsky fell on the sofa, close to hysteria.

We waited a little, until Dostoevsky calmed down, and then waited for Maikov to recover, since he was close to fainting at this point. Then the three of us ran out into the street. At present our people are used to the series of assassination attempts, but you couldn't possibly imagine what went on in St. Petersburg the night of 4 April 1866 after the first shot was fired at the Tsar. It was the first shooting of its kind that had ever happened in Russia. Everyone ran out into the streets. There was a huge mess of people. Everyone was running somewhere, with most of the people hurrying to the Winter Palace. You could hear people here and there screaming, "Karakozov! Komissarov!" reviling the first and praising the second [the names, respectively, of the assassin and the officer who saved the Emperor]. Groups of people were singing "God Save the Tsar!" Several orchestras which had been thrown together were playing the national anthem....

I parted from Maikov and Dostoevsky quickly. They mingled with a huge crowd, and we lost each other. The next day, I found out that Maikov had a patriotic inspiration and had hurried home to write a poem dedicated to the event....

Pyotr Veinberg: Literary Spectacles with Dostoevsky as an Actor

(From P.I. Veinberg, "Literaturnye spektakli" Iz moikh vospominanii" ["Literary Spectacles. From My Memoirs"] in *Ezhegodnik Imperatorshikh Teatrov* [*Annual Review of Russian Royal Theaters*] Vol. 3, 1893– 1894, pp. 96–107.)

The Society for the Support of Writers and Scholars in Need, also known as the Literary Fund, commenced its activity in 1860. Literary artists were making a real difference at the time. They were highly respected and well treated by society, and for good reason: in our group were writers such as Nekrasov, Maikov, Goncharov, Grigorovich, Turgenev, Dostoevsky, Derzhavin, Pisemsky....

I remember that as soon as the Society was founded, we held a literary evening for charitable purposes.... The theater completely sold out. It was virtually packed with people, and the crowd burst out in a storm of cheers and ovations when they welcomed the reading of each literary artist....

I became a member of the board of the Literary Fund at the very outset of its existence. The activity and the purpose of this organization were things with which I sympathized ardently. Since I knew that society, as well as our literary artists, supported the fund, I decided, with the participation of our writers, to stage an amateur theatrical production....

It was important to invite our so-called "great writers," and most of them agreed to participate to some extent in this enterprise. Several people even agreed to play principal parts in the performance. But most of the writers were not professional actors, had not acted on stage before, and did not have the courage to make a new start in this field....

The only famous writer who agreed to take an active part in the production of the play was Fyodor Mikhailovich Dostoevsky, who had recently returned to St. Petersburg [from prison and exile]. Not only did he agree to appear briefly on stage, as most writers did, but he also expressed his complete willingness to play a major role.

"This is a good thing to do, I tell you, this is a very important thing to do," he told me, his voice full of joy. While I was making all the necessary arrangements, he visited me several times, in order to find out whether everything was all right.

It goes without saying that both Pisemsky, my adviser and associate, and I myself gave Fyodor Mikhailovich complete freedom in choosing the kind of role he wanted to perform. Without any hesitation, he agreed to play the role of Shchepkin, the post office director [from *The Inspector-General* by N. Gogol].

He said: "This is one of the most comical images not only in Gogol's works, but in all of Russian literature, and, besides, it has social significance.... I do not know whether I can handle this role properly, but I will do the very best I can by putting into it my love...."

So, it was decided that Dostoevsky would play the postal officer. But what about the other writers? And, most importantly, how could other big writers be involved? Without their participation, the effect of the performance, as I saw it, would be much weaker.

Therefore, I decided to include them all into a silent delegation of tradesmen and merchants who came to visit Khlestakov and the Major. They all agreed to this, so I had a very impressive company: Turgenev, Grigorovich, Maikov, Druzhinin, Kraevsky, and Vasily Kurochkin! One cannot imagine the joy of a producer who has such people in his cast! ...

The theater lovers of St. Petersburg already knew Dostoevsky as a good literary elocutionist who could give superb readings of his own literary works. Here, Dostoevsky also displayed a great gift for acting. I think that no one who knew Fyodor Mikhailovich during the last years of his life could have imagined him as a good comic actor. Yet, he was not merely an actor, but a very good one, who could make the audience laugh in a very Gogolean manner. In fact, Dostoevsky-Shchepkin was an actor above reproach....

After one rehearsal, namely, after the official breakfast at the Major's house, Dostoevsky was especially satisfied: "This is Khlestakov! He is both a tragic and a comic figure!" he said in all seriousness, and, after he noticed a puzzled expression on the faces of the people present at the rehearsal, he exclaimed: "Yes, yes, it is tragic as well ... 'Tragic' is surely the right word here." Many years afterwards, Fyodor Mikhailovich recalled this scene to me saying that it should be staged exactly the way we did it... Our rehearsals proceeded well, and two days before the performance, we put up a poster....

Need I say that it was truly sensational? It was an unusual event not only for St. Petersburg, but for all of Russia. My position as cashier at the event became a most unpleasant one. We were faced with many demands, all sorts of people wanting to make reservations, ranging from the highest ranking officials, statesmen, and nobility to junior office clerks and civil servants. The doors of my apartment were not closed for a minute, and the person I hired to distribute tickets was completely at a loss, having more work than he could cope with. Even if the hall could have taken three times the viewers, the tickets would have been sold out well in advance of the show.

The performance was held as scheduled. The theater hall was simply packed with people; every space, from the stage to the back wall, was filled with chairs, and every seat was occupied. Every more or less important person, everyone interested in the literary and artistic world of St. Petersburg was there. Grand Prince Konstantin Nikolaevich Romanov and several senior officers were seated in the first row....

At the very beginning of the performance, just as the curtain rose, revealing Pisemsky, the audience burst into applause which lasted for several minutes. Dostoevsky received the same warm welcome.... One can hardly describe the applause and enthusiasm with which the theater audience greeted the group of famous professional writers when they appeared on stage. I have rarely ever heard such a loud and lengthy applause in my life, even when the best actors have appeared on stage. The applause lasted so long that I, who played Khlestakov [a principal character] meeting the delegation of merchants, had to go aside, sit down, and wait for a long time until the ovation stopped.

There was good reason for this applause. For example, the character played by Turgenev was the first to attract everybody's attention. He had a pince-nez on his nose, held a big sugarloaf in order to bribe the Mayor, and was dressed in a huge, long uniform.... The applause lasted for a long time and the people shouted: "Thank you!"

Evgeny Opochinin: How Dostoevsky Took Plots of His Novels from Real Life

(From E.N. Opochinin, "Besedy s Dostoevskim" ["Talking to Dostoevsky"], *Zvenia* [*Chains*] Moscow, 1936, Vol. 6, pp. 457–484.)

Most of Dostoevsky's works have criminal plots, which he derived from real life....

Fyodor Mikhailovich told me a story about a murderer he met in a Siberian prison.... A robber killed an old man who was just walking along a quiet village road, close to Barnaul. The killer told Dostoevsky that "the old man did not even stir a hand" when he was slaughtered. He simply fell down after the first stroke, as if he were a rotten tree trunk. The murderer explained: "So, I got the old man and then I took all his money, about two roubles [the equivalent of a few dollars], and then I went away. But then I remembered that the old man had been slaughtered like a calf. I had killed him with my knife—and he had been so calm and quiet, that I became angry at him and went back.... I saw him lying there quietly, face down and motionless. I did not have much to do there, so I just spat on the old man several times, simply because I was mad at him."

Fyodor Mikhailovich finished his speech by saying that the most difficult thing for a man is "to confess to himself what he has done." And such a confession, such an understanding of what he has done, is the first step in repenting his sins before God. "You cannot find peace, either with yourself or with God, until you do this."

Another time I met him, Fyodor Mikhailovich spoke about sexual differences. He spoke about this with such excitement and was so absorbed in his speech, that I understood that he was intensely interested in the subject. I will not relate everything here, it would be too indiscreet....

Among other things, he said: "In the man-woman relationship, there is always one who suffers, someone who is abused. This is especially true when it happens between two young people ... either an honest man meets a dishonest, dirty woman, and smears himself with this filth; or a bad man, a scoundrel, a sophisticated and mean person meets a young, innocent woman with a pure soul, and abuses her.

"Well, sometimes one cannot do much about it. One can't help it. A beautiful flower can be immersed in mud. And what really scares me is that this happens all the time, everywhere in life. And do you know that even a prostitute, yes, the cheapest prostitute, can be abused by a man very easily, because men have a more sophisticated mind in this respect."

Chapter 6. Three Love Stories in the 1860s, in Russia and Abroad

"...Then he struck her again and yet again, with all his strength, always with the blunt side of the axe, and always on the crown of the head. Blood poured out as if from an overturned glass and the body toppled over on its back. He stepped away as it fell, and then stooped to see the face: she was dead. ... The blow fell on her skull, splitting it open from the top of the forehead almost to the crown of the head, and felling her instantly."

(*Crime and Punishment*)

"There were moments ... I would have gladly given half of my life for the pleasure of strangling her! I swear that if I had a chance to bury a sharp knife slowly in her breast, I probably could have reached for that knife with great pleasure.... But she told me to play roulette and make money."

(*The Gambler*)

I N ST. PETERSBURG DOSTOEVSKY, who was 41 at the time, secretly met with a 22-year-old student named Polina Suslova, an admirer, a beginning writer, and a passionate lover. It was his obsession with this woman that led him to leave his first wife, Maria, who was dying from tuberculosis, to take his second trip abroad to Western Europe.

In Paris, in August 1863, Dostoevsky again secretly met with Polina, with whom he was already deeply in love. Later she became the prototype for many of his characters, including Dunia, Raskolnikov's sister in *Crime and Punishment*; Aglaia in *The Idiot*; Liza Drozdova in *The Demons*; Akhmakova in *The Raw Youth*; and, definitely, Katerina Ivanovna in *The Brothers Karamazov*. Polina tortured him constantly, being a hot-tempered and selfish young woman. He described her as "a big egoist. Her most prominent features are egoism and selfishness. She asks for everything, for absolute perfection from people.... I still love her, but I do not want to love her any more. She doesn't deserve this love...." (*Complete Works*, Vol. 28, part 2, p. 121).

Most of Dostoevsky's books are based on real stories: either they are autobiographical, such as *The Gambler*, telling a story of his gambling and his love for Polina Suslova; or they reflect the most famous criminal cases of the time, such as *Crime and Punishment*, one of the most renowned novels in world literature, which depicts the psychology of a killer.

During the trip abroad with Polina Suslova, Dostoevsky developed a passion for roulette which would return to plague him later in his life. In Baden-Baden, he played roulette and "lost absolutely everything." As he wrote in one of his letters to Russia, "I go to the bottom line in everything, and throughout my entire life, I have crossed this bottom line" (*Complete Works*, Vol. 28, part 2, p. 207). In October 1863, he returned to Russia to his mortally sick wife, with whom he lived for about a month in Vladimir, and then until April 1864 in Moscow. Maria died from tuberculosis on April 15, 1864.

His brother Mikhail was the first person whom Dostoevsky informed of her death: "My dear brother, at seven o'clock, Maria Dostoevsky died and wished us all a long and happy life (these were her last words)" (*Complete Works*, Vol. 28, part 2, p. 92).

Dostoevsky's relationship with his first wife had been both passionate and complicated. As he wrote, "Because of her strange, suspicious and fantastic character, we were definitely not happy together, but we could not stop loving each other; and the more unhappy we were, the more attached to each other we became" (*Complete Works*, Vol. 28, part 2, p. 116).

Not long after the death of his wife, Dostoevsky lost his brother, Mikhail who died on July 10, 1864. In a letter to his younger brother Andrei, Dostoevsky wrote, "This man loved me more than anything in the world." After Mikhail's death, Dostoevsky assumed the burden of both paying off his deceased brother's debts and supporting his family, as he wrote to Chumikov on January 13, 1865: "After my brother died, he left a journal.... Notwithstanding all his debts, both I and she [the brother's wife] decided to pay them *all* back" (*Complete Works*, Vol. 28, part 2, p. 110).

As a consequence of this decision, Dostoevsky was short of money for many years, a situation which caused him a great deal of stress and took its toll on his health. On March 31, 1865, Dostoevsky wrote to his friend Vrangel, "So, I am left alone, suddenly, and I am scared. My whole life has been broken into two pieces... I feel coldness and emptiness around me" (*Complete Works*, Vol. 28, part 2, pp. 116–17).

Dostoevsky tried to continue *Epoch*, the journal he and Mikhail had begun in 1864, but sagging subscriptions in 1865 forced him to close the journal. This was a difficult period for Dostoevsky. He was in his middle forties and he was alone, without his wife and without Polina. In a small space of time he desperately proposed to several women.

One of these women was Anna Korvin-Krukovskaya, the daughter of General Vasily Korvin-Krukovsky, who had submitted several pieces to *Epoch* in 1864. Dostoevsky had accepted these stories and responded to them with words of encouragement. In the spring of 1865, Dostoevsky was a frequent visitor at the home of the General. Anna Dostoevskaya wrote in her memoirs that Dostoevsky and the young woman were engaged for several months. However, Anna's sister Sophia Korvin-Krukovskaya wrote in her memoirs that Dostoevsky received an immediate rejection. In any case, their different views on the role of women made them unsuitable marriage partners. Towards the end of July 1865, Dostoevsky went to Wiesbaden, Germany, where he wrote in a letter to his publisher Katkov about an idea for "a psychological report of a certain crime" which later became his famous novel *Crime and Punishment*.

Dostoevsky spent the summer of 1865 in Liublino at the summer cottage of his sister, Vera Ivanova, preparing *Crime and Punishment* for its publication in *The Russian Herald*. He wrote, "The murderer faces questions he cannot answer. Unexpected feelings torture his heart. God's truth, the law of the earth take their course, and the murderer is forced to report himself. He is forced to do this because it is better for him to die in prison, yet join humanity" (*Complete Works*, Vol. 28, part 2, p. 137).

Dostoevsky described many typical social characters of St. Petersburg of the time in *Crime and Punishment*. His major task was "to find the man within the man." He explained his motto in these words: "They call me a psychologist—this is not true; I am a realist in the highest meaning of this word, that is, I depict the deepest regions of a man's soul" (*Complete Works*, Vol. 27, p. 63). This psychological novel, based on a criminal plot, enjoyed a tremendous readership. In *The Fatherland Notes* (1867, no. 1) it was written, "The novel *Crime and Punishment*, by Dostoevsky, was without doubt the greatest literary event of our time."

In 1866, in the midst of his work on *Crime and Punishment*, Dostoevsky was forced by a deadline with his publisher to write a novel in thirty days. The result of his efforts was a book called *The Gambler*. Dostoevsky dedicated this novel to "a Russian abroad as compared to complete Europeans (French, British, Germans, etc.)." In it he partially depicted his own experience traveling abroad with his lover Polina Suslova in 1863. While writing *The Gambler*, Dostoevsky was so pressed for time that he hired a stenographer and dictated to her, for 25 days between October 4 and October 30, 1866, his experience of gambling abroad. In a letter to Polina Suslova dated April 23, 1867, Dostoevsky revealed that writing *The Gambler* brought an enormous and unexpected benefit: "My stenographer, Anna Grigorievna, was a very young and rather nice looking twenty-year-old woman with a kind heart. When we concluded work on the novel, I noticed that my stenographer loved me sincerely, though she never told me about it. I also liked her more and more.... I proposed to her and we got married" (*Complete Works*, Vol. 28, part 2, p. 182).

After marrying, the Dostoevskys traveled abroad for four years to escape creditors and to improve Fyodor's health. From mid–1867 to July 1871, they lived abroad in Berlin, Dresden, Prague, Milan and Florence. During this time, Dostoevsky worked on his novels *The Idiot*, *The Eternal Husband* and *The Demons*. In 1871 the couple made a firm decision to return to Russia.

Polina Suslova: The Years of My Intimacy with Dostoevsky

(From Polina Suslova, *Gody blizosti s Dostoevskim, Dnevnik* [*The Years of My Intimacy with Dostoevsky: A Diary*]. Moscow: Sabashnikov, 1928.)

August 19, 1863.
I just received a letter from Fyodor Mikhailovich. He will arrive in several days...

August 27, 1863.
As soon as I wrote these lines in my diary, Fyodor Mikhailovich arrived. I saw him through the window....
"I thought that you wouldn't come because I had written a letter to you," I said.
"Which letter?"
"The letter in which I asked you not to come here."
"Why?"
"Because it is all over."
He lowered his head, "I must know everything. Let us go somewhere

and you will tell me everything, otherwise I will die." I suggested going to his place....

When we entered his room, he fell on his knees at my feet and started to cry, to embrace and to press my knees, screaming: "I have lost you, I knew it!" A bit later he became more quiet, and he started to ask me who the man was. "He may be young, handsome and a good speaker. But, nevertheless, you will never find a heart as true as mine." I did not want to speak for a long time.

"Did you surrender to him completely?"

"Why do you ask this? It is not good to ask such things," I said.

"Oh, Polina, I do not know what is good and what is bad. Who is he: a Russian? A Frenchman? Is he my doctor? (The same one?)"

"No, no." I told him that I was deeply in love with this man.

"Are you happy?"

"No."

"How can this possibly be? You are in love and you are not happy. How can this be?"

"He does not love me."

"He does not love you!" he cried out, clutching his head with both his hands in despair. "But don't you love him as his slave? Please, tell me the truth. I want to know this. You would follow him to the ends of the earth, wouldn't you?"

"No, I ... I will go away to the countryside," I said, my eyes filled with tears.

"Oh, Polina, why are you so unhappy? This had to happen, you falling in love with another man. I knew it. You fell in love with me by mistake, because you are very sensitive and have a big heart. You have been waiting for [happiness for] twenty-three years. You are the only woman who does not ask for promises or the fulfillment of duties. This is what it means: a man and a woman are different. She takes, he gives."

When I told Fyodor Mikhailovich what kind of man he [Salvador, a Spanish student] was, he said that he felt disgust; but he felt that this was not a serious man, not a Lermontov [a famous Russian poet] type. We talked about many other things. He said that he was happy to have got to know someone like me. He asked that we remain friends, and that I write to him when I was very happy or unhappy. Then he asked me to follow him to Italy, and said that he would behave with me as a brother.

When I said that he would probably work on his novel most of the time, he replied: "Who do you think I am? Do you think you will have no effect on me?" I promised to visit him the next day. I felt better after I had spoken to him. He understood me. And I had not received a letter from Salvador....

I could not sleep all night and the next morning, at 7 A.M., I went to visit Dostoevsky. He was asleep when I came. After he opened the door, he went back to bed and covered himself with a blanket. He looked at me with both astonishment and fear. I was rather calm. I asked him to come to my place immediately. I wanted to tell him everything and to ask him to be my judge. I did not want to stay at his place, though, because I was waiting for Salvador.

A little later, when Fyodor Mikhailovich arrived at my house, I was having my breakfast and I met him at the door with a piece of bread in my hand.

"You see. Now I am calm," I said.

"Well, I am glad. But is there anyone who can understand you?" he said.

I started to tell him about my love affair [with the Spanish student Salvador] and my meeting the day before. Fyodor Mikhailovich said that I should take it easy, that I had got my hands dirty and that all this had happened quite by chance, and that Salvador was a young man who simply needed a lover. I just happened to come by, and he used me. Why wouldn't he use such a chance? A pretty woman who satisfies everybody's taste. Fyodor Mikhailovich was right. I understood this and agreed with him.

My travels with Fyodor Mikhailovich have been rather amusing. Yesterday he made a scene at the Vatican embassy while we were applying for our visas. All the way he spoke in verses. At least he found a hotel with two separate rooms and two beds.

He signed the hotel register as "An officer" and we laughed. He plays roulette all the time and behaves in a careless and casual way.

He told me that he had hope for our future, something he did not have before. I did not respond to this, but I knew that it was not to be. He was glad that I had agreed to leave Paris. He had not expected it. But one can't make too many plans and build hopes based on this.

Yesterday he was furious for a while. At 10 P.M. we had a cup of tea. I felt tired and went to bed. Then I asked him to move closer to me and to sit on my bed for a while. It felt so good. I took his hand and held it in mine for a long time. He said that he felt very good to sit like this. I told him that I had been unfair and rude with him in Paris....

He suddenly stood up and wanted to go, but stumbled on the slippers that were on the floor next to my bed. He turned around and sat in his former place.

I asked him, "Where did you want to go?"

"I wanted to close the window."

"Please do that if you wish."

"No, there is no need. Do you know what has just happened to me?" he said in a strange voice.

"What is it?" I looked at him.

He was so excited. "I wanted to kiss your leg."

"Oh, but why?" I said with great excitement and fear, pulling my legs closer together under the blanket.

"I just wanted to do this very much and I decided that I would kiss it."

September 17, 1863.

I again feel tenderness toward Fyodor Mikhailovich. I despised him for a while, but then I felt that I had been wrong and became more tender. He responded with such tenderness and joy that I was touched and excited, and felt even more tenderness towards him. When I sat close to him and looked at him, he said: "I recognize this glance, I have not seen it for a long time." I put my head on his chest and cried. ...

September 29, 1863.

Yesterday Fyodor Mikhailovich again tried to get close to me. He said that I have to take love more seriously. I said that there was one reason which I had not mentioned before.

"It's not true, it's not what you think," I told him. He thought that I wanted to torture him.

"You know, when you refuse a man all the time, he can put an end to his efforts to possess a woman." I could not help but smile....

He stood up and went to the bed. I started to walk across the room. My thoughts had shifted direction. I had hope, I was not too ashamed to have hope.

When he got up later, he was loose and joyful and followed me around. It seemed as if he was trying to forget about his inner abuse and to take revenge on me.

I looked at his strange behavior with puzzlement. He wanted to make a joke of it. He wanted to tease me, but I only looked at him with my surprised eyes. "You do not look good," I said simply.

"Why? What did I do?"

"Well, in Paris and in Turin you were better. Why are you so..."

"This joyfulness is not sincere," he said and left. Soon after he returned.

"I feel terrible," he said in a sad and serious voice, "I look at everything [at the love affair] as if I am obliged to do this, as if I am a student at a lesson. I wanted at least to entertain you."

I embraced him with passion and I told him that he did many good things for me and that I felt good with him.

"No," he said with sadness, "you will go to Spain."

I felt scared and full of pain, and at the same time thrilled by his hints about Salvador. What had happened between me and Salvador was a very wild thing! Salvador's attitude to me was very contradictory.

When Fyodor Mikhailovich was leaving my room, he made a joke out of our situation, just as he used to. He said that he was ashamed to leave me like this. (It was one o'clock in the morning and I lay completely naked in bed.) He said, "The Russians never surrender...."

Paris, October 22, 1863.

On the ship in Naples, while on our way to Paris, we met Herzen and his entire family. Fyodor Mikhailovich introduced me as a member of his family, but in very vague terms. He treated me as if he were my brother or even closer.

All this surprised Herzen. He listened attentively as Fyodor Mikhailovich told him many things about me. I spoke to Herzen's son too. He seemed to be a desperate young man. I told him how I felt about traveling abroad, that I found unpleasant things everywhere. He tried to convince me that it was the same everywhere.

While we talked, Fyodor Mikhailovich passed by us without stopping. I asked him to join us and he was very glad to hear this.

The young Herzen told me that he would be in Paris in the winter and that he would like to visit me. He asked for my address, but added that he could get it later, from Mr. B. I told Fyodor Mikhailovich about this and he advised me to give him my address, thereby expressing my respect for his father.

When we said good-bye in Livorno, I gave Herzen my address. Fyodor Mikhailovich saw him to his hotel. When he returned, he was excited and he told me that I should write to him and inform him if Herzen visited me. I promised I would. He did not say much about the young Herzen, but when I began to speak about him, Dostoevsky became critical. He also said that at the Herzens' he had seen a photograph of me which I had presented to Herzen earlier, with my address on it. On the photograph there was an inscription, a phrase by the father Herzen, written in Aleksandr's handwriting: "People would not have gone very far, if they had only used their logical minds."

When we left Naples, I had a quarrel with Fyodor Mikhailovich, but on the same day, on the ship, under the impression of our meeting with Herzen, we became friends again. Our point of contention was the emancipation of women. After this we did not have any quarrels. I treated him almost as before, and it was a pity to say good-bye.

*October 27, [1865]**

I received a letter from Fyodor Mikhailovich yesterday. He had been gambling and lost everything. He asked me to send him some money.

*December 5, [1865]**

I hate Paris, but I can't get away from this city. Maybe this city offers

---

Polina Suslova did not put years in her Diary, *only date and months.*

something special to people who don't have a certain place or purpose in life. I want to see America. This is my constant wish. In spite of the many faces and activities around me, I am constantly haunted by one thought, one image. What did I see in him?

September 15, [...]
People talk to me about Fyodor Mikhailovich. I simply hate him. He has caused me so much suffering. Especially when one considers that it could have been avoided. I see clearly now that I cannot fall in love again, I cannot find happiness in the pleasures of love, because the tenderness of men will always remind me of my former insults and suffering.
Something new could distract me from these thoughts though....

November 6, [...]
Fyodor Mikhailovich visited me. There were three of us, him, A.O. and myself. We talked a lot. I said that I would become a saint, that I would walk barefoot across the Kremlin Garden in Moscow and that angels would talk to me....

Sofia Kovalevskaya: How Dostoevsky Proposed to Anna Korvin-Krukovskaya

(From S.V. Kovalevskaya, *Vospominaniia i pis'ma* [*Memoirs and Letters*]. Moscow: Academy Press, 1961, pp. 102–121, 122–132.)

I saw a letter which read: "I can tell you definitely ... that your story will be published, and I will do this with great pleasure, in the next issue of my journal.... Yours sincerely, F. Dostoevsky."

When I read this letter, I could not concentrate. It was a great surprise for me. The name of Dostoevsky was well-known; of late, it was often mentioned at lunch, during my sister's [literary] discussions with our father. I knew that Dostoevsky was one of the most prominent Russian writers, but why did he write to Aniuta and what did all this mean? For a moment I thought that my sister had written a fake letter to poke fun at me.

When I finished reading the letter, I looked at my sister in silence and did not know exactly what to say. She was pleased with my astonishment.

"Well, you see," Aniuta said, her voice full of excitement, "I wrote a story, and, without saying a word to anybody, I sent it to Dostoevsky. And, here we are, he found it interesting and he is going to publish it in his journal. My dream has come true. Now I am a Russian woman writer." She almost screamed with pride that she could not hide....

The first success of Aniuta encouraged her greatly and she started to write a second story which she published several weeks later. This time her hero was a young man named Mikhail. He had been brought up far away from his family, by his monk uncle, in a monastery. Dostoevsky considered this second story a more mature work and admired it better than the first one. There was some similarity between this character, Mikhail, and Alyosha from *The Brothers Karamazov*. Several years after this, when I read the novel which was published in a literary journal at the time, I mentioned this similarity to Dostoevsky. I met him often at the time.

"Well, you know, maybe it is true," said Fyodor Mikhailovich, and he slapped himself gently with his palm against his forehead. "But, believe me, I forgot about Mikhail when I was creating my Alyosha" [a major character of *The Brothers Karamazov*].

Dostoevsky was very graphic in his speech. Sometimes he forgot that he was speaking in the presence of ladies, on occasion scaring my mother. For example, he started telling us about one of the novels that he had wanted to write when he was younger. The main character was a landlord in his best years, a well educated man. He went abroad, he read clever books and he collected pieces of art, such as paintings and lithographs. Although in his youth he led a very dissipated life, he later became a serious man, he created a family, he had a wife and children and grew to be a well-respected gentleman.

One day he woke up in the morning and saw the sun coming into his bedroom. Everything around him was so good, neat and cozy.

He felt as if he were remembering something, so he concentrated hard, and his memory started to show him pictures from the past. Suddenly he remembered a certain incident, very realistically, and in great detail, and he felt disgusted. He felt as if it had happened to him just the day before, and not twenty years previously. He remembered how, after an evening party, heated by his drunken friends, he raped a ten-year old girl. ...

[Dostoevsky made friends with Korvin-Krukovskaya parents and started visiting the family on a regular basis.]

After I entered another room, I felt that there was something wrong.... There was nobody in the second room either. Then I opened a big curtain which separated the lobby from a small dining room in the corner. Oh my God, what I saw there! I saw there Fyodor Mikhailovich and Aniuta.

They were sitting together on a small sofa. The room was hardly lit by a shaded lamp. The shadow fell on my sister so I could not see her face well. I saw Dostoevsky's face; it was pale and excited. He held Aniuta's hands in both of his hands and spoke to her in a passionate whisper which I knew so well and which I loved so much: "My darling Anna

Vasilievna, please understand me. I fell in love with you from the very moment I saw you. I even had this feeling before we met, from your letters. I do not treat you as a friend, but I love you with all my heart, with passion."

My heart fell, and I experienced a feeling of complete solitude and absolute anger with him. It seemed that, after I heard this, my blood started to circulate more quickly and that a hot wave moved, first to my heart, and then to my head. I felt myself blush. I dropped the curtain and ran out of the room to the clatter of a falling chair which I knocked over on my way....

Late at night, before going to bed, I asked her: "Do you love this man?" Aniuta said to me, "Well, you see.... I do not love him, really."

Anna Dostoevskaya: *Memoirs*

(From A.G. Dostoevskaya, *Vospominaniia* [*Memoirs*]. Moscow: Gosizdat, 1925.)

Our teacher of stenography, P.M. Ol'khin, sat on the class bench next to me and asked: "Anna Grigorievna, would you like to have a job? Someone asked me to find a stenographer, and I thought that maybe you would like to have this job."

"Yes, and very much so," I answered. "I have dreamt about such work.... And with whom should I work as a stenographer?" I asked.

"With Dostoevsky, the writer. He is working on a new novel, and he wants to write it with a stenographer's help. Dostoevsky plans the novel to be about seven printing signatures, and he has suggested a payment of fifty roubles for the whole work."

I instantly agreed. I had known Dostoevsky's name since childhood; he was my father's favorite writer. I too admired his works and had cried over his *Notes from the House of the Dead*. I felt very excited and happy for the chance to know a talented writer better and to help him with his work.

Ol'khin passed me a small sheet of paper folded twice, on which the address was written: "Stolyarny Street, on the corner of Meshchanskaya Street, Alonkin House, Apartment No. 13, ask for Dostoevsky."

Ol'khin told me: "Visit Dostoevsky tomorrow, at 11.30 A.M., as he told me today, 'neither sooner, nor later'...."

Apartment 13 was situated on the second floor. I rang the doorbell, and an old woman servant opened the door. She had a green gingham shawl on her shoulders.

I had recently read *Crime and Punishment*, and I thought that this shawl was perhaps the prototype for the same shawl which played such an important role in the Marmeladov family.

I asked the servant to tell her master that I had come from Mr. Ol'khin, and that her master should know about my visit....

Then Fyodor Mikhailovich appeared. He apologized for the delay and asked me: "For how long did you study stenography?"

"For about half a year."

"How many students are in your class?"

"At first there were more than 150 people who enrolled in the course, but now only 25 persons remain."

"Why so few?"

"Well, many people thought that it was easy to study stenography, but they dropped the course after they saw that it is impossible to learn the subject in a few days."

"This happens all the time," said Fyodor Mikhailovich, "People start some new enterprise with enthusiasm, and very soon they drop it. They see that they have to work, and who wants to work hard?"

At first, Dostoevsky seemed to me a rather old man. However, when he started to talk, he looked younger, and I didn't think he was older than thirty-five to thirty-seven. He was of average height, and he held himself erect. He had light brown, slightly reddish hair, he used some hair conditioner, and he combed his hair in a diligent way. I was struck by his eyes, they were different: one was dark brown; in the other, the pupil was so big that you could not see its color. (Later I found out that Dostoevsky had fallen and injured his eye during a fit of epilepsy.) The strangeness of his eyes gave Dostoevsky some mysterious appearance. His face was pale, and it looked unhealthy. It seemed very familiar to me because I had seen his portrait many times before. He had a dark blue jacket on; it was rather worn out, but accompanied by a perfectly white and fresh shirt....

We were served tea, and Fyodor Mikhailovich started to dictate to me. It seemed that it was very difficult for him to get involved in the work: he often stopped, thought it over, and asked me to read again the passage which I had just written down....

In this way, our work began. I usually went to Fyodor Mikhailovich at twelve and stayed until four. During this time, he dictated some material, in three sessions, each about half an hour, and in the intervals we drank tea and talked. It was with pleasure that I noticed that Fyodor Mikhailovich had started to get used to this new type of work, and that he became more satisfied with every visit.

Every day, Fyodor Mikhailovich treated me better and with more kindness. He often called me "my dear" (his favorite pet name), or "my dear Anna Grigorievna," or "my lovely." I thought that these words

Dostoevsky's parents and childhood home. TOP: *Maria Fyodorovna Dostoevskaya and Mikhail Andreyevich Dostoevsky, both in 1823 portraits by Popov.* BOTTOM: *The Marinskaya Shelter for the Poor in Moscow.*

A sketch of young Dostoevsky by Konstantin Trutovsky, his classmate at the Engineering Academy.

TOP: *The cottage in Darovoe where the family spent summers.* BOTTOM: *The St. Petersburg Military Engineering Academy, where Dostoevsky studied from 1838 to 1843.*

Scenes from the darkest period of Dostoevsky's life. TOP: *The Alexeev single cells of the St. Peter and Paul Fortress, where he was held for eight months in 1849 after his arrest.* BOTTOM: *An artist's depiction of the mock execution of members of the Petrashevsky Circle, December 22, 1849.*

CLOCKWISE FROM TOP LEFT: The cover page of Dostoevsky's file compiled by the 3rd Section of the Secret Police; the Omsk prison where Dostoevsky was incarcerated from 1850 to 1854; the outer wall of the Omsk prison; a drawing of Semipalatinsk, the Siberian town where Dostoevsky served in the army upon his release.

The Dostoevsky Museum in Semipalatinsk, a house where he lived while serving in the army.

An 1857 portrait, in his junior lieutenant's uniform.

*Two photo-
graphs from
the early
1860s; the one
at left, from
1861, is by
M. Tulinov.*

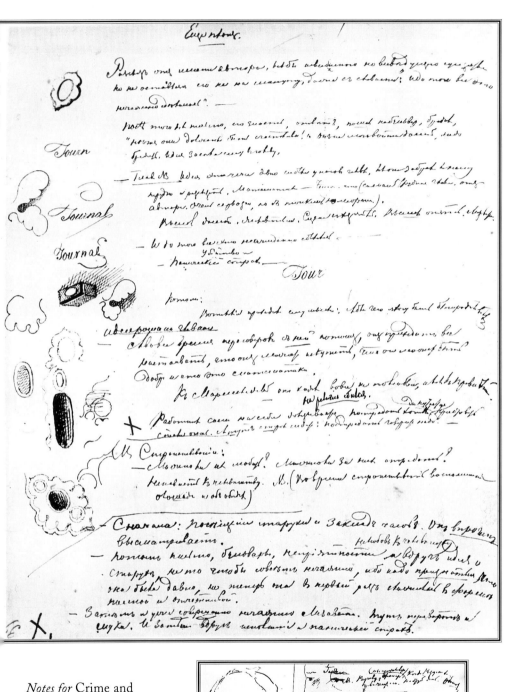

Notes for Crime and Punishment. *ABOVE: a handwritten outline of the novel. RIGHT: A detail from a page of notes showing Dostoevsky's sketches of characters.*

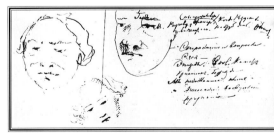

Anna Dostoevskaya (née Snitkina), Dostoevsky's second wife, in an 1871 photograph taken in Dresden.

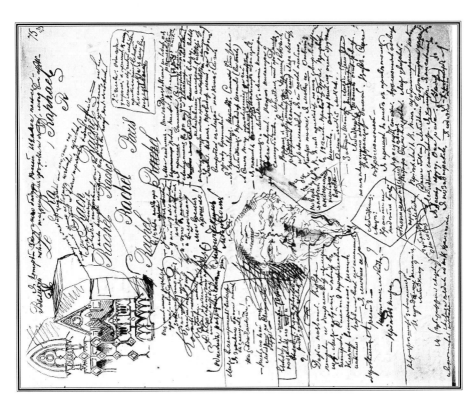

Notes and drawings for The Idiot *(left) and* The Demons.

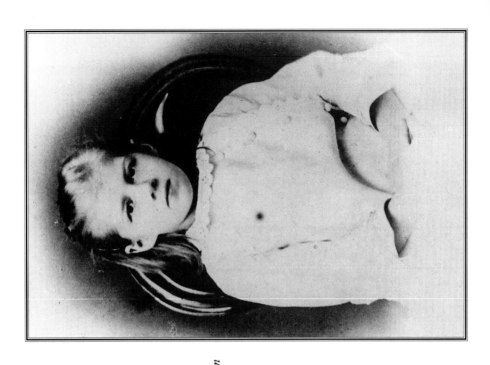

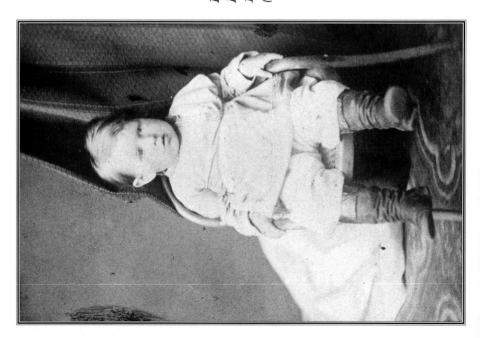

Dostoevsky's children Fyodor (left, circa 1872) and Liubov (mid–1870s).

An 1878 photograph by N. Lorenkovich

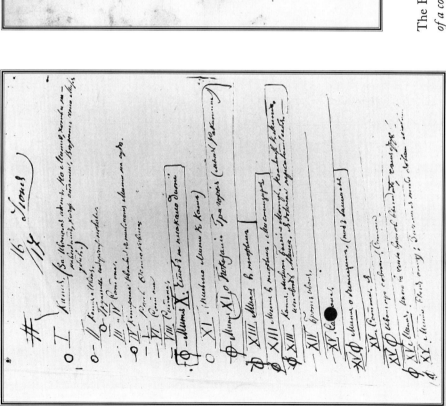

The Brothers Karamazov: early notes (left) and the title page of a copy autographed to Ivan Aksakov, St. Petersburg, 1881.

TOP: *Dostoevsky's study at his summer home in Staraya Russa; here he wrote most of* The Brothers Karamazov *and* A Writer's Diary. BOTTOM: *An artist's depiction of Dostoevsky's funeral procession, January 31, 1881.*

Probably the most famous portrait of Dostoevsky, an 1880 photograph by M. Panov. In her memoirs Anna Dostoevskaya wrote, "At this photograph the face of Fyodor Mikhailovich became even more meaningful, more deep and tragic.... I think that this is the best photograph of Dostoevsky. My husband's mood was changing all the time. In this portrait I saw the expression of his face that I saw many times when he experienced pleasure or happiness."

referred to my young age, as I looked like a young girl in comparison to him. It was pleasant for me to help him in his work, and to see that my work helped him finish the novel by the deadline and raised his spirits. I was even secretly proud that I was able to help my favorite writer, that I could improve his mood. All this raised my own opinion of myself as well.

I was not afraid of "the famous writer" anymore, and I spoke to him freely and openly, as if he were my uncle, or an old friend. When I asked Fyodor Mikhailovich about different events in his life, he gladly satisfied my curiosity. He told me in detail how he spent eight months in the St. Peter and Paul Fortress, and how he communicated with other prisoners by knocking on the wall. He told me about his life in prison, and about the criminals who were in prison with him. He reminisced about his trips abroad and his meetings with different people there; and about his family in Moscow whom he loved so much. He told me that he had been married, that his wife had died three years ago, and he showed me her portrait. I did not like it.... Fyodor Mikhailovich often complained about his debts, the absence of money and his difficult financial situation. In the future I found out more about his financial affairs.

All of Fyodor Mikhailovich's stories were rather sad, and one day I could not stop myself from asking him, "Dear Fyodor Mikhailovich, why do you remember only misfortunes? Tell me more about the times when you were happy."

"Was I happy? I have never been happy, at least I did not ever possess that happiness about which I dreamt. I expect it in the future. Recently I wrote in a letter to a friend of mine, Baron Vrangel, that, in spite of all my misfortunes, I still dream about a new happy life."

It was so strange for me to hear that this talented and kind man, already in old age, had not found the happiness he deserved, and that he only dreamt about it.

One day Fyodor Mikhailovich told me how he proposed to Anna Korvin-Krukovskaya. He was so happy that he received a positive answer from this clever, kind and talented young woman; it was difficult for him to return his promise, when he understood that it was impossible to create happiness with such divergent views on life.

One day, when he was rather excited, Fyodor Mikhailovich told me that he was facing a difficult choice regarding his future: to go east to Constantinople and to Jerusalem, and, maybe, to stay there forever; to go abroad and start playing roulette, a game which he liked very much, and which completely absorbed his attention; or, the last variant, to marry for a second time and to seek happiness and joy in family life.

Fyodor Mikhailovich expressed great concern with these questions which could completely change his life, so unhappy before. He recognized that my attitude towards him was friendly, and he asked me for advice in the matter.

To tell the truth, it seemed difficult for me to provide an honest answer to this question. His plans to go to the East, or his desire to become a gambler, all these seemed unclear and phantastic to me. However, I knew that there were happy families among my friends and relatives, so I advised him to marry for a second time and to find happiness in a family.

"What do you think?" Fyodor Mikhailovich asked me. "Can I marry again? Will anyone agree to marry me for the second time? What kind of wife should I choose: a clever one or a kind one?"

"Certainly, a clever one."

"Well, no, I do not agree with you. If I could choose, I would take a kind wife, who would love me and take care of me." Then Fyodor Mikhailovich asked me about the possibility of me marrying and why I hadn't yet. I answered that there were two men who would like to marry me. They both were wonderful people and I respected them very much, but I did not feel love towards them, and I should be in love with my future husband.

"Yes, you definitely must be in love with the man you marry," agreed Fyodor Mikhailovich passionately. "Respect alone is not enough for a happy marriage." ...

The more we worked, the more Fyodor Mikhailovich became involved in the work. He did not dictate directly anymore, creating his work on the spot, but worked at night, dictating to me by day from his manuscript. Sometimes we managed to write so much during the day that I had to sit and work way past midnight, rewriting the material he had dictated to me during the day. But the next day I was so happy to tell him the number of new pages which had been added to the novel! I was so happy when I saw a satisfied smile on Fyodor Mikhailovich's face when I assured him that the work was proceeding according to schedule and that, without doubt, it would be finished by the deadline.

We both started to share the lives of the major characters in the novel, and both Fyodor Mikhailovich and I liked some of them and disliked others. I felt sympathy for the old lady who lost a fortune gambling, and for Mr. Ashtly, and I hated Polina and the main character, because I could not excuse him for his weak will and his passion for gambling. Fyodor Mikhailovich liked "the gambler" and told me that he himself had experienced many of these emotions. He also told me that a person can have a strong character, and can prove it with his life, but at the same time have no power to fight with the passion for playing roulette, the passion for gambling....

November 8, 1866, was one of the most important days in my life.

On this day Fyodor Mikhailovich told me that he loved me and that he would like me to become his wife. Almost half a century has passed since that day, but I remember every detail of it, as if it happened a month ago.

It was a clear frosty day. I went to Fyodor Mikhailovich by foot, and because I was walking, I was half an hour late.

It seemed that Fyodor Mikhailovich had been waiting for me for a rather long time. He appeared in the corridor as soon as he heard my voice.

"At last you came!" he said welcomingly, and he helped me to unbind my shawl and to take off my coat. We went into his study. It was well lit, and I noticed that Fyodor Mikhailovich was excited about something. His face looked exhausted, and it made him look younger. "I am so glad that you came," Fyodor Mikhailovich said. "I was afraid that you had forgotten about your promise."

"Why do you say this? If I make a promise, I keep it."

"Excuse me, I know that you always keep your word, I am so glad to see you again."

"And I am glad to see you as well, Fyodor Mikhailovich...." Then I asked Fyodor Mikhailovich what he had been doing for the last few days.

"I am thinking about writing a new novel."

"Will it be an interesting novel? What will it be about?"

"Yes, it should be a very interesting novel indeed. But I can't figure out the end of the novel. It is about the psychology of a young woman.... If I were in Moscow, I would ask Sonechka, my niece. Now I will ask you for a piece of advice."

I prepared to listen carefully to the famous writer. "And who is the major hero of the novel?"

He is an artist, not a very young man. Well, he is my age, actually."

"Tell me, tell me, please," I was very much interested in his new work. After I asked him this, he started his brilliant improvisation. Never before had I heard anything of this sort from Fyodor Mikhailovich, nor would I ever again hear a more inspirational story than his story that day. The more he narrated, the more convinced I became that he was telling me the story of his own life, just making small changes, here and there, to minor characters and circumstances. This story contained everything he had told me about himself before, and it also explained a great deal about his relationship with his first wife and his family.

In the new novel, the hero had the same childhood; he lost his beloved father early, had some sad experiences which distracted him from his work (a serious illness), then returned to life, fell in love with a woman, lost his wife and his sister, experienced poverty, death, etc. The inner state of the hero was one of solitude and disappointment with the people who surrounded him. He fervently desired to start a new life, feeling a necessity, a need to love, and passionately wishing for new happiness.

All this was described in such a detailed way ... that it was obvious that the hero was not merely a fantasy, that the author had suffered these things himself in his actual life. Fyodor Mikhailovich used dark, gloomy colors to describe his hero. He said that his hero was a man who had become old too early. He had an incurable illness (his right arm was paralyzed), and was a gloomy and suspicious person.... However, he had a kind heart, though he could not express his feelings. He was a real artist, but he could not put his ideas in the forms he dreamt of and he suffered from this.

I saw that the hero of the novel was Fyodor Mikhailovich himself and I asked him: "Why did you dislike your hero? I see that you do not like him."

"No, on the contrary, I like him very much, he has a wonderful heart. Just think about how many misfortunes he had in his life, and he survived them all without complaint. Any other person who had suffered so much would have become cruel, but my hero, on the contrary, loves people and wants to help them. Do not treat him badly."

"Yes, I agree that he has a kind and loving heart, and I am glad that you understand him."

"Well," Fyodor Mikhailovich continued his story, "during the decisive period of his life, the artist meets a woman of your age, or a couple of years older. Let us call her Anna, so we will avoid using 'The Heroine.' This is a good name." ...

The portrait of a heroine was made in completely different colors from those of the hero. Firstly, Anna was a humble, clever, kind, optimistic and very tactful person. In those years I paid much attention to a woman's beauty and I couldn't help asking him, "Is she a beautiful woman, your heroine?"

"Well, she is not a striking beauty but rather a nice looking woman. I love her face...."

"Fyodor Mikhailovich, you idealize your Anya too much. Is she really like this?"

"Oh yes, I have studied her well. The artist met her at different artistic circles and the more often he met her, the more he loved her. He became more and more confident that he could find happiness with her. But this dream seemed impossible to him. What could he give to this young, healthy and optimistic young woman? He was an old and ill man and had many financial debts. Maybe the young woman's love for the artist would turn into sacrifice and she would regret in the future that she had connected her life with his life. In general, is it possible for a young lady to fall in love with my artist? They are so different in character and in years, that maybe I have made here a psychological mistake. What do you think about this, dear Anna Grigorievna?"

"Why do you think it is impossible? If this is true and you feel that your Anya is not just a coquette but that she is a nice person and has a responsive heart, why do you think she can't fall in love with your artist? It does not matter much that he is ill and poor. People fall in love not only for appearance or money. And what is her sacrifice? If she loves him, she herself will be happy. She will never have to regret this!"

I spoke with passion and Fyodor Mikhailovich looked at me with excitement.

"Do you really believe that she can truly fall in love with him? For the rest of her life?" He was silent for a while as if he were hesitating. "Just put yourself into her place for a moment," he said with a trembling voice. "Imagine that this artist was me. And that I told you that I loved you and wanted you to be my wife. How would you answer me?"

I saw an expression of great embarrassment on Fyodor Mikhailovich's face. It was an expression of inner torment and at last I understood that this was not merely a literary conversation, and that I would cause a severe blow to his self-esteem and his pride if I gave him an indirect answer. I looked at the excited face of Fyodor Mikhailovich that was so dear to me and I said, "I would tell you that I love you and that I will love you for the rest of my life."

Here I will omit the tender words, the words full of love which Fyodor Mikhailovich said to me in those unforgettable moments. They are sacred for me.

I was so stunned and overwhelmed by this huge happiness that I couldn't believe it for a long time. I remember that about an hour later, Fyodor Mikhailovich started to discuss our plans for the future and I answered him, "Do you think I can discuss my plans now? I am too happy by all this!"

We did not know what the circumstances would be and when our marriage would take place, so we decided not to tell anyone except my mother. Fyodor Mikhailovich promised to come to me the next day and to spend the whole evening. He said that he would be looking forward with impatience to seeing me. He saw me to the corridor, and carefully bound my shawl around my shoulders....

We spoke about so many things during those happy months. I asked Fyodor Mikhailovich to tell me in detail about his childhood, the Engineering Academy, his political activity, his exile to Siberia and his return.

"I want to know everything about you," I said. "I want to know all your past and to understand your soul." Fyodor Mikhailovich gladly told me about his happy, cloudless childhood; he described his mother whom he loved so much. Most of all he loved his elder brother Mikhail and his sister Varen'ka [Varvara Mikhailovna Dostoevskaya, after marriage Karepina, 1822–1893]. The younger brothers and sisters did not impress him very much.

I also asked Fyodor Mikhailovich about his earlier love affairs. It seemed strange to me that in his younger years he had not seriously loved any woman. I explained this by the fact that he started his intellectual life rather early. He had been so involved in the creative process that his personal life became less important to him. Afterwards he was involved in a political conspiracy for which he seriously suffered.

I tried to ask him about his deceased wife, but he did not like to talk about her....

Fyodor Mikhailovich and I both were so involved in our happy relationship that we forgot about *Crime and Punishment*. Indeed, about one-third of the novel remained unwritten. Fyodor Mikhailovich remembered it only in late November, when the editor of *The Russian Herald* asked him about the continuation of the novel. We were lucky that at the time journals in general were rarely published in time, and that *The Russian Herald* also appeared with some delay. The November issue appeared in late December, the December issue appeared in early February. Therefore, we had some time.

When Fyodor Mikhailovich brought me the letter from the editor and asked for my advice, I suggested that he close his doors to visitors every day and work from 2 to 5 P.M., and then come to me in the evening to dictate the manuscript.

So we decided to work like this. After chatting with each other for about an hour, I would sit at the writing desk, Fyodor Mikhailovich near me, and he would start dictating. Our work was often interrupted by jokes and laughter. Our work proceeded successfully, and the last part of *Crime and Punishment*, which was about seven printed signatures long, was written in four weeks. Fyodor Mikhailovich assured me that never before had he proceeded with his work so easily, and he said that the success was due to my cooperation.

What became a habitual joyful and happy mood of Fyodor Mikhailovich influenced his health positively. During the three months prior to our marriage, he had no more than three or four fits of epilepsy. I was satisfied by this, and it gave me hope that he would feel better, having a healthy and happier life. It was as I thought. His fits of illness, which had occurred almost every week, became weaker and less frequent....

The major and most important topic of conversation between me and Fyodor Mikhailovich was our future married life. I was so happy when I thought that I would not have to part with my husband during the day, that I would take part in his work and take care of his health and save him from all his frequent and irritating visitors. Sometimes I was ready to cry over the fact that it wouldn't happen sooner. The day of our marriage depended very much on the decision of the publisher of *The Russian Herald*. Fyodor Mikhailovich was going to visit Moscow for Christmas to suggest to Katkov a future novel. He had no doubt that *The Russian Herald* would like his new work to be published because his *Crime and Punishment*, published in 1866, had been a big event in literature and had attracted many new subscribers to the journal. The question was whether or not the journal could spare several thousand roubles, without which we could not make a new start in life....

If the business trip to Moscow were to fail, it could postpone our marriage for a long time, maybe for a whole year. I became very agitated whenever I thought about this....

Besides having many debts, Fyodor Mikhailovich was forced to approach journals about new works all by himself, and he received much less than other well-established writers, such as Turgenev or Goncharov. For example, Fyodor Mikhailovich received 150 roubles a signature, while Turgenev for his novels published in the same journal, *The Russian Herald*, received up to 500 roubles a signature.

The most discouraging thing was Fyodor Mikhailovich's endless debts. All the time he had to be in a hurry doing his work. He had neither the time nor the opportunity to complete his works in a perfect form, as he would have liked. It was a very painful thing for him. Some critics reproached Fyodor Mikhailovich for the lack of perfection in the style of his novels. Sometimes there existed several novels included in one, with the events awfully mixed up, and many things remaining incomplete. These strict critics probably did not know the conditions in which Fyodor Mikhailovich had to work. It sometimes happened that the first three chapters of a novel were already published, the fourth was in print; the fifth was sent by mail, the sixth was being written, and the remaining chapters had not even been discussed or thought over. Many times, I saw Fyodor Mikhailovich in a desperate situation where he suddenly understood that he had spoiled an idea which [he] loved so much, and could not correct his mistake.

I was upset about the difficult material situation of my groom, and comforted myself with the fact that in the near future I would be more able to help him seriously, and that I would receive ... a part of my inheritance, my father's house.... While a groom, Fyodor Mikhailovich never accepted my financial help. When I told him that, if we love each other then we must equally share everything we possess, he answered: "Yes, certainly, it will be like this when we get married, but until then I do not want to take from you a single rouble."

The Trip Abroad.

After two days in Berlin, we moved to Dresden. My husband had difficult literary work ahead, and we decided to stay there for not more than a month. Fyodor Mikhailovich liked Dresden, most of all its famous art gallery and the wonderful gardens in the suburbs, and he always visited them there when he traveled here. There were many museums in the city. Fyodor Mikhailovich knew my curiosity, and he thought that I would be interested in them, and I wouldn't miss Russia too much, which he was afraid of during our first time abroad.

We stayed in Neumarkt District, in one of the best hotels in town, the Stadt Berlin. As soon as we arrived, we changed and went at once to the art gallery. My husband wanted to introduce me to this place before any other artistic sight. We got to the gallery less than one hour before closing time, but we decided to enter it. My husband quickly went through all other halls of the gallery and brought me to the *Sistine Madonna*. This was the painting which he considered to be the highest expression of human genius. Afterwards I saw how my husband could stand for hours in front of this beautiful painting, being deeply touched by it and admiring it. I must say that the *Sistine Madonna* produced an overwhelming impression upon me right away. It seemed that the Holy Mother, with the infant in her hands, flew in the sky, moving closer to the people standing in front of her.

Fyodor Mikhailovich considered works of Raphael to be the finest paintings, and he treated the *Sistine Madonna* as his best work. He appreciated very highly Titian's talent, especially his famous painting *Christ with a Coin*. He could stand there for a long time, in front of it, without moving his eyes from the portrait of the Savior.... Usually at 6 P.M., after having a rest, we went out for a walk in the Grossengarten. Fyodor Mikhailovich liked this huge park very much, most of all for its beautiful meadows in the English style and its gorgeous greenery. It was about six to seven miles from our house to the park. My husband liked to walk. He appreciated these walking tours even in the rainy weather, saying that it produced a good impact upon us.

At that time, there was a restaurant in the park.... It was called Green Wirtschaft. Every evening some military music, trumpet orchestras, or other instrumental music was played. Sometimes programs for the concerts were rather serious. My husband was not an expert in music, but he liked the musical pieces by Mozart, Beethoven (*Fidelio*), Mendelssohn (*Wedding March*) and Rossini (*Stabat Mater*), and he experienced great pleasure while listening to his favorite pieces. Fyodor Mikhailovich did not like the works of Richard Wagner at all.

Usually, during such walks my husband rested from his literary and other work, and would be in a very good mood: he would laugh and make jokes.... When we decided that as soon as we received some money, we would go to Baden-Baden for two weeks, Fyodor Mikhailovich became more quiet, calm, and started to redo and finish the work which was moving with great difficulty. This was the article about Belinsky in which my husband expressed everything which he felt about this famous literary critic. Belinsky was a person whom Fyodor Mikhailovich appreciated ... very highly, even before he got to know him personally, as he said in *A Writer's Diary* (1877). He appreciated highly Belinsky's gift as a literary critic, and he felt grateful towards him for the support of his literary talent. However, Fyodor Mikhailovich could not excuse Belinsky's mocking and blasphemy of the Christian faith and religion. It was obvious that the views of Fyodor Mikhailovich were not settled, for he had to think the article over again and again; he hesitated in making judgments. He wrote and rewrote his article about Belinsky five times, and in the end, he was not satisfied with it. In a letter to A. Maikov dated September 15, 1867, Fyodor Mikhailovich wrote, "The thing is that I just finished this cursed article 'My friendship with Belinsky.'"

This article experienced a sad fate. We lived abroad and we did not know whether the article was published or not. In 1872 Fyodor Mikhailovich received from some bookseller a request to send to him an article which had been written for K.I. Babikov on spec, and he informed us that the anthology had not been published because K.I. Babikov had died. Fyodor Mikhailovich was very much upset that his article had been lost, because he had put a great deal of work into it, and though he had not been satisfied with it, it was important to him.... The article disappeared without a trace....

At the end of June, we received money from the publisher of *The Russian Herald*, and we decided to move at once. I left Dresden with regret, because I had been happy when we were living there, and I vaguely felt that there would be many changes as new circumstances arose. My feelings regarding the future came true. When I remember our five weeks in Baden-Baden and when I read the notes which I wrote in my day-book, I remember that something terrible took possession of my husband and did not release him from its heavy chains. All the hopes of Fyodor Mikhailovich as to becoming a big winner playing roulette in the casinos, following his theories of the game, all this was wrong. One could achieve luck only on the condition that this method were used by some cold-blooded and balanced Englishman or German, but not by a nervous man like my husband was; a man who felt passionate about many things, who was always going over the edge....

A person who plays roulette with anything but a cold and balanced mind must have some financial means in order to face the unfavorable during the play. Fyodor Mikhailovich did not have extra money, and there was very little chance of our receiving any extra money if we lost what we had. It was less than a week after our arrival that Fyodor Mikhailovich lost all his cash and started to think about where to get money in order to continue the game. We had to pawn our possessions. But even after we pawned our possessions, my husband could not restrain himself, and sometimes he lost everything we had received for our pawn. It was very painful for me to see how Fyodor Mikhailovich suffered: he would return home, pale and exhausted after playing roulette (he never took me with him, because he thought that a gambling hall was not a good place for a young and decent woman); he could hardly walk on his feet; he would ask me for some money (he had given all the money he had to me); go away and in half an hour return even more disappointed to take some more money, and this went on to the point where he lost everything we had.

Then he had no money for roulette, and could not get any money. Fyodor Mikhailovich at this point was so depressed that he started to cry. He knelt in front of me, asking me, imploring me to pardon him for his behavior, for torturing me with his actions, and he appeared as if he were in a state of complete despair.

It took a lot of energy and talking to calm him down, to explain that our situation was not hopeless, to find some way out, to direct his thoughts onto something else. And I was very happy and satisfied when I managed to do this—when I took him to the reading-hall of the local library to look through the newspapers, or when we went out for lengthy walks, which almost always had a healthy impact on my husband. We walked for many versts until we received money.

Once Fyodor Mikhailovich visited I.S. Turgenev who lived in Baden-Baden at the time. When he returned, he was very irritated and told me about their conversations in detail....

When we went to Geneva, we at once started to look for some furnished rooms to rent.... Only late at night did we find an apartment which suited us.... Here, as well as in Dresden, we had a fixed schedule for the day: Fyodor Mikhailovich worked during the night, and got up after eleven; I had breakfast with him and we went out for walk, as I had been recommended to do by the doctor, and then Fyodor Mikhailovich continued his work. At three o'clock we went to the restaurant to have dinner, after which I took a nap. My husband saw me home then went to a cafe at Rue de Mont Blanc where they received Russian newspapers and spent two hours reading Golos ("The Voice"), *The Moscow News* and *The St. Petersburg News*. He also read a few foreign newspapers.

In the evenings, at about seven o'clock, we went out for lengthy walks. So that I would not get too tired, we often stopped in front of the windows of fashionable shops, and Fyodor Mikhailovich showed me the jewelry which he would give me as a gift if he were a rich man. I must say that he had artistic taste, and all of the jewelry he selected was delicious.

I spent evenings writing down a new work dictated to me, or I was reading French books. My husband kept track of my systematic reading and study of the works of a certain particular author, without distracting my attention to the works of other authors. Fyodor Mikhailovich greatly appreciated the works of Balzac and George Sand, and little by little, I read all their novels. During our walks we discussed what I read, and my husband explained to me all the advantages or weak points of the works I had read.

I was surprised that Fyodor Mikhailovich could forget things which had happened recently, but remembered in detail all the plots and the names of major heroes from the novels of his favorite authors.

I remember that, most of all, he appreciated the novel *Père Goriot*, from the series of "Les Parents Pauvres." Fyodor Mikhailovich himself, during the winter of 1867-68, read again the famous novel by Victor Hugo, *Les Misérables*....

At the beginning of September 1867, the Congress of Peace was held in Geneva, and Guiseppe Garibaldi arrived for the opening. People attributed great importance to his visit, and the city prepared a wonderful reception for him. We were interested in the World Congress, so we went to the second sitting and listened to the speeches for two hours. Fyodor Mikhailovich was depressed by the speeches and he wrote to Ivanova-Khmyriova the following: "They started by saying that in order to reach peace on Earth, we have to destroy Christianity, to destroy big states, to destroy the capitals, so that everything should be the same, etc.... And after everything is destroyed, then there will be peace...."

Fyodor Mikhailovich in autumn 1867 was very busy with his work. He was writing his novel *The Idiot*, which was supposed to be published in the first issue of *The Russian Herald* in 1868. The idea of the novel was an old and favorite one—"to describe a positively excellent person"—but it seemed to Fyodor Mikhailovich that it was a very difficult task to handle. This irritated him....

The whole winter passed for us quickly, in hard work without intervals, in the writing of the new novel. In February 1868, we had the exciting event which we have been expecting for a long time. Our dream at last came true, and a new creature, our first child, appeared in this world. But we did not enjoy our happiness for long.... In the first days of May, the girl caught a cold, and the same night she developed a fever and a cough. We were greatly alarmed, and our worst expectations came true: during the day on May 12, our dear Sonya died.

I cannot express the desperation we felt when we saw our nice young daughter dead…. It was impossible to stay in Geneva, where everything reminded us of Sonya, so we decided immediately to fulfill our old wish and to move to Vevey, situated on the other side of the same Lake Geneva.

During the fourteen years of our marriage, I cannot remember a summer as sad as that which I spent with my husband in Vevey in 1868. It seemed as if life had stopped for us. All our thoughts, all our conversations were concentrated on the memory of Sonya, on that happy time when she lit up our lives with her presence.

Every child we met reminded us of our loss, and in order to save myself from torment, we went out for walks outside of the city where we wouldn't meet children….

Fyodor Mikhailovich continued to work on his novel, but the work did not console him. To our sad mood was added our alarm about lost letters. On several occasions letters addressed to us were lost in the mail, and it was difficult for us to maintain communication with members of our families and with friends. This had been our only consolation….

In the autumn it became obvious to us that we had to change our difficult mood, and at the beginning of September we decided to move to Italy and to stay in Milan for the first few days….

The autumn of 1868 in Milan was very cold, and it was impossible to take the lengthy walks which my husband liked so much. There were no Russian newspapers and books in the local libraries. Fyodor Mikhailovich was very bored living without newspapers and news from the home country.

Consequently, after two months in Milan, we decided to go to Florence for the winter. Fyodor Mikhailovich was there some time ago, and he had good memories of the city, mostly of its artistic treasures. We often went to Palazzo Picti, and he was excited by the painting *Madonna della Sedia* by Raphael…. After the visit to the art gallery he, by rule, had to see the statue of Venus in the same building (Uffizi Gallery)…. This statue, my husband said, was a work of genius. In Florence, to our great happiness, we found a wonderful library with Russian newspapers, and my husband went there daily to read after dinner…. He also borrowed books in French, which he could read and speak perfectly….

In 1869 our financial circumstances were very difficult and we were in need…. We missed the company not only of Russian people, but people in general; we did not have a single acquaintance in Florence with whom we could talk…. They were alien, unfriendly people for us, and this complete separation from people was difficult for us…. We discussed the question of where we could go and where Fyodor Mikhailovich could find intelligent society.

So, in the beginning of August we went to Dresden and rented three furnished rooms. My mother visited us again, to help me during labor. We settled in the English part of the city, in 5 Victoria Strasse.... Here, on September 12, 1869, a happy family event took place: the birth of our second daughter....

After finishing his novel *The Eternal Husband*, Fyodor Mikhailovich sent it to the journal *Zaria*, where it was published in the first two volumes for 1870.... This was a response to my husband's stay in the summer of 1866 in Lublino, near Moscow, where he lived close to the summer cottage of V.M. Ivanova, his sister. In the members of the Zakhlebin family, Fyodor Mikhailovich depicted the Ivanov family.... Even in Velchaninov were some features of Fyodor Mikhailovich himself—for example, in his description of different games Velchaninov created when he arrived at the summer cottage. Nikolai Fon-Fokht remembered him as a participant of such summer evenings and amateur performances when Fyodor Mikhailovich was a very joyful person, a young and creative member of this group of people.

In the winter 1869–1870, Fyodor Mikhailovich was busy creating a new novel which he wanted to name *The Life of a Great Sinner*. This work, which my husband planned, was to consist of five big stories, each of 15 signatures. Each would be a piece of art in itself and could be published in a journal or as a separate book. In all five stories, Fyodor Mikhailovich was going to ask an important and tormenting question which he had been thinking over his entire life; that is, the question of the existence of God. Fyodor Mikhailovich put many great hopes into his novel, and regarded it as the end of his literary activity.

Many of his plans were realized, because many of the heroes he created for this novel became part of *The Brothers Karamazov*. However, at that time he could not fulfill his plans, because he was involved in some other work, about which he wrote to Strakhov: "I have big hopes for the work which I am writing for *The Russian Herald*, not only from the artistic, but also from the journalistic point of view ... even if my artistic side suffers in the process." This was the novel *The Demons* which appeared in 1871. This topic was a reaction to the arrival of my brother from Russia. Fyodor Mikhailovich was interested ... in the mood of the student's world. Here an idea appeared to Fyodor Mikhailovich—to describe the existing political movement in one of his novels. He took a student named Ivanov, called Shatov in the novel, as one of his major heroes. My brother spoke about the student Ivanov as a clever and outstanding person with a firm character, a man who had completely changed his former views. My brother was deeply affected when he read in the newspapers about the murder of Ivanov, for whom he had felt great attachment. Fyodor Mikhailovich took the description of the Peter's Academy, the park and the cave in which Ivanov was killed from the words of my brother.... The material for this novel was taken from reality. As usual, Fyodor Mikhailovich was not satisfied with his work; he changed it many times, and he destroyed fifteen signatures. The journalistic novel was not in the mainline of his creativity.

Time passed, and in April 1871, we celebrated the fourth anniversary of our stay abroad, and our hope of returning to Russia appeared and disappeared. In the end, my husband and I made a firm decision to return to St. Petersburg....

Chapter 7. Socialists Become "the Demons." The Citizen, A Writer's Diary, The Idiot *and* The Brothers Karamazov. *Friendship with the Royal Family.*

"We will proclaim destruction.... Russia will weep for its old gods.... I am a scoundrel, and not a socialist, of course."

(*The Demons*)

"Rogozhin whispered: 'I'll make a bed here.... So let her lie there now beside us, beside you and me....' 'Yes, yes!' the prince assented warmly.... 'Listen to me: what did you kill her with? The knife? The same one?' 'Aye, the same.... There's something else that was funny: you see, the knife only went in three or four inches, just under the left breast, and no more than a tablespoon of blood came out on her chemise, not a drop more.'"

(*The Idiot*)

"...The blood was flowing, flowing terribly, and instantly poured its hot stream over Mitya's trembling fingers. He remembered snatching from his pocket the new white handkerchief, and putting it to the old man's head, senselessly trying to wipe the blood from his forehead and face. But the handkerchief instantly became soaked with blood as well. 'Lord, why am I doing this?' Mitya suddenly came to his senses.... 'If I have killed him, I've killed him.'"

(*The Brothers Karamazov*)

I n 1871, Russian newspapers reported a violent murder in Moscow which became the most famous criminal case of its time. This incident was depicted by Dostoevsky in *The Idiot*, in which the lover-murderer and the former husband sleep together with the corpse of the freshly slain wife and lover.

Dostoevsky tried to escape his creditors by making another trip abroad. He warned the Russian people about the danger of revolution; he compared the socialist nihilists with devils in his novel *The Demons*, in which he predicted the Russian Revolution and the ensuing terror almost fifty years before the actual events took place. He decided to study Russian life in detail and started publishing *A Writer's Diary*, in which he commented on the latest political events and literary publications and the most notorious criminal cases.

In 1872, the Dostoevskys spent the whole summer in Staraya Russa, which thereafter became the place where they spent most of their summers. In 1876, the Dostoevskys bought a house in this provincial Russian town.

In 1872, Dostoevsky attended parties at the home of Prince Vladimir Meshchersky, the publisher of the newspaper *The Citizen*. At these meetings, he met with Konstantin Pobedonostsev, the future minister of the Tsar, who would be his friend for many years and who would later introduce him to the Royal family.

In December 1872, Dostoevsky agreed to become the editor of *The Citizen*. He "took this position temporarily, to take a rest from creative work and to acquaint himself better with everyday life" (Anna Dostoevskaya, 1981: 253). The work of the editor took too much of Dostoevsky's time: "We do not have a secretary ... I proofread articles by myself. It takes much of my time and is ruining my health. I feel that I am sacrificing my time, which is being taken away from more important artistic work.... I spend all my time on the journal" (*Complete Works*, Vol. 29, part 1: 262).

In the spring of 1874 Dostoevsky quit his editor's job. His advancing emphysema forced him, following his doctor's advice, to go to Ems, a water resort in Germany.

In 1875, Dostoevsky published his new novel, *The Raw Youth*, in Mikhail Saltykov's journal *The Fatherland Notes* (1875, nos. 1, 2, 4, 5, 9, 11, 12). He described it as "a novel about contemporary children, contemporary fathers and the relationships between them." Dostoevsky's own family was at the center of his attention.

In 1875, at the end of the year, Dostoevsky started *A Writer's Diary*, which he continued with occasional interruptions until his death. He called it "a chronicle of events," "a real diary in the fullest meaning of the word." The *Diary* included Dostoevsky's fiction, journalism and literary criticism, and reviewed the latest political events in Russia and abroad.

In 1877, Dostoevsky was elected a member of the Academy of Sciences.

In the late 1870s, he often read his works at literary evenings and became a regular visitor at literary parties and salons of St. Petersburg.

At the end of 1877, Dostoevsky announced in *A Writer's Diary* that he was planning to start working on a particular artistic piece which had been slowly germinating for two years. It was his largest and last novel, *The Brothers Karamazov*, which he worked on for almost four years. The plot was based on a sensational criminal case of patricide, but Dostoevsky wove in a great number of other stories connected with love, religion and children. He created a real encyclopedia of Russian life of that period. The novel was hugely popular at all levels of Russian society.

By this time Dostoevsky's political opinions had changed, and in the late 1870s he developed a close personal friendship with the royal family and became a regular guest at the Winter Palace in St. Petersburg. It had taken him almost thirty years to change his views on tsarism, from his involvement into an anti-government conspiracy in the secret socialist circle of Petrashevsky in the late 1840s to his becoming an ardent monarchist in his final years.

Naturally, this facet of Dostoevsky's career was never mentioned by Soviet biographers. Indeed, hardly any information on this subject has been available until recently, with the opening of the archives of the Tsar's family. The extremely negative and critical view of the socialist movement in Russia that Dostoevsky expressed in his later years did notee coincide with the official Soviet "party line," a fact which was impossible for the officials of Soviet propaganda to admit. Thus for many years, especially between 1930 and 1950, Dostoevsky's name was unwelcome in the view of state officials and absent from school programs. Even in the guides provided for high school teachers in Russia, Dostoevsky was referred to as "a bourgeois follower with an old-fashioned capitalist ideology."

Many of the documents in this chapter, which have been translated into English for the first time, shed additional light on Dostoevsky's relationships with socialism and the Russian monarchy.

One of the turning points in Dostoevsky's career was his trial and incarceration in the Omsk prison. It is important to stress that he often spoke of these events with his friends during the last years of his life. In her memoirs Katerina Letkova wrote,

> It happened in the winter of 1878-79 at the home of the Polonskys who had literary evenings each Friday.... Suddenly, among the people standing in front of me, I saw a man with a grey face, a small dark-blonde beard, fearful suspicious eyes and his shoulders hunched, as if he were cold. It was Dostoevsky!...
>
> I knew the same man from the portraits at high school. In my imagination that man was a giant with flaring eyes and a bold tongue; this man in front of me, however, was small, quiet and looked as if he were guilty of something. I could see that this was Dostoevsky—but I could not believe my eyes....

He told a story about the day he stood on the Semyonovsky Parade Grounds facing his execution on December 22, 1848. ... Here is his story:

And then some unknown voice pronounced: "You are sentenced to execution by shooting." We were surrounded by a crowd of several thousand faces, red from the cold, and thousands of inquisitive eyes.... All were excited.... All were excited about life. And we had to face death.... I did not believe it. I did not understand it until I saw a priest carrying a cross.... I then clearly understood that death was inevitable. I wanted everything to be over as soon as possible.... Suddenly I became indifferent to everything.... It all seemed so insignificant in comparison with transferring to another state, to some darkness.... Without any joy whatsoever, without emotion, we received the announcement that the execution had been cancelled....

He became pale and yellow at this point, as if he were made of wax; his eyes moved inside their sockets and his lips became pale and white as he remembered his sufferings. Then he smiled.

And in my imagination, I saw all the way to his Golgotha—his expectation of death, then his sufferings in the maximum security prison, his House of the Dead with all its horrors: the huge iron chains which he had on his legs for several years and which he was not even allowed to remove while taking a bath, the foul odor of the prison, the uncontrollable behavior and tortures undergone by the prisoners at the hands of prison guards.

This man had endured a terrible life... I wanted to kneel in front of him and bow before his sufferings [Katerina Letkova, "About F.M. Dostoevsky," in *Zvenia*. Moscow: Academia, 1932, Vol. 1, pp. 459–462].

Dostoevsky inserts this episode of his memoirs in *A Writer's Diary* and again and again reminisces about these events to his friends and colleagues.

Probably one of the turning points in the Tsar's attitude toward Dostoevsky occurred in February 1880, when the writer was elected the vice president of the Slavic Charity Society in St. Petersburg. At a meeting of the society on the twenty-fifth anniversary of the reign, Dostoevsky read his "Special Greeting Letter to the Russian Tsar" on behalf of the society. His address stated, "We believe in real, complete, living freedom, not in the formal freedom of this country..." ("The First Fifteen Years of the Slavic Charity Society," *Bulletin*, St. Petersburg, 1883; *The Old Times*, XV, p. 119).

Practically the next day, February 15, 1880, the Ministry of State decided to stop the surveillance of Dostoevsky by the secret police. Dostoevsky received a letter stating "there are no obstacles to stopping all police surveillance of you." He had remained under police surveillance for almost twenty-five years after his release from prison in 1856 (Grossman, *Zhizn' i trudy Dostoevskogo* [*Life and Works of Dostoevsky*], Moscow: Academia, 1935, p. 293).

Dostoevsky combined his monarchist views with repeated demands for the freedom of press. Orest Miller wrote about Dostoevsky at the time he was working on the January 1881 issue of *A Writer's Diary*, recalling that "He was very upset: 'If the censors don't let me publish these lines, everything is ruined'" (O. Miller, *Biography*, 1883, pp. 72–73).

Dostoevsky already had some influence at court and in the upper echelons of Russian society. As soon as he asked the minister of the press and censorship to change the censor for his *Writer's Diary*, Minister Abaza replied that "he would personally take care of this issue"; that is, he would read and censor the manuscript himself (*Peterburgsky Listok*, 1881, no. 24).

It is telling that during one of Dostoevsky's last meetings with the publisher Alexei Suvorin, several days before his death, he spoke again on the freedom of the press, repeating his conviction that "We should have complete freedom of the press in Russia ... complete freedom. We need more freedom than anybody else; we Russians have much work to do" (*The Northern Star*, 1881, II, pp. 139–140).

Among those who introduced Dostoevsky to the royal family was Konstantin Pobedonostsev, a senior state official who was, at different times, a professor of law at Moscow University; the teacher of the Tsar's children, the future Alexander III and Nikolai II; and eventually, one of the Tsar's ministers. He was a great admirer of Dostoevsky's works; besides, he understood that the Russian government would benefit from a friendship with a famous writer who greatly influenced and to a large extent formed public opinion in Russia.

Konstantin Konstantinovich Romanov, the Great Prince of Russia, was a great lover of literature. He often attended literary evenings and organized such receptions in the Winter Palace. Pobedonostsev became the intermediate man. He wrote to Dostoevsky on December 9, 1880, to say, "Thank you for your gift, the book *The Brothers Karamazov*. Let me recommend that you present this book to the Royal family." Having received Dostoevsky's consent, Pobedonostsev wrote another letter in about a week: "Dear Fyodor Mikhailovich, I wrote in a letter to the Great Prince that tomorrow, at noon, you will visit the Royal Palace to see him and his wife. As you enter, please announce your arrival to the guard. These matters are quite simple. Most sincerely yours, Pobedonostsev" (Rumiantsev Library Archives, Grossman, 1935, p. 313).

Dostoevsky visited the Royal Palace on a regular basis in 1879-80. His daughter Liubov Fyodorovna remembered that "the carriages with the royal guard used to pick up Father" and that "he came back after such meetings in good spirits." In her memoirs there are interesting observations about her father's behavior in the royal circle:

> It is interesting that Dostoevsky, who was a passionate monarchist at that time, did not want to follow court etiquette. He would be the first to speak in His Majesty's presence; he would sit down when he wanted; he would go out of the room with his back to the monarch. Alexander II was not offended by this and spoke about Father with respect and sympathy [L. Dostoevskaya, *Dostoevsky v izobrazhenii ego docheri* (*Dostoevsky in the Reminiscences of His Daughter*). Moscow, 1922, p. 105].

Konstantin, the Great Prince of Russia, personally wrote several brief invitations to Dostoevsky, with such wordings as "I invite you to attend a literary evening in the Winter Palace" or "Let me impose upon your freedom and ask you to visit us this Thursday at 9 P.M." (*Literary Heritage*, Vol. 86, p. 306).

While reading his works, Dostoevsky always had a great impact on his listeners, including the royal family. In his daybooks for March–May 1880, which have become available with the opening of the Russian archives, the Great Prince Konstantin wrote, "Today I had a meeting with Dostoevsky in the Mama's Pink Room.... Eugenia (the Princess) was very glad and spoke to him the entire evening. ... Dostoevsky's reading 'was much appreciated' by the Princess..." (*Literary Heritage*, Vol. 86, p. 137).

At such meetings, other members of the royal family were often present, including the Tsar, Alexander II; Sergei, his son; Helen, the daughter of Nikolai I; and Prince Konstantin. Dostoevsky often read pieces from *The Brothers Karamazov*, as Konstantin Romanov recollects: "I asked Dostoevsky to read the confession of monk Zosima.... Helen was crying, tears rolled down her cheeks" (*Literary Heritage*, Vol. 86, pp. 306–7). Besides his readings, Dostoevsky was eager to express his views on Russian and Slavic questions to the future Russian Tsar Alexander III, who himself was interested in the patriotic Russophile movement (Russian Archives, V).

Dostoevsky's new attitude toward the Russian royal family, and his praise of Orthodoxy and the monarchy were not a secret to anybody at the time. Many young radicals were quite critical of him during this period. As Katerina Letkova, one of the organizers of the women's movement in Russia remembered,

> When Dostoevsky was finishing *The Brothers Karamazov* he reached the height of his creativity, but in *The Diary* he was so foreign to many of his young readers that they could forget all his artistic skill and treat him as a political enemy....
> In spite of all this there has not been a single Russian writer who was as popular in society as Dostoevsky was during the last year of his life.
> Neo-slavophiles were becoming more and more popular; people were afraid of new terrorist acts; this fear caused a certain antipathy towards the students who were often associated with the socialists; faith in the godly, divinely oriented mission of the Russian people filled the hearts of people with pride and joy....
> This all resulted in the huge popularity of Dostoevsky. He was practically mobbed; he received hundreds of letters and answered them; he had visitors every day, old and young, seeking answers to the questions that tormented them or wishing to show their admiration for him; he received everyone; he thought it was his obligation not to refuse anyone... [K. Letkova "About Dostoevsky," *Zvenia*, 1932, Vol. 1, pp. 471–72].

Even in Dostoevsky's famous Pushkin speech, a speech concerning the history of Russian literature and the Russian national character, students could trace "the fine irony" directed against socialists:

The youth were very critical of Dostoevsky after his "patriotic" articles in *The Diary of a Writer* and *The Possessed*. We glanced at each other when Dostoevsky spoke about "the unhappy wanderers" in our native land ... now they no longer join the gypsy tribes, they do not seek for ideals among the gypsies at present....

They move to socialism ... they go about with the naïve faith that in their fantastic activity they will find happiness for themselves and for the whole world....

"A Russian man will not settle for less than the whole world."

This was said with such an artistic, fine irony ... all knew that Dostoevsky belonged to the supporters of the monarchy and that his *Diary* was read by the upper echelons of Russian society [Ibid., p. 469].

The final assertion certainly was true. As well, the *Diary* was read by practically every intellectual in Russia. In December 1880 and early January 1881, one month before his death, Dostoevsky reflected on current political events in the last edition of *A Writer's Diary*. He praised the Russian people, the Orthodox church and the Russian monarchy, and included a strong critique of the nihilist-socialist movement: "The nihilists appeared in Russia because we all are nihilists. This is a story that is washed with blood.... The Tsar for the people is not an eternal force. The Tsar is the personification of his people, of their ideas, hopes and beliefs" (*A Writer's Diary*, January 1881).

Dostoevsky's meditations on the political future of the country are prophetic, as they are in the novel *The Demons*, in which he had predicted the Russian Revolution: "The machine is more important than kindness. The governmental machine is what we have in Russia. We must change the formulas of the administration. It is necessary to do this." At this point in the manuscript, Dostoevsky wrote three crosses and six exclamation signs on the margins. With his deep knowledge of Russia, he probably sensed the weakness of the existing government and the threat of a socialist uprising.

Dostoevsky was harshly critical of socialism. In the chapter called "I Start Talking About Spiritual Things Because of Ignorance" and in the notes to the last issue of *A Writer's Diary*, he expressed the opinion that Russian socialism and the Russian future were continued in Christianity, "in brotherly love in the name of Christ" (*Complete Works*, Vol. 27, pp. 12–15). On the same pages, he compared socialism to Anti-Christ: "Socialism and Christianity. Try to define where one ends and the other begins.... Socialism ... will completely destroy Christianity and civilization. The Anti-Christ will come and have a victory for some time..." (pp. 49, 59). Dostoevsky called socialists "villains" in his notes about terrorism and went on to write, "Blood. Only those things become firm that are washed in blood. But they forgot that it becomes firm not for those who shed blood, but for those whose blood is shed. This is the law of blood on earth" (*Complete Works*, Vol. 27, p. 46).

The question of terrorism and blood was an important one in Russian society at the time, especially during Dostoevsky's last years. Several assassination attempts on the Russian Tsar and other senior state officials were made by the terroristic socialist group "The People's Will" ("Narodnaya Volia") between 1878 and 1880. On August 26, 1879, the Executive Committee of this secret terrorist group sentenced Alexander II to death. The assassination took place on March 1, 1881, one month after Dostoevsky's death. The following are excerpts from Russian newspapers of the time describing various earlier assassination attempts:

> The Tsar was walking around the Winter Palace when a poorly dressed young man approached the Emperor…. He drew a revolver from his pocket and shot at His Majesty several times. The Tsar was not injured.

> An explosion on the Moscow-Kursk Railway. The Tsar's private train misses the explosion by chance.

> Another assassination attempt fails: after preparing a bomb explosion, Stepan Halturin forgets to close the doors to the basement of the Winter Palace. The results of the explosion: 10 people dead and 50 injured.

> From the speech of the Russian Archbishop: "We do not know why His Majesty was late in his dining room for lunch that day. The angels have stopped him" [see Volgin, I. *The Last Year of Dostoevsky*, Moscow 1986, pp. 110–112].

Dostoevsky was very upset, since by that time he had become an ardent supporter of the monarchy. Alexei Suvorin, a journalist, friend and publisher, recalled the plans Dostoevsky expressed at the end of his life, under the influence of the revolutionary terror in Russia: "He said that he would write a new novel with Alyosha Karamazov as the main hero. He wanted to take him to the monastery and then make him a revolutionary. He would commit a political crime and then be executed…" (Suvorin 1923, p. 16).

And political criminals were indeed executed. Alexander Soloviev, the Tsar's attacker, was hanged in St. Petersburg. By a new order of the Tsar, the governor-generals across Russia received special powers to govern the country according to the rules of wartime. It was a sad time. During the wave of terrorism that came to Russia in 1879, there were sixteen executions of terrorists and three assassination attempts on the Tsar.

Many people in St. Petersburg awaited February 1880 apprehensively, but surprisingly there were no assassinations on February 19, the twenty-fifth anniversary of Alexander II's accession. The Tsar made a statement that he planned "to give more opportunities for society to participate in the discussion of state affairs" (*The Northern Star*, 1888, 11, p. 143). Everything was relatively quiet. However, on the next day, February 20, there was an assassination attempt on General Mikhail Loris-Melikov, the minister of the interior, in front of his house. The General was not injured in the shooting and even managed to catch the assassin himself.

Alexei Suvorin, a literary critic, a friend of the royal family and one of the most important Russian publishers, visited Dostoevsky on the 20th. They talked for about for two hours. Dostoevsky expressed his hope that, after the terrorist activity of the socialists and nihilists, a peaceful time in politics would be coming:

> On the day of the assassination attempt on General Loris-Melikov I visited Dostoevsky. He lived in a small poor apartment.... We did not know about the assassination yet.... Dostoevsky believed in changes for the better: "It will make a difference. I am not a prophet, but you will see for yourself" [Alexei Suvorin, *The Diary*. Moscow–St. Petersburg: Frenkel, 1923, pp. 15–16].

At the same time Dostoevsky was afraid that the official course for democratic reforms in Russian society initiated by the Tsar would be interrupted. The would-be assassin, Ippolit Molodetsky, faced a military tribunal the next day and was hung in two days. Molodetsky was brought through the streets of Petersburg in an open cart to his place of execution. On his chest the words "State Criminal" were written in big letters. Dostoevsky was present at the public execution in the center of St. Petersburg together with many other Russians.

Though he was a supporter of the monarchy and had depicted violent death in many of his novels, Dostoevsky was devoutly opposed to capital punishment. He had himself experienced the feelings of a person condemned to death, and this produced a great impression on him. As he wrote earlier, in his novel *The Idiot*, "It is written in the Bible 'do not kill.' To kill for a killing, or to execute a person, is a bigger punishment than the crime itself.... You cannot do such a thing with a human being."

Several days after the execution of the assassin, Konstantin, the Great Prince of Russia, wrote about his meeting with Dostoevsky in the Winter Palace:

> Fyodor Mikhailovich said that he saw the execution of the assassin of General Loris-Melikov and was upset.... Maybe he wanted to relive the feelings of his own near execution....
> He also said that the person to be executed is not afraid of future pain or future sufferings, he is afraid of moving into a new, unknown state... [*Literary Heritage*, Ibid].

Under the influence of the growing socialist terror in February 1880, Alexander II created a special commission to restore state order. Hopes for a peaceful future were expressed by many Russian intellectuals. Elena Stakenshneider, a friend of Dostoevsky and the hostess of a literary salon, reflected on the prevailing mood at the time: "It seems that the nihilists have become more quiet; I can't believe that this is true. Perhaps many of them have been caught by the police. God save us, maybe they are just getting quiet before they commit some new terrible acts..." (Elena Stakenshneider, *Diary and Notes: 1854–1886*. Moscow: Academia, 1934, pp. 425–441).

The Case of the Sixteen (sixteen terrorists charged with planning assassinations) ended in November with the executions of Kviatkovsky and

Presniakov in the St. Peter and Paul Fortress in St. Petersburg. Elena Stakenshneider wrote the following about these events:

> The court hearings that investigated the case of the sixteen criminals in
> Petersburg have just finished. These people committed three major crimes—
> three bomb explosions—one which was intended to blow up the Tsar's train,
> the other of which took place in the Royal Winter Palace....
> Two criminals, Kviatkovsky and Presniakov, are executed....
> This makes a bad impression even on the liberals..." [Ibid.].

Dostoevsky, in a grim mood because of this execution, remarked in *A
Writer's Diary* in January 1881, "Why can the state not grant an amnesty to
them? What is an execution? An execution for a political crime becomes a
sacrifice for an ideal." Unfortunately, he was right: the executions could not
stop the wave of terror in Russia. Dostoevsky died at the end of January 1881,
several days before the January 1881 edition of his *Diary* was published. Only
one month passed after the publication of these words before Russian society faced a decisive event: the assassination of the head of state, Tsar Alexander II. General Bogdanovich was indignant when he wrote on March 4, 1881,
"A terrible crime has happened. The Emperor is mortally wounded, two guard
officers are killed and eight are wounded.... The bomb exploded when the
Tsar was on his way to the palace.... How can we bear such a shame? All
society is indignant. We all mourn..." (Alexandra Bogdanovich, *Journal de
la General Bogdanovitch: chronique du temps des trois derniers Romanof.* Paris:
Payot, 1926).

The nation's mourning over Dostoevsky lasted for almost a month, until
it changed abruptly into mourning over Tsar Alexander II.

More than thirty-five years later, during the Red Revolution of 1917, the
prophesy of Dostoevsky was fulfilled: the socialists came to power in Russia,
bringing with them the destruction of old Russian values, Russian culture and
Christianity.

Vladimir Meshchersky: He Was the Most Loyal, Dedicated and Conservative Monarchist

(From V.P. Meshchersky, *Moi vospominaniia* [*My Memoirs*]. St.
Petersburg, 1898, pp. 175–182.)

> At the end of *The Citizen*'s first year of publication, we came to the
> conclusion that, starting the next year, I would have to find another edi-
> tor-in-chief. The situation was critical.

Dostoevsky approached me, asking, "Do you want me to be your editor?" At first, I thought that Dostoevsky was joking, but then I realized with joy and satisfaction that he was in earnest, and was sympathetic to my enterprise. This was not all. Dostoevsky expressed his magnanimity. Although he was Dostoevsky, a famous writer, he was also a poor man. At the same time, he knew that my financial resources, both personal and editorial, were limited. Therefore, he told me that he wanted only the smallest, most necessary salary, in order to cover his living expenses, he himself naming the sum of 3,000 roubles, plus payment for his own writing.

Early in the new year, we discovered a young new talent. When Dostoevsky was visiting me, he told me that he had a story by a certain Mr. Nemirovich, a man from the north of Russia. We started an interesting correspondence with this talented author. He was living in exile, in the Arkhangelsk region. His talent was genuine, and his eloquent letters made us decide to ask the authorities for amnesty on his behalf. Prince Palen, the minister of justice at the time, entertained our request, and the young author received amnesty.

Dostoevsky always rejoiced when he found the smallest traces of talent in the writing of others. Once he came to me and told me that he had found another talent, another Gogol, while he was looking through a pile of manuscripts. It was true. Moreover, this author possessed a real talent for humor, which showed itself in his story, *The Boots*.

Dostoevsky discovered that the author was a humble civil servant who lived in Okta, in the suburbs of St. Petersburg, and we began working with him. However, the man made no progress after this story, and everything he wrote later was very poorly conceived.

Dostoevsky was one of the most interesting and original people I ever met. From beginning to end, he story of his life was a story of great misunderstandings. It was one of the most unusual and original life stories I have ever heard. He was sent to Siberia and deprived of all civil rights for his political disobedience. It was rumored that he had participated in a conspiracy against Nikolai I.

Never in my life have I met a more complete, loyal, dedicated, and conservative monarchist, or more fanatical supporter of the Tsar than Dostoevsky. And this was the same Dostoevsky who went to Siberia, to a maximum security prison, for a political crime! I could not understand how all this could have happened. I have also heard from his own lips the following sad facts about this gloomy period in his life. He was a young military engineer who had become involved and was consequently arrested in connection with the so-called Petrashevsky case. I came to the conclusion that the main reason for this dramatic episode in Dostoevsky's life was his pride and strong character. He could not submit to any compromise. He did not stir a finger to defend himself. He did not utter a single word to betray anyone who had involved him in this dramatic misunderstanding. During the period of his incarceration he remained a very proud man. Later, in the 1880s, I heard from his friends that over there, in Siberia, Dostoevsky, the author of *Notes from the House of the Dead*, was really a fanatic apostle and defender of the Russian Tsar and of the monarchy, and that the speeches he made in prison had a great impact on the young people who had lost direction in their lives.

I had a special feeling for Dostoevsky, which was compounded with a bond of friendship and gratitude. This new feeling was one of admiration for this martyr ... whose soul was completely devoted to the Russian Tsar.

I have never met a more dedicated and complete conservative ... all our views seemed petty beside those of Dostoevsky. Some people, though, saw Dostoevsky as an idol for a revolutionary movement, or a symbol for the liberals. Dostoevsky loathed these self-styled admirers with all his heart and intellect. He hated Russian revolutionaries with all his might. But this made no difference, because of his other personal qualities; I have rarely met a person as filled with love as was Dostoevsky.

Samarin, for instance, hated Russian landlords because he lacked love. Dostoevsky, on the contrary, hated revolutionaries because he had too much love and respect for real ideas and for real truths. Therefore, he despised all kinds of lies.... There were two types of hatred that Dostoevsky felt towards revolutionaries: first, anger at all the damage they did to the Russian people and secondly, hatred for the great falsity of their views.

There was not a kinder person than Dostoevsky. He was ready to share everything he had, in order to help; at the same time, I have heard that there was hardly anyone more ill-tempered than he.

At the parties I gave, Dostoevsky showed himself to be a charming person. He told his stories, and he displayed his wit and humor, as well as his unusual and original way of thinking. As a new person entered the room however, Dostoevsky became silent for a moment and looked like a snail retreating into its shell, or like a silent and evil-looking pagan idol. And this lasted until the newcomer produced a good impression on him.... If the stranger engaged Dostoevsky in conversation, one generally heard him make some rude remark, or saw a sour look on his face.

Dostoevsky was opposed to the so-called "Women's Question." At that time, this movement took the form of eccentric behavior and attire on the part of some women, such as very short haircuts, dark blue spectacles and other fads. Among other things, these ladies did not notice that Dostoevsky disliked them, and they revered him as their teacher.

Several times, I was present at such meetings. A contemporary woman entered the room. She failed to notice the forbidding expression on Dostoevsky's face. She did not hear his cold tone of voice or his formal question, "What do you want?" This lady, filled with her own motives, began to tell her story, with animated and shining eyes and flushed cheeks.

Dostoevsky listened to her attentively. His expression became very nervous, and I saw that every feature of his face had become very tense, as if he had a volcano burning within. I sensed that he was restraining himself. As soon as this woman finished her discourse on the Women's Question, she waited for a word of support from Dostoevsky. At this point, the resolute enemy of the Women's Question put to her his own question, "Have you finished?" "Yes, I have finished," replied the lady with the short haircut.

"So, listen to me. My speech will be much shorter than yours. I want to tell you this: all that you told me now was very stupid and banal. Do you understand me? It was stupid. It would be better to dispense with you, in this matter, but your family, your children and your kitchen cannot survive without a woman ... a woman has only one main purpose in life: to be a wife and a mother ... there is no, there was no, and there will not be, any other 'social purpose' of a woman. This is all stupidity, senseless talk, and gibberish. All that you have told me here is nonsense, do you hear me? It was nonsense, and I am not going to say anything else to you."

This was the conversation I witnessed, and which I remember. He was equally strict and uncompromising with regard to all other fashionable, liberal, social questions, and he hated these issues because he considered them to be false. Dostoevsky greatly influenced people, and at the end of our first year of friendship, I understood that I had not been conservative enough before, and I felt that thanks to him I had developed my conservative views even further. He had a great and profound impact on me for the rest of my life.

Vsevolod Soloviev: Memoirs of a Close Personal Friend

(From Vsevolod Soloviev, "Vospominaniia o Dostoevskom" ["Memoirs About Dostoevsky"], in *Istoricheskii Vestnik* [*The History Herald*] 4 [1981]: 839–853.)

I knew Fyodor Mikhailovich well. He was not just a friend of mine, but a spiritual teacher; I confessed to him. A coincidence of very special circumstances helped to form our friendship which started from our first meeting. It all started from the early period of his life, when he was rather lonely in his relationships and had a very limited circle of friends.

The publishing of *Crime and Punishment* had been a great event for me. I read this book day and night, again and again. I had just graduated from the university, moved from Moscow to St. Petersburg and published several short plays.

At the end of 1872 I read in the newspapers an advertisement about the appointment of Mr. F. Dostoevsky as the new editor-in-chief of *The Citizen*.

A maid opened the door for me. At first I was so excited that for a while I could not utter a word. The maid asked me what I wanted.

"Is Fyodor Mikhailovich at home?" I uttered at last.

"Yes, but his wife is away, she is at the theater." I climbed the narrow dark stairs, took off my fur coat and put it on a chest in the small corridor.

"Please go inside, open the door, he is in," said the maid and went away.

I went through the dark room, opened another door and went into his study. You could hardly use the word "study" to describe this tiny, crowded, poorly furnished room where one of the greatest literary artists of all time wrote his works!

A simple writing table stood in front of the window. Two small candles on the table lit the room. You could see here several newspapers, old and new, some books ... a pen which looked old and cheap, a can for tobacco and some rolling paper for cigarettes. There was a small bookcase standing near the table. On the other side of the room, close to the wall, there was a sofa with red upholstery, the same sofa which served as a bed for Fyodor Mikhailovich ... several simple chairs, another small table and nothing more. I noticed all this later, but at that time I saw only his figure. He was sitting at the table. He turned around and stood up when he saw me.

He was a short man, rather skinny, but with wide shoulders. He seemed to be younger than his fifty-two years. He had a thin fair beard, a tall big forehead, greyish, thin and soft hair, light grey eyes, and a simple, plain, ordinary face. But this was only the first impression, because after seeing his face once you remembered it for a long time. His face produced a great impression; it betrayed a profound spiritual life.

You could see some traces of illness. For example, his skin was pale, as if made from wax. I have seen such faces only in prison; it looked as if it were the face of a religious fanatic. Later, I got used to his face and did not pay much attention to it, but the first time I saw it, it greatly impressed me.

I introduced myself. Dostoevsky shook my hand firmly, smiled to me with a tender and encouraging smile and said in a quiet voice: "All right, let us have a talk...."

I wanted to find out some details about his illness, that is, his epilepsy. I had heard that Dostoevsky suffered from this illness, and I wanted to ask him about his state of health, but I did not know how to start the conversation. However, it seemed that he guessed my intentions and he himself started to talk about his illness. He told me that he had just recently had a fit of epilepsy.

"My nerves have been shattered since my youth, you know," he said. "It happened two years before Siberia, during my literary quarrels and all that excitement. At that time I acquired a strange and painful nervous illness. I cannot even accurately express the unpleasant, disgusting feeling I experienced, though I remember it quite clearly. It would seem to me that I was dying, that it was actually death which came to me, and then left me alone and went away. I was afraid of falling into a lethargic sleep. It is strange that as soon as I was arrested, my strange disease disappeared and I never experienced it again, neither on my way to Siberia, nor in the prison itself. It was strange, but I became fresh, quiet and strong during my stay in prison. Though it was in prison that I had my first epileptic fit, and this illness has not left me since then...."

"I remember everything that ever happened to me before this first epileptic fit, every small occasion of my life, every face, every detail, everything I ever heard, I ever met, or read, I remember all the details. It all started after the first epileptic fit. I started to forget the people I knew so well, I started to forget faces. Moreover, after prison I forgot everything that I wrote. For example, when I finished writing *The Demons*, I had to read it from the very beginning, because I forgot even the names of the major characters...."

He spoke about the last four years of his life which he spent abroad. He told me about Russian men abroad who started hating Russia and who became Europeans. He mostly spoke about one particular person [Turgenev]. He also spoke about his passion for gambling, about roulette and about his love. He confessed to me, "Well, those people who fall in love, they forget about logic. You probably know how people can love!" His voice trembled and he started to whisper passionately. "If you have a true love, a pure love, you may think that the woman you love is as true and as pure as your love is. But imagine that suddenly you find out that she is a fallen woman, that she is dissipated, and that she is cheating on you. Then you start to love in her this distrustful, loose behavior which you hate at the same time, but you love even this.... And such a love can happen!"

It was late and we said good-bye....

The warm reception which I received from Dostoevsky during our first meeting, during our first evening together, this sincere attitude helped our friendship develop very quickly. Every time I had a few free minutes, I went to visit him, and, though we met often, every time we felt as if we had not seen each other for a week or so, and he reproached me for neglecting him.

He was in the habit of working late at night, going to bed about seven in the morning, and then getting up at 2 P.M. At this time I usually met him in his small and gloomy study. I saw him change apartments several times during the last eight years of his life, and all these places were very gloomy. As a rule, he had a tiny little room for his study, with hardly any free space inside.

After he had finished washing his face and combing his hair, he usually sat in front of a small writing table, in his old coat, rolling his terrible thick cigarettes. He chain-smoked while drinking the strongest possible tea, or even stronger coffee. Almost every time I entered his room, he looked gloomy and was in low spirits. You could see this right away: his eyebrows were knit, his eyes glowed, his face was as pale as wax, and his lips were pursed.

In such cases he usually started with the same ritual. He silently and peacefully shook my hand and then pretended he did not notice my presence in the room at all. I knew him well and did not pay any attention to this either. I sat down quietly, smoked a cigarette and took any book from the table. The silence usually lasted for a long time. It was only from time to time, when he made a pause between rolling another cigarette or looking at the newspaper, that he looked at me through the corner of his eye, blew his nose and coughed slightly.

I loved him dearly during these moments. Very often I could not help smiling. He certainly noticed that I was looking at him. He waited, taking his time, but my persistence always won. At last, he used to put aside his newspaper and turn his face to me. It was a nice face which he pretended was gloomy.

"Do you think that a respected gentlemen can behave like this?" he asked me. "You came here, you took my book, you sat down and did not say a word."

"Respected gentlemen do not behave like you either." I answered to him while moving slightly closer. "You shook my hand, then you turned your back to me, and kept silence all the time." Every time he smiled at this point. ...

Little by little, he became more and more friendly. His thoughts moved from one object to another and he expressed interesting, unusual points of view every time he spoke about anything. He sometimes started to daydream loudly and passionately about the future of all people, all mankind, as well as about the future of Russia. These dreams were often unusual, or paradoxical. But he spoke with such passion, such inspiration, and in such a prophetic tone that listening to him made me tremble. I followed his thoughts, his imagination, and asked him questions which heated his imagination even more....

After two or three hours of such conversation, I left his apartments with shattered nerves, as if in a fever. It was the same feeling I had when I read his novels....

Dostoevsky worked as editor-in-chief of *The Citizen* for only about a year, and all this time he seemed to be very tired. He had too much work to do. He worked very slowly, he was not created for this job. At last he came to the conclusion that he could not get from this job what he expected. He simply could not have two full-time jobs at the same time. At the time he was going to start writing a big novel. He had collected enough material and it was time to write, to create images, to do big artistic and creative work.

In the beginning of 1874, he complained to me about his terrible financial situation more and more often, and at last he said that he would work only until the next spring and then quit the editor's job. Due to the different circumstances, I did not see him very often at the time, that is, during the spring of 1874....

At the beginning of 1875 he came to St. Petersburg for several days, and he paid me a visit. I saw him in a completely new role, in a new environment. He was full of many new projects and new commitments. After my meeting with him, my apathy disappeared. We had several things to discuss, and I had been very glad to see him. When he entered my room, I saw at once that he was upset by something.

He told me the reason for his bad mood right away: "Tell me honestly, do I look like I am jealous of the glory of Leo Tolstoy?"...

I was surprised to hear such an unexpected opener of the conversation, though he always liked to start our meetings with some strange remark....

"I do not exactly know your feelings towards him, whether you are jealous or not of Leo Tolstoy, but you do not have to be," I said. "You both have your own ways. There is no competition between you, and therefore no cause for jealousy from your side. Please, tell me, who accused you of this?"

"Yes, accuse is the word. They accuse me, they are my friends who have known me for a long time, probably for about twenty years...." And he named these friends.

"Did they tell you about this straight to the eye?"

"Yes, almost.... They are so obsessed by this thought that they cannot hide it, and they speak about it all the time." He was very irritated, constantly walking from one corner of the room to another. "Well, you know, I really do feel jealous, but in a different way. It concerns my working conditions, right now. It is difficult for me to work, but I work. It is difficult for me to be constantly in a hurry.... Oh my God, it repeats all the time.... Recently I read my *Idiot* again. I had forgotten it completely, I read it as if I were doing this for the first time. There I found several good chapters and some good scenes. Well, for example, do you remember Aglaia meeting the Prince, there on the bench? And I saw that it was good, it was written as I wanted it to be, but there were so many things which were done in a hurry, things which should have been improved.... I am forced to write in a hurry all the time, again and again.... I never speak about this, but I suffer from this constantly.

"And he [Leo Tolstoy] is a wealthy man, he has everything, he is not concerned with how and where to make some money tomorrow. He can take his time while writing and improving his works, and this is very important.... So, I am jealous of him in this way. Yes I am jealous...."

I feel now that it's important for me to remember this conversation. It reveals a sad side of Dostoevsky's life. There were times when he was completely desperate, because money was absent from his pocket, because he lacked the means to support his family. I know what I am talking about. Throughout his entire life, Dostoevsky was in need of money, he could never relax and rest, not even for a moment....

All these facts influenced his literary work, and he was not entirely happy with the quality of all of his major creations. When he worked, he was constantly in such a hurry that sometimes he did not even have time to read what he had written before submitting it to the publisher. And, remember, he did not write simple, easy stories, such as coffee-table books. In his works there are many great pages and many chapters filled with real inspiration and great poetic scenes. And this was not enough for him; he added to his works serious psychological substance and he suggested original solutions to moral questions. With this kind of work, inspiration was not enough. He needed to work quietly and to concentrate, but his circumstances did not allow him to work peacefully.

Consequently, there are many unclear, unexplained, and mixed up things in his novels. Many of his works, especially his latest novels, contain great ideas, but sometimes they produce the impression that you have only read the draft of a book which is to be written in the future....

He was ill, tortured by his work, and getting increasingly tired. He was tired not only morally or mentally, but simply physically. It was difficult for him to work so hard, so extensively, and, so, he worked slowly. He often sold his new novels in advance, and the public waited for the consecutive chapters to be published. The publishers asked him to send the manuscript quicker, before the deadlines. He became irritated and excited, and he was always in a hurry.

Sometimes he forgot a few important details which had occurred at the beginning of a novel. Sometimes he saw, while finishing a novel, that several earlier pages should be changed and rewritten again, but often these pages had already been published. Certainly, there were great pieces in every novel, but in general, his novels were not completed units. The writer understood all this, he talked about it many times in our private conversations.

Aleksandr Briullov: Dostoevsky Speaks About Italian Art

(From A.P. Briullov, "Vstrecha s F.M. Dostoevskim" ["Meeting Dostoevsky"] *Nachala* [*Beginnings*] 2 [1922]: 264–265.)

My father, the painter Pavel Briullov, told me about his meeting with Dostoevsky in the late 1870s, in the house of the famous woman mathematician S.V. Kovalevskaya....

My father met Dostoevsky and another visitor, a young man from India.... He could speak English and French and was on his way to Western Europe, and Dostoevsky in connection with this started to discuss his views on the importance of European nations in the cultural process [of mankind]. The major message of his speech was that the creators in Europe were only Roman nations, and Germans did not create anything of their own, but only commented on and developed that which had been created by the Romans.... Dostoevsky said, "The notion of god in ancient Greek society was expressed by the *Venus de Milo*, and the Italians created the real Mother of God, the *Sistine Madonna*, but what kind of Madonna was created by the best German painter, Holbein? Is it a Madonna? She is a woman from the bakery! A bourgeois woman! Nothing more!..."

We took an example from literature. Someone said, "Excuse me, but *Faust* by Goethe, is it not an original piece of art which reflects the German creative spirit?..."

"*Faust* by Goethe? It is only an interpretation of the book of Jonah. Read this book and you will find everything important in *Faust*."

"Excuse me," countered my father, "but in that case, the *Sistine Madonna* is an interpretation of the antique notion of beauty."

"How do see this?" [asked Dostoevsky].

"I see it in everything, in every fold of her cloth...." He regretted that he pronounced these words. Something terrible happened to Dostoevsky ... who jumped from his seat, clutched his head in his hands and ran, his face distorted by convulsions and he repeated with indignation, "a piece of cloth." I thought that he would have a seizure... Everyone became silent. But Dostoevsky sat down, became completely silent and soon after, went away.... He could not even bear the thought that the *Sistine Madonna* could be reduced to a piece of cloth.

Elena Stakenshneider: Dostoevsky at Literary Parties

(From E.A. Stakenshneider, *Dnevnik i zapiski [1854-1886]* [*Diary and Notes: 1854–1886*]. Moscow-Leningrad: Academia, 1934, pp. 269-270, 281, 456–465.)

Yesterday we had a party, as we usually do on Tuesdays. As a rule, our guests do not stay after three o'clock, but this was a special occasion. Literary readings alternated with singing, and we did not notice how quickly the time passed. Several people read literary pieces: Dostoevsky, Masha Bushen, Zaguliaev, Sluchevsky, and Averkiev. Countess Dondukova sang, and her sister, Liadova, played the piano....

Dostoevsky was marvellous when he read "The Prophet." We all were touched....

He is an odd, but rather sophisticated old man! He is like something from a fairy-tale, full of unexpected wonders, frightening monsters and magic.

Sometimes he becomes gloomy, and he just sits quietly in the corner. He is easily disappointed by mere trifles. He could have interrupted any conversation and stopped it, but he simply could not find a pretext, and, besides, he does not have enough courage when he is in company. Some people do not agree with this, but I know that he does not feel comfortable in society. He sits quietly, thinks of how to intervene, and hesitates. His head is bowed, his eyes move around in their sockets; his lower lip parts from the upper lip and curves down. He does not speak much on such occasions, and gives laconic answers to any questions you may put to him. At such times, he can easily mock or tease anyone. Then, as if by magic, his mood quickly changes, so that he smiles and starts to talk....

Dostoevsky became famous not because he was in prison, not because he was the author of *Notes from the House of the Dead*, not even because of his novels, but mainly, because he created *A Writer's Diary*.... This work made his name well known to all Russian youth, and not only to youth, but to everyone interested in the accursed question [of the Russian Revolution]. Everything that is going on now can be explained by this. ... [Here Stakenshneider refers to the wave of revolutionary terror in Russia.]

His real glory started rather recently, about two or three years ago, when he started publishing *A Writer's Diary*. His former imprisonment and his other works compound this effect, but they are not the major reasons for his popularity.

His role as a teacher is so new that even he himself does not understand it completely. I pray to God to give him a long and a healthy life! Help him, Lord, and prolong his days! He can do many good things, make our faith more firm, and show us the way to the truth. People follow him because they are eager to listen to him; they do not know what to do. ... Long ago, when he had just returned from prison, and had written *Oppressed and Humiliated*, people were indifferent.

Everybody wants to be with him now. As soon as he appears, all eyes are on him, and the whisper can be heard in the hall: "Dostoevsky! Dostoevsky!" Yet, quite recently, only a brief while ago, he could sit quietly at our parties and our young guests would sing or play music, and not pay any attention to him. At the time, we often invited a lot of young people; when a group of students was released from the prison, we all danced. At that time his niece, Maria Mikhailovna, a pretty young lady and a good musician, occupied the attention of the young people much more than Dostoevsky....

He told us many stories about Siberia, about his life in prison, in exile. I can remember all these stories; many of them were reproduced in *Notes from the House of the Dead* and some in *A Writer's Diary*.

I remember very well only one story which was different. He told us how happy he was when, after his stay in prison, he was transferred to a place where he was to live in exile. The day he moved, he was going along a long road together with other former convicts. And on the way, they met a caravan which was carrying ropes and the people from the caravan gave him a lift. For several hundred miles he traveled sitting on these ropes. He told us that he had never been so happy, nor had he even felt as good as during this time, when he was sitting on the hard and stiff big rolls of ropes, with the blue sky above him, fresh air around him, and the feeling of freedom in his soul.

In 1862 we left St. Petersburg ... in the early 1870s, thanks to Mikhail Pavlovich Pokrovsky, we resumed our friendship and for a long time were on good close terms with Dostoevsky, becoming better and better friends until his death....

He was an outstanding man. He comforted some people, and irritated others.... All people searching for truth wanted to see him, although most of his colleagues and literary artists, with few exceptions, did not really like him....

Some people were of the opinion that he put on airs, that he thought too much of himself. I can say for sure that he himself underestimated himself, that he himself did not know his real potential. Otherwise he would have been more balanced and reserved, and would never have been irritated by so many small things, and people would have liked him more. Because it really impresses others when you have a high opinion of yourself.

He did not know his real spiritual power, but he could feel it and saw its impact on others, especially during the last years of his life. He knew a great deal about the human soul; indeed, he could describe the slightest movements of the human soul in his works, but sometimes he did not really understand the people who surrounded him....

He was easily hurt by innocent, casual remarks, for example, an enquiry about his health, and after such remarks would spend the rest of the evening in silence.... His favorite writer was Dickens.

Mikhail Alexandrov: Memoirs of a Publishing House Worker

(From M.A. Alexandrov, "Dostoevsky v vospominaniiakh tipografskogo naborshika." ["Dostoevsky in the Memoirs of the Publishing House Worker."] *Russkaia Starina.* [*The Russian Past*] 4 [1892]: 117-207.)

When I saw him for the first time, it seemed to me that he was not a typical intellectual, but a simple and a rude man.... However, I knew that he was one of the most intellectual persons I ever met.... He looked as a typical Russian....

He was very suspicious of people when he met them for the first time.... In one of his works he wrote that he was very slow to get close to new people, to start new relationships.... When he met a stranger, an average simple man, Fyodor Mikhailovich assumed that, since he was known to many people, this person would know the history of his imprisonment and exile, but he also understood that many people did not know *why* he was in prison, and that people simply looked at him and treated him as a former criminal.

Therefore, he was very stern and serious when dealing with strangers. He began to trust a person only after he had made sure that there was no animosity towards him.

For example, he trusted me [a technical publishing house worker] completely, because he knew that I was never rude to him. With other people in the publishing house with whom he had to work, he was on very official terms. All his financial matters he delegated to his wife....

I would like to write a few lines about the literary activity of Dostoevsky in *The Citizen*. He did not write much at the time; *A Writer's Diary* had only fourteen issues, but even this small journalistic work was difficult for him.... At the same time he simply had to write. Writing was Dostoevsky's life, it was the major source of income for him and for his family, and the editor's salary was not enough. Therefore, [after writing his novels] Fyodor Mikhailovich tried out the other genre of literature, writing political reviews, and he was satisfied with this kind of work; he succeeded in it.

The writing of political reviews and editorials for *A Writer's Diary* was not a simple thing to do, but nevertheless it was urgent and necessary.

In the *Diary* he could write whatever he wanted and omit important events, though in general, in a political periodical, especially one which reviewed international events, he could not omit much. This urgent job was difficult for Fyodor Mikhailovich, and it exhausted him both emotionally and physically.

He was a famous novelist, and he understood perfectly well that if he continued to work all the time like this, he would have to write routine on-spec work, doing reviews all the time. He understood that he would waste his great talent for nothing, for small routine things, and that he would not be able to create other significant literary works....

He understood this well, and I presume it was a real nightmare for him with only one way out: to quit his editorial job at *The Citizen*, a weekly journal where he worked.

He made this decision at the end of 1873, and wrote an official letter to the authorities stating that he would like to quit as the editor of *The Citizen*. His last political review was published in the first issue of 1874....

He wrote with his blood, with all his heart....

He brought his works to the publishing house by himself....

In spite of the great popularity of *A Writer's Diary*, and in spite of the great desire of Fyodor Mikhailovich to participate in social life as a journalist, in the second half of 1877, he made the decision to stop the publication of *The Diary* as of the next year. It was due to the same reason for which he had forced himself to quit his editor's job in *The Citizen*: the necessity of creating serious literary work. Certainly, Fyodor Mikhailovich was a hard-working writer, but his inspiration, his muse, did not suit a journalistic career, so to speak.... He did not like to glide on the surface, he always went into the depth, into the heart of the matter, down to the bottom-line, and it was impossible for him to do this while he was doing journalistic work, with its routine and its deadlines....

Fyodor Mikhailovich announced his decision in an article addressing his readers directly.... In a private conversation with me he told me that he hoped to see me again and to work with me in about two years. He said: "I will take a short rest, and then I return to work. I have been obsessed with an interesting idea for a long time and I want to develop it..., but it is impossible while writing *The Diary.*"

"Is it a novel?" I asked him.

"Yes, a novel, if you want to know," he smiled back.

The new idea materialized in a novel which was published about two years later. It was the new great novel, *The Brothers Karamazov.*

Liudmila Simonova: Dostoevsky Talking to Activists of the Women's Movement in Russia

(From L. Simonova, "Iz vospominanii o Dostoevskom." ["From the Memoirs About Dostoevsky"] *Tserkovno-obschestvennyi vestnik* [*Church and Society Messenger*] 16 [1881]: 4-5.)

Fyodor Mikhailovich was a very nervous, sensitive man who was easily irritated by anything. At the same time he was very kind and sincere person, and he responded to every friendly attitude. He could quickly change his aspect from one of friendship to the explosions of a bad temper caused by his unbalanced and shattered nervous system, long imprisonment and epileptic illness. But even in the periods when he was in a bad temper, he noticed a nice person, and even if he saw this person for the first time, he changed his attitude and behaved as a good friend....

I decided to visit him, but I postponed my visit because I knew that he was a nervous man and I was afraid to meet him in a bad temper. In the long run, in April 1876, I entered his study. My heart was beating loudly, and I felt embarrassed.

He lived in the neighborhood of Pesky, close to the Greek church, in a small apartment on the third floor. I remember his study, a small room with one window. Among the furniture was a leather sofa, a writing table with numerous piles of books and newspapers on it, several straw chairs and a small table by the wall. Among the other objects which were always present at his table were a glass of cold tea and some glasses containing medicine....

He was very pale, with a yellow complexion, and he coughed all the time and spoke in a whisper. I really do not remember whether I explained to him the reason for my visit. It was not necessary. He could cast a brief glance at a person and understand what was going on inside his or her soul. On that day he simply took me by the hand and we sat on his sofa. He started to talk about his *A Writer's Diary*. Three issues of this work had already been published at the time.

"By the way, my novels *The Idiot* and *The Raw Youth* are not understood even now," he said.

When he said this, I remembered that *The Raw Youth* was a novel about atheism and that it had greatly impressed me. His thoughts were so good, fresh and original that I could quote them everywhere.

The novel was about people who had lost their faith in God.

"And suddenly people understood that they remained alone, completely alone, and they felt as if they were orphans. So, people started to move closer to each other, they were filled with love, they took each other by the hand and they understood that they meant so much to each other...." I reminded him of these pages from *The Raw Youth* and then I expressed my surprise that sometimes the atheists reminded me of the early Christians.

"Yes," he said, "I would like them to be like this, but this is a dream. Without God people will start killing each other." And then he added: "They will call everything a paradox, even this thought."

Whom did he mean by "them?" ... As I understood, he meant literary critics. I tried to calm him down, and I said that, in spite of all the literary critics, his readers appreciated his works, and that young people and women especially read his work with special attention.

When I spoke about women, he made a comment: "I have thought about women for a long time. You see, several women like you have visited me, and several women activists have written me letters."

Anatoly Koni: Most Novels Were Based on Criminal Cases Taken from Real Life

(From A.F. Koni, "Vsterchi s Dostoevskim." ["Meetings with Dostoevsky"] *Vestnik Literatury* [*The Literary Herald*] 2 [1912]: 2-8.)

In the early 1870s, I was the prosecutor at the St. Petersburg District Court. One day, I received a letter from Mme. Kulikova, the sister of a good friend of mine, containing a personal request to help Dostoevsky....

He was the editor of *The Citizen* at the time....

I replied to Mme. Kulikova immediately, asking her to tell Dostoevsky that his conviction could be postponed until such a time as he found convenient. Shortly afterwards, I received a letter from Dostoevsky, in which he expressed his gratitude to me. His visit followed after the letter. When I made a return visit to him, I was greatly surprised by his very modest apartment, by the poverty of the rooms in which one of the greatest Russian writers lived.

We talked for a long time and he asked me many questions. He was very interested in the workings of the jury, and in the differences between the city courts and district courts. Dostoevsky was interested in the work of the Ministry of Justice and in several of the most famous criminal cases....

On October 15, 1876, St. Petersburg City Court convened to deliberate the case of Katerina Kornilova. This peasant woman, four months pregnant, was very much irritated by the reproaches and critical remarks of her husband, who kept repeating to her that his first wife had been a much better housekeeper. The woman lost her temper one day and threw her stepdaughter, a six-year-old girl, out of the window on the fourth floor. The girl was lucky enough to survive; she was not injured, only slightly scared. Dostoevsky was very much interested in this case....

He devoted several pages of *A Writer's Diary* to this criminal case. In those pages, he performed a deep psychological analysis of the human soul, and of the Russian national character. He made observations about the Kornilova case, and then wrote about the purpose of criminal courts in general....

He supported a "non-guilty" verdict for Kornilova, and he often visited my office in the Ministry of Justice... At last she was found not guilty....

Twenty years later, Leo Tolstoy depicted a similar case in his novel *Resurrection....*

Dostoevsky wrote about the Kornilova case that he felt proud to be the only person who had had enough courage to support the victim in public, to stand up against a judicial error, and to win the case....

Soon after this case I saw Dostoevsky again in the corridors of the Ministry of Justice. Dostoevsky was very much interested in the colony for teenage criminals situated in Okta, in the suburbs of St. Petersburg, behind the military factories, and I granted his request and took him there in 1872.

V. Pribytkova: Dostoevsky and Spiritualism.

(From V. P-va [V. Pribytkova] "Vospominaniia o Dostoevskom" ["Memoirs About Dostoevsky"], *Rebus* [*Puzzle*] 25 [1885]: 230-231.)

I would like to tell you my own recollections of Dostoevsky's attitude towards spiritualism. He did not like it at all, and he asked me several times to quit this practice which was harmful in every respect. In spite of Dostoevsky's negative attitude with respect to spiritualism, he was interested in it, and he criticized those people who simply mocked and laughed at spiritualism in public. Quite often he had rather lengthy discussions with me on the subject, but, in the long run, we usually did not find common ground.

He personally knew all the famous spiritualists, such as Aksakov, Butlerov and Vagner, and treated them in a friendly way, maybe because he liked their scholarly attitude towards the phenomenon of spirituality.

He believed in the events which occurred during the meetings at the spiritual seances, though, at the same time, he wrote in *A Writer's Diary* (April 1876) that he did not want to believe in all this.

However, he wrote: "You cannot stop those who want to believe in spiritualism…" also in *A Writer's Diary*. Dostoevsky undoubtedly was a great writer who knew people's hearts and psychology….

I remember the sixth week of Lent before Easter, when I visited Dostoevsky to say good-bye before going from St. Petersburg to Moscow. His wife was at home, and Fyodor Mikhailovich met me in the corridor. He told me that he could not talk to me for long, because he was busy finishing another issue of *A Writer's Diary*, though he would like to discuss some questions on spiritualism with me later. "This is not a big deal, your trip. You will not go to Moscow forever, there is no need for you to go there. We will observe Lent, and then please come and visit me at Easter; we will talk."

It worked out as he had said. I stayed in the city, and on the Easter holidays I visited Fyodor Mikhailovich again, following his invitation. He was at home. It seemed to me that at first he was not happy with my visit. I have rarely seen him with a face as gloomy as on that day. "You came in vain," he said. "I do not want to talk about spiritualism." I was not surprised by this cool welcome, and I said that I had come not to see him, but to see Anna Grigorievna.

At this moment his wife appeared in the corridor. She was confused by the rude behavior of her husband, and she invited me in. She offered me a seat and we started talking about spiritualism. Fyodor Mikhailovich disappeared at once.

In less than five minutes, though, he returned, with his usual cup of tea in his hands. He sat close to us and started listening to what we were talking about.

I told him about the spiritualists' meeting of our circle, and he continued: "This is all your nonsense, this is all your fantasy."

Then he told us how the family of his friends moved the table. The table turned, banged on the floor and answered the questions they asked, and then the table lifted in the air and moved across the room several times, here and there.

"Dear Fyodor Mikhailovich, what was it, a fake, a trick, or something of the sort?" I asked him. "Maybe your friends have had too much practice preparing tricks?"

"Well, you forget that, as I told you, it happened to the family of my close friends. They have never lied to me," he said, in a gloomy voice.

"Then how can you explain all these events, if you admit they did not lie to you?" I asked.

Dostoevsky was very disappointed, did not say a word, turned around and went out of the room. He returned several minutes later, when I was talking to his wife about something else. When we parted, he agreed, at the request of his wife, to visit one of the meetings of our spiritualists' circle.

It was interesting to observe the contradictory attitude of Fyodor Mikhailovich towards spiritualism. While he himself said that he did not like to explain some facts through mysticism, at the same time he sometimes displayed great interest in these questions....

Spiritualism irritated and attracted him at the same time.

Anatoly Alexandrov: Fyodor Mikhailovich in Staraya Russa

(From A.A. Alexandrov, "Fyodor Mikhailovich Dostoevsky [stranichka vospominanii]" ["F.M. Dostoevsky: A Page from the Memoirs"] *Svetoch i dnevnik pisatelia* [*Candle and Diary of a Writer*] 1 [1913]: 53–56.)

My meeting with Fyodor Mikhailovich Dostoevsky was one of the brightest events of my life. It was one of those events which seem to be small, unimportant, unnoticeable and rather quiet, but then, after they occur, become a part of your soul, stay in it for the rest of your life, and slowly, little by little, unnoticeably and quietly, make great changes in you, forming your outlook and influencing your way of thinking.

This meeting happened under circumstances which were very favorable to me. I got to know Fyodor Mikhailovich Dostoevsky in Staraya Russa where he came with his family during the last years of his life to have some rest from his hard work and from the busy everyday life of St. Petersburg.

This was during the second half of July 1878. As you know, this was the year during which we were at war with Turkey, when all directed their attention to the Danube and the Balkans where the Russian soldiers performed their heroic deeds. All Russian people and all of Russian society felt patriotism as they watched the noble struggle for the liberation of our brother Slavs.

Dostoevsky was fifty-seven years old, and I was eighteen. He was a famous writer at the height of his fame and of his genius and was publishing at this time his famous novel *The Brothers Karamazov*. It was published in *The Russian Herald*, edited by Mikhail Katkov. It was the time of his greatest fame: the time of his "swan song," his Pushkin speech. I was then a very humble young man, unknown to everybody, a student in the senior classes of Moscow College, and a great lover of literature who had just started writing poetry secretly. I knew Dostoevsky as a writer; I had read his novels and I loved him passionately.

The director of the college, Mr. M. Katkov, was at the same time the publisher of "The Moscow News" and *The Russian Herald*. Following the recommendations of doctors, he had sent me to Staraya Russa for the summer, where I could receive some baths [water resort treatment]. I was accompanied by one of the best assistant college teachers, a friend of mine, Kuz'ma Filippovich. Before my departure from Moscow, Mr. Katkov told me that Mr. Dostoevsky would stay in Staraya Russa the whole summer, and that he would write about me to Dostoevsky, so that the writer would visit me from time to time.

My teacher found me a very small house in Staraya Russa, where we stayed. It was a small and modest building, and it corresponded with our financial means. The floor was not painted, and it sloped to one side. However, it was situated right in front of the park, and it was very convenient for me with my illness.

One day, a very nice day in July, Kuz'ma Filippovich, who usually went with me to the bath and waited for me somewhere nearby, came into my bathroom and pronounced that family name which is known to all of Russia. However, he did mispronounce this name and reported that some writer, Mr. Dostroemsky, had asked about me and had ordered him to ask me whether he could pay me a visit the next day, and at what time it would be most convenient. I was very happy to hear this news, it was very easy for me to set up the time, and Kuz'ma Filippovich went out with my answer to Fyodor Mikhailovich who was waiting for me outside.

On the next day, at the appointed time, the writer entered my small house. As I waited for the visit of this man, I had felt very humble and excited, and had counted every minute, but during the first few moments of seeing him, and at the first sound of his voice, all my humbleness and excitedness disappeared. In five minutes it seemed to me that we were very good friends, and not only good friends, but that we had known each other for a long time and loved each other, and that there was nothing for us to do other than treat each other in a simple, sincere and open way, believe in each other and love each other.

He was not a young man by far, but he was very optimistic and full of energy. He dressed simply, and had a typical Russian face, with a touch of grey in the beard, he moved quickly and had a very spiritual, big forehead, a very nice friendly voice and wonderful eyes.

These were very attentive eyes, brimming with life and energy, and it seemed as if they penetrated into your soul, seeking out all of its curves and secret places. His glance contained no hint of mockery, nor was it cold and evil. It did not speak of reproach, but rather of something very friendly and very nice which asked for sincerity, trust and understanding.

One got the same impression while listening to his voice, which was hearty and sincere. In fact, it seems to me that I hear this voice even now, as I speak about him, and that his eyes, thoughtful, encouraging and kind, look directly into my soul.

He started off by apologizing for not being able to visit me immediately after receiving the letter from Mr. Katkov. His reason was a fit of epilepsy, after which it had taken him a rather long time to feel better. He asked me, "Do you have any knowledge of this illness?" I answered that I knew about it from its description in his novel *The Idiot*. He started to talk about his literary work; he was very much involved with the topic of *The Brothers Karamazov*, in which he wanted to show several new types, and he did not know whether he would be able to achieve his desired effect. His comments about this were very short and simple, free of any exaggeration, or any attempt to look important and to show himself at his full height. He went on to the story of Staraya Russa, our water resort. He knew about the doctors, and he praised Dr. Rochel. When he spoke about me and about my illness, he tried to comfort me and to encourage me. He said that I would be cured and that my health would improve in the future.

One outstanding and very rare quality possessed by this great man, this wonderful story-teller, greatly surprised me. It was his ability not only to speak well, but to listen well. He listened to the person he spoke to with such great interest and attention, with such involvement and meditation, that the other person, in turn, spoke with more sincerity and inspiration. This was my first meeting with Dostoevsky and I regret that it was the last one. When I left Staraya Russa, I did not see him again. When I returned to Moscow, I commenced reading his works thoughtfully and attentively. The more I read his books, the more I understood his great role as a symbol of our social conscience, and as a great expert of the human soul in general, and the Russian soul in particular.

Dostoevsky brought Russian society with him to the Orthodox Church, which this society had forgotten. He brought the exhausted and tired Russian intellectual with him, asking him to walk with him along the great historical Russian way and to shed the tears of the prodigal son, and he said: "Be humble, you proud man! Be hard-working, you lazy man!"

Dostoevsky addressed the Russian intelligentsia on behalf of simple Russian people, saying: "Love not me, but what belongs to me, our shrine and our past. Bow in front of it and take it into your empty and tormented soul."

Orest Miller: The House and the Study of Dostoevsky

(From O. Miller, "Dom i kabinet Dostoevskogo" ["Dostoevsky's House and Study"], *Istorichesky Vestnik* [*The History Herald*] [1887]: 572–574.)

In early June 1885, I was lucky enough to be invited to spend several days at the Dostoevskys' summer cottage. This cottage had provided the writer with a quiet escape during the last years of his life, years full of hard work. Anna Grigorievna [Dostoevsky's widow] invited me to stay in the bedroom next to Dostoevsky's study. As I entered the writer's room, I experienced feelings of sadness and admiration. Every time I passed Dostoevsky's table, I stopped for a second. This was the table at which Fyodor Mikhailovich had often worked late at night. He had liked this place better than St. Petersburg....

After his Pushkin speech, the celebration and glorification of Dostoevsky had quickly and regrettably turned to criticism. What was even more surprising was that the criticism of Dostoevsky came from his close friends, from the people who had been the first to shake his hand after his famous speech, and the first to express their admiration and sympathy.

It was from this study that Dostoevsky wrote me a letter expressing his deep regret regarding these events. He was upset that I hadn't been able to participate in the celebrations in Moscow, adding, "I was strongly criticized in the press, as if I had committed a theft, or a fraud, or had done some other mean thing, or as if I had robbed a bank. Even Jukashev was not criticized more severely." This was one of the last strokes of misfortune that sent Dostoevsky to his grave.

Dostoevsky visited Staraya Russa for the first time in May 1872, during his first summer in Russia after four years abroad. He chose the town of Staraya Russa for his summer stay following the advice of his doctors, who recommended the local spa for his children.

During the first summer he stayed on Pyatnitskaya Street, in the house of Ivan Rumiantsev, the local priest. Staraya Russa seemed beneficial to the health of his children, and Fyodor Mikhailovich decided to go there again the next summer, in 1873. This time the family stayed at the Gribbe house. At that time Dostoevsky was busy editing *The Citizen* (although he soon quit this job). Consequently, he could not live in Staraya Russa permanently, but instead, visited his family several times during the course of the summer.

Fyodor Mikhailovich liked the simple and quiet life of the town. When he visited it in 1874, he decided to stay for the winter of 1874-75. Here Fyodor Mikhailovich wrote his novel *The Raw Youth,* which was published in *The Fatherland Notes* in 1875....

In August 1875, his son Alexei was born (he died in 1878). From this time on, there grew around the house very special memories for the Dostoevsky family. When A. Gribbe, the owner of the house, died in 1876, and Mrs. Eliseeva, his heir, wanted to sell it, Fyodor Mikhailovich took advantage of this opportunity. Although Dostoevsky's financial situation was not entirely secure, the family bought the house for the moderate sum of 1,150 roubles.

The Dostoevsky house stood on the bank of the Pererytitsa River, in what was the Kolomets District. From the windows of the house, there was a wonderful view of the river and a small village situated on the opposite bank. In front of the house, along the river, were several huge old trees which had been planted in the time of Arakcheev. Behind it was a large backyard, a garden, and an orchard. On the same piece of land there were several wooden outbuildings: a horse stable, an icehouse, and a bathhouse. The summer cottage afforded all the comforts of country life.

There were six rooms on the second floor—not large, but cozy. The writer's study occupied the corner room with three windows.

Fyodor Mikhailovich liked Staraya Russa very much. He usually arrived in early May and sometimes stayed for the whole summer, until late October. Very few people knew him in Staraya Russa, so he enjoyed complete solitude. For the most part, he immersed himself for days on end in literary work, his favorite activity. Dostoevsky's health always improved in Staraya Russa. The salt-filled air was good for his weak chest. Besides, he liked to be there because his children became healthier and stronger in the fresh air.

Because of his deteriorating health, Fyodor Mikhailovich had to go abroad every year for several weeks, to a spa in Ems, Germany. He did so in 1875, 1876, 1878 and 1879. He always tried to finish his medical treatment as soon as possible, in order to return to his family in Russia. There was only one summer during which he did not go to Staraya Russa, in 1877, the year he went to the Kursk region. Dostoevsky wrote several works at the house in Staraya Russa, such as *A Writer's Diary* (1876), part of *The Brothers Karamazov* and his Pushkin speech.

The Dostoevsky house in Staraya Russa belongs at present to his family.... The house, as well as its interior design, is preserved as it was during the writer's lifetime. Only one addition has been made by members of the Dostoevsky family: the walls of the house have been decorated with portraits of the writer.

In its simplicity, Dostoevsky's house typified the monk Zosima's humble attitude to life: "I cut away all redundant and unnecessary needs." There never was and could never have been anything redundant in Dostoevsky's life....

... During his last years in St. Petersburg, Dostoevsky lived in the Kinkostrom house (No. 2–5), on the corner of Kuznechny and Yamskaya streets.

Fyodor Mikhailovich rented the Kinkostrom apartment in the fall of 1878 and lived there until his death.... He wrote major portions of his novel *The Brothers Karamazov* and *A Writer's Diary* (1881) there. On the walls hung pictures of Fyodor Mikhailovich and his children, and on the bookcase stood a portrait of his wife. On the wall over the sofa hung a copy of the *Sistine Madonna*. Fyodor Mikhailovich considered this painting by Raphael to be the greatest of all works of art....

The apartment was not at all luxurious. Dostoevsky did not know what luxury was. Those readers who criticize Dostoevsky too often mention, for example, the financial concerns voiced in his letters from abroad, but they do not know that all the money he made from his literary work went to pay off the debts of his late brother and to meet the basic expenses of the writer and his family. The author of these lines met and appreciated Fyodor Mikhailovich only during the last years of the writer's life, yet I can say this of him: "This man did not profit from other people's lives, like the people about which on occasion he wrote. This man lived the life he depicted. He had every right to speak about the things he wrote."

Vladimir Korolenko: Dostoevsky Speaks About Russian Writers

(From V.G. Korolenko, "Pokhorony Nekrasova i rech' Dostoevskofo na ego mogile" ["Nekrasov's Funeral and Dostoevsky's

Speech on His Grave"], in V.G. Korolenko, *Sobranie sochinenii* [*Works*]. Moscow: Gosizdat, 1953, pp. 197–200.)

> Nekrasov died at the end of 1877.... Dostoevsky wrote in his *Writer's Diary* that the last poems by Nekrasov were as good as his early, best poems....
>
> When Nekrasov died (27 December 1877), his funeral turned into an impressive demonstration. The mood of our youth coincided with the mood of all educated people, and St. Petersburg had never seen such a huge funeral procession before. The funeral started at 9 A.M. ... and the immense crowd finally dispersed late at night...
>
> I was lucky when, together with a couple of friends, I managed to get fairly close to the grave, to the stone fence of the cemetery. I climbed atop this cemetery wall, where I grasped the branches of a tree, in order not to fall, and I heard and saw everything.
>
> Dostoevsky spoke in a quiet voice, but in a very emotional way. His speech produced a variety of responses in the press. He put Nekrasov's name on the same level with those of Pushkin and Lermontov, and some people in the crowd did not agree with him.
>
> "He is better than those poets," yelled someone from the crowd, and two or three voices supported him.
>
> "Yes, he stands higher, because others merely continued the Byronic tradition in Russian literature" [replied Dostoevsky]....
>
> Dostoevsky certainly did not agree with all of his listeners or admirers. Later, he said that people recognize only those poets who respect the values of the people, that is, the throne and the church. But these were his later observations. On that day, I remembered Dostoevsky's words about the great social changes which would occur in our society, about revolution. He was a prophet who spoke about people and about [world] history....

I. Iasinsky: Dostoevsky's Meeting with Anti-Christ

(From I.I. Iasinsky, *Roman moei zhizni. Kniga vospomianii* [*The Novel of My Life: A Book of Memoirs*]. Moscow: Gosizdat, 1926, pp. 117–119, 168–169.)

> A short man in a fur coat with his head thrown and his hand outstretched came into the room without greeting us and screamed hurriedly, "I am still waiting for my royalties! And royalties there are not! And royalties were promised today!"

At this moment, the publisher of the journal, Mr. Kliuchnikov, came in from the next room ... and started to explain why the royalties had not been sent.... Actually, they discussed not the royalties but the advance for a future novel....

The man in the fur coat made the comment that they had let him down in their promise to send him money. Kliuchnikov went out for a moment and quickly returned bringing an envelope with the money....

Maikov introduced me to Fyodor Mikhailovich.... Fyodor Mikhailovich threw me a brief glance. "Poems? ... It is a pity, Apollon Mikhailovich, that you did not go to the Tolstoys' last party," Dostoevsky said. [At the time Dostoevsky often visited Sofia Tolstaya, a distant relative of Leo Tolstoy.]

"...They had a party," continued Fyodor Mikhailovich. "Representatives of high society were walking in front of me.... Ministers, secret advisers, top rank officials, high society ladies...

"I saw a very pleasant young man who looked very fashionable. How can I tell you? Maybe he was the ambassador from a great country like France or a rich businessman. He looked very smart.... I couldn't take my eyes off him and what is most strange is that from the very beginning I thought, may he was an anti–Christ? And as soon as I thought this, I noticed a piece of beautiful fur tail that appeared from beneath the folds of his suit. Yes! You can laugh at me; though you are secretly religious, you are known as atheists, and I understood that it was an hallucination.... I didn't trust my eyes and I decided to use the sense of touch. As he was gracefully passing me, moving his body in a beautiful way and approaching a woman standing close to me to kiss her hand, at this moment, I dared to catch him by his tail! And what do you know, it was definitely a real tail, almost like sable, living, warm and even containing some electricity. And he himself looked at me welcomingly, as if he had known me for a long time, as if he wanted to say, 'Did you recognize me?' and then he disappeared. I truly cannot remember how he disappeared. He vanished into thin air. But this definition does not fit. It happened much quicker than that. He disappeared not in a second, but in one-tenth of a second...."

"What is your explanation? Was it a vision or a real event?" asked Maikov.

"A vision? This was a fact!" repeated Fyodor Mikhailovich excitedly. "I do not make conclusions, but I have no doubt that he is coming and his kingdom is at hand."

He stood up quickly and went to pick up his coat. "Well, Fyodor Mikhailovich, where are you going? Would you care for a cup of tea?"

"Do I want tea? Why would I want tea? This is slander. I wanted to share this topic with you. Anti-Christ, that is, the most terrible thing, is coming to this world little by little, and I wonder who will chop away his tail?..."

When Fyodor Mikhailovich left, there was a brief silence. I was the first to break the silence: "Who was this man?"

"It was Dostoevsky."

N.F. Bunakov: According to Dostoevsky, the Idea of Socialism Was Alien to Russia and Was Brought from the West

(From N.F. Bunakov, *Zapiski. Moia zhizn* [*Memoirs. My Life*]. St. Petersburg, 1909.)

> *[From the book of rare memoirs of a teacher, anthropologist and journalist who was a member of the revolutionary terrorist organization "Land and Freedom." He worked with Dostoevsky on his periodicals* Time *and* Epoch.*]*

Dostoevsky invited me to contribute to the journal *Time*. Once he invited me to a party where I met the editorial staff of the periodical. Fyodor Mikhailovich was very nervous, he was pacing back and forth across the room in small baby steps, and occasionally said something, almost in a whisper. Everybody became silent at the time when he spoke. It seemed that he was the prophet of this literary circle, and everybody admired him. He spoke about the purifying force of sufferings, about the greatness of the Russian people, about the impossibility of hatred and violence.

He also strongly criticized ideas borrowed by the contemporary generations from the books brought to Russia from the West. All these ideas were alien to Russian life.

V.M. Peretz: Scars Left by Prison Shackles Were Displayed in Public

(From Dostoevsky, *A One-Day Newspaper of the Russian Bibliogical Society*. Moscow, 30 October 1921.)

> *[Memoirs of a member of Russian Academy of Sciences, a famous Russian linguist.]*

At the end of the 1860s, Dostoevsky became immensely popular among the reading public. His every word was commented on and listened to. His readings at literary evenings gathered a great number of listeners. Dostoevsky spoke about the Russian soul, the future of Russians, and developed his ideas which he later used in his artistic works. He criticized fashionable materialism.

One of the students asked him a question, in a very sharp and blunt manner: "Who gave you the right to speak like this, on behalf of all Russian people?"

Dostoevsky made a quick and unexpected movement, and displayed a part of his feet from under his pants, and answered to the greatly amazed audience, by showing the scars made by the prison shackles on his feet, "This is my right to speak like this."

A.G. Shile: Frequent Epileptic Fits— A Terrible Experience

(From *Birzhevye vedomodsti* [*The Stock Exchange News*] 12144 [27 January 1911].)

Almost forty years have passed since I met Dostoevsky for the first time, when he took the editorship of the *Epoch* journal, after the death of his elder brother Mikhail.

I came to his apartment on the Ekaterininsky Channel. He was deeply in meditation about something. His face was pale; he looked at my face and did not recognize me. He had some strange expression in his eyes.... In less than ten minutes, Fyodor Mikhailovich had an epileptic fit. His face was completely changed by a painful grimace, and he hit his head against the armchair in which he sat. A foam appeared from his mouth, and he made such a snore that I felt terrified. I could not leave him; I was afraid that something worse could happen. I asked for the landlady. She came with a white cloth in her hands and covered the face of the suffering man. It seemed that she got used to such fits of illness, because afterwards she went back into her room and left me alone with the sick man. I could not go, I felt such a pity for him.

In half an hour, a bell rang at the door, and a young man came in. He was a student and a nephew of Fyodor Mikhailovich. He came to his uncle and took the white cloth from his face. Fyodor Mikhailovich breathed quietly, and he fell into a sound and deep sleep.

V. Vasiliev: Meeting with the Royal Family During the Creation of *Crime and Punishment*
(From *Stolichnaia molva* [*The Rumors in the Capital*] 341 [9 December 1913].)

[From the memoirs of Maria Ivanova, Dostoevsky's niece.]

This was in Lublino, near Moscow. During the night, Dostoevsky worked there on *Crime and Punishment*.... During the day he was busy with his family, his friends and with the routine of life at the summer cottage.... It was strange that such a great psychologist was very naïve in the high society relationships and accepted the etiquette of high society as a sincere friendship. For example, he participated in the amateur theater performances which were organized by members of the royal family. He was often invited to the rehearsals at the Winter Palace, and he invited his young nieces with him, saying, "Please join me, let us go together. They [the Tsar and his wife] are such simple people, and they would be happy to see you."

Once he told us an interesting story about his visits to the Royal Palace. He was a very good speaker, and when he spoke, he had a bad habit of holding the buttons, or sides of the dress of the person he was talking to. Once he spoke in person to the Empress, Maria Fyodorovna. They had an interesting question to discuss, and he was completely involved in the conversation. Suddenly he noticed that he was holding Her Royal Majesty at the button of her dress, and they were standing at the entrance to her bedroom. It turned out that the Empress was trying to escape from the speaker, and slowly stepped back into her room. She could not interrupt him, though, because she was interested in his speech, so that tears rolled along her face. Fyodor Mikhailovich started to apologize, but the Empress asked him not to feel embarrassed and to continue his conversation....

I. Izmailov: Anna Dostoevskaya Recollects About Writer's Epilepsy
(From *Birzhevye vedomodsti* [*The Stock Exchange News*] 15350 [28 January 1916].)

A terrible illness could destroy all our happiness. The greatest interval between the fits of his illness was four months; sometimes they happened

every week. There were terrible cases such as when he had two fits during the week, and sometimes he had two seizures, one following another
with an interval of several hours.

He uttered a terrible, inhuman cry, a noise a normal person cannot
make. Very often I ran from my room to his room and held him standing in the middle of his room with his face contorted by convulsions,
his body shaking all over. I embraced him from the back, and then we
went down on the floor together. Usually the catastrophe happened at
night.... Therefore, he used to sleep on a wide and low sofa, in case he
might fall down. He did not remember what was going on when he
regained his consciousness. And then he asked a question, "Was it a
seizure?" "Yes, my darling," I replied. "How often do I have them? It
seemed to me that I had one recently." "No, you did not have them for
a long time." I tried to calm him down. After the seizures, he fell asleep,
but he could be awakened by the slightest noise—for example, a sheet
of paper falling from the table. Then he jumped up and uttered some
words which nobody could understand. You know, one could not cure
this illness. All I could do was to loosen the upper button of his shirt
and take his head into my hands. But it was painful for me to see the
convulsions on the face of my beloved man, his face turning blue, the
arteries filled with blood. I saw him agonizing, but I could not help him.

I had to pay for the happiness of being close to him with my sufferings.

Maria Stoiunina: The Dostoevsky Family: Romance Which Never Ended
(From *Novoe Russkoe Slovo*, New York, 15709 [1 May 1895.])

I remember well Dostoevsky's wife, Anna Grigorievna, who was my
closest friend. They had a very close connection; they adored each other.
She spent thirty-five years of her life after the death of her husband dedicated to the distribution of his ideas, his fame. She never parted with
Dostoevsky's letters to her, and brought them with her wherever she
went.

Once I remember how Dostoevsky received royalties, about 250 or
300 roubles. Then he went to the central shopping center in St. Petersburg, to the Morozov Jewelry Shop, and bought a big golden bracelet,
and made this a gift to Anna Grigorievna. She told me that she managed to convince him to get rid of this gift. She told him, "Our children
do not have good shoes, do not have enough clothes, and you bought
me such a precious bracelet." He felt desperate. "I was so happy that I

made some money, and that I could buy a gift for my beloved wife! I implore you, please keep it with you...." In the middle of the night she got up from her bed, [saying,] "But we have to think about our children first." And they had this tender drama during the whole night....

Dostoevsky could suffer physically when he saw the suffering of other people. Once he read in the newspaper that a woman killed her small baby and threw the dead body in the garbage. After this, Dostoevsky could not sleep for a night or two, and he tortured himself thinking about this woman and about her child. He could not bear the suffering of the children.

P.I. Karepin: A Story About Dostoevsky's Brief Incarceration in the 1870s
(From RGALI Archive, File 553–1–1077.)

In the 1870s I worked as a prison guard at the Hay Market Prison [Sennaya]. It was a very boring service, I had the same kind of work every day, and I could hardly make a living for my family. I remember the writer Dostoevsky was in the prison cell.... He prayed every night before going to bed. He stood in the dark corner for a long time, with his hands crossed on his breast. After he finished his prayer, he went down on his knees, took a cross from his neck and kissed it, and then, without saying a word, went to bed.

They spread rumors that Dostoevsky was a Jew. I do not know this exactly, but he was not pure Russian....

During the day, Dostoevsky read a lot, or wrote letters. He gave me some money to buy him the writing paper; it was allowed for the officers to leave the prison for a short time during the day. Once Dostoevsky received money for his publications, he wanted to pay me for my service, but I refused. I told him, "Though it is against the prison regulations, I am helping you, but I do not do this for money, never...." Soon Dostoevsky was released from prison.

V.A. Sevastianova (Dostoevskaya): My Meeting with My Uncle, Fyodor Dostoevsky
(From IRLI Archive, Institute of Russian Literature, File 56–1.)

My father had a very long conversation with my uncle [Fydor], and I was so happy to be present.... Both brothers had a feeling of love, respect, similar views.... My uncle spent most of the time in his study, and I could hear him coughing slightly. Then he went out, walking quietly, with his curved back, with a tired and pale face, carrying a cup of tea. He went to the living room, greeted us, and sat down in an armchair, near Anna Grigorievna. We spoke about their plans to purchase a country estate.... Fyodor Mikhailovich said, pointing at Anna Grigorievna, "Her brother found an estate for us in the Kursk region [in the south]. But is it real Russia? I want a place in the heart of Russia, so that I can see birch trees, but there is only oak growing there. But I love birch trees, and small Russian forests. What can be better than small birch leaves, sticky in the springtime!" ... He saw us off into the corridor and spoke to us for a long time. We listened to him, and he was holding me by the button of my coat and talking. About what? Certainly not about everyday life; about some theories, and some philosophy. He was interested in such things....

K.I. Maslennikov: Memoirs of a Senior Officer from the Parole Department of the Ministry of Justice

(From *Novoe vremia* [*The New Times*] 1 [12 October 1882].)

In October 1976, the public of St. Petersburg discussed two criminal cases. In one case, Katerina Kornilova threw her small, six-year-old stepdaughter out of the window of her fourth floor apartment. The second case was about Ms. Kornilova, who was accused of the premeditated murder of architect Malevsky, and who had intimate relationships with the murderer. All were greatly surprised that in the first case, the accused pleaded guilty, despite the indication that she was not completely normal mentally; and in the second case the woman was acquitted.... These doubts were expressed by Dostoevsky in *A Writer's Diary* (October 1876). He stressed, "Can we change the Kornilova verdict? It seems that it is a mistake, a judicial mistake! It seems to me all the time..."

The highly artistic work of Fyodor Mikhailovich made such a great impression on St. Petersburg society, both on the public opinion and on the members of the jury, that the judge addressed a special word to the jury and asked them "not to be influenced by a certain talented literary artist," but "to discuss the case according to their own considerations."

... But what could these official words mean to the members of the jury, when they were all under the impact of Fyodor Mikhailovich? A very short and artistic picture created by Dostoevsky was instilled in our imaginations, when he asked, "Is it possible to acquit? Just take a risk and to acquit?" ... Fyodor Mikhailovich was present in the court hall when he heard the final verdict of the jury, "No, not guilty!"

N. Pruzhansky: My Visit to Dostoevsky's Apartment in St. Petersburg
(From *The New People* 2 [1 March 1910].)

I vistited Dostoevsky who lived at the Pesky [a district of St. Petersburg]. He had a very humble house; when you entered his house you had to enter from the backyard, which was far from a clean place. When I entered, a pale and thin woman opened the door for me. I looked at her dress and thought that she was a servant. Later on, I understood that she was his wife. I never saw a servant in his place. Then I entered a very dark entrance hall, which had two doors, one leading directly to the kitchen, and the other to the living room. When I entered the living room, I was surprised by its poor furniture. I remember it: bare walls covered with old wallpaper, old and shabby chairs, two armchairs, a small round table in front of the sofa—that was all.

Everything indicated that our great writer did not have a very comfortable life. Such an apartment could be rented by a low class civil servant.

N. Repin: Dostoevsky and the Beggar
(From *The St. Petersburg Newspaper* 333 [4 December 1903].)

This incident happened to our famous writer, Fyodor Dostoesvsky, twenty-five years ago. Once our famous writer-psychologist went along the Nikolaevskaya Street. It was the weekend. As usual, he was concentrating, looking at the ground in front of him as we walked. At the corner with Stremiannaya Street, a beggar approached him and asked, "Can you spare some change for me?" Maybe Dostoevsky did not hear him, because he continued on his way without paying any attention. The beggar hit Dostoevsky in his head with his fist. The blow was so strong that our famous writer fell on the sidewalk, several meters from the place.

The police officer who was at the nearest corner came to Dostoevsky and helped him to stand up.... The beggar started running along the street, but he was caught by some people. In several days, Dostoevsky went to the local court. "Witness, Fyodor Dostoevsky, do you really want to drop charges against Mr. Egorov from Kolpino, who abused you with his actions?" "Yes, I refuse any accusations," said Dostoevsky. "I do this for two reasons. First, I cannot say for sure that it was this man who hit me, and not the other man, because I did not see the face of this man. The second reason—I cannot understand that a man in his clear conscience could hit his neighbor with his fist in the head. It shows that this is an ill man and you should send him for medical treatment, and not punish him...."

"We will send him to prison for one month. We know what to do better than you," said the judge. Dostoevsky replied, "This will remain on your conscience. But please take these three roubles from me and give the money to this man...." When Dostoevsky left the courtroom, the judge asked the beggar, "Do you know whom you hit? You hit the greatest among the Russian writers and the kindest man among the Russian people!"

Anna Dostoevskaya: Rare Reminiscences from the Personal Diary

(From S. Poshemanskaya, "Anna Dostoevskaya: A Decipherered Stenography," *Literary Heritage* 86 [1973]: 155–290.)

During the early years, Dostoevsky liked wide ties with bright colors, especially red ties.... He liked to read Walter Scott, *Prisoner of Edinburgh* and *Rob Roy*. He liked to read Charles Dickens, with his *Oliver Twist*, *Nicholas Nickleby* and *The Old Curiosity Shop*. He did not like Thackeray. He liked to read Balzac, *Le Cousin Pons*, *La Cousine Bette*.... He made preparations for bed for a long time, about two hours beforehand. He took care of the night toilette of the children, gave them drinks, had his supper, checked whether all the doors were closed, then went to the washroom, brushed his teech, did his physical exercises, prayed, and prepared his watches, matches, and a candle not far from the place where he slept. When he went to bed, he covered himself completely, with his head under the sheets, with two blankets, and even covered his feet with an old coat.... He read prayer with the children, said several tender words to them, kissed them on their foreheads and their lips, and said, "Have a good sleep, my dears...." He liked only black ink, and good, big, thick sheets of paper....

He had a project—to build a huge ship, not an oval one, but of a square form, with a flat bottom, so it would be impossible to move fast in the water. To make an expensive engine, so that the fuel would cost at least a hundred thousand per month. To use as many precious stones as possible in the interior. And to send this ship sailing into the sea which would be our proof and a sign of good-will to Europe, our demonstration that the Russians are fighting for peace.... This ship was intended to be used by the Russian diplomats and the whores serving the high society.

Chapter 8. The Pushkin Speech: Triumph in Moscow.

"This is an obscure and fantastic criminal case, a contemporary case, something that could only have happened in our day, when the heart of man has grown troubled, when people quote sayings about blood that it 'refreshes,' when all of life is dedicated to comfort."

(Crime and Punishment)

"The destination of the Russian man is to be a European man: a citizen of Europe, a citizen of the world. To become a real Russian, a complete Russian, means to become the brother of all humanity...."

(Pushkin speech, June 1880)

D URING HIS LAST YEARS, Dostoevsky maintained a busy social life. He organized the work of the Slavic Charity Society, read his works in public at numerous literary gatherings, and supported the aggressive wars of the Russian Tsar in Southern Europe and in Asia, calling them "the liberation of people by the Orthodox faith and the Russian monarchy."

On May 1, 1879, Dostoevsky received a brief but extremely important letter inviting him to attend the Pushkin Festival to be held in Moscow on June 8, 1880. The speech he delivered at this event proved to be a crowning achievement of Dostoevsky's final years, indeed a milestone in his biography. The public's enthusiastic reception of his Pushkin speech elevated him to the rank of prophet, and he was now celebrated in literary circles as the greatest contemporary Russian writer.

His invitation to the festival came from Sergei Iuriev, the president of the literary society at the University of Moscow, and read as follows: "On behalf of the members of the Society of Lovers of Russian Literature of Moscow University, from whom you will receive an official invitation ... I ask and implore you to give us the honor of attending the meeting of the Society." Three days later, at the sitting of the Slavic Charity Society, Dostoevsky was unanimously elected to represent the society at the unveiling of the monument to Pushkin in Moscow.

On May 23, Dostoevsky arrived in Moscow to participate in the unveiling of the monument to Alexander Pushkin. Several of the leading Russian journalists, including Sergei Iuriev, Iakov Lavrov, and Ivan Aksakov met him at the railway station. Hundreds of delegates poured into Moscow from different associations, scholarly societies, universities, and newspapers. Representatives of 106 delegations from across Russia arrived, ranging from the Russian Choir Society to the Society for the Acclimatization of Animals and Plants. A heated discussion over the future of Russia was expected between the Westernizers, headed by Turgenev, and the Slavophiles, led by Dostoevsky and Katkov.

On June 7, Turgenev established the theme of the festival in the introduction of his speech at the opening of the Pushkin monument. "There is no doubt," he said, "that Pushkin ... created our literary language and created our Russian literature." The following day the Society of Russian Lovers of Literature convened for its second sitting. Here Dostoevsky delivered his famous speech on Pushkin as the father of Russian literature. The speech was immensely successful and brought much public acclaim. There are numerous testimonies of the tremendous impact that Dostoevsky's Pushkin speech made on his contemporaries. The response was overwhelmingly positive, though there was disapproval in some quarters. Excerpted below are accounts of the speech from the reminiscences of participants in the Pushkin Festival, including some of the attacks it provoked.

Katerina Letkova-Sultanova, a writer, a translator, and one of the organizers of the women's movement in Russia, beautifully described the hypnotic effect that Dostoevsky had on the audience: "There is really nothing that can be compared to that day of June 8, 1880. There was such a huge roar in the hall ... see, it already seemed that the walls would fall" (Letkova, "About F.M. Dostoevsky," pp. 459–477).

Russian writer, publisher and journalist Gleb Uspensky (1843–1902), a Westernizer, was struck by Dostoevsky's extraordinary persuasiveness: "When his turn came, he 'quietly' came to the podium and within five minutes he had complete control over the entire audience, all their hearts, their thoughts, all the souls of the people who came to the meeting.... Dostoevsky, after his speech, did not receive just an ovation, but rather the apotheosis of an idol...."

Dostoevsky departed from Moscow on June 10 and arrived the next day in his summer cottage in Staraya Russa. Here he wrote the greater part of his last and greatest novel, *The Brothers Karamazov*. He had taken time out from the writing of the novel to compose his Pushkin speech. It, like the novel, expressed Dostoevsky's religious views, stressing the messianic mission of Russia and the universal brotherhood of mankind. After working very hard for three weeks on the novel, producing three printing signatures, he again interrupted his labors to answer some of the negative reviews of the Pushkin speech that had begun to appear in the press.

In August 1880, although he had planned to publish only his Pushkin speech in *A Writer's Diary*, he decided to add his answer to the critics of his speech. Shortly after the speech, Professor Grigory Gradovsky of Moscow University had charged that the speech offered "many things about morality, but not a hint of social ideas." Dostoevsky answered Gradovsky with a big article in which he wrote,

> You have to know, dear professor, that there are no social ideals that are not connected with morality; there are not now, there never were and there will never be such a thing.... The most conservative part of our society is as shitty as any other part. So many villains have joined it: Filonov, Krestovsky and a general, stupid fool... [*A Writer's Diary*, 1880].

This article, "My Reply to Professor Gradovsky," constituted an entire chapter in the *Diary* and took several weeks of his work. Shortly afterwards Anna Dostoevskaya wrote to St. Petersburg to her husband in Staraya Russa to report the new issue of the *Diary* was "selling madly," with people simply tearing it from her hands. In three days some 3,000 copies were sold in St. Petersburg alone. What was the secret of such a huge success? How did Dostoevsky manage to attract the attention of practically all Russian people? How Dostoevsky became a living prophet for Russian intellectuals? The following memoirs collected in this chapter partially answer these questions.

N. Firsov: In the Editorial Office of *The Russian Speech*

(From N. Firsov: "V redaktsii zhurnala *Russkow Slovo* ["In the Editorial Office of *The Russian Speech*"], *Istoricheskii vestnik* [*The History Herald*] 6 [1914]: 897–899.)

I would like to set down Dostoevsky's comments about articles on Pushkin after they had been published in *The Russian Speech*. I often met Fyodor Mikhailovich at A. Pleshcheev's house, because my uncle and Dostoevsky were schoolmates and had been close friends since early childhood. Everyone knew that Dostoevsky and Pleshcheev were close.

Once (at the very end of 1858 or at the beginning of 1859) I visited Pleshcheev and met Dostoevsky there. Fyodor Mikhailovich was pacing back and forth in the hall without making the slightest noise, as he tended to do, because he liked soft shoes. A thin old lady, the host's mother, sat on the sofa. Pleshcheev spoke about the direction of some "thick" literary journals of the time—in particular, about the sections of literary criticism.

He paused rather often, as if he wanted to entice Dostoevsky to speak, but the writer was silent, perhaps because he was indifferent to the subject, perhaps because he was thinking over one of his future novels. This was his habit—to think over his literary work while other people were talking. I already knew that when he paced, his work on his novels was going on successfully and that sometimes he could be completely immersed in his thoughts under very unusual circumstances.

For example, several years after this, we were at a water resort of Staraya Russa. Fyodor Mikhailovich used to take his evening walk in the town park where the brass orchestra played very loudly. He circled around the playing orchestra, slightly dragging his feet and holding his hands behind his back, with his back hunched, in complete solitude, without saying a word to anyone. It seemed that he did not notice the noise of the military brass orchestra, that he did not pay any attention to the thick crowd of people talking loudly.

People who were close to him told me that as soon as he returned home, he used to pace across the room and start dictating several new pages of the novel he was writing at the time.

D.I. Stakheev: Dostoevsky's Portrait in Society

(From D.I. Stakheev: "Gruppy i portrety" ["Dostoevsky's Portrait in the Society: Pages from My Memoirs"], *Istoricheskii vestnik* [*The History Herald*] 1 [1907]: 84–88.)

The old monk led a secluded life; he was a hermit and lived in complete solitude, in a specially built small house situated far from other buildings of the monastery. Fyodor Mikhailovich Dostoevsky, on visiting the monastery contrary to his plans of listening to the speeches of the old monk ... spoke himself; he passionately argued with the old man, explaining to him the meaning of what he had just told him, and instead of being a listener, he became a speaker and a teacher.... Vladimir Soloviev [who visited the Optina Pustyn' Monastery with Dostoevsky] told me ... that Fyodor Mikhailovich was very excited, as was usual before a seizure of epilepsy, and then he became very nervous and talked a great deal without stopping....

In general, Dostoevsky was very sharp and even rude in his speech.

"Once," said Apollon Nikolaevich Maikov, "Fyodor Mikhailovich came to my study for evening tea. He liked such private conversations with his friends." They talked for ten or fifteen minutes, and then suddenly they heard the doorbell ringing. Fyodor Mikhailovich roused himself. "Is this a guest?" he hissed, became gloomy and frowned.... "I hate such casual visitors...." Dostoevsky was excited during the previous conversation, but he suddenly looked drawn and haggard and became as silent as a snail moving inside of his shell. They heard the steps of a person approaching the doors of the study.... "I will sit here," whispered Dostoevsky, raising himself from his armchair and indicating a chair which stood behind the open door. "Maybe you will be lucky, God help you, and you will get rid of your guest quickly," he added in a whisper, hiding himself behind the door and sitting on the chair.... The visitor, I do not want to mention his name, did not have any literary talent.... He used to publish small articles here and there, sneaking everywhere and trying to please publishers in every way.... This time he started to praise Maikov as soon as he entered the study: "I have read your last poem in *The Russian Herald* and it was so beautiful.... It was great, wonderful, amazing! ... Goethe and Shakespeare—who are they as compared to you.... You are Maikov, you are our glory!" The visitor's enthusiasm and delight were boundless.

Dostoevsky was sitting behind the door. He could not endure this flattery, so he stepped from behind the door, nervously waved with his both hands in the air and hissed in an angry voice, "Who is the scoundrel who talks like this?..." Fyodor Mikhailovich could behave in such a way when he was nervous.... The guest became embarrassed after Dostoevsky appeared and confronted him. He did not dare to find any explanations and he chose to depart right away.... He just muttered, "Excuse me, Apollon Nikolaevich, but I am in a hurry and have to go," and he grabbed his hat and rushed out of the study without even looking at Fyodor Mikhailovich.

D.N. Sadovnikov: A Reading by Dostoevsky

(From D.N. Sadovnikov: "Vstrechi s Turgenevym" ["Meetings with Turgenev"], *Russkoe proshloe* [*The Russian Past*] 1–2 [1923]: 74–83.)

[The author of this piece recollects literary readings in 1878 with Turgenev and Dostoevsky.]

After a brief intermission Dostoevsky, a short man, went out on the podium and started to read chapters from *The Brothers Karamazov*. He started in a weak and boring manner, as if he spoke about some nonsense, and I thought that he reminded me of Lord Redstock telling about the apocalypses.

But everything changed when he started to read the confession by Dmitry Karamazov. The audience became completely still. The evil character of this terribly dissipated man was described by the writer in such an impressive manner that [I felt that] I have never heard anything like this before.

Dostoevsky was wonderful when he read his prose and verses, when he inserted the words addressed to the brother, when he imitated the trembling voices, and [when, by] increasing the speed of reading in the scene of the suicide in the most dramatic place, [he] created an effect of accelerated time. The audience, as far as I remember, called him five times for encores.

E.M. Garshin: Memoirs About Turgenev and Dostoevsky

(From E.M. Garshin, "Vospominaniia o Turgeneve i Dostoevskom" ["Memoirs About Turgenev and Dostoevsky"], *Istoricheskii vestnik* [*The History Herald*] Vol. 14, 11 [1883]: 386–388.)

That year we spoke a lot about Dostoevsky. This was after we had buried Dostoevsky with tears in our eyes. People did not cry that much after they buried Turgenev.... Once ... Ivan Sergeevich [Turgenev] depicted a not very sympathetic image of Dostoevsky: "He was not a very kind person, because he could not endure other people's success. He was not content by depicting me in Karmazinov [in satirical form], but why did he mention Granovsky, who was dead by that time?"

He stressed that Dostoevsky could not treat people without personal attitudes, and he told me about their personal quarrel.

... It was in Baden-Baden.... Dostoevsky was gambling all the time and he lost ... all the money he had, to the last penny. He borrowed a small sum of money from Turgenev. Soon he won some money playing roulette, and returned his debt ... to the man whom he did not like [Turgenev was speaking of himself]; he was especially irritated by the notorious novel *The Smoke.*

When Dostoevsky took this book into his hands, he said: "This book should be put into fire by the hands of the executioner." Turgenev inquired about the reasons for this. [The scene happened between the two of them, without any witnesses.] Dostoevsky responded with a big speech, in which he accused Turgenev of hating Russia, of not believing in its future, etc.... Turgenev listened in silence; he did not make any comments and waited until Dostoevsky left....

After some time, Turgenev received a letter from Mr. Bretenev, the publisher of *The Russian Archive*, saying that Dostoevsky had addressed the journal with a letter in which he reproduced the same dialogue, but this time not as his accusation, but as Turgenev's personal confession, namely: "I hate Russia," etc. Besides, Dostoevsky asked the publisher to publish this letter not earlier than after a certain period of time, about ten to fifteen years, as far as I remember. Bretenev asked Turgenev what he should do with all this, and Turgenev answered that he could do whatever he wanted.

S.A. Vengerov: Four Meetings with Turgenev

(From S.A. Vengerov, "Tchetyre vstrechi s Turgenevym" ["Four Meetings with Turgenev"], quoted in V. Rosenberg, "Tchetyre vstrechi s Turgenevym" ["Four Meetings with Turgenev"], *Biriuch Petrogradskikh gosudarstvennykh teatrov [Review of St. Petersburg State Theaters]* 2 [1918]: 43–44.)

I met with Turgenev in 1879, at a famous ceremonial dinner which was organized in his honor, and where the famous incident with Dostoevsky occurred. Many speeches were made....

The dinner made a very pleasant impression on everybody, except for the incident with Dostoevsky which occurred at the end of the evening. Turgenev made a speech about the "crowning of the building of the reforms made by Alexander II." He meant the new constitution when he used the term "crowning the building." Everybody understood well what he [Turgenev] meant by his speech, and only Dostoevsky asked a sharp question in a loud voice: "What do you mean by 'crowning the building'?"

The people who were present at the dinner treated Dostoevsky's remark in a rather strict way.... Everybody knew about the animosity which existed between two writers. Dostoevsky was sharply criticized in *The European Herald* after this event.... Everyone was so indignant about Dostoevsky's behavior that I had to find excuses for myself, saying: "But I love Turgenev as well, you see, I came in a tuxedo for the occasion...."

S. Bobchev: About the Unveiling of the Pushkin Monument in Moscow

(From S. Bobchev, "Informatsiia o torzhestvakh po povodu osviashcheniia pamiatnika Pushkinu v Moskve" ["About the Unveiling of the Pushkin Monument in Moscow"], *Godishnik na Sofiiskii universitet* [*Proceedings of the Sofia University*], Vol. 54. Philology Series. Sofia, 1961: 813–815.)

The Pushkin Festival was the focus of attention of all Russian intelligentsia. An important result was achieved by the festival, because it united all Russian intellectuals ... all [political and artistic] groups and parties were united. The importance of this event was great. The Russians showed that they appreciated their best men.... Russian writers and scholars understood the importance of the event. It was proved by the speeches made at the two meetings of the Society of Lovers of Russian Literature. About 2,000–3,000 people were present at each of these meetings. This was the most important part of the festival....

Turgenev spoke about Pushkin as the first really national Russian poet ... who made the same great influence [on Russian literature] as Goethe made in Germany, Molière made in France and Shakespeare made in England....

I felt embarrassed when I start talking about the second day of the festival. You have to be very self-confident to have the courage to express the effect produced on the audience by Dostoevsky after his talented and prophetic speech.

Aksakov, a grey-haired Slavophile, rushed to the speaker in ecstasy, kissed him and expressed his congratulations. Many members of the society did the same. The audience yelled, "Hurray!" The applause did not stop. Many women cried, some of them even fainted. A young man, a student, ran out to the podium to greet the speaker, fainted and fell on the floor. They instantly collected money for a laurel wreath, and in half an hour, several very beautiful women, students from the Women's College, presented the wreath to Dostoevsky.

At last it was time for Aksakov to make a speech, and he went to the podium. The famous Slavophile was very excited, and his beautiful and honest face was gleaming. He said that Dostoevsky's speech was a big event and that he didn't dare speak after it.... "Before," said Aksakov, "we could have had some doubts about Pushkin's greatness, but now this issue is solved by the prophetic speech made by Dostoevsky."

However, the audience applauded Aksakov and forced him to make a speech.

M. Kamenetskaya: Dostoevsky in the Seventies

(From M. Kamenetskaya, "Vstrechi s Dostoevskim" ["Meetings with Dostoevsky"], in *Sbornik pamiati A.P. Filosofovoi* [*A Collection of Articles Dedicated to A.P. Filosofova*]. St. Petersburg, 1915, pp. 258–259.)

Certainly, I remember Dostoevsky well, especially during the last two or three years of his life, when he and my mother became very good friends. They understood each other, because they both had experienced many hardships. Although I do not know exactly where I met him for the first time, I remember well that my mother was with Dostoevsky when his younger son died from epilepsy. As far as I remember, it was the young boy's first seizure, and the fit was so severe that it killed him. This affected Fyodor Mikhailovich deeply. He visited my mother only occasionally, when they had some business to discuss. Well, to be exact, it was not only a matter of business, but also the need to talk to each other, to listen to each other, to communicate. I will try to tell you what I recall.

At the time I was about fourteen years old.... Once, Fyodor Mikhailovich visited us when my mother gave a small party. There were about five or six people in all; all had different views and preferences, and were of different social standings. As usual, we all sat in my mother's living room and she served tea. She poured the tea herself. The uniformed butler, in livery, brought us the teapot and cups....

On this particular day, Aleksandr Alexandrovich Navrotsky, a lawyer from St. Petersburg's Military Court, was in the center of attention. He was the author of the song "The Rock," which was very popular among the students at the time. He also wrote many poems, both long and short. That evening he spoke about the "World Soul" and "World Wisdom." He maintained that the life exists only on our planet, but that the Earth will soon be frozen, just as the Moon froze ages ago. I was fascinated by him, and, after his words, I could not even stir a finger. Incidentally, at the time, I was standing behind Dostoevsky, who was seated on a chair.

Navrotsky addressed the ending of his speech almost solely to Dostoevsky. For a moment, Fyodor Mikhailovich was silent, then he turned around and said, as if to escape from the previous conversation, "Dear Mary, what about your small turtle, is it still doing well?" Then he turned to my mother, and began to explain the reason for his visit. He needed our assistance....

I remember the time Fyodor Mikhailovich attended a big charity concert organized by our mother. At the end of the event, when he exited the big, heated hall where he had spoken, our young people surrounded him at once. He did not like to give interviews, and seldom spoke on serious topics, and furthermore, he often looked very tired, indeed practically exhausted....

I also remember lengthy discussions he had with my mother. Neither of them knew how to debate in a polite way; they became excited too quickly, and Fyodor Mikhailovich would start to speak in a very loud voice. My mother often argued with him about his "Orthodox God." Dostoevsky had published *A Writer's Diary* at the time. My mother told him heatedly: "Congratulations, you have won. You can stay sitting here alone with your Orthodox God!" After such "feminine arguments," as he called them, Fyodor Mikhailovich used to burst out laughing very loudly, and then addressed my mother with a friendly tone of voice: "Dear Anna Pavlovna, I am sorry! We were too excited, as if we were two young people...."

When I was only sixteen, and had just graduated from high school, I was in the habit of running though the numerous rooms of our huge apartment. Once, when I was running about like this, I collided with Fyodor Mikhailovich as I rushed into the lobby. I started to apologize, but then I realized that it was not the right time for this. He was very pale and he was wiping sweat from his forehead, for he was out of breath by the time he had hurriedly climbed our stairs. He asked me, "Is your mother at home? Well, here we are, thank God!" Then he took my head between his hands and kissed my forehead, repeating: "Thank God, you are here! I have just been told that you were arrested...." This was shortly before we went to Wiesbaden [Germany]. Just after our return [from abroad], I attended his funeral, together with my father. My mother was still abroad at the time.

D. Liubimov: From My Memoirs. Dostoevsky's Speech About Pushkin

(From D. Liubimov, "Iz vospominanii. Rech' Dostoevskogo na Pushkinskikh torzhestvakh" ["From the Memoirs. Dostoevsky's Speech at the Pushkin Festival"], *Voprosy Literatury* [*Problems of Literature*] 7 [1961]: 156–166.)

It was exactly twenty-five years ago, in the same hall, behind these columns, that I experienced emotions which I will remember for the rest of my life. It was June 8, 1880, during the celebrations dedicated to the opening of the Pushkin Monument in Moscow....

The huge hall was filled with rows of chairs; every place was filled with the rich and well-dressed public; crowds of people stood in the aisles and in the galleries.... Admission was restricted to those who had tickets; these tickets were free, and they had been distributed long before the opening of the festival. Many respected guests went to the hall that day, among them representatives of literature, science and art. One could see all who were famous and outstanding. "All of Moscow," so to speak, was there.

The Pushkin family sat in the first row ... and close by, the mayor of Moscow ... after him was the minister of education.... A group of people sitting next to them attracted everyone's attention. They were, simply, an apotheosis of Russian music. The two Rubinstein brothers were present, both of them directors and founders of conservatories, Anton in St. Petersburg and Nikolai in Moscow....

Pyotr Tchaikovsky was present; at the time he was living in Klin, near Moscow, and he had recently staged his *Evgeny Onegin*. Only two days before the Pushkin Festival, he conducted an orchestra playing his symphony, which enjoyed great success....

On the other side of the chairman, with his profile turned to the public, sat Ivan Aksakov, a man who was very famous in Moscow.... He was the publisher of *Rus'* [*Russia*], and at the same time, he had also been the president of the Moscow Bank of Commerce for 25 years....

Next to Aksakov sat a man who was deeply immersed in reading some notes on sheets of paper in front of him: this was Fyodor Mikhailovich Dostoevsky. He would be the future hero of this meeting, but nobody knew this at the time. He looked tired and unwell.

I had seen him recently; he visited my father and they discussed the publication of the last chapters of the novel *The Brothers Karamazov*, which was published in *The Russian Herald*. All the major works by Dostoevsky, including *Crime and Punishment*, *The Idiot*, *The Raw Youth* and *The Brothers Karamazov*, appeared in this periodical published by my father, a professor at Moscow University, together with the publisher M. Katkov. ... I remember that during the conversation, Dostoevsky explained the main idea behind his Grand Inquisitor. ... It was about the necessity of matching the high truth of the New Testament with the understanding of ordinary people and their everyday life.

... My skeptical neighbor explained to me that Count Leo Tolstoy was absent. He had become a "simple man from the crowd" and was spending all his time on his estate at Yasnaya Poliana [situated not far from Moscow]. The organizers had sent him three invitations, but he had replied that he considered every festival to be a sin....

The chairman announced: "And now, ladies and gentlemen, Fyodor Mikhailovich Dostoevsky, an honorary member of our society, will make a speech."

Dostoevsky stood up, gathered the sheets of paper on which he had made his notes, and slowly went to the podium. On his way, he reshuffled his notes; most likely they contained his speech. Later, however, he did not refer to them. On this day, he looked even more tired than he had the day before. His coat hung loosely on him as on a hanger, his shirt was wrinkled, his white tie was askew and seemed as if it might come loose at any moment. He dragged one foot. My enthusiastic neighbor started to explain, "He acquired this strange gait in prison; for many years he had cannon balls and huge chains attached to his feet...."

Dostoevsky was greeted by a storm of applause, which started as soon as he ascended the podium. I remember all the details so well. He stretched out his hand, as if trying to stop this ovation. After the audience became quiet, he started without any introduction, and without any formal salutation, such as "Dear ladies and gentlemen."

He spoke straightforwardly: "'Pushkin is an outstanding and unique phenomenon of the Russian spirit,' said Gogol. And, I would add, he is also a prophetic phenomenon."

Dostoevsky quoted from Pushkin by heart several times. "Yes," he exclaimed, "Pushkin, without a doubt, could feel our great destiny. He was a real prophet! To be a real Russian is to become a brother to all mankind, to become a real man.... All our parties, such as the Slavophiles or the Westernizers, are based on a great misunderstanding. Our entire

history is proof of this. We have always served Europe more than ourselves.... Pushkin died at the height of his creative powers, and he took
with him to the grave a great mystery. And now we are trying to solve
this mystery."

Dostoevsky pronounced the last words of his speech in an excited
whisper, and began his descent from the podium surrounded by a complete, deadly silence. All of the audience was utterly silent, as if waiting
for something more.

Suddenly, there was a hysterical scream from the last row: "You have
solved this mystery!"—and it was repeated by several women's voices in
the gallery. The whole crowd seemed to awaken. "Yes, yes, you did it!
You solved it!" people screamed. The storm of applause began, mixed
with sounds of clapping, stamping, cheers and women's screams. I think
that the walls of the House of Nobility in Moscow had never heard such
a stormy ovation as on that day; nothing like this had ever happened,
nor would it happen again. Everyone was shouting and applauding, both
those on the stage and those in the hall. Aksakov rushed to embrace Dostoevsky. Turgenev spread his arms wide and approached Dostoevsky as
well. And when he walked across the stage, he looked like a big bear. A
young man rushed to the stage, pushing everyone aside, struggling
though the press and screaming, "Dostoevsky, Dostoevsky!"; as he ran
out on to the stage, he fainted and fell to the floor in front of the audience. Some people took him away. Dostoevsky was simply carried behind
the curtains. He was supported by Turgenev and Aksakov, and had
become very weak; Grigorovich ran in front of them, waving his white
handkerchief in the air, for no apparent reason. The whole crowd was
extremely excited....

The chairman desperately rang his bell, repeating several times that
the meeting should continue, and that Ivan Sergeevich Aksakov should
make a speech. The audience became a little quieter, but Aksakov himself looked extremely excited. He ran to the podium and announced:
"Ladies and gentlemen! I cannot, and I do not wish to, make my speech
after Dostoevsky! His speech has been a great event. Everything has
been explained, everything has become clear now...."

I also was very much excited by Dostoevsky's speech, and by all of
the events surrounding it....

Gleb Uspensky: Writer's Report About Pushkin's Festival: "A Great, Overwhelming Success"

(From G.I. Uspensky, "Prazdnik Pushkina" ["Pushkin Festival"], in G.I. Uspensky. *Polnoe sobranie sochinenii* [*Complete Works*]. Moscow: Academy Press, 1953, pp. 407–430.)

Yesterday, on the eighth of June [1880], the four-day Pushkin Festival in Moscow began with a musical and literary concert in the House of the Russian Nobility. Ivan Aksakov, a man of great and varied education, an intellectual and talented person ... made a speech after the minister of education's opening address.

No one would have guessed that [after Aksakov's speech] one of our contemporaries would secure the undivided attention of the great throng which filled the huge hall of the House of the Russian Nobility. This feat was accomplished by Fyodor Mikhailovich Dostoevsky, who sat quietly near the podium, writing in his notebook.

When his turn came, he calmly mounted the podium, and in less than five minutes won the complete possession of the hearts, minds, and souls of the people present at the meeting. He spoke in a very simple way, as if to a circle of friends, without long phrases or sharp, dramatic movements of his head. In a very simple and clear manner he told the public what he thought of Pushkin and what we, all the people present at this meeting, should expect from him. He, managed, so to speak, to bring Pushkin into the hall. It seemed as if it were the poet himself who was telling our society about its present state and its present problems. No one had seen anything like this before, and this led to great, overwhelming success.

... It is a well-known fact that after the speech, Dostoevsky received more than just ovation; it was more a special ceremony, which could be termed "the creation and adoration of an idol." One young man managed to squeeze through the crowd and jump on the stage; he was so excited that, after he shook hands with the writer, he lost consciousness and fell to the stage floor.... The sincere and lengthy speech by Dostoevsky really impressed many people. The young man fainted on the stage because he understood the Dostoevsky speech exactly as we understood it. I have to apologize, however, because I am unable to interpret his speech adequately here. Dostoevsky is a wise man, as I said, although he recently compared a group of people (he glorifies them now) to a herd of swine and predicted that they were doomed to drown in the depths of the sea.

It is hard to understand a man who is so contradictory in his judgments, and it is obvious that his speech produced a completely different impression after being published in the press.

Gleb Uspensky: A Few Days Later

(From G.I. Uspensky, "Prazdnik Pushkina" ["Pushkin Festival"], in G.I. Uspensky, *Polnoe soloranie sochinenii* [*Complete Works*]. Moscow: Academy Press, 1953, pp. 407–430.)

Dostoevsky's speech has appeared in *The Moscow News* No. 162. I read it several times, but it is not that easy to understand, and I came to the conclusion that there was something in his speech that made it sound like a riddle which I do not want to solve. This puzzle made the speech lose its meaning. The reason for this is that Mr. Dostoevsky has added so many considerations of the "hare variety" to the entirely human meaning conveyed by the figure of the Russian traveler.

... He combined such words as "perhaps" with "always" and "for a long time." Sometimes he combined words such as "fantastic" and "prosaic," etc. Such "hare jumps" transform what is basically a dull speech into a real flight of fancy.

Little by little, from one hill to the next, leap by leap, our hare moves into such a thick forest that you lose all sight of him, you do not see even his tail.... There is no doubt that those young ladies who brought a wreath for Mr. Dostoevsky did not do this as a token of gratitude for him having advised them to spend their lives sitting at home and taking care of elderly husbands.... Dostoevsky did not explain his thoughts in a simple manner.

Alexei Slivitsky: Those Were Really Unforgettable Days!

(From A.M. Slivitsky, "Iz moikh vospominanii o Polivanove. Pushkinskie dni" ["From My Memoirs About Polivanov: The Days of the Pushkin Festival"], *Mosvkovskii ezhenedelnik* [Moscow Weekly] 46 [1908]: 41–45.)

Dostoevsky's speech was a real event. When he went to the podium, the whole audience was electrified. The creator of [*Notes from*] *The House of the Dead* was standing before us: pale, his back bent, his hands hanging down loosely, and the walls of the hall trembled from the ovation....

People who read his [Pushkin] speech afterwards were very surprised at the shocking impression it made on the audience. Several women and a young man became simply hysterical, confusion reigned in the hall, and a great many people ran to the stage to kiss the writer's hands. The meeting was interrupted for at least half an hour. They called him back on stage again and again.

When Dostoevsky went out to answer one of these ovation calls, a group of young women held behind him a huge laurel wreath....

I was fortunate enough [to be delegated] to bring this laurel from the House of the Russian Nobility to the Loskutny Hotel, where Dostoevsky was staying. We both reached the hotel at almost the same time, and I entered the room right after him. He kindly offered me a seat, but he was so pale and, probably, tired that I was inclined to make my visit brief. I remember well that he was holding in his hands a small notebook which contained the draft of his speech and that he kept repeating, "Why all this success? I did not expect it!..."

I remember the dinner in less detail.... I do recall one moment however: when the dinner was over and the people stood up from their seats, members of a "Shakespearean Literary Circle" went up to Dostoevsky and surrounded him, talking to him. I remember that he complained to them about the illness which constantly interrupted his work: "After every seizure, I completely forget what I have written on earlier pages, which I have already sent to the publisher. I have to continue writing, but I do not remember whether I have said this or was going to say it...." I now think that all the lengthy descriptions and repetitions you encounter in Dostoevsky's novels are the result of his terrible illness....

He was silent for a while, and then he added: "I will write a new novel, *The Children*, and I then will die." He was planning to write another novel, which would be a continuation of *The Brothers Karamazov*. The major heroes of this new work would have been the children from this previous novel....

I remember also that Dostoevsky was in a hurry that day, because he had promised to visit old friends who lived far away, in a remote part of the city—perhaps, of a rather poor family. We implored him, "Please, Fyodor Mikhailovich, stay with us for a while!" He answered: "No, I have to go, otherwise they will wait for me in vain, and they may be offended. They will say that I have become too proud to visit them."

On the same day, at nine in the evening, there was a literary-musical concert.... Those were really unforgettable days!

Anna Suvorina: More About the Pushkin Speech

(From A.I. Suvorina, "Vospominaniia o Dostoevskom" ["Memoirs About Dostoevsky"], in *Dostoevsky i ego vremia* [*Dostoevsky and His Time*]. Leningrad: Nauka Publishers, 1971, pp. 295–296.)

The following day [after the Pushkin speech], we gave a breakfast at the Testov Restaurant.... We had a small meal for a select company of close friends. I was the only woman present, and I sat halfway down the table, with Dostoevsky sitting on my right, next to me. There were really very few people: myself and my husband, Ostrovsky, Grigorovich, Maksimov, Gorbunov and N. Berg. The breakfast was going well, and we were talking about literature and politics, when, suddenly, Fyodor Mikhailovich asked me if I had read Dickens. I was ashamed to have to answer that I hadn't yet read any of the works of this writer. He was surprised, and fell silent for a moment. The others continued talking about something else. Then, suddenly, Fyodor Mikhailovich proclaimed in a loud voice: "Ladies and gentlemen! The happiest person in the world is among us!"

I looked around at the people sitting at the table, and I was very surprised. All these men were well advanced in years, and I did not see much happiness in their faces. After a brief silence, Dostoevsky said: "This is Anna Ivanovna, my neighbor." I got flustered because of this unexpected turn of meaning of his phrase. "Yes, yes, it is she. Gentlemen, Anna Ivanovna is happy because she has not read Dickens and she has this happiness to look forward to! Oh, how I would like to be in her place. To once again read *David Copperfield*, and all the rest of Dickens, would be such a pleasure...."

I explained to him why I had not read Dickens, though in general, I read a great deal. I had tried to read his works, but could not finish them, because I cannot bear to read about the sufferings of children or animals.... Dostoevsky laughed and said, "You must read Dickens. When I am too tired, or when I do not feel well, nothing calms me down better, or gives me more joy than this writer, one of the best in the world!" Certainly, I promised him that I would read Dickens.

In St. Petersburg we had parties on Sundays. We usually started serving tea at nine, then we would dine, and later, at twelve, several actors would join us after their theater performances.... We had many interesting people, and everyone liked to talk, mostly about literature and politics.

Fyodor Mikhailovich liked to come to our Sunday parties, and he often stayed for dinner. After dinner, we had short performances, singing and dancing, or invited gypsy singers or street musicians to entertain us....

Fyodor Mikhailovich liked jokes, he liked to laugh, and I remember his face well, as if it were yesterday. However, even when he laughed, he remained a little too serious, and even a bit gloomy. To be more precise, he looked at one with his piercing eyes in a special way.... His eyes had a very special expression. It seemed as if he peered deep into an object or a person, as if he could read one's soul. He had a strange influence on me. I understood well that he was an outstanding writer, that he was our national glory, but I did not really like his work....

I remember Fyodor Mikhailovich and I.S. Turgenev reading their works at one of the literary meetings. I remember their success and the admiration of the audience. As usual, Dostoevsky was better than anyone else. Turgenev was the first to read, and he read his story "Knock, Knock!" The applause and cheers did not subside for a long time after he finished. It seemed to me that it was the heartiest ovation one could receive.

Then Dostoevsky appeared. Everyone became excited, the crowd was magnetized, and we listened to his reading with rapt attention. He read, from *The Brothers Karamazov*, the chapter entitled "Confession of an Ardent Heart." In this chapter Mitya tells his brother about how Katerina Ivanovna came to him to borrow some money to save her father.

The last words read by Dostoevsky produced an overwhelming effect on the audience. Here is this piece from his novel: "She trembled, looked at him, then suddenly became very pale, and, without saying a word, bowed to him. She bowed to him not as a lady, not as a female student, but as a Russian woman...." These last words Dostoevsky did not read, but screamed throughout the hall in a terrifying, shattering way. At the same moment, all those present jumped from their seats and started to cheer, to applaud, and to shout, "Bravo!"

Fyodor Mikhailovich stood before them, out of breath. He was tormented by the emotions of his heroes. This was the power of his talent!

I also remember a story about Fyodor Mikhailovich my husband told me after he had visited him. Before this visit he had felt poorly and was depressed. When he called on Dostoevsky, he found the writer recovering from a severe bout of illness. Dostoevsky was lying on his leather sofa, restless and shaken, his forehead wet with sweat and his eyes feverish, and he spoke in a stumbling, weak voice.

My husband was so alarmed by this sight, and by the state of Dostoevsky's health, that he did not dare to start speaking to him. Fyodor Mikhailovich told him that unfortunately he had lost control and had fallen on the floor during a seizure, but, thank God, had not hurt himself. My husband asked whether it was possible to predict these fits of epilepsy, and to take preventive measures in order not to fall.

"No," said Fyodor Mikhailovich. "Suddenly it seemed to me, for a brief second, that over there, in the corridor, there was a dark spot ...

and I fell down...." This story had a terrible, depressing effect on both of us.

K.M. Staniukovich: The Pushkin Anniversary and Dostoevsky's Speech

(From K.M. Staniukovich, "Pushkinsky jubilei i rech' Dosto-evskogo" ["The Pushkin Anniversary and Dostoevsky's Speech"], *Delo* [*Business*] 7 [1880]: 106–120.)

The greatest event of our poor social life during the past period was the unveiling of the monument to the great Russian poet....

I would like to make a few remarks about Dostoevsky's speech, a speech which produced a great impression on the listeners and which was called "an event" by I. Aksakov.... The most passionate ovations at this event, as we know, were dedicated to Turgenev and Dostoevsky, especially to the latter.

Mr. Dostoevsky produces a strange impression. There is no doubt that this speech is a talented one, passionate and sincere, but there is a spirit of mysticism which pervades it.... It is obvious that it impressed more the hearts than the minds of the audience.

In general, Mr. Dostoevsky is an expert in stirring up emotions. The "profession de fois" which he expressed in his speech is not big news to us. We find the same things in many of his works; he transmits these words through the lips of his characters ... it is a sermon of love with a certain odor of mysticism and the additional smell of the sunflower oil. We find the same things in that part of his speech where he speaks about the position of an artist.... You can see a great love for his people in his speech, but at the same time you are puzzled, you see a kind of mist, you do not know exactly what the artist wanted to say. You cannot, so to speak, translate his ideas into understandable language. Sometimes you see the truth, you find some original thoughts in which you see that here is a talented writer who has meditated a great deal, but in general, I repeat, there is something in this speech without flesh....

The language of Dostoevsky's speech really looks like a sermon. He speaks with the tone of a prophet. He makes a sermon as a pastor; it is very deep, sincere, and we understand that he wants to impress the emotions of his listeners. ... The young people gave Dostoevsky an ovation. I would like to know why.

Chapter 9. Dostoevsky's Last Month: January 1881.

"Let us be kind and honest; and then, let us not forget about each other."

(*The Brothers Karamazov*)

"From the zenith to the horizon stretched the forked outlines of the faintly visible Milky Way. A cool, silent, motionless night had enveloped the earth.... Alyosha ... suddenly fell to the ground.... He did not know why he was embracing the earth ... he kept kissing it as he wept and sobbed, drenching it with tears.... Threads from all of God's countless worlds had converged into his soul."

(*The Brothers Karamazov*)

*T*HE LAST MONTH OF DOSTOEVSKY'S LIFE, above and beyond its intrinsic interest, is of crucial importance in several respects. A great many events were concentrated in this short period of about twenty-five days, and key features of Dostoevsky's life and character were highlighted. For example, he published the last issue of his *A Writer's Diary*, a work on which he had toiled for many years. These days are also important for the insight they give us into Dostoevsky's attitude toward his family, his complex and ambivalent opinion of Tolstoy, and his relationships with other writers, colleagues and friends.

With the huge popularity Dostoevsky achieved by the publication of *A Writer's Diary* and his Pushkin speech, he became the most respected writer in Russia. He died at the height of his fame, at the age of sixty, and all Russians mourned his death. His funeral became the largest gathering in Russian history, attracting a crowd of about 50,000 people.

At the beginning of the month there was nothing alarming in the Dostoevsky family. Dostoevsky enjoyed an active social life: he participated in the activities of the Slavic Charitable Society, he worked to prepare the first 1881 issue of *A Writer's Diary* for publication, and he rehearsed his role for an amateur performance at Sophia Tolstaya's literary salon.

The best account of Dostoevsky's last days appears in Anna Dostoevskaya's memoirs. On the morning of January 25, 1881, Dostoevsky met the editor of *The History Herald* and spoke about the political situation in Russia. He had many visitors during the day, including Apollon Maikov, Nikolai Strakhov, and Orest Miller. Anna Dostoevskaya recollected that "In the morning he was healthy and happy; there was no indication of what would happen in several hours.... During lunch we spoke about *The Pickwick Papers* by Charles Dickens, then he went out for a walk. This was his last walk" (Anna Dostoevskaya, *Vospominaniia* [*Memoirs*], Moskow: Nauka, 1971, pp. 371–372).

At 3 A.M. on January 26, Dostoevsky suffered an internal hemorrhage, in which blood trickled from his mouth. Anna Dostoevskaya mentions in her 1923 memoirs at least three different possible causes for the hemorrhage that caused her husband's death: (1) late at night he moved a heavy bookcase in order to get his pen-holder; (2) he had a heated discussion about his works with a visitor, "a good and kind friend"; (3) there was a scene and a stormy dispute between Dostoevsky and his sister about their aunt's inheritance.

Dostoevsky spent most of the 26th and 27th in bed. J. von Bretsel, a family doctor, came to examine him at 5:30 P.M. During the examination another massive bleeding suddenly started. The family sent for the pastor, who arrived in half an hour, at 6 P.M., to administer confession and holy communion. For the rest of the day and the night it was expected that Dostoevsky's health would improve. The next morning he got up at 7 A.M., which was very early for him. Telling his wife that he would probably die that day, he asked her to open the Bible at random. She opened at Matthew, III: 14 and read, "But John held him back saying, I need to be baptized by You, and do You come to me? But Jesus replied to him, Do not hold me back, for thus it is fitting for us to fulfill a great truth." Dostoevsky said that the words "do not hold me back" indicated that he had to die.

During the day Dostoevsky slept, and later he talked to several close friends and members of the family. In the evening, at 7 P.M., he asked for his children and presented his copy of the New Testament to his son Fyodor (Anna Dostoevskaya, *Memoirs*, 1923, p. 377). His daughter Lily was very emotional; she understood everything and cried, "My dear father, I will remember you forever, you will be with me for the rest of my life" (George Friedlender, editor, *Materialy i issledovakia*, [*Materials and Proceedings*], Vol. 1, p. 289).

Anna Dostoevskaya remembered the last minutes of her husband's life and his last words:

> He spoke some tender words to me and thanked me for the happy life we had together: "Remember Anna, I always loved you passionately and was never unfaithful to you, even in my thoughts." ... Suddenly without an obvious reason Fyodor Mikhailovich trembled and moved up a little on his sofa. ... I had his hands in mine and I felt how his pulse became weaker and weaker.... At 8:38 P.M. (January 28, 1881) he went to eternity... [Anna Dostoevskaya, *Memoirs*, [*Vospominaniia*]. Moscow: Nauka Publishers, 1971, pp. 376–378].

On the next day, January 29, the news about Dostoevsky's death quickly spread across St. Petersburg. Thousands of visitors went to pay their final respects to the great writer. The Tsar issued a special order granting a substantial pension to Dostoevsky's widow, and minister Konstantin Pobedonostsev offered money for the funeral (Alexandra Bogdanovich, *Journal de la General Bogdanovitch: chronique du temps des trois derniers Romanof*. Paris: Payot, 1926, p. 23).

On January 30, professors of St. Petersburg University suspended their lectures as a sign of mourning. In a letter to Ivan Aksakov about Dostoevsky's death, Pobedonostsev wrote, "At 10 A.M. all of Kuznechny Street, St. Vladimir's Plaza and the neighboring streets were filled with people who came to see Dostoevsky.... The crowd of people was not less than fifty or sixty thousand people, and it extended all the way to the monastery cemetery" (Grossman, 1935, pp. 322–323; *The New Times*, no. 12118). Similarly, Aleksandr Miliukov wrote, "Tens of thousands of people came to his funeral.... Delegations from St. Petersburg City Council, the mayor's office, the Russian court, many ministers, and representatives of about sixty-four organizations sent their delegates to pay their last tribute to Dostoevsky" (*The World in Illustrations*, 1881, no. 631).

On January 31, 1881, the funeral procession with Dostoevsky's coffin, wrapped in golden cloth, went across St. Petersburg. According to the newspapers, it was the biggest such public gathering in Russia in the nineteenth century, with about 50,000 people paying their last tribute to the great writer. Detailed accounts of the funeral appeared in all the major Russian journals and newspapers, including *The Russian Herald, St. Petersburg News, Moscow News,* and *Voice.*

The burial ceremony took place on February 1, 1881, at the Tikhvin Cemetery, close to the tombs of Russian poets Zhukovsky and Nekrasov. During the next month Russian society mourned the loss of the great writer. Special meetings of the Russian Literary Fund, the Russian Lawyer's Association and other organizations were devoted to Dostoevsky (*The New Times,* 1881, no. 1773). At one of these meetings the famous Russian composer Mussorgsky played music dedicated to Dostoevsky:

> During a literary evening on Fyodor Dostoevsky ... they brought before the audience the deceased writer's portrait edged in black; Mussorgsky sat down at the piano and improvised a funeral knell similar to that heard in the last scene of *Boris Godunov....* This was the next-to-last public appearance of Mussorgsky [A. Orlova, *Mussorgsky's Days and Works: A Biography in Documents.* Ann Arbor: UMI Research Press, 1985, p. 633].

In February and March of 1881, a special commission was formed, headed by Anna Dostoevskaya and consisting of Russian writers, poets and literary critics. The goal of the commission was to prepare the publication of the complete works of Fyodor Dostoevsky (*The New Times,* 1881, no. 1852). In April 1881 the Caucasus Medical Society set up a Dostoevsky fellowship for work on the topic "The Etiology of Madness in Russia, Based on the Works of F. Dostoevsky" (Grossman, 1935, p. 327). The name of Dostoevsky was recognized by more and more people in Russia and abroad.

Among the well-known stories surrounding Dostoevsky's death is the correspondence between Tolstoy and Nikolai Strakhov, a literary critic and former friend of Dostoevsky. After Dostoevsky's death he wrote to Tolstoy, "I feel as if the earth trembled under my feet.... Feeling great emptiness, as if half of St. Petersburg has disappeared, half of our literature has died" (*Correspondence Between Leo Tolstoy and Strakhov,* Moscow, 1914, p. 266). But the next letter from Strakhov to Leo Tolstoy about Dostoevsky was completely different. In his letter Strakhov made a remark to which Tolstoy did not reply. Strakhov characterized Dostoevsky as "an unhappy and bad man" and accused him of many evils including a sexual assault on a nine-year old girl in a public bath house (*The Contemporary World,* October 1913). This letter was kept in the archives of Tolstoy's family until it was published in 1913. Anna Dostoevsky read Strakhov's letter with disgust and indignantly denied all accusations in her 1923 *Memoirs,* replying that "My husband was the most kind and responsible human being" (Anna Dostoevskaya, *Memoirs,* [*Vospominaniia*]. Moskow: Nauka, 1971, p. 405).

The First Posthumous Edition of Complete Works of Fyodor Dostoevsky in Fourteen Volumes was published in 1881. Two years after his death Dostoevsky's first biography appeared, edited by Professor Orest Miller. Other editions of *Complete Works* followed in 1894–1895, 1904–1906, 1910, 1926–1930, and 1974–1985.

Dostoevsky's works combine exciting criminal plots with meditations about such basic questions of human existence as life, death and religion. His books have been translated into all major languages and remain today among the best-selling classics. He is considered to be one of the world's best novelists. Dostoevsky is one of the most contradictory, exciting and mysterious figures in Russian literature.

There were two dating systems existing in Russia during this period, with a 13-day difference. Readers will note in the following what appear to be discrepancies in the dates of Dostoevsky's death and funeral. Using the old style he died on January 28, 1881; his funerals took place January 29, 30 and 31, 1881. By the new style Dostoevsky died on February 10, 1881, with his funerals occurring February 11, 12 and 13, 1881.

A. Toliverova: Dostoevsky: In Memoriam

(From A. Toliverova, "Pamiati Dostoevskogo" ["Dostoevsky: In Memoriam"], *Igrushechka* [*The Toy*] 6–7 [1881]: 182–183, 238–240.)

Fyodor Mikhailovich liked children very much…. He was exhausted from illness and from his hard life, but when he was among children he behaved like a child. He used to play their games. Once he dressed as a white polar bear, got on all fours and crawled across the room and the children sat on the ice-floes (on the white stools) imitating poor ice-bound travelers. The room was filled with wild screams every time the terrible bear appeared. The bear rushed to the children and hugged them….

I got acquainted with Fyodor Mikhailovich … under some unexpected circumstances. He did not know me personally, but he helped me when I was in a very difficult situation. When I came to visit him to express my gratitude, he was very excited.

It seems to me that he stands in front of me now. He was pale and had a long jacket on. He came to me and took both my hands in his hands and said: "I am sorry for you, but these are the regulations of censorship…." He offered me a seat and himself remained standing. I felt awkward being seated in his presence and wanted to get up, but he wouldn't let me do this and said: "Do not pay any attention to me, sometimes I simply cannot sit."

Most of all I was impressed by Fyodor Mikhailovich's eyes. They were dark brown, deeply set, and his head was covered with dark-brown hair with some grey in it. His eyes made a great impression…. Sometimes his eyes glittered as if in a fever, sometimes this glitter seemed to die out, but they produced a great impression always. Fyodor Mikhailovich always used to look straight in the eyes of the person to whom he spoke, and maybe this habit of his produced this effect. He was not always in the same mood, but he was always sincere, and you felt very special, you felt very good being with him....

... When Fyodor Mikhailovich visited Darovoe [his father's village], he assembled all the peasants who had known him when he was a child and he went together with them to all the places he had liked so much during his childhood.... He went with the peasants as if they were his old, favorite friends, and they spoke for a long time about everything. And it was so good. He understood them, and they understood him.

A. Doganovich: A Student Meets Dostoevsky

(From A. Doganovich, "Is vospominanii feldsheritsy" ["From the Memoirs of a Nurse"], *Nabliudatel'* [*Observer*], October 1885: 332–334.)

After Christmas, when everybody was having some fun, we worked hard ... we organized the ball ... Vereshchagina and I had to invite several famous writers to our evening, and Dostoevsky was among them.... We went to visit him.

"He is having dinner," said the maid.

"We will wait. Just tell him that we're here, please."

"All right, I will do this." She disappeared, and almost immediately Fyodor Mikhailovich ran out. His face kept twitching and he looked very excited.

"I am not a young boy, dear ladies, I am an old man," he interrupted us. "I must have peace when I have my dinner. If you do not give me time for this, how could I possibly survive, how could I sustain myself? I asked you a question, didn't I?..."

My friend was confused and moved back up toward the entrance.... He [Dostoevsky] was gesticulating and walking aggressively towards us: "My body needs rest! It really needs some rest!..." I pulled the door handle.

"No, do not go away just like this," Dostoevsky stopped us. "Explain why you came."

"We are students ... and we wanted to ask you to read your works for us," shouted Vereshchagina from behind the door.

"Well ... you can come in then.... Enter here, please. Come on in," he repeated when he saw that we were hesitant. "Please excuse me, I am an old man.... I am sick and unwell now." At this point he softened, showed us the way to his study, and offered us seats in front of his writing table. "At what college do you study?"

"At the Medical Nurses School [College]," we answered with hope....
"Are there many students there?"
"Lots of students."
"Then I will read.... All right, I promise." His face expressed suffering. His irritation disappeared as quickly as it had appeared. In a moment we saw a completely different man sitting right in front of us. We thanked him on behalf of all our friends.

... The hall was packed with people that night, and it was filled with lights. Famous literary artists appeared on the podium one after another and they were met with a storm of applause.... The whole evening was a success.... Dostoevsky read his works best of all.

D.S. Merezhkovsky: A Childhood Encounter with Dostoevsky

From D.S. Merezhkovsky, "Avtobiograficheskaia zametka" ["Auto-biographical Notes"], in S.A. Vengerov, ed., *Russkaia Literatura XX veka* [*Russian Literature, 20th Century*], Vol. 1, Moscow, 1914, p. 291.)

In 1880, in St. Petersburg, my father got acquainted with Dostoev-sky in the home of Countess Tolstaya, the poet's [Alexei Tolstoy's] widow. Soon after, my father brought me to Dostoevsky's home. I remember a tiny apartment on the Kuznechny Street, with low ceilings and a small hall filled with copies of *The Brothers Karamazov*. Fyodor Mikhailovich was sitting in a small study reading the proofs of his manuscript. I recited to him my simple childish poems, and soon I blushed, stumbled and became pale. He was impatient and annoyed and listened to me in silence. It seemed to me that we were interfering with his work.

"Everything you read was weak, unimpressive, bad and very poorly written," he said at the end. "In order to write well, you have to suffer, you have to suffer."

My father contradicted him: "It would be better for the child if he didn't write if he has to suffer."

I remember the transparent and piercing glance of his pale-blue eyes when Dostoevsky shook my hand as we parted. I never saw him again and soon afterwards I found out that he had died....

A. Kruglov: A Writer Remembers the Funeral

(From A. Kruglov, "Pyostrye stranichki: Iz literaturnykh vospominanii" ["Pages from the literary memoirs"], *Istoricheskii vestnik* [*The History Herald*], Vol. 62, no. 11 [1895]: 473–483)

After visiting Fyodor Mikhailovich in his editor's office, I did not dare to visit him again, but we met in "Rossiia" quite by chance. I greeted him. He answered and looked at me attentively....

"Do you recognize me, Fyodor Mikhailovich?" [I asked.]

"I have seen you ... somewhere...."

"I brought my novel to you..." and I told him my name.

"Oh, yes, yes, nice to meet you.... Write ... but do not neglect other people.... Love people ... and, what is most important, love those who work honestly.... Love and respect people.... Your stories are very good...." This was my last meeting with Fyodor Mikhailovich....

I was struck by the news of his death. Everybody felt the terrible loss. As N. Strakhov remarked, and many people felt this way, a great part of our literature, maybe half of our literature went to the grave with Dostoevsky's death.... Never before had any writer been buried in such a ceremonial manner. Everybody was struck by the event. Even the most passionate admirers of Dostoevsky had not expected this crowd of thousands of people.... This procession formed naturally, without any preparation, without any invitations, because nobody expected his death.... It occurred naturally, all of a sudden, because it was the death of the Teacher, to which thousands of Russian people responded.... It was a national Russian funeral of a Russian national writer.

A. Moshin: Dostoevsky in Literary Gatherings

(From A. Moshin, *Novoe o velikikh pisateliakh* [*New Memoirs About Great Writers*], 2nd ed. St. Petersburg, 1908, pp. 71–81.)

Literary artists gathered several times a year: M.E. Saltykov-Shchedrin, F.M. Dostoevsky, N.A. Nekrasov, I.S. Turgenev (when he was in Russia) and P.I. Veinberg.... Saltykov made jokes, sometimes very witty and merciless. Everybody treated him with some caution.... If he created a nickname for someone, it would stick.... He gave a nickname "klikusha" [a hysterical woman] to Dostoevsky [for his] manner of finishing his discussions in a very excited manner, screaming and yelling....

When he argued on the so-called "cursed questions," Dostoevsky was shattering, shrieking and cursing his accusations, sometimes using dirty language. "'Klikusha,' please calm down," they told him.

"'Klikusha?' answered Dostoevsky. "If you have suffered as much as I have, then you can be like this." Several times when we had men in our company, Dostoevsky raised the bottom of his pants and showed his bare knees above his stockings. "Have a look. Here!..."

His bone was covered not by flesh, but, it seemed, by a very thin and transparent layer of skin. This was a terrible trace made by a cart during his prison labor.

Sometimes Dostoevsky read his works. Every time it produced a shattering impression. When his listeners told him about this, he answered, "Do you think I read with my voice? I read with my nerves! With my nerves!..."

He was rather tall, thin, looked ill and had a hunched back. Dostoevsky nevertheless made a good impression by his glance, which was very kind, meek and quiet. His eyes were never ill-tempered, even in the moments when he was irritated by someone.... His glance became only sad, but it never ceased being gentle and amiable....

Dostoevsky and Bunin decided to go to Staraya Russa for medical treatment, and in 1878 or 1879 went there along the Volkhov River by boat. They stayed in the two neighboring rooms at the Staraya Russa Inn and visited each other several times every day. They lived like this for about two months. Dostoevsky cured himself with the vapor baths. He had a very amiable attitude toward everyone he met there.

Dostoevsky liked to remember the nature of the country where he spent his hard times [in Siberia]. Dostoevsky spoke about cedars, about taiga.... He liked birds with passion; he liked to see them free, and did not like cages. Flocks of sparrows came to his window, and he treated them with bread.

As soon as Dostoevsky heard the birds singing, he stopped for a while; he could distinguish a bird by its voice. He liked to remember the local names given to the birds in Siberia....

Most of all he loved pigeons; when he saw pigeons, he stopped and looked at them, with a quiet and happy smile on his face.

I.I. Ianzhul: Dostoevsky in the Late 1870s

(From I.I. Janzhul, *Vospominaniia* [*Memoirs*] Vol. 2. St. Petersburg, 1910, pp. 25–27.)

I saw Dostoevsky three times, at the height of his glory.... I tried to talk to him several times, but he escaped conversation with me, behaving like a Buddha who accepted the admiration of his worshippers and kept quiet. During the tea, we sat at a huge table and started to talk about the pleasures of the country life.... My neighbors listened to me with interest, making occasional remarks. Suddenly we heard Dostoevsky's screaming voice. He yelled from the other side of the table, where he sat close to the hostess Eugenia Karlovna, exclaiming: "Professor, hey, you, professor!" [addressing me in such a rude way] though I had been introduced to him by my full name. "Professor, tell us, are you involved in the dull activity of growing vegetables, even though growing fruits is a much more pleasant and joyful thing?..." He said these words in such a rude and malicious tone, that those sitting at the table exchanged glances, and Schelgunov, with his usual straightforwardness and without any trace of shyness, made a remark, looking directly into Dostoevsky's eyes [and addressing another person, the host of the party]: "Dear Ivan Ivanovich, how do you find our famous writers? I think we have spoiled them by letting them say whatever they want." Mr. Geideburov, the host, looked with imploring eyes at Schelgunov, who got up and went out into the neighboring room. I followed him.

Count G. De Vollan: Sketches of Dostoevsky

Count G. De Vollan, "Ocherki proshlogo. F.M. Dostoevsky"
["Sketches from the Past. F.M. Dostoevsky"], *Golos Minuvshego*
[*The Voice of the Past*] 4 [1914]: 123–125.)

I saw him at the Slavic Committee. I liked his tired face with its martyr expression.... I wanted to get to know him closer, but I did not know how to do it. I took my booklets, as if a pretext to start a conversation, and I was lucky. Dostoevsky spoke with me for several hours.... Dostoevsky was very close to the Slavophile point of view and he was seeking salvation in Christianity, in the spiritual truth. Dostoevsky told me, "I can gather in my periodical [*A Writer's Diary*] all sincere and honest people who love Russia. The Russian youth wrote to tell me that I could be a banner, a symbol for them...."

I also spoke to him later, but for a brief period of time. I showed him books I was planning to send to the Belgrade library. He stared at Dobroliubov's name: "You should not send this, this is bad, this is poison," etc. I expressed my surprise at these words of his. He told me that some time ago he had been under the influence of the Petrashevsky Circle, but he had been cured of this illness and had started to hate revolutionaries with all of his heart. ... He seldom spoke in society. He looked with suspicion at every new face around him. He produced a hard, depressing impression; there was something unnatural, abnormal, in his behavior. Dostoevsky had a psychiatric problem: this was the conclusion I came to.

Nikolai Strakhov: Memories of a Close Associate

(From N. Strakhov, "Iz vospominanii o Dostoevskom" ["From the Memoirs About Dostoevsky"], *Semeinye vechera* [*Family Evenings*], February 1881: 235–248.)

> I have been very close to F.M. Dostoevsky for the past twenty years ... working at his journals.... Sufferings, desperation, crime, illness— these were recurrent topics in Dostoevsky's works. And what were the major conclusions? ... During his burial we remembered several words: compassion and love. I think that was the major honor which he [Dostoevsky] deserved. Christian ideals—this was the major thought which he so passionately expressed in his *Diary* and in his last novel....
>
> Everybody knows that the ideal image of Christ was the highest ideal for another of our artists, Count L.N. Tolstoy.... They did not know each other personally, but they wanted to get to know each other. Let me quote here from a letter written by Lev Tolstoy in September of last year: "Recently I read *Notes from the House of the Dead*.... It is a good book.... When you see Dostoevsky, please tell him that I love him." I brought this letter to Fyodor Mikhailovich in person, and I witnessed one of the beautiful moments. Therefore, the love of their people, the love of the people's ideals, the ideal of Christ, was the meaning of the works of our two best literary artists.

Alexei Suvorin: About the Deceased

(From A.S. Suvorin "O pokoinom" ["About the Deceased"], *Novoe Vremia* [*The New Times*], 13 February 1881: 1771)

> When you read these notes, Dostoevsky's body will be buried in the ground. I am compelled to write here about this man, whose death has affected so many people....
>
> We did not pay much attention to his illness. Dostoevsky looked rather young, younger than his years; he was always lively, enthusiastic and excited, and so full of plans that he did not even think about taking a rest. It never occurred to me that he might die from ruptured arteries. I have heard that many people live and very quickly recover from this illness. But Dostoevsky's body was worn out, and that is why his death came so suddenly.
>
> On Monday he had a hemorrhage first in his nose, and then in his throat. He was alarmed, but only slightly, and he felt that there was no real danger. All of us were upset, but we somehow felt that the situation was under control. Furthermore, Dostoevsky was used to such things

because he had had many illnesses during his life. He had suffered from epilepsy since youth. Something very terrible which he could never forget had happened to him in his childhood, and epilepsy was the result.

During the last few years of his life, the epileptic seizures were not frequent and were less severe than formerly, yet he constantly suffered from different things, such as the intensity of his work, the disappointments and failures of his life, and all the cruelty which existed in the Russian literary world....

Certainly, we all know that we are doomed to die, but we think about death and fear it only when we are threatened by some immediate danger.

Dostoevsky was under this threat every day of his life. It seemed as if he was faced with death all the time and that every enterprise, every literary work, and every image or idea which he created and nourished for a long period of time—all this could be destroyed in one blow. In addition to people's usual illnesses and prospects of possible natural death, he had his own personal illness, and it was impossible for him to grow accustomed to it. The fits of epilepsy were very severe. He knew that he might die in convulsions, after losing consciousness, and that this could happen at any time, and that the whole process would last no more than five minutes.

It required great courage to work under this constant threat, yet he worked like this all the time.

Because he was constantly subjected to this nagging threat to his existence, he developed his own attitude in the face of death: it was one of panic, and of fear.... After his fits passed, he usually became very talkative and was in a good mood.

Once I visited him when he had just experienced a fit of epilepsy. He was rolling his cigarettes, and it looked to me as if he were drunk.

"Please do not be alarmed," he said. "I have just had a seizure." Something similar happened to him when he had felt ill the previous Monday. He imagined that he had to face death, sudden death, and that he had to hurry to prepare for it. He confessed and took Holy Communion. He asked for his children, a boy and a girl, to be brought to him. The girl, the elder of the two, was eleven years old. He told his children that they should live without him, that they should love their mother, the truth and work, and that they should also help and respect the poor.

The loss of blood [from the hemorrhaging] made him very weak; he bowed his head and his face became dark. He regained some of his strength during the night.

On Tuesday, he felt better and did not think about death. The doctors advised him to remain completely quiet which is necessary in such cases. However, because of his nature, he was unable to stay quiet; his brain was constantly working.

As usual, he kept himself busy all the time. One moment, he would be considering his death, and would make final arrangements with respect to his family. The next moment he would be planning future works and dreaming about the future, when his children would be grown up, and he would take care of their education. He believed that the younger generation should have a better future, that they should live happy lives and do many good things in order to make other people happy.

M. De Vogue: Dostoevsky as a Psychologist: Notes by a French Literary Critic

(From M. De Vogue, "F.M. Dostoevsky kak psikholog pod sudom frantsuzkoi kritiki" ["F.M. Dostoevsky as a Psychologist: Notes by a French Literary Critic"], *Epokha* [*The Epoch*] 2 [1886]: 93–96.)

With your permission, I will proceed with the story of my acquaintance with Dostoevsky.... Due to special circumstances, I had the pleasure of meeting with Fyodor Mikhailovich fairly often during the last three years of his life, and I would like to say, with respect to both his appearance and his novels: once you encountered either, you could never forget the experience....

He was the reflection of his works, of everything he saw and of everything he experienced. He was a small, gaunt man and seemed to be made out of nerves. Dostoevsky did not appear to be aging, but rather, so to speak, to be fading away. He had a long beard and fair hair, and he looked like a sick person of indeterminate age. Nevertheless, he moved about very quickly, and he used to say that he was "quick as a cat."

He had the face of a typical Russian peasant: a rather flat nose and small eyes which were sometimes fiery and sometimes tender. He had a wide, high forehead covered with wrinkles, and small whiskers. All these features were grouped around his wrinkled mouth, which gave mute testimony to the tribulations he had endured.

Never in my life have I seen a man who personified such great suffering. It seemed to me that all the troubles and misfortunes he had ever encountered in his life had left their mark on his face.... His eyes, eyebrows and eyelashes twitched as if he had a nervous tic. Sometimes his face was filled with rage and you would swear that you had seen it before, either in the courts, on the bench where the accused convicts sit, or among the beggars soliciting alms in the streets. There were other moments though, when he looked like one of the saints depicted on the old Slavic icons.

This man was the reflection of the Russian national character. He was some inexplicable combination of rudeness, calmness, and intellect—typical features of many Russian peasants. There was something very unusual about his face; perhaps it was the look of concentration on the face of a simple worker.

At first sight, he produced an unpleasant, hostile impression, but soon you found yourself charmed by the enigmatic inner force which flowed from and surrounded him.

Dostoevsky was usually silent at first. Presently, he would start to talk, quietly and slowly, but with ardor and passion; little by little he would become inspired, as he expounded and defended his views, and at such times he could be very rude.

For example, once, when he was supporting his favorite thesis about the superiority of the Russian people, he said to a woman, "You do not deserve to belong to the worst of the males." He concluded all his literary discussions with me [a French writer] with the brusque declaration: "We have the genius of all peoples, added to the genius of Russian people. Therefore, we can understand you, but you cannot understand us."

Now—and I am sorry to say this—I think that he was wrong, and that the opposite is true.

I regret saying this, but Dostoevsky looked on life with somewhat naïve eyes. I remember how one day he became very critical of Paris. It happened one evening, when he was especially inspired. He spoke like a prophet in the Bible, like Jonah the Prophet speaking against Nineveh. Here are his words: "The day will come when a prophet will come to the *Café Anglais*, and he will write in burning letters on its walls. This will be the sign for the fall and destruction of Paris, with all its pride, its theaters and its English cafes, and the city will be destroyed in a deluge of fire and blood."

In his imagination, it was the city of Sodom, an inferno of wild damnable orgies. He prophesied loud and long on this topic.

Fyodor Mikhailovich often quoted Jean-Jacques Rousseau. In him was the same morality, the same combination of rudeness and idealism, of sensitivity and savagery, and at the foundation of it all a boundless love of humanity, for which the writer deserved the admiration of his contemporaries.

In public Dostoevsky was gloomy, but at the same time, he was an idol to the Russian youth. Young people waited impatiently for his every new novel and newspaper article; they came to visit him, to receive moral support and to hear his kind words. During the last years of his life,

Fyodor Mikhailovich was very busy with correspondence. He had piles of letters to answer; he had to support people in their sufferings.

One had to live in Russia during that gloomy era to understand the great influence which Dostoevsky exerted on the ordinary people in their search for ideals in life.

Turgenev's glory as a writer of fiction was fading. Tolstoy was influential as a philosopher because he was closer to logical understanding.

Dostoevsky addressed people's hearts and so acquired great influence. By the time of the Pushkin Festival in 1880, his popularity had grown greater than that of any of his literary rivals.... His greatness became fully apparent only at the time of his death.

I must describe the apotheosis which occurred then. The impression those few days produced on me was stronger than that effected by any literary criticism; this event [Dostoevsky's funeral] showed us just what this man had meant to his country.

On 10 February 1881, Dostoevsky's friends told me that he had died after a brief illness. We went to his apartment on Kuznechny Street, to be present at the preliminary funeral service. The crowd around his house was so dense that we could hardly squeeze through to the apartment to see the body.

In a small room we saw many sheets of paper piled here and there, in complete disorder. The room was filled with visitors standing around the coffin. It was the writer's first real rest, and for the first time I saw a tranquil expression on his face, a face usually filled with suffering. Finally he lay perfectly still, in a sea of flowers. The crowd grew every minute; here and there, weeping women and agitated men could be seen among the moving multitude of people. It was very hot in the room.

Suddenly, all the candles around the coffin flickered and went out.... There remained only a dim light issuing from a small incense burner in front of an icon. On the stairs, there was some movement, then a crowd of people came in, jostling those who were already standing in the room; they, in turn, pushed against the coffin. The poor widow, who stood with her children on the other side of the table on which the coffin rested, leaned over the body, trying to prevent it from falling.

It seemed to me, for an instant, that the coffin might be overturned. It was balancing on the edge of the table, where it had been pushed by the crowd. In a moment, as if in a flash, I saw in my imagination the life and works of the deceased in their entirety. I remembered the characters in his novels and the images of the different people he created. It seemed to me that these people were surrounding me then and that they were taking part in this frightful scene. Even after his death, the people he depicted in his novels tormented him. It was exactly the same kind of characters he had created in his works that came to his funeral, and who showed, through their very rudeness, their feeling and compassion for the writer.

Two days later, I witnessed a similar scene, but on a much larger scale. It was on 12 February 1881, the day of Dostoevsky's funeral. Russia had never seen a greater, more impressive funeral, and those who witnessed the procession could see in it all the shades of the Russian land and its people.

There were an abundance of speeches made by senior officials, students, Slavophiles, Liberals, journalists, and poets. Everyone emphasized his opinion of Dostoevsky, stressing the importance of this writer, although many people, as is typical on such occasions, simply nourished their own egos....

The February wind blew away the powdery snow, the dry leaves fell from the trees, and there was the sound of the beautiful speeches. I stood in silence, trying to understand the importance of this man and his work. It was difficult to pass judgment. Dostoevsky had awakened in his people feelings of compassion and love. He achieved this result gradually, by extraordinary diligence and tenacity. He had given his whole heart to his people, in spite of the fact that he did not apply logic to his emotions.

I thought about this for a long time, and then I remembered the story of Dostoevsky's life. Born in a charity hospital for the poor, his early years were dogged by need, poverty, and misfortune. Siberia brought him even more physical and moral suffering coupled with hard physical toil. It was then that I realized that his oppressed soul could not be understood and analyzed according to the usual criteria because he truly was a phenomenon unto himself....

B. Markevich: A Brief Report About Dostoevsky's Death

(From B. Markevich, "Neskolko slov o konchine Dostoevskogo" ["Several Words About the Death of Dostoevsky"], *Moskovskie Vedomosti* [*The Moscow News*], 1 February 1881.)

I was present for the last minutes of Dostoevsky's life. My hands can hardly move as I write these lines, being fresh under the impression which this death has made upon me. This is a great loss to all Russian society. It is the loss of a Russian thinker.

Recently, I spent an evening with the deceased at the home of Countess S.T. [Sofia Tolstaya], whom he visited very often and respected. He was very lively and joyful. We talked about the three scenes of a trilogy by Count Alexei Tolstoy. The amateurs were going to perform there, and Fyodor Mikhailovich had taken the role of the monk in *The Death of Ivan the Terrible*. I left before him and, saying good-bye to him, asked him whether we would see him again the next Monday (on Mondays, the Countess had her parties).

"Possibly," he said. I shook his hand, and I would not have believed it if somebody had told me that this handshake would not happen again in this life. He did not look like a man who would die in the next few days. On Monday, however, he did not come. I noticed this and asked the hostess about him. "I don't know, he had planned to come," she told me. "Maybe he is busy with his *Diary*," which was forthcoming soon, and she added: "He had dinner with us recently, and he took a copy of the trilogy in order to learn his role by heart."

Today, on Wednesday, before dinner, I read in *The New Times* that Dostoevsky was seriously ill. In spite of the alarming tone of the newspaper article, I did not believe the words....

Around eight o'clock, I rang the doorbell of his modest apartment at 5 Kuznechny Street. From the stairs I heard a strange noise. Someone opened the door and rushed at me crying, "Call the doctor! Quickly, quickly!" in a piercing voice. (It was the stepson of Fyodor Mikhailovich, the son of his first wife by her first marriage.) Before I answered, a ten-year-old blonde girl ran into the corridor screaming, "You are the doctor! For God's sake, please save my father. He cannot breathe."

"I am not a doctor," I answered quietly.

At the same moment Apollon Nikolaevich Maikov, with a pale face and feverish, blinking eyes, came into the corridor. "Oh, it's you," and he called my name. ...

He had also read about Fyodor Mikhailovich's illness in *The New Times*. Maikov had come to visit Dostoevsky about half an hour before me, and it seemed that everything was over....

On Monday he had some hemorrhage from the mouth. His family said that he had lost about 1½ pounds of blood and had become very weak. Yesterday he stopped bleeding. He slept well, was in a good mood and spoke about his *Diary*. He even made jokes: "I will live longer than all of you." However, he wanted to take Holy Communion and to confess. This morning he became nervous, then he started bleeding again and then.... Apollon Nikolaevich was not able to continue, because he was too excited.

"Can I see him?"

"Come with me!..."

I will never forget this picture! ... Dostoevsky was on the sofa, at the far end of a poor and rather gloomy dark room, his study. He was dressed and had a pillow under his head. The dim light of a lamp, or that of a candle (I do not remember well) standing on the night table fell on his completely pale forehead and cheeks, and on the dark-red spot of blood on his chin which had not been washed off.... His breath moved with a brief whistle and through the convulsively opened lips.

His eyelids were half-closed, as if mechanically. This was the convulsion of the seriously ill body. This face was well-known to me. It was tormented by thought; it looked as if it was burning from the inside by a passionate flame, and you could not see the physical torment in him. It seemed that he was completely unconscious....

His wife was kneeling in front of him desperately. She fell onto his arm which fell lifelessly from the sofa and had the words of prayer on her lips..... It tore my soul apart....

Two children, the son and the daughter, were kneeling close to her and were crossing themselves in a frightened way. The girl rushed to me, desperately, and took my hand: "Please, I implore you, pray. Pray for my father, so that if he had any sins God will forgive them," she said these words with some unusual, not childish expression, and hysterical tears started to fall from her eyes. I took her from the study. She was trembling with fever, but she released herself from my arm and ran back to the dying man.

Apollon Maikov tried to convince the mother to leave Dostoevsky and to calm down for a while.... She obeyed, at last. She wanted to release her moans, because he could not hear them from the other room. She could only say, "Oh, whom am I losing," falling into the armchair. "And whom is Russia losing," Maikov and I said simultaneously. We gave her some water to drink. "He wanted to live more. Life, at the very least, was becoming better for him. He was going to say many things...."

We heard voices: "The priest ... the doctor ... they have arrived." Several people who had been sent for the doctor and the priest came into the room. The doctor hurried into the study. He asked for the window to be opened ... and to be left alone, together with Dostoevsky's stepson, at the bed of the ill man. Maikov and I stayed with Anna Grigorievna. Several minutes of inexpressible and difficult waiting followed.

The doctor opened the door which he had closed a while ago, and he went out. "Is this the end?" cried the poor woman, jumping from her place.

He put her into her seat and took her hand. "It is not over yet, but it will be over soon. And it is my duty to tell you that the last sense which is preserved in a dying man is his ears. So please, do not torment him during his last minutes with your cries of torment."

"Oh, doctor, I will not make a single noise, but please let me see him!" And they ran to the dying man, and they knelt in front of him. Everything was deadly silent. You could not hear his breath anymore.

The priest came in, and he started to whisper a prayer over the dying man.... The doctor bowed over him, listened, unbuttoned his shirt, put his hand under it, and bowed his head. This time it really was the end.... I took out my watch. It was 8:36 P.M.

He died, and all of thinking Russia responded to this great loss with a feeling of great and painful woe. He was a great talent and he had a great soul. This was a great, fearless and undefeatable fighter for Jesus Christ, for his people, for the best and the most holy ideals. He fought for these ideals throughout his life and, as if from the purifying torment, he brought such a great spirit, such a great force of sermon, such a great power to influence people's souls that even his worst opponents were silent.

Do we have to remember how popular he became in Russia during the Pushkin Festival?... The youth felt, saw and accepted him as a teacher. And his influence on the youth, on these children of Bazarov-the-father, grew from year to year, stronger and stronger.... For this youth, he renewed the publication of his *Diary*, but his death interrupted this. Wednesday, 11 P.M.

Vladimir Davydov: Russian Actors at Dostoevsky's Funeral

(From V.N. Davydov, *Rasskaz o proshlom* [*A Story from the Past*]. Moscow: Academia, 1931.)

Savina invited me to listen to Dostoevsky. He read the *Greedy Knight* [a novel by Pushkin] very badly. Nevertheless, a few moments after meeting its favorite writer, the audience went quite wild. Then he read "In the Springtime." It was also poorly done, but he was still called back for an encore.

Finally, he began to read "The Prophet." When he started to read this poem, he changed completely and became quite unrecognizable.

Before this, he had looked weak and tired, and his back was bent, but he suddenly changed into a powerful giant, a man of steel. His hoarse voice rang throughout the hall, as if it were a brass trumpet, and he read the last verse of the poem with flashing eyes, gazing beyond us at some point in the distance, with an expression of great inspiration and a voice choked with tears.

The audience moaned with admiration. Dostoevsky became very pale, and it looked as if he might faint. It seemed to me, as far as I recall, that the crowd carried him off the stage.

Everything that happened after Dostoevsky was so bland and unimpressive that I simply forgot it. Soon afterwards, the writer died, and I went to bid my last farewell to his remains. I was accompanied by Savina, an actress of whose acting he was very fond. I remember that on the way from the theater to his house, we were both silent. Without saying a word, we arrived at his home, and went up the narrow, dirty stairs crowded with young people.

It was a poor apartment, and the writer had been put into his coffin by the time we came. I saw Pobedonostsev [a minister of the Tsar], who bowed his head very low, close to the face of the corpse. He had been a great friend of Dostoevsky.

P. Gnedich: Dostoevsky's Last Public Appearances

(From P.P. Gnedich, *Kniga zhisni. Vospominaniia. 1855–1918 gody.* [*The Book of My Life: Memoirs, 1855–1918*] Leningrad: Priboi, 1929, pp. 121–122, 130–133.)

One day I visited the Hall of the Russian Nobility where a benefit concert to support the Literary Fund was being held. There were so many famous names in the program that if the same event had been repeated three times in a row, the tickets would still have been completely sold out.

The writers who read from their works were Saltykov (Shchedrin), Dostoevsky, Turgenev, Polonsky, Pleshcheev and Alexei Potekhin.

Dostoevsky read best of all. At the time *The Brothers Karamazov* was being published in *The Russian Herald*. That night, he read the scene from the novel in which Katerina Ivanovna meets Grushenka. He read wonderfully; I have never heard anything like it before or since. It was not merely a reading, or a theatrical performance; it was a horrifying depiction of real life, an epileptic's nightmare.

Dostoevsky was tremendously successful. This performance occurred prior to his famous speech ... during the unveiling of the Pushkin Monument in 1880.

I remember now how in the autumn of 1880 many young people, impressed by Dostoevsky's speech, began saving their money in order to buy a new edition of Pushkin's works. The youth began to read his works again, and he became popular once more.

Three months later, in January 1881, Dostoevsky died. The news was a real blow for young people.... Everyone had known that Fyodor Mikhailovich was suffering from epilepsy, but many people live for a long time with this illness.

The Demons engendered a negative attitude towards Dostoevsky among our youth. His other novels *The Idiot* and *The Raw Youth* were not understood at first, but *The Brothers Karamazov* was hugely successful.

Dostoevsky died in his apartment on Kuznechny Street.... At his funeral, a huge crowd of people showed up. His small apartment—several rooms on the second floor—did not have enough room for all the visitors. People kept coming; they went up the stairs, [through the rooms], then out into the street, and then along the huge fence in the marketplace where the merchants sold dry wood for fireplaces.

The weather on the day of Dostoevsky's funeral was bright and frosty. One can find the procession depicted in *The Illustrated World.**

Hundreds of wreaths were carried along the Kuznechny Street, then the procession went into the direction of the church on the Vladimirsky Prospect, and then turned right, along the Nevsky Prospect....

This was "the triumph of the heart." Loris-Melikov [Minister of the Interior] did not want to restrict "the people's lamentations" and did not place any restrictions or obstacles in the way of the procession. As if by chance, however, a Cossack military exercise was being held on the Cossack Parade Ground [in the center of the city], and several military units were kept on alert.

Dostoevsky's family was left without any means of support. Due to the merits of the deceased, however, his family was granted an annual pension of 3,000 roubles.

The main source of income for Dostoevsky's family came from the energy and the practical wit of Anna Grigorievna, who started to publish Dostoevsky's works. An example of her tenacity was when, twenty years later, Mr. Mark, the publisher of the journal *The Field*, offered her 100,000 roubles for the copyright to all of Dostoevsky's works, she flatly refused. For this sum, she gave the publisher permission to release the works for a limited period of two years only, which allowed Dostoevsky's works to be published as a special bonus for subscribers to *The Field....*

Vsevolod Soloviev liked to live in a large apartment, to which he invited many of his friends. He told me that during his first years in St. Petersburg, Dostoevsky was among his frequent visitors. He usually visited Soloviev after an epileptic fit.

---

*This famous illustration is included in this work in the glossy insert.

Once when he came to Soloviev's home on such a visit, he was gloomy and ill-tempered, saying that after his seizures he could not go anywhere else. On another occasion when Dostoevsky was in an especially bad mood, Nikolai Vagner arrived. Dostoevsky looked at him with a puzzled gaze. The host introduced the visitor by name, and Dostoevsky responded: "Nice to meet you."

Vagner was completely incensed, replying, "What, don't you still recognize me?"

Dostoevsky replied, "This is the first time I have ever seen you."

"I am Dr. Vagner, professor of zoology, and my pen-name is the Cat's Meow."

"This is the first time I have ever seen you."

"How can this possibly be? You once worked at my journal, *The Light*."

"Never."

Dostoevsky had just had a fit of epilepsy, and he was trying to make fun of Vagner, whom he somewhat disliked. The man grabbed his hat and left instantly. Then Soloviev asked Dostoevsky, "Did you really forget Vagner?" Fyodor Mikhailovich thought for a while and said, "It seems to me that I do know him. But I did not remember him right away."

I.P. Pavlov: Letters to the Bride About Dostoevsky's Funeral

(From I.P. Pavlov, "Pis'ma k neveste" ["Letters to the Bride"], *Moskva* [*Moscow*] 10 [1959]: 175–178.)

Yesterday, I went to Dostoevsky directly from the railway station. I fought my way through the crowd for about an hour. Out of breath and drenched with sweat, I could hardly see anything for the huge mass of people. Completely exhausted, I came home and spent the entire evening with Sergei....

At 11 A.M. I was at Dostoevsky's apartment. My dear Sarah, I have never seen anything like this before. A huge mass of people and an endless line of laurel wreaths above the heads of these people, maybe from forty to fifty wreaths, from different educational institutions starting with high schools and ending with universities, from different societies, from associations of lawyers and judges ... from newspapers, etc. Each wreath was accompanied by a delegation representing a certain organization. Each wreath had an inscription made from flowers on it, with the name of the organization, titles of nobles, Dostoevsky's initials or mottoes such as "to the Russian man" or "to the Great Teacher" or "to the friend of truth." The coffin was covered with a golden cloth and was carried high above the heads of the people. Three to four meters around the coffin, people carried in their hands chains of fresh flowers....

The people sang without pause, "Holy Is Our Lord." It was sung not only by several professional church choirs, but by groups of people who spontaneously burst into song, university and high school students....

We went for three hours. If the deceased could have felt this, he would have been satisfied. By his death he elevated the soul of every thinking and feeling person in St. Petersburg....

You could enter the church only if you had a ticket. I was lucky to have one. The wreaths stood on supports on either side of the coffin along the whole length of the church. Most of the people were young. There were, however, several ladies (from high society) and members of the royal family....

Yesterday the January issue of *A Writer's Diary* was released. We look forward to reading it with excitement....

I enclose news about Dostoevsky's funeral from different newspapers....

There were more than 70 wreaths. *The New Times* reported that about 30,000 people participated in the funeral procession....

I.F. Tiumenev: From the Diary of a Composer

(From I.F. Tiumenev, "Iz dnevnika" ["From the Diary], *Literaturnoe nasledstvo* [*Literary Heritage*] 86 [1973]: pp. 339–345.)

29 January 1880.

We found out from the newspapers that Dostoevsky died yesterday at 8:00 P.M. We all grieved. In two days we gathered 110 roubles, put aside the money necessary for the wreath, and decided to send the remainder to *The New Times* where they had already started to accept donations for the monument.

30 January.

A deputation of student representatives from our college visited Dostoevsky's apartment. During our evening classes we made all the necessary preparations for tomorrow. We discussed where and when we should meet. About sixty students have agreed to go—most of them painters and designers—from the department of visual arts...

31 January.

At 10 A.M. we met at St. Vladimir's Church. The adjoining square was entirely filled with people. There were about twenty or thirty wreaths, and together they formed a line from the church to the house where Dostoevsky had lived.

Around one of the wreaths stood a group of high school students. Vladimir Soloviev said that the students of the First High School had not been allowed to attend the funeral by the school principal, but they had collected the money for the flowers, and several senior students had left their classes secretly in order to participate in the procession.

Another wreath was surrounded by students from the Central Technical School. Next to them was a wreath from the Bestuzhev Female Courses, surrounded by a group of young women. Further on, a short distance away, there was a wreath from the Art Exhibition Society. Kramskoi, Lemokh and other artists stood close by this wreath. Behind them there was a wreath from the Russian Opera Theater. There we saw a tall figure of V.J. Vasiliev-Senior talking to Morozov and Melnikov. Later on we found out that Melnikov was reproached [punished] by Kister, the theater director, for going out without permission. He could have caught cold, fallen ill, or become hoarse, and they would have had to cancel the performance. Beyond the opera company was a wreath from the Russian Drama Theater Company. There we saw Brodnikov, Sazonov, Petipa and other actors. Karazin from the Artists Club was also there....

The group of students from St. Petersburg University arrived making a lot of noise. They carried a huge wreath decorated with palm branches and shaped in the form of a lyre. This group stood right in front of us....

We heard the chimes of the huge bell of St. Vladimir's Church Tower and the singing of "Holy Is Our Lord." It was the University Choir who sang, accompanied by dozens of voices from the huge, moving throng. At the first words of the prayer everyone took off their hats. This slow, sad music was so touching that many of us felt tears in our eyes. I too was greatly impressed by the singing....

The Nevsky Prospect [the central street of St. Petersburg] was completely packed with people. The carriages could hardly move in the two narrow lanes and the rest of the street was filled with the procession; another huge mass of people stood on both sides of the street, on the sidewalk. One old woman asked, "Whose funeral is it?" And one of the students answered: "He was a prisoner." At one point, there was a stir in the crowd and we heard voices announce, "Gentlemen, please let the President pass." The people stepped aside to create an open space and an old man in a fur coat with a large grey beard, a bit confused, went forward. This was Beketov, the president of St. Petersburg University.

The procession was immensely long and resembled a huge parade: the coffin was only just moving onto the Nevsky Prospect, but the first wreaths approached Znamenie [a distance of about three kilometers or nearly two miles]. All the sidewalks, balconies and windows were packed with people. The streetcars were forced to a halt and some people climbed onto their roofs. Along the way two more delegations with wreaths joined the procession; these were students from Moscow University and Katkov College who had just arrived by train from Moscow.

The wreath from the Russian Drama Theater Company was carried by Sazonov and Savina [famous actors], and most of us liked their respectful attitude toward the deceased.... The young people behaved properly; they were very polite, though some of them smoked cigarettes together with actors and passersby. At Znamenie there was another huge church service.

During the service we all stopped and kept silent for a moment, then several voices commanded "Let's go!" and we again started singing "Holy Is Our Lord" and marched on.

At the Lavra Square I stepped onto the sidewalk and let the whole procession pass me by. Following the coffin were many wreaths from literary artists and journals. A wreath from *The Russian Speech* was brought to the Dukov Church, borne above the crowd. I saw wreaths from *The New Times*, *The St. Petersburg Herald*, *The Illustrated World*, and other newspapers and journals. I do not now remember them all, there were so many of them.

The coffin was surrounded by people who carried a huge chain of fresh flowers connected to the wreath of the Slavic Charity Society, which was carried in front of the coffin.

I bowed to the dear departed and then looked at the coffin for a long time. Its lid was covered with a golden pall and richly decorated; it seemed like it was flying above the crowd....

When the procession approached the gates of the cemetery, there were moans and cries. As the crowd started to pass through the gates, I turned around and went home....

That night I spoke with my friends about idealism, realism and art; we drew parallels between Dostoevsky and Shchedrin, between Schiller and Heine, and our discussion lasted until 7.30 A.M. Such things had never happened to us before!

Pyotr Tchaikovsky: "I Wept as I Have Never Wept Over a Book Before"

(From P. Tchaikovsky, *Letters to His Family*, trans. by G. von Mekk. London: Dobson, 1972, pp. 216–217.)

From a letter to Anatoly Tchaikovsky, dated 15–27 February 1879 and written in Paris:

> I am at the moment very much under the influence of Dostoevsky's *The Brothers Karamazov*. If you have not yet read it, run and get the January *Herald* where there is a description of Father Zosima receiving visitors in his monastery. In this episode a woman is struck down by the grief of losing all of her children. After she lost the last one she left her husband to wander, full of anguish, all over the country. When I read this, the woman's words and her hopeless agony after the death of her last child, I wept as I have never wept over a book before. It has made the deepest impression on me....

Letter to Modest Tchaikovsky, 23 August 1881:

> I am reading *The Karamazovs* and long to finish it as soon as possible . Dostoevsky is an author of genius but I find him anti-pathetic. The more I read him the more he weighs me down.

Katerina Letkova: About Dostoevsky Reading His Works and His Funerals

(From K.P. Letkova-Sultanova, "O F.M. Dostoevskom. Iz vospominanii" ["About F.M. Dostoevsky. From My Memoirs"], *Zvenia* [*Chains*]. Moscow: Academia, 1932, Vol. 1, pp. 459–477.)

This happened at a literary evening in support of the Literary Fund. Several famous literary artists were reading from their works, and Dostoevsky was to be among them....

I went there with some excitement. Yet my expectations of the magnitude of the effect Dostoevsky would have on me were more than realized. I saw him as a great writer, suffering for me and for all of us, for humanity. When he read "The Prophet" [a poem by Pushkin], it seemed that it was about Dostoevsky that Pushkin had written these lines: "Prophet, you must burn the hearts of the people with your words."

Applause and cheers were not necessary after his quiet, deep voice. As I went out into the lobby, I ran into Pyotr Veinberg, the organizer of these concerts. He said, "Let's go to the actors' rooms in the back, behind the stage. You will find some friends there."

Actually, I met Grigorovich and Goncharov, whom I had recently met at the home of my sister, J.P. Makovskaya.

Dostoevsky sat in the corner, looking tired to the point of exhaustion.... I did not have the courage to go and talk to him. I did not know whether he remembered me. But then he looked at me. I bowed, he stood up, and I approached him. He had a very special, "official" way of shaking hands, and he usually spoke in a reserved tone when he met a stranger. I felt a bit awkward because he was so tired and I was forcing him to stand, so I said: "Please sit down, Fyodor Mikhailovich!"

But he did not want to sit down, and merely to say something. He said, with a slightly ironic smile, "Jakov Petrovich told me that you write something from time to time...."

"I try to do my best."

"By fasting and prayers?" he asked me with the same irony.... Suddenly he became serious and said, "It's good that you write.... It is a good thing to do." His mood was changing rapidly. It seemed that there were two different men in him; he produced such a diverse and contradictory impression on people....

Dostoevsky's funeral has been described by so many people. It was truly a great event, and deeply symbolic. From all walks of life and from every party, people came to say their farewells to him. There were the young and the old, writers, generals, actors, and simple people: "the oppressed and humiliated," people from "basements and slums," those he had written about. And, most importantly, there were the many young people who had felt the truth [he told them] ....

These young people did not let the police keep order at the funeral. Instead, they formed a chain around the crowd, holding each other's hands. The procession following the coffin was led by A. Pleshcheev, a man who, together with Fyodor Mikhailovich, had been sentenced to death long ago. Close to him walked General Tcherniaev, our Serbian hero and Dostoevsky's friend; then followed many painters, and certainly all our literary artists.

Representatives from many delegations and societies (more than seventy) followed this group of people. They were carrying laurels and flowers and were singing "The Eternal Glory." An immense crowd followed them in awe and silence....

Dostoevsky was buried as "one of our friends."

"Today we bury a great artist," said Ivan Shishkin as he approached our delegation....

"And a great patriot," someone added.

All the troubles, discussions and quarrels which had existed before the death of Fyodor Mikhailovich disappeared that day. We all were united; we all understood that a great man had been lost, a writer of genius who had created many artistic masterpieces for humanity.

When it was late at night, we returned home from the cemetery. Many speeches had been made throughout the day, and they still echoed in our ears. Life was going on noisily along the Nevsky Prospect [the central street of St. Petersburg]....

Alexander Nikolaevich Pleshcheev said, at the first meeting dedicated to Dostoevsky's memory,

I did not know a man who was more unhappy in this life.... He was ill and weak, and, consequently, could hardly endure all the hardships of prison.... He always was in need of money, and he suffered from this too.... And what is even more serious, he suffered at the hands of the critics.... You cannot even imagine how sensitive he was to every unfriendly phrase.... How he suffered! He suffered for all these reasons, not for only one or two years, but for decades ... to his dying day.... This was the terrible drama of his life.

Nevertheless, time has passed its own judgment.... Dostoevsky's name is not forgotten; indeed, it becomes more and more respected. This name survived through the rabid criticism of the '60s, the sharp political changes of the '70s, the silence of the '80s; it survived through many new literary trends (decadence, symbolism, individualism, etc.), and through all the storms that shook our world, and this name shines brighter and brighter.

Anatoly Alexandrov: To the Memory of Dostoevsky

(From A. Alexandrov, "Pamiati Dostoevskogo" ["To the Memory of Dostoevsky"], *Moskovskie vedomosti* [*Moscow News*], 28 January 1910: 22.)

Every time we celebrate the anniversary of the death of a person who was close to us, we remember this person's life and we want to talk about him.... Dostoevsky died on 28 January 1881 at 8:38.

You experienced even stronger feelings [of grief], if you were close to the man....

People of our generation had a very special feeling, because he was close to our generation, to the people who were formed in the late 1870s and early 1880s. He was a very sensitive, impressive, responsive person. He loved youth and he understood its interests; he shared its concerns, its pains.

He could carry youth away with his passionate, sincere and excited speeches. During the last years of his life, that is, during the publication of *A Writer's Diary*, he was flooded with correspondence from young people of both sexes.

Crowds of young people followed him everywhere. He became a teacher, a leader of our youth. Many young men and women, including the author of these lines, had the happiness of knowing him personally, of communicating with him, and we store the best memories of this man in our souls. He was called "simply a Christian" by K. Leontiev who was a great scholar and a great person of the time, who was the supporter of the traditions of the true old Orthodoxy and who was brought up in the spirit of Athos and Optina [two Russian shrine monasteries]. He was a true Christian, and he asked others to follow him, to admire the idea of the greatness of the Russian people....

He was a turning point for our intellectuals who were lost on their way to find the truth; he was on his way to the real Orthodoxy taught by Leontiev.... "Love not me, but my holy shrine": he addressed this message to our intellectuals, and in addressing them, he represented the whole Russian people.... He asked them to work for the people.

"Be humble, you proud man! Be hard-working, you lazy man!" He inspired us with such words. Today these words sound as important as they were at that time—for those people who understand him.

Apollon Maikov: Several Words About Dostoevsky

(From A.N. Maikov, "Rech' na torzhestvennom obshchem sobranii St. Petersburgkogo Slavianskogo Bogotvoritelnogo Obshchestva" ["Speech Made at the General Special Meeting of the St. Petersburg Branch of the Slavic Charity Society"], *Rus'* [*Russia*] 18 [1881]: 14–15.)

At Dostoevsky's funeral, many people asked me the same question about my recollections of the deceased. I answered that it was too hard for me to bring it to my mind. Today, several weeks later, I feel the same way. Perhaps the reason for this is the fact that I shared a very close and lengthy friendship with Dostoevsky... Our relationship dated from the publication of *Poor People*. It was then interrupted in 1849, for many years, but resumed again after Dostoevsky's return from Siberia. During the years he spent abroad, from 1867 to 1871, we kept up an intense correspondence, and it brought even closer together our respective views, preferences, and dislikes. It was natural that, after his return from abroad, we wanted to see each other more often. We had conversations which lasted many hours, we argued, we worked out many new ideas, we discussed each other's works, and, as a result, we helped each other to understand things. We discussed everything: current events, small incidents from our personal life, great events in our country and throughout the world—we discussed everything on a grand, historic scale. All smaller, unimportant things we logically connected to great events of general significance. The major goal of our discussion was to understand the past, to interpret the present, and to guess at future events.

He always wanted to get to the heart of the matter, to an understanding

of what was most essential in life. We both wanted this, and he helped others to achieve this goal.

"Oh, if only people could understand, then there would be Paradise on Earth," he used to say. What exactly did he mean, "to understand"? Yes, dear ladies and gentlemen, I hope you have guessed correctly. He spoke about people in general, about all of humanity.... He once explained, "Yes, just try to understand! But well, they often do not understand! If our people do something right, they do it without a deep and sound understanding of the matter. They just follow their instincts, like St. Nicholas.... "What do you think, do many people understand us? 'It is all peanuts! Chauvinism! Mysticism! Art for art's sake!' they scream."

After all the applause, shouts and cheers from the crowd which followed readings of his work before large audiences, he used to repeat, "Yes, yes, this is good, but you do not understand the most essential things." Now that the official funeral ceremony, the long ovations, and all the laudatory newspaper articles have passed, I remember the question Fyodor Mikhailovich asked so often: "How many people understand, and do people understand it at all?" He meant those things which he called "the heart of the matter."

I do not have a real answer to this. But I would like to finish, as Dostoevsky used to do, with an anecdote.... A respected high-ranking state official once met Dostoevsky at a high society party. This man had known Dostoevsky before the Petrashevsky case, but he had not seen Fyodor Mikhailovich in the many years since the latter's return from Siberia. The two old friends were reintroduced to each other. They remembered old times and began to talk. The elderly official asked him: "Your punishment and several years in Siberian prisons was an injustice?"

Dostoevsky answered, "It was justice. Maybe the Divine Spirit had to bring me to that prison, so that I could find out something that is the most important thing in the world; things without which we cannot live, otherwise people will eat each other with their materialistic development.

"So I had an understanding of these most essential things, because the answer is hidden in our own people. I reflected that there were many people who were drunkards, thieves, murderers, so I had to bring this knowledge back with me and tell others, and so at least some of those others became a little better, or at least began to understand some things."

PART II

*Chronology of
Dostoevsky's Life*

1 8 2 1

October 30   Fyodor Mikhailovich Dostoevsky's birth in Moscow at the Marinskaja Shelter for the Poor, to the family of a doctor. He is the second child in the family.

1 8 2 3

From the memoirs of Anna Dostoevskaya: "Fyodor Mikhailovich remembered himself from the age of two years old, when his mother gave him sacred wine in the village church and he saw a pigeon flying from one window of the church to another."

1 8 2 5 – 1 8 3 3

Fyodor receives his first education from tutors hired by his father.

1 8 3 0

Summer   The rape and subsequent death of a nine-year-old neighbor girl deeply affects young Dostoevsky. He will depict this case in his writings several times.

1 8 3 1

The Dostoevsky family buys Darovoe, a small estate about 150 kilometers (125 versts) south of Moscow where they will spend each summer.

1 8 3 4

September   With elder brother Mikhail, enters the Chermak Private High School in Moscow. Writes to his mother, one of his first letters.

1 8 3 7

February 27   Mother's death at age 37.
May   With Mikhail, D. goes to St. Petersburg to enter the St. Petersburg Military Engineering Academy.
July 1   Father resigns and moves to live with his younger children at Darovoe, his country estate.
September 1   The brothers are introduced to General V.L. Sharnhorst, the director of the Military Engineering Academy.

1838

January 16   D. enters the St. Petersburg Military Engineering Academy. Among major subjects in the curriculum are mathematics, physics, military engineering, fortification, French and German.

1839

June 6   Father, Mikhail Andreevich, is killed by village serfs.
June 22–   D. spends the summer in a military camp in Peterhoff, a sub-
August 8   urb of St. Petersburg.

1841

August   D. becomes a junior officer and moves to junior officers' class.
October   Brother Mikhail moves to Narva City.

1842

January   The marriage of brother Mikhail. In November their son Fyodor is born. Dostoevsky becomes the godfather of his namesake nephew.

1843

August   D. graduates from the St. Petersburg Military Engineering Academy and is given officer rank as a junior lieutenant. Starts his work as a draughtsman.

1844

March   D. translates *Don Carlos* by Schiller and *The Last Albina* by
through May   George Sands.
September   D. works on the first draft version of *The Poor People*.
October   D. resigns from his job as a draughtsman to become a professional writer. By chance, he meets in the street D. Grigorovich, his friend and a young writer who has just published his story *Street Organ-Grinders of St. Petersburg*. They start to share an apartment. Dostoevsky works on his first novel, *Poor People*. He destroys the first version of the novel; he works very hard, often all night long. During a walk with Grigorovich he experiences a serious epileptic fit.

1845

January– April	D. rewrites first novel, *Poor People*, several times.
End of May	D. gives his work to his friend Dmitry Grigorovich for evaluation. Grigorovich and famous Russian poet N. Nekrasov read the novel and tell him that he is a great writer.
June 1	D. is invited to visit the famous Russian critic Belinsky: "This was the most wonderful moment of my life."
June 7	Nekrasov agrees to publish the first novel by D. in his almanac. He gives the manuscript to the censor with a remark: "The novel is really outstanding."
Summer	D. travels to Revel to visit his brother's family. Starts to write *The Double*.
Autumn	D. pays repeated visits to Belinsky. The renowned literary critic gives the young artist some advice on how to become a professional writer.
October	Nekrasov organizes a humor magazine, *Zuboskal*. D. submits writings and meets many famous Russian writers, including I. Turgenev and V. Odoevsky.
November	D. writes *The Novel in Nine Letters* in one night; Nekrasov buys it for 125 roubles.
November	D. reproached by friends Turgenev and Belinsky for "leading a loose life."
December	D. reads *The Double* at a literary party at Belinsky's home.

1846

January	D. is introduced to Siniavina, a famous female singer, at a party hosted by the Vilegorsky family. Excited by the woman's beauty, he faints during the introduction. Turgenev and Nekrasov write an epigram on this occasion.
January 2	Belinsky writes to Grigorovich that D. will write a story for his literary almanac.
January 24	First novel, *Poor People*, is published. It enjoys a tremendous, overwhelming success among readers and literary critics. Later in the year, *The Double* and *Mr. Prokharchin* are published.
January 24	D. finishes writing *The Double*.
March 5	Nekrasov's new almanac publishes the story "It Is Dangerous to Have Day-Dreams."
April 1	D. writes a letter to his brother about his sensitivity to critics.
April 26	D. becomes very ill, suffers a nervous breakdown and almost dies.

Late May	D. develops friendship with Dr. Ianovsky.
Summer	D. works on "Mr. Prokharchin": "I suffered during the whole summer." For various reasons, mostly financial, D. moves three times to different apartments during a brief period of time.
October 5	D. makes acquaintance of A. Herzen.
October–December	D. works on *The Landlady* and *Netochka Nezvanova*; sends his stories to literary journals to be published.

1847

January–April	D. quarrels with Belinsky.
February 19	Belinsky writes to Turgenev that he "did not like *The Novel in Nine Letters* and … could hardly read it to the end."
Spring	D. makes money by preparing several articles for *The Starchevsky Encyclopedia*.
July 7	A serious epileptic fit. Dr. Ianovsky meets D. in front of St. Isaac's Cathedral in St. Petersburg and helps him.
Late October	D. starts visiting the Petrashevsky Circle.
November–December	Negative reviews on the novel *The Landlady* by several leading literary artists: Belinsky, Nekrasov and Aksakov. *The Novel in Nine Letters* is published. D. attends secret meetings of the Petrashevsky socialist circle.

1848

	During the year, several stories and short novels are published in literary journals: "Weak Heart," "Somebody's Wife," "Mr. Prokharchin," "The Jealous Husband," *The White Nights*.
February 15	Belinsky writes a letter to P.V. Annenkov: "We were mistaken and my friend Dostoevsky is not a genius."
February 26	Cartoon on D. by N. Stepanov appears in Russian newspapers.
Spring–Summer	D. continues to attend meetings of the Petrashevsky Circle at which socialist theories, mostly of the French socialists, are discussed.
May 13	D. attends a literary party hosted by Apollon Maikov, a poet and a friend of his. After a sudden dispute he displays his bad temper and leaves.
May 26	Belinsky dies; D. has an epileptic fit late at night.
Autumn	More frequent visits to the Petrashevsky Circle.

October– November	D. organizes with Sergei Durov, his friend a separate secret group where they discuss socialist ideas.

1849

January	D. tries to entice his friend Apollon Maikov in organizing with him a secret socialist publishing house.
April 1	Dispute about freedom of the press and liberation of serfs at the Petrashevsky Circle. Late at night, after the dispute, D. experiences an epileptic fit.
April 23	D. is arrested together with 34 other members of the Petrashevsky socialist circle.
July 18	D. writes to his brother from prison: "I am not allowed to write here.... I have plans for at least three big stories and two novels."
August	D. wins permission to read books.
September 10	D.'s brother sends him three books: the Bible, *The Works of Shakespeare* and the latest almanac with D.'s novel.
September 30– November 16	Court hearings on the Petrashevsky case. The verdict of the military tribunal: execution for most of its members, including D. His new novel *Netochka Nezvanova* (unfinished) is published.
December 22, 7 A.M.	The mock execution at the Semyonovsky Parade Grounds in St. Petersburg. During the last minutes before the execution the Tsar's amnesty is announced. The death penalty is changed to four years in a maximum security prison and an indefinite term of army service in Siberia.
December 24	D. departs for Siberia in a sledge with his feet shackled, accompanied by a police officer.

1850

January 11	D. arrives at Tobolsk. He meets there the wives of Decembrists, members of an anti–Tsar rebellion of December 1825, and receives from them a gift, the New Testament, the only book he is allowed to read in prison. He keeps this book for the rest of his life as a precious treasure.
January 23	D. arrives in the maximum security prison at Omsk where he will spend more than four years.
April 24	D. dreams about his childhood, remembering his meeting with a peasant named Marei.
Spring	Twice D. goes to work at a brick factory located several miles from the prison.

1850–1854

D. incarcerated in the Omsk maximum security prison.

1854

February 22   D. writes to his brother, "Almost a week passed after I am out of prison."

March 2   Having served his sentence in prison, D. is enrolled in military service as a private in the Siberian 7th Infantry Battalion in Semipalatinsk.

Spring   D. is allowed to read the books he missed so much during his imprisonment.

Summer   D. gets acquainted with the Isaev family, civil servant Aleksandr Isaev and his wife Maria. They spend the summer together in the city suburbs.

July 30   D. writes to brother Mikhail about his service in the army.

November 20   Baron Vrangel's arrival in Semipalatinsk. A new military chief prosecutor of the city, he brings Dostoevsky letters and some money from the family.

1855

February 18   Death of Nikolai I.

April–May   Vrangel's *Memoirs*. D. lives at Vrangel's summer house. He works in the orchard and in the garden. They go together riding horses and swimming in the Irtysh River.

June 14   Baron Vrangel attempts to forward a poem written by D. "On the Death of Nikolai I," to General Gasfort, the commander of the Siberian Army Corps.

August 4   Isaev dies from alcoholism. D. has fallen in love with the widow.

August 30   The birthday anniversary of the new Tsar, Alexander II. D. celebrates it together with Baron Vrangel and other officers.

September   D.'s patriotic poems are passed to the minister of defense by Dostoevsky's friends in St. Petersburg.

1856

February   Baron Vrangel visits St. Petersburg, the Russian capital. He finds some influential friends who agree to help D., including General E. Totleben.

March 24   D. writes to his brother Mikhail about Maria Isaeva. Also writes to the Tsar asking for permission to be dismissed (due to his poor health) and to be published.

May 19   P. Spiridonov, governor-general of Semipalatinsk, sends to the commander of the Siberian Army another poem written by D. and dedicated to the coronation of the Tsar.

June 12   D.'s poem is passed by Baron Vrangel to the Tsarina Maria.

October 1   Sergeant D. receives the rank of a junior lieutenant, but, according to the order of the Tsar, has to continue his army service in the same military unit.

November 24   D. proposes to Maria Isaeva; they plan their wedding for December.

December 22   D. writes to brother Mikhail about his plans to marry Maria Isaeva.

1857

February 6   D. marries Maria Isaeva.

Mid-   A strong epileptic fit leaves D. ill for several days.
February

March 25   D. achieves the rank of lieutenant.

November 3   D. writes Mikhail about his work on a new novel.

1858

January 15   D. asks to be allowed to resign: "Please let me be dismissed due to illness."

Spring   D. writes to Katkov, a Moscow publisher, and promises to send him a new novel.

June   D. asks for permission from the authorities to be the editor of the journal *Time*.

September 31 Permission granted to work as editor of *Time*.

1859

March 18   The minister of defense issues an order for D. to be dismissed, with the provision that he live in Tver City rather than in the capitals (Moscow and St. Petersburg).

April 11   D. writes his brother about his new novel, *The Village Stepanchikovo and Its Inhabitants*.

May 7   Letter from the governor-general of Tver about the secret police surveillance over D. upon his arrival.

May 8   D. dismissed from the army due to his illness.

July 2–   The Dostoevskys leave Semipalatinsk, Siberia, for Tver, a
August 19   provincial city in central Russia, situated about 150 kilometers (125 versts) (1 versta = 3,500 feet) north of Moscow.

August 26	Letter from Nekrasov to Mikhail Dostoevsky: "I always respected and loved your brother and it will be a pleasure for me to publish his works."
September	D. meets with Baranov, governor-general of Tver. He likes literature and agrees to help D. get permission to live in St. Petersburg.
October	Plans to publish *Collected Works in Three Volumes*.
October 23	D. writes a letter to Heibovich, his former commander, about his travel from Siberia to Tver.
Autumn	In notes about literary plans and topics for 1860, D. names several stories and novels: *Minion, Spring Lovers, The Double* (new edition), *Prisoner's Notes* and *Apathy*.
November	D. plans to publish a new literary journal.
November 23	Plans for a new novel, *Fatum* (not fulfilled).
November 25	D. receives permission to live in St. Petersburg.
December	Letter from brother Mikhail. Members of the family find a furnished apartment for D. on his arrival in St. Petersburg.
Late December	Arrival in St. Petersburg after almost eleven years of prison and exile. At a literary party, D. gets acquainted with the literary critic Strakhov, who will be one of his first biographers and his friend for many years.

1860

March 14	D. writes A. Schubert about his arrival in St. Petersburg.
April 14	The Literary Fund stages an amateur production of a play by Nikolai Gogol; D. plays the part of a post office clerk.
May 1–2	D. visits his brother in St. Petersburg.
May 24	D. writes in the album of Mrs. Miliukov, his friend's daughter, a story about his arrest on April 23, 1849.

1861

March 5	The Tsar's *Manifesto* about the abolition of serfdom in Russia is published in the press. D. writes, "We started a completely unknown period." He is critical of the reforms and supports traditional Russian values of the period before Peter the Great.
July 9	D. finishes his novel *Oppressed and Humiliated*.
July 31	D. writes to poet Polonsky about his dreams about Italy and literary plans.
September	A short story by Polina Suslova is published in *Time*.
December 26	Letter from Turgenev praising *Notes from the House of the Dead* and *Petersburg Dreams in Poetry and in Prose*.

1862

Early January An agreement with publisher A. Bazhunov about the publication of *Notes from the House of the Dead* in book form.

February   A note in the January issue of *Time*: "Further publishing of the novel is interrupted due to the illness of the writer." First book reviews on the novel in press.

March 2   D. reads his works at a literary-musical charity event in support of poor literary artists and scholars.

Early May   D. finds a socialist leaflet at his door with the words, "Kill the monarchists! Kill them in the streets and squares if they dare to go out! Kill them in small and big cities! Kill them in the villages!" Dostoevsky is furious; during the years in Siberian prisons he completely changed his views and turned from socialist to passionate monarchist.

Mid-May   Huge fires in St. Petersburg burn hundreds of wooden houses. D. visits Chernyshevsky, one of the leaders of the socialist movement in Russia and a literary critic. "You know the people who set the city on fire," D. says. "You can influence them. Please stop them."

Late May   An article in *Time*, published by the Dostoevsky brothers, is banned from publication by the censorship.

June 7   D. goes abroad and lives in Paris.

June 27   D. goes to London to visit Herzen, one of the Russian revolutionary leaders abroad.

Late July–   D. travels across Germany, Switzerland and Italy.
August

Winter   D. becomes intimate with Polina Suslova.
1862-63

1863

January 5   Letter to M. Belinskaya: "I am married, ill with epilepsy, edit a journal...." An announcement in the January issue of *Time*: "We plan to publish *Confession*, a big new novel by Dostoevsky."

February–   D. takes an active part in the activity of the Literary Fund, a
March   charitable organization supporting poor writers. He often reads his works at literary parties.

April 12   A medical certificate is issued by the Russian Royal Medical Academy for Junior Lieutenant F. Dostoevsky stating that "he is ill with epilepsy and he is recommended to swim in the sea and in the ocean."

May 24–26   *Time* is closed after Strakhov's politically controversial article.

Early summer   Polina Suslova, D.'s lover, goes to Paris.

June 27   D. is allowed to go abroad for medical treatment.

July 24   The Literary Fund gives D. money to go abroad.

August 14   D. arrives in Paris.

August 15–19   D. meets Suslova. She tells him about her love for Salvador, a Spanish student. D. becomes almost mad. The student leaves her in several days and they decide to travel together across Europe.

September   D. and Suslova go to Baden-Baden. He plays roulette.

September 10   Dostoevsky pawns his watch in Geneva to play roulette, gambles again and loses almost everything. The lovers travel to Genoa-Leghorn-Rome.

September 18   Letter to Strakhov about plans for *The Gambler*.

October 6–15   D. and Suslova meet the Herzen family in Naples.

Mid-October   D. parts with Polina Suslova. She goes to Paris. He gambles for several days, loses everything and returns to St. Petersburg.

November 15   Letter to brother Mikhail. Plans to publish a new literary journal, *Pravda* (*Truth*). Later the name is changed to *Epoch*.

December   D. returns the money he borrowed from the Literary Fund.

1864

January 14   Dostoevsky contributes 545 roubles to the Literary Fund.

January 24   Tsar grants D. permission to publish *Epoch*.

March 21   First issue of *Epoch* is published.

April 15   Maria Dostoevskaya dies of tuberculosis.

April 17   D. writes to Polina Suslova.

July 10   Death of brother Mikhail. *Epoch* is not published for two months. D. decides to continue the journal.

Mid-July   The widow of Mikhail Dostoevsky allows D. to continue *Epoch* with A. Poretsky as publisher.

August   Saltykov writes "Strizham" ["Addressing the Martians"], an article sharply critical of Dostoevsky.

September   D. begins corresponding with Anna Korvin-Krukovskaya, a young writer.

December 31   D. spends New Year's Eve at the home of his sister, A. Golembovskaya.

Year's End   D. develops a close relationship with Martha Brown.

1865

January	Letter from Martha Brown: " I am not sure whether I can satisfy you in the physical respect and whether we will find intellectual harmony...." D. meets his brother Andrei and tells how *Time* was closed by the officials.
March 7	In a general meeting of the Literary Fund, D.'s bid for money is discussed. D. is deeply in debt after the closing of *Epoch* and the deaths of his wife and brother.
March–April	D. visits the Korvin-Krukovskaya family three or four times every week. *Epoch* folds.
Early May	D. proposes to Anna Korvin-Krukovskaya; she agrees but he soon changes his mind.
June 5	D. is invited to debtor's court.
June 7	The Literary Fund partially pays Dostoevsky's debts.
July 24	*The Complete Works* of D. are published, including *The White Nights*, *The Crocodile* and other stories and novels.
July 29	D. arrives in Wiesbaden.
August 10–24	D. is engaged in gambling at the casinos. He writes letters to Luslova and A. Vrangel to borrow some money in order to survive.
September	D. writes to publisher Katkov about starting a new novel, *Crime and Punishment*.
Mid-October	Return from abroad.
November 2	D. meets Polina Suslova in St. Petersburg, speaks of marriage.
Late November	D. burns the first version of *Crime and Punishment*, later remarking, "I liked a new form and I started my writing all over again."
December	Notes on *Crime and Punishment*.

1866

January	Notes on *Crime and Punishment*.
January 12	A student named Danilov kills a pawn shop owner named Popov and his servant Nordman in Moscow. This criminal case influences the plot of *The Idiot*.
January 14	In a letter to D. General V. Korvin-Krukovsky writes about sending him the manuscript of a story written by his daughter Anna and thanks D. for his flattering review of the manuscript.
February 18	Letter to Vrangel about *Crime and Punishment*.
February 23	Notes about *Crime and Punishment*.

Late February Negative reviews appear in *The Contemporary*, a leading Russian literary journal, about D.'s current novel *Crime and Punishment*. Nekrasov, the editor, informs D. that he published this very negative review because D. published a cartoon on him two years earlier.

March 14 J. Grot invites D. to participate in the next meeting of the Literary Fund; D. answers that he will gladly participate at the meeting of Russian Literary Fund and that he will read from his latest novel, *Crime and Punishment*.

March 21 Visit to publisher Katkov in Moscow. D. receives an advance of 1,000 roubles.

March 26 Dostoevsky proposes to Maria Ivanchina-Pisareva; she rejects him.

April 4 The assassination attempt on the Russian Tsar by Karakozov. In the middle of the day D. runs into the apartment of his friend, poet Apollon Maikov, and tells him about the assassination attempt.

Late April Letter from D. to Anna Korvin-Krukovsky about *Crime and Punishment*. Parodies of *The Double* appear in the magazine *Spark*.

May 9 Letter to Vrangel: "My publisher Katkov is not a socialist."

July D. lives in the country, in the Moscow suburb of Lublino, in the summer house of his sister's family. According to the memoirs of his sister, D. proposes to his sister's sister-in law, Elena Ivanova, but he does not receive a direct answer. He works on the fifth part of *Crime and Punishment* and writes the outline of his novel *The Gambler*.

July 10–15 Letter to A. Miliukov about the publishing of *Crime and Punishment* after Katkov objects to the ninth chapter, in which Sonia, one of the main characters, becomes a prostitute in order to save her family from starvation.

August 29 The first French translation of *Crime and Punishment* appears in *Courrier russe*.

September 1 Conviction of Karakozov, the Tsar's would-be assassin.

September 3 The execution of Karakozov, whose case greatly influences D.'s notebooks and the plot of *The Demons*.

October 1 Miliukov, a friend of D., finds out that D. has signed an agreement with Stellovsky, a publisher in St. Petersburg. One of the items in the agreement is that if Dostoevsky does not deliver a new novel for the Stellovsky Publishing House at the end of October, the publisher will have the copyrights for all of D.'s works. Miliukov understands that it is impossible to write a novel in a month and suggests that D. find a stenographer.

October 4	At 11 A.M. Anna Snitkina, a young stenographer, visits Dostoevsky's apartment for the first time. They have a brief talk and arrange a meeting later in the day. At 8 P.M. Dostoevsky starts to dictate his novel *The Gambler* to his new stenographer. They work together all through October, four to five hours every day.
October 29	The novel *The Gambler* is finished.
November 1	D. brings the manuscript to Stellovsky's home, but the publisher is away on the pretext of a business meeting. The deadline upon him, D. takes the manuscript to the local police station late at night and leaves it for Stellovsky to satisfy the agreement.
November 3	D. pays his first visit to Anna Snitkina's family.
November 8	D. proposes to Snitkina. Starting from this day he visits her home every day.
December 9	In a letter to Snitkina, D. explains that after hard work on *Crime and Punishment* he has had a fit of epilepsy and cannot go to her birthday party.
December 29	D. goes from St. Petersburg to Moscow to visit his sister and to inform her about his decision to marry Anna Snitkina.

1867

January 1	Dostoevsky celebrates New Year's Eve at his sister's home in Moscow. During the bingo game he receives a letter from Anna Snitkina and feels an approaching fit of epilepsy. He leaves in the middle of the party.
January 2	D. writes to Anna about the advance from his publisher Katkov which makes their marriage possible in the nearest future.
February 15	Wedding ceremony of Fyodor Dostoevsky and Anna Snitkina at St. Petersburg. Two witnesses at the wedding are D.'s friends D. Averkiev and N. Strakhov.
Late February	Several severe fits of epilepsy.
March 30	The Dostoevsky family moves to Moscow. Moscow newspapers report the violent murder of a famous jeweler, Ilya Kalmykov, by his former friend Marurin, a respected city citizen. This criminal case is reflected in the novel *The Idiot*.
April 7	D. wins permission of the Russian government to leave the country for Germany to be treated for epilepsy at the Western European clinics.

April 10–12	D. receives an advance from his publishers. Anna pawns her jewelry and furniture to get money to go abroad.
April 14	The Dostoevskys start their trip abroad, traveling from Moscow through Vilnus and Berlin to Dresden. Instead of making a brief voyage as planned, they stay abroad for four years.
April 20	Visit to the Dresden Art Gallery. D. is greatly impressed by the masterpieces of the Western European painters.
April 23	D. writes his former lover Polina Suslova, the main prototype for the novel *The Gambler*, about his recent wedding.
May 4	D. receives a letter from Suslova.
May 5	D. travels from Dresden to Homburg and starts to play roulette in the casino.
May 5–15	D. gambles every day. He wins 100 guldens the first day, a real fortune at that time. During the next two weeks he loses everything, including his wedding ring and his coat.
May 11, 13	D. sends letters to his wife and asks her to send him more money for gambling.
May 15	D. returns to Dresden to his wife.
May 24–26	D. reads *The Old Curiosity Shop* and *Nicholas Nickleby* by Charles Dickens.
May 25	Assassination attempt on Russian Tsar Alexander II in Paris by Berezovsky.
Summer	The Dostoevskys travel to Dresden, Frankfurt and Baden. D. plays roulette practically every day, losing everything and pawning all possible possessions, including his and Anna's clothes and her jewelry.
August 29	D. visits the First Congress of Peace and Freedom in Geneva with Garibaldi and Bakunin as invited speakers.
September 14–October 30	D. works on the general plan of his novel *The Idiot*, outlining the chapters, making occasional notes and putting down psychological observations concerning the major characters.
October 9	D. writes to Maikov about the lonely life in Geneva, critical opinions about the Swiss people and the city, work on the novel, and the political situation in Europe.
October 11	D. writes to his sister-in-law Emilia Dostoevskaya about several fits of epilepsy during the summer, his gambling losses, and his plans to publish a magazine.
November 5	At 4 P.M., D. arrives in Saxon-les-Bains and goes to a casino. He wins 110 francs. Between 5 and 8 P.M., he returns to the hotel and writes a letter to his wife. At 8 P.M. he goes to a casino again and loses all his money.
November 6	At 3 P.M., D. pawns his wedding ring and his winter coat.

He loses everything. In another letter to his wife, he asks her to send 50 francs to pay for his stay at the hotel.

November 22 D. destroys the first version of *The Idiot* and creates several new outlines for the novel.

December A secret letter from Police General Mezentsev goes to customs officials at all major checkpoints on the Russian border instructing them to search Dostoevsky on his way home from abroad and, if necessary, to arrest him.

December 6 D. writes to his mother-in-law, A. Snitkina, and begins the final version of *The Idiot*. His main idea is to "to depict a positively beautiful man."

December 24 Letter to the publisher of *The Russian Herald* about sending him the first five chapters of *The Idiot*.

December 31 Letter to Maikov about his work on the novel *The Idiot* and his impressions of Geneva.

Winter 1867-68 D. reads *The Moscow News* and *Voice* daily, makes notes about unwritten works titled *Emperor* and *The Obsessed Man*.

1868

January 1 D. writes to his sister Vera Mikhailovna Ivanova about his life in Geneva and his relationship with *The Russian Herald*. Also writes to his niece S. Ivanova about the general idea of *The Idiot*.

January 7 Letter from Maikov to Dostoevsky with the latest literary news.

February 18 Letter to Maikov about work on *The Idiot*, life in Geneva, Saltykov and Russian liberals: "there will be a new world created by a new Russian thought."

February 22 Daughter Sonya born.

March Dostoevsky meets Herzen in Geneva. "We spoke for five minutes with a politeness and animosity and said 'good-bye.'"

March 1–10 Changes in the general outline of *The Idiot*. Hard work leads to several epileptic seizures.

March 10 Dostoevsky reads in *Voice* that a family of a merchant named Zhemarin from Tambov has been killed by a home tutor named Gorsky. This criminal case is referred to in the second part of *The Idiot*.

March 23 D. writes to his wife in the afternoon. By 8 P.M. he has begun playing roulette and losing everything. At 9:30 P.M. he writes another letter to his wife.

April 19 Anna's mother arrives in Geneva.

May 12 Daughter Sonya dies.

Summer	D. works on *The Idiot*.
September	The Dostoevskys move to Milan, Italy.
September 8	Notes to *The Idiot*.
October 26	In a letter to Maikov D. expresses disappointment with his work on *The Idiot*.
Early December	The Dostoevskys move to Florence. D. reads reports about the Mazurin criminal case in *The Moscow News* and *Voice*. The materials are used in *The Idiot*.
December 11	Letter to A. Maikov about finishing writing *The Idiot*.

1869

July 22	Travel from Florence to Venice, Bologna and Vienna. A fit of epilepsy at the beginning of the trip. After ten days the Dostoevskys arrive in Prague. They spend three days in Prague, cannot find a proper place to live and go back to Dresden.
August 18, 23; September 1, 14, 30	Fits of illness.
September 14	The birth of daughter Liubov in Dresden.
September 17	Letter to Maikov about literary work.
Mid-October	The brother of D.'s wife, I.G. Snitkin, visits D. in Dresden and tells him about the atmosphere of the student life and about one of his close friends, Ivanov, who will later be killed by Nechaev, his former friend and associate in the revolutionary circle. This criminal case will form the basis for the plot of *The Demons*, the strongest indictment of the revolutionary terror in Russia.
October 20	D. receives a letter from brother Andrei about an inheritance from their aunt, A.F. Kumanina.
Late October	*The Dawn* magazine in Moscow advertises "a new novel by Dostoevsky."
November 9	First notes on *The Demons*: "1) Search for the novel... 2) The end of existence... What can we do? Revenge..."
November 21	The head of the revolutionary "Society of People's Revenge," Sergei Nechaev, organizes the murder of Ivan Ivanov, a student of Petersburg Academy and member of the circle, for refusal to follow his orders.
November 27	The murder of Ivanov is discovered.
Late December	D.'s daughter Liubov (Lily) is baptized. The godfather is A. Maikov, the godmother V.M. Ivanova.
December 5	D. sends the manuscript of *The Eternal Husband* to *The Dawn* magazine.

December 8   D. makes a note in the notebook concerning the outline of a novel to be called *The Life of a Great Sinner*.

December 10   D. writes to his stepson P.A. Isaev about the contract with the publisher Stellovsky.

December 11   D. goes to the Russian consulate in Dresden to send an official letter of transfer of copyrights for the novel *The Idiot* to his stepson P.A. Isaev.

December 14   Letter to S.A. Ivanova about work on *The Eternal Husband*, life in Dresden, etc.

December 20   The first brief notes about "the prince" appear in the notebooks and on the outline of the novel *The Life of a Great Sinner*.

1870

January 1   "Strong fit of epilepsy" noted in D.'s daybook.

January 8   *The Moscow News* reports that "The German press pays great attention to the nihilistic revolution in Russia and the Nechaev case."

January 11   *The Voice* reports, "All speak in St. Petersburg about ... the murder of student Ivanov."

January 15   D. works further on the outline for *The Life of a Great Sinner*.

February 4   A new plan for the novel *The Demons* appears in the notebooks. A note: "The main idea of the novel: A novel writer. In the old age, because of epilepsy, became stupid, and later, very poor."

February 6   More notes on *The Demons*.

February 11   A fit of epilepsy at dawn.

February 26   Letter to Strakhov about *The Eternal Husband*.

March   Letter to the editor of *The Dawn*, V. Kashpirev, concerning publication in the next year of D.'s his new novel, *The Demons*.

March   Notes on *The Demons*.

March 25   In a letter to Maikov, D. describes working on the big novel against nihilists and the plan of the novel *Atheism*, or *The Life of a Great Sinner*.

April 17   D. arrives in Homburg.

May 28   Letter to Strakhov about the philosophical character of his articles.

June 11   Letter to Strakhov with a negative review on Turgenev's work *The Tropman's Execution*. Notes to *The Demons*: "A fantastic page."

June 16   In the daybook: "I finished the fifth chapter of the novel. In my dream I saw my brother Mikhail and my father."

July 1	A fit of epilepsy at dawn. During the day D. reads newspapers and telegrams, predicts "there will soon be war between France and Prussia."
July 2	Letter to S.A. Ivanova about happiness in family life and plans to go back to Russia and travel to the East.
July 5	"I work on the first part of the novel and become more desperate. Anna is exhausted. Lyuba is very nervous...."
July 13, 16	Fits of illness.
July 30	D. makes notes about his illness and about the novel *The Demons*.
August	"I found a new hero. The whole novel should be rewritten."
August 4	"Everything is in Stavrogin's character. Stavrogin is everything."
August 12–22	Notes on *The Demons*.
August 17	Letter to S.A. Ivanova about work on *The Demons*, the usefulness of wars, and the political situation after the war in Europe.
August 28	A fit of illness in the morning.
September 19	Letter to publisher M.N. Katkov about his work on *The Demons*.
October 7	Letter to *The Russian Herald* about sending the first part of *The Demons*.
October 8	Letter to M.N. Katkov about the Nechaev case as the material for *The Demons* and about Nikolai Stavrogin.
Early October	I.G. Snitkin leaves Dresden.
October 9	Letter to Maikov about Russian liberalism and about the novel; letter to S.A. Ivanova about *The Demons*.
October 20	Notes: "The novel: think about the main plot. Main remarks."
December 2	Letter to Strakhov about D.'s literary work, the negative review of *The Dawn* magazine and Turgenev's works.
December 13–15	Final changes in the general plan for *The Demons*.
December 15	Letter to A. Maikov about *The Demons*.
December 30	Official letter of credit to A. Maikov about receiving the money for *Crime and Punishment* from the Stellovsky Publishing House.
December 31	D. spends New Year's Eve at a ball in the Russian consulate in Dresden.

1871

| January 7 | In a letter to Maikov, D. asks him to receive money from publisher Stellovsky for *Crime and Punishment*. |

January 18, 26	Letters to Maikov praising Leskov and expressing a critical attitude towards the militarization of Germany.
February 3	Notes about plot developments in *The Demons*.
February 17	More notes about *The Demons*.
March 31	D. experiences a strong epileptic fit at night.
April 1	D. receives a telegram from A. Maikov inviting him to St. Petersburg and advising him to ask for some money from the Russian Literary Fund and from the publisher Stellovsky for *Crime and Punishment*.
April 12–19	D. goes to Wiesbaden for a week to play roulette.
April 16	At 1 A.M. D. receives some money to pay for the hotel and a letter from his wife. He writes her back. At 4 P.M. he goes to play roulette. Late at night he writes another letter to his wife about losing all the money that she sent. He promises not to play in the casinos anymore.
April 17	D. writes another letter to his wife, describing his plans to return to Russia.
April 21	Letter to Maikov in which D. announces his decision to return to Russia.
May 1	Notes about Tikhon and the Prince in the notebooks. Notes about "the principle of Nechaev."
May 13	D. makes notes which he declares to be "the last remarks" on *The Demons*.
Late June	The Dostoevsky family packs for Russia. The editors of *The Russian Herald* send some money.
July 1 through September 1	At special meetings of the St. Petersburg City Court hearings are held on the political conspiracy against the monarchy. The charges are "the massive conspiracy in the different parts of the Russian empire directed on the overthrowing of the existing government" and the murder of student I. Ivanov. On trial are a group of people from the underground socialist circle including S. Nechaev, P. Uspensky, A. Kusnetsov, I. Pyzhov, N. Nikolaev and others. Reports of this renowned criminal case are published in all Russian newspapers. The materials and many details of the case are used by D. in *The Demons*.
July 3	Before his trip to Russia, D. burns the manuscripts of *The Idiot*, *The Eternal Husband* and *The Demons*.
July 5–8	Dostoevsky family goes from Dresden to Russia via Berlin.
July 8	Arrival in St. Petersburg after four years' absence.
July 8–15	The seating of the jury at the Nechaev criminal case. Some revolutionary materials are made known to the public, among them "Program of the Revolutionary Actions."

July 15	The members of the conspiracy are sentenced to long terms in prison in Siberia.
July 16	Son Fyodor is born.
Late July–Early August	D.'s trip to Moscow to receive payment for his publications from *The Russian Herald*.
August 18	Visit to Semenov-Tian-Shansky.
Mid-August	Notes to the second part of *The Demons*.
September	Newspapers note D.'s arrival in Russia. After this news, his financial creditors start visiting him very often. One of the creditors wants to put him into debtor's prison, but the writer's wife Anna settles the dispute.
September 12	Notes: "Great Ideas."
September 17	*Russky Vestnik* informs D. of the publication of his novel *The Demons*.
November 20	D. asks Maikov and F. Filippov to prepare for him some information about the history of the Russian church for use in his future novels.
December 10	The St. Petersburg Court of Commerce invites D. for a hearing on the case of his debt of 500 roubles to merchant Ginterlach.
December 16	D. presents to the court documents about his illness from his doctors. He does not go to court, but it is ruled that he has to pay this debt.
December 31	D. spends New Year's Eve at the home of his sister Vera in Moscow.
Year's End	Anna Dostoevskaya finds a basket full of D.'s old notes and diaries. She keeps them for the future.

1872

January	D. meets Konstantin Pobedonostsev, a future minister and a close associate of the Tsar who will become D.'s close friend and will introduce the writer to the royal family.
January 1	A visit to Katkov, D.'s publisher in Moscow.
January 4	During another visit to Katkov, they discuss the publication of *The Demons* in *The Russian Herald*.
January 20	Letter to princess Obolenskaya about staging *Crime and Punishment* in Russian theaters.
February 17	A literary evening at the D.s' apartment. Among the guests are Polonsky, Maikov and Strakhov.
March 31	Russian art collector Pyotr Tretiakov writes asking D.'s permission to paint his portrait for Tretiakov's art collection.
April 5	Letter from Liubimov about publishing *The Demons*.

May	D. meets several times with Russian painter V. Perov, who works on his portrait.
May 16	Arrival in Staraya Russa at a summer cottage.
May 20–21	Sudden departure to St. Petersburg. An urgent medical operation is necessary because daughter Liubov's broken arm healed wrong.
June 12, 14	In letters to Anna, D. expresses his concern about *The Demons*.
July 19	D. sends Chapter V, Part II of *The Demons* to Liubimov.
September	D. returns from Staraya Russa to St. Petersburg.
October 1–10	D. pays a visit to his publishers in Moscow to discuss the publication of the third part of *The Demons* in the year's last issues of *The Russian Herald*.
October 9	D. visits painter Perov in his house.
November	After a year's interval, *The Russian Herald* resumes the publication of *The Demons*.
November 14	Publisher Liubimov writes a letter to D. asking him to accelerate the writing of the final part of *The Demons*.
December	At a literary party at the home of his friend Prince Vladimir Meshchersky, D. agrees to assume the editorship of the journal *The Citizen*.
December 15	D. signs an official letter to the Ministry of Press stating that he would like to take the position of the editor of *The Citizen*.
December 20	Dostoevsky writes, "On the 20th of December I found out that everything was settled, that the decision was made and that I am the editor of *The Citizen*."
Late December	D. delivers the first chapter of *A Writer's Diary*, to be published in *The Citizen*.

1873

Early January	Dostoevsky works on the proofs of *The Demons* to be published in a book format.
January	Avertisement in *St. Petersburg News*: "Mr. F. Dostoevsky, the editor of *The Citizen*, has office hours from 2 to 4, Monday–Friday."
January 12	The newspaper *Voice* publishes a negative article about the art exhibition at the Academy of Fine Arts where D.'s portrait is displayed.
January 21	D. is elected a member of the Slavic Charity Society.
January 22	*The Demons* is published in book format.
January 29	An article, "Deputies from Kirgistan in St. Petersburg," is published in *The Citizen* without the censor's permission.

February 29	*Voice* publishes ads for Dostoevsky's new novel *The Demons*.
April	Anna Dostoevskaya moves to a summer cottage in Staraya Russa. D. stays in St. Petersburg, busy editing *The Citizen*.
May 20	D. makes a visit to Moscow to settle matters about the inheritance of his aunt, Aleksandra Kumanina.
June 11	D. is asked to the court for publishing Meshchersky's brief article "Deputies from Kirgistan in St. Petersburg" in his journal *The Citizen* without the censor's permission.
June 12, 22	Letters to Anna.
June 25	The court reaches a verdict regarding the article in *The Citizen*. D. is fined 25 roubles and ordered to serve two days in prison.
July 8	A.N. Snitkina, D.'s mother-in-law, pays a visit to D.
July 12	D. writes to Anna that he is very tired with the editor's work.
July 20	D. receives a rude letter from Prince Meshchersky.
July 30	D. writes a brief article in memory of Russian poet Fyodor Tiutchev.
August 9	D. arrives in St. Petersburg from Staraya Russa. He writes in a letter that he slept for two hours during the day and then worked until 3 A.M.
August 29	Pobedonostsev writes a letter about *The Citizen*.
October–November	D. writes a series of political articles for *The Citizen*, mostly about international affairs in Europe.
October 18	Retail sales of *The Citizen* are forbidden by the authorities.
November 3	D. has an epileptic fit.
December 20	*The Idiot* is published in the book form; the first printing of 2,000 copies is a success. It is sold out in several days.
December 27	A severe fit of epilepsy. In winter Dostoevsky moves to an apartment in Ligovsky Prospect in St. Petersburg to be closer to *The Citizen's* office. He has edited this journal all year while also publishing some editorials and his *Writer's Diary*.

1874

January	D. informs Prince Meshchersky that he wants to quit editing *The Citizen*.
February 14	D. is present at the meeting of the Slavic Committee.
March 3–28	Ads in *Voice* about publishing *The Idiot*.
March 19	D. writes a letter to the Ministry of Press stating that he is resigning from editing *The Citizen* because of his poor health.

March 19	D. signs a document transferring the copyrights for all of his works to his wife. This proves a wise decision; Anna Dostoevskaya will settle many financial matters for the family after she organizes the publishing business.
March 21–22	D. spends two days in prison for publishing an article in *The Citizen Alekseevich* that was not censored.
Mid-April	Visit from D.'s friend Nikolai Alekseevich Nekrasov, who asks D. to give him a new novel to be published in *The Fatherland Notes* and offers good royalties.
April 16	A severe fit of epilepsy.
April 22	D. officially resigns as editor of *The Citizen*.
April 24	D. goes to Moscow to negotiate the publishing of his new novel, *The Raw Youth*, in *The Fatherland Notes*.
May	The Dostoevsky family lives in Staraya Russa.
May 7	D. plans to make a visit to a children's prison with Anatoly Koni. He is interested in the topic of young criminals.
June 4–9	D. follows the advice of his doctor, Professor Koshlakov, and goes (via St. Petersburg and Berlin) to Ems, Germany, a spring resort, for medical treatment.
June 12– July 20	During his stay in Ems, D. takes mineral water treatment. He writes lengthy letters to his wife very often, practically every other day.
August 10	D. returns to Staraya Russa.
August 11	D. asks Putsykovich to collect newspaper reports on the Dolgushin criminal case, saying "I need these materials for a literary project."
Fall–Winter 1874	D. stays in Staraya Russa, working most of the time on his novel *The Raw Youth*. Writes a letter to Nekrasov.

1875

January	Starting in January 1875, *The Raw Youth* is published in monthly installments in *The Fatherland Notes*.
January 4, 11	Fits of epilepsy.
February 5	D. goes to St. Petersburg, visits *The Citizen* and meets with Nekrasov, his friend and publisher of *The Raw Youth*.
February 6	Most of the day and all night D. reads the proofs of his latest novel.
February 8	D. writes to Anna that Nekrasov visited him and "expressed his admiration" for the first part of *The Raw Youth*.
February 16–17	D. returns to Staraya Russa.
February– May	D. works on *The Raw Youth* in Staraya Russa.

May 28–July 3 D. takes medical treatment at a water resort in Ems, Germany.

September 15 D. returns from Staraya Russa to St. Petersburg.

October An article in *The Citizen* reports that the St. Petersburg Slavic Committee will publish a collective monograph on Slavic questions. D. is among the contributors.

November 6 D. starts making notes to resume *A Writer's Diary*.

November 21 Death of Russian sergeant Foma Danilov during the hostilities in Turkestan. D. admires his heroism in *A Writer's Diary*.

December 27 D. visits a prison for young criminals with his friend, prosecutor A. Koni.

December 30 The Russian Society for the Protection of Animals celebrates its tenth anniversary. D. writes a big article about abused animals, dedicated to this event.

1 8 7 6

January Ads in *Voice* announce that the publication of *A Writer's Diary* by D. will be resumed.

January 15–30 D. expresses his strong interest in the two most spectacular criminal cases of the time, the Perova and Kronenberg cases. He works on a new article about child abuse.

February 14 Spiritualistic seance at the Aksakovs'. D., Leskov, Butlerov and others are present.

March 1 *The New Times* publishes a report about the seance of February 14.

March 3 D. receives a letter from women's activist Christina Alchevskaya.

April D. writes an article in *A Writer's Diary* defending the honor of his deceased brother Mikhail.

May 18 Anna makes a joke with a letter that she received from a fictitious lover. D. is very upset.

May–June D. visits Alchevskaya several times.

Summer The Dostoevsky family spends the summer in Staraya Russa.

July 8–
August 20 D. goes to the water resort in Ems, Germany, for a medical treatment.

Late August S.A. Ivanova, Dostoevsky's niece, marries D. Khmyrov, a high school teacher. She was very close to D. in the early 1860s; he even proposed to her, and dedicated his novel *The Idiot* to her.

September–
November D. works at *A Writer's Diary* in St. Petersburg.

October 15 D. takes an interest in the criminal case of Katerina Kornilova, a woman who threw her six-year-old stepdaughter from a window of a tall apartment building. He defends Kornilova in his articles, stressing that a pregnant woman cannot be held responsible for such a crime under the circumstances.

November   D. works on his story "The Meek One" ("Krotkaya") about a woman who commits suicide by throwing herself out a window.

November 13   Konstantin Pobedonostsev, a minister of the Tsar and friend of D., writes a letter to D. in which he recommends, "It can be good if you send *A Writer's Diary* to the royal heir."

December 6   Demonstration of Russian youth in downtown St. Petersburg. Police beat protesters and disperse the crowd. D. writes about this event in *A Writer's Diary*.

1877

January–   During most of the year of 1877, D. works on *A Writer's Diary*.
December

January 13   D. writes a letter to poet Pyotr Bykov and meets him in about two weeks.

February 11   *The Moscow News* publishes an editorial by Katkov about "terrible oppression of Christians in Turkey." D. calls it "a wonderful article."

February 21   D. asks for permission from the Ministry of the Press to publish *A Writer's Diary* without any further censorship. He receives permission very quickly, a sign of official recognition of his loyalty and his growing influence at the royal court.

March   The Dostoevskys buy a summer cottage in Staraya Russa.

April 12   D. reads newspaper reports that Russia has gone to war with Turkey for the liberation of Slavic people, including Bulgarians and Serbs. He immediately goes to the Kazan' Cathedral, a major church in St. Petersburg, to pray for the Russian victory.

April 20–24   D. visits the second court session dedicated to the Kornilova case. The defendant is acquitted on the basis that during the pregnancy she could not control herself. D. has written an article in defense of the accused woman, prompting the chief of the jury to instruct the court not to "fall under the influence of some talented literary artists."

May   D. reads the last chapters of *Anna Karenina* by Leo Tolstoy and greatly admires this work in *A Writer's Diary*.

June   The Dostoevsky family goes for the summer to the countryside in the Kursk region in southern Russia, close to the estate of I. Snitkin.

July 5–17   D. makes a brief visit to St. Petersburg to coordinate publication of the summer issues of *A Writer's Diary*.

July 20–21   On his way to his family, D. visits Darovoe, his father's estate where he spent his childhood. He is very excited after this visit.

Late July   D. returns to St. Petersburg.

October 14   *The Moscow News* publishes an article about the suicide of falsely convicted General Gartung during a court session. D. responds with an article in *A Writer's Diary*.

November 28   D. writes to Anna Filosofova, "Almost all the month I was ill and had a fever."

December 2   D. is elected a member of the Russian Academy of Sciences in the section of Russian language and literature.

December 17   In a letter to Stepan Ianovsky, D. expresses satisfaction with *A Writer's Diary*.

December 24   D. writes in his *Notebooks*: "Memento, a task for the rest of my life." He resolves to write at least three big novels during the next ten years.

December 27   The death of Nikolai Nekrasov, Russian poet, publisher and D.'s close friend. Dostoevsky spends the whole night reading all three volumes of Nekrasov's works.

December 30   D. makes a speech at Nekrasov's funerals.

1878

January 12   Arseniev, a tutor of the Tsar's children, pays a visit to D. He relays the Tsar's wish to arrange a meeting between the Great Princes and the writer so that D. can make a positive influence on the young royal heirs.

February 6   D. receives a diploma stating that he is elected a member of the Russian Academy of Sciences.

March 14   D. receives an invitation to the International Congress of Literature to be held in Paris.

March 31   D. is present among the press representatives at the trial of terrorist Vera Zasulich in St. Petersburg City Court. She fired a revolver into one of the chiefs of the city police but is acquitted of the charges.

April 24   D. visits Great Princes Sergei and Paul, children of Alexander II.

May 16   Alexei, D.'s three-year-old son, suffers a sudden severe fit of epilepsy that lasts more than three hours. The child dies.

May–June	Philosopher Vsevolod Soloviev is among few close friends who try to console D. in his grief. They often visit each other.
June 23–29	D. and Soloviev make a pilgrimage to a remote Russian monastery, Optina Pustyn'. On the way D. tells his friend Soloviev the general plan and the main ideas of his future novel *The Brothers Karamazov.*
August 4	The assassination of General Mezentsev, chief of the St. Petersburg police, by the members of a revolutionary society. D. repeatedly expresses strong criticism of the revolutionary movement and reiterates his support of the monarchy.
October 19	D. is present at an official dinner in honor of General Fyodor Radetsky, the hero of the Russian-Turkish War at the Balkans. Dostoevsky studied with the general during his early years at the Military Engineering Academy. During this reception the writer glorifies Russian victories in southern Europe.
November 7	D. goes to Moscow to meet with his publishers Katkov and Liubimov to discuss the publication of his future novel *The Brothers Karamazov.*
December	D. makes a detailed outline and writes 10 printing signatures (160 pages) of *The Brothers Karamazov. The Moscow News* announces that *The Russian Herald* will start publishing a large new novel by D. in its January issue.
December 14	The Bestuzhev Courses for Women, one of the first higher education institutions in Russia to admit women, organizes a literary evening. D. reads from his *Oppressed and Humiliated.* He enjoys great success among the public.
Winter 1878-79	D. leads an active social life, paying weekly visits to the literary salons of Polonsky and Stakenshneider and participating often in literary gatherings by reading his works.

1879

1879–80	D. reads often for different charities despite working hard on *The Brothers Karamazov.*
January 30	Letter to Liubimov. D. sends his publisher the third chapter of *The Brothers Karamazov*, requesting that he "please publish this whole chapter in one issue so as not to break the harmony and artistic impression."
February 4	Assassination attempt by Alexander Soloviev on Russian Tsar Alexander II.
February 5	An evening commemorating the anniversary of the founding

	of St. Petersburg University. Dostoevsky is invited to the reception.
February 24	Archbishop Simeon of Russia gives Konstantin Pobedonostsev, the Tsar's assistant, a description of burial ceremonies at Russian monasteries. The material is forwarded to D. so that he can incorporate it into his novel.
March 9	A meeting of the Russian Literary Fund. D., Turgenev, Saltykov and other famous Russian writers read excerpts from their works.
March 10	In a letter to A. Kireev, one of the chiefs of the Russian police, L. Maikov declares, "There are no obstacles against lifting the secret police surveillance over Dostoevsky." The writer has been under police surveillance for almost 25 years after being released from prison in 1856.
March 13	A group of prominent Russian professors and writers hold a reception in honor of novelist Ivan Turgenev. D. stops Turgenev in the middle of his speech, with a loud remark: "Now tell me, what is your ideal in life?" Then, without waiting for an answer, he stands up and leaves the room. This tactless behavior was typical of D.
March 15	Konstantin, the Great Prince of Russia, asks D. "to attend the literary evening at the Royal Palace."
March 16	Meeting of the Russian Literary Fund. Turgenev, D. and Savina read their works.
March 17	Literary evening at the home of Duchess S.A. Tolstaya, a distant relative of Leo Tolstoy.
March 20–23	Reports in *Voice* about the court case of A. and E. Brunst, two German parents living in Russia who were systematically torturing their daughter. D. writes, "What can you say of parents who put shit all over a poor five-year-old child and lock her in a dark and cold washroom for the whole night...?" This case affects him, and he uses this material in *The Brothers Karamazov*.
April 3	D. brings his children to a children's party. He reads his story "Boy at the Christmas Party" at the meeting of the Slavic Charity Society. Great success.
April 5	Nikolai Lebedev-Morskoi, a young writer, brings D. his novel *The Aristocracy of the Guest Yard*.
April 30	D. sends his publisher N. Liubimov a chapter of *The Brothers Karamazov* with a note: "This is the most important part of the novel and I wrote it with a special diligence."
May 1	In a letter to the Literary Congress in London, D. declines an invitation to attend the congress for health reasons.

May 17   In a letter to Nikolai Liubimov, D. writes, "In *The Brothers Karamazov* there are many characters for whom I was reproached for being fantastic; and then, would you believe, they were all justified by reality.... Everything that my protagonist says in the text that has been sent off to you is based on reality. All the stories about the children actually occurred, took place, were printed in the newspapers, and I can show where.... Nothing has been invented by me. The story about the general who hunted down a child with dogs was a true story."

May 19   In a letter to Konstantin Pobedonostsev about *The Brothers Karamazov*, D. writes, "God's creation, God's world and its meaning are rejected as strongly as possible. That's the only thing that contemporary civilization considers ridiculous.... Many critics have reproached me for generally taking up in my novels themes that are allegedly wrong, unreal and so forth. I, on the contrary, don't know anything more real than precisely these themes.... May God send you tranquility of thought—I don't know any wish that could possibly be better than this."

May 28   Alexander Soloviev, the Tsar's attacker, is hanged in St. Petersburg. A new order of the Tsar: the governor-generals across the country receive special powers to govern the country according to the rules of wartime.

June–July   From the memoirs of Dr. Miliutin, the minister of defense: "I found in St. Petersburg a strange mood.... Nobody believes in the state order...."

Summer   The Dostoevskys live on their estate in Staraya Russa.

June 3   A new foreign passport is issued for D.

June 9   D. finishes writing one of the most important chapters from *The Brothers Karamazov* and sends it to Nikolai Liubimov, his publisher.

June 9–14   The International Literary Congress in London votes to elect D. as an honorary member. The president of the congress is Victor Hugo; two other members from Russia are Leo Tolstoy and Ivan Turgenev.

July 1   Doctors recommend that D. undergo medical treatment at the mineral springs resort in Ems, Germany.

July 20   D. goes abroad from Staraya Russa to Ems via St. Petersburg.

July 24   D. arrives at Ems. Doctors diagnose emphysema.

July 24   St. Petersburg City Court hears the case concerning the division of the huge estate of Aleksandra Kumanina, aunt of D., who is among the heirs.

July 30　　　　D. writes to Anna "I can work only two hours a day because of my poor health."

Summer　　　　While D. is receiving medical treatment in Germany, Anna visits the estate of his late aunt and chooses the Dostoevskys' part of the inheritance: about 300 acres of forest and 100 acres of arid fertile land.

August 7–8　　D. sends off the sixth chapter of his novel *The Brothers Karamazov* to his publisher: "I view this chapter as the tensest point in the whole novel."

August 9　　　Letter from Dostoevsky to Konstantin Pobedonostsev: "This is the sixth chapter of the novel and it is called 'The Russian Monk'.... I wrote this chapter with a few selected readers in mind and I think it is the culmination of my work." Letter from Kramskoi to Tretiakov: "After reading *The Brothers Karamazov* (and during the reading) I looked around me in horror several times and I was surprised that everything was going on as it was before. I asked myself, after the Karamazovs' reunion, or after the monk Zosima, or after the Great Inquisitor, how can we have people who rob their neighbors, how can we have people with double standards, people telling lies...?"

August 26　　　The Executive Committee of "The People's Will" (*Narodnaya Volia*) a secret socialist terrorist group, sentences Alexander II to death. The assassination will take place on March 1, 1881, a month after D.'s death.

August　　　　D. writes to Anna from Germany almost every other day, telling her that he desperately misses her at the mineral springs in Germany and that he is "obsessed with buying an estate for the children."

September 1　　D. returns from Germany to St. Petersburg.

September 8　　Letter to Nikolai Liubimov: "The last chapter, the seventh, is probably the most important place in the whole novel."

October 30　　D.'s birthday. Anna Dostoevskaya remembered in her *Memoirs*, "Once Dostoevsky told me ... that the painting he appreciated most of all was the *Sistine Madonna* by Raphael. I presented him with a reproduction on his birthday, 30 October 1879.... So many times I saw him standing in front of this painting during the last year of his life...."

November 10　The fifth edition of *Oppressed and Humiliated*.

November 16　Letter to Nikolai Liubimov about sending the eighth book of *The Brothers Karamazov*, in which "many new faces appeared."

November 19 Another assassination attempt on the Russian Tsar, in the form of an explosion on the Moscow-Kursk Railway at 11 P.M. The Tsar's private train misses the explosion by chance.

December D. reads parts of his new novel *The Brothers Karamazov* at concerts organized by the Russian Charity Society at St. Petersburg University and at Higher Women's Courses. "I went to listen to Dostoevsky reading his works. What happened was much more impressive that I expected.... A wild storm of applause and yells from the crowd were not necessary after his quiet inner voice" (K. Letkova, *About Dostoevsky*). "I felt a great happiness after listening to one of Dostoevsky's readings in 1879.... Never again have I met such a deadly silence in a hall packed with people, such a complete attraction of a spiritual life of a huge crowd of thousands of people by the mood of one man" (S.A. Vengerov, *Memoirs*).

Winter 1879-80 D. often visits the Stakenshneiders, where he meets with other literary figures: Apollon Maikov, Iakov Polonsky, Nikolai Strakhov, Dmitry Averkiev, Konstantin Sluchevsky and Fyodor Berg. They organize literary readings and amateur plays and discuss questions of literature and art.

December "The year comes to an end. A terrible year. This period has been carved into the heart of every Russian," laments *The Fatherland Notes* in its December editorial. The year has brought Russia a wave of terrorism that culminates in sixteen death penalties and executions and three assassination attempts on the Tsar.

December 18 Letter to Nikolai Liubimov: "The book's [*The Brothers Karamazov's*] theme has grown longer and more complicated, and most important, most important—is that this book turns out to be most important for me in the novel.... The novel is being read everywhere, people write me letters, it's being read by young people, it's being read in high society, it's being criticized or praised in the press, and never before, with the impression produced all around, have I had such a success."

1880

January 1 Announcements in the St. Petersburg newspapers: "Starting from January 1, 1880, a new book trade company of Fyodor Dostoevsky is founded. ... We send by mail orders the following works of the writer: *Oppressed and Humiliated* (5th edition), *The Demons, The Raw Youth, A Writer's Diary.*"

January 2   D. sends as a gift several copies of his works to Russian libraries in Bulgaria.

January 17   Dispute between the French literary critic M. De Vogue and D. The Russian writer claims, "We have the genius of all people plus the Russian genius; therefore, we can understand you, but you cannot understand us." De Vogue has the impression that "this Russian [thinks] himself to be more important than the whole of Europe."

January 17, 21 Articles in *The Warsaw Herald* about the torture of children. D. is outraged and writes several furious letters.

February 2   D. reads from his works at the Kolomenskaya female high school.

February 3   D. is elected vice president of the Slavic Charity Society in St. Petersburg.

February 5   An assassination attempt on the Tsar fails when Stepan Halturin forgets to close the doors to the basement of the Winter Palace. An explosion leaves 10 people dead and 50 injured. From the speech of the Russian archbishop: "We do not know why His Majesty was late in his dining room for lunch that day. The angels have stopped him." D. is very upset, having become an ardent supporter of the monarchy.

February 14   At a meeting of the Slavic Charity Society, D. reads a special greeting letter to the Russian Tsar for the occasion of the twenty-fifth anniversary of the reign. The text of the letter was written by D: "We believe in real, complete, living freedom, not in formal freedom in this country...." Russian newspapers publish a special order issued by the Tsar about the new Supreme Executive Commission to protect state order and law.

February 15   The Ministry of the State decides to stop secret police surveillance of D.

February 19   The twenty-fifth anniversary of the rule of Alexander II. The Tsar plans "to give more opportunities for the society to participate in the discussion of the state affairs."

February 20   An assassination attempt on Mikhail Loris-Melikov, the minister of the interior. Only slightly injured after the shooting in front of his house, the general catches the gunman by himself. D. is afraid that the course of democratic reforms started by the Tsar will be interrupted.

February 20   Publisher Alexei Suvorin and D. talk for two hours. D. is confident that a peaceful time in politics will be coming: "It will make a difference. I am not a prophet, but you will see for yourself."

March 20, 21, 28   D. reads from his novels at literary evenings sponsored by the St. Petersburg Charity Society, the Children's Charity Fund and the Russian Literary Fund.

March 21   At a literary concert at the Higher Pedagogical Courses for Women, D. reads a scene from his novel *The Raw Youth*. One present reported, "Dostoevsky made an unfortunate choice for his reading. The plot of the story which he read was about a young woman who had arrived from a small provincial town and who is looking for tutoring lessons to make her living in a big city. She gives ads to a newspaper, but receives an offer to be a paid mistress and at the end, by a lie finds herself in a public house. ... This story made a depressing effect on the public, especially on the young female students, who constituted the majority of the audience." Yet as always, his presence exerted a powerful effect: "Dostoevsky read at the podium ... with such a touching voice that you felt scared, as if you were living part of the scene.... At the end of the reading ... the audience yelled, knocked, broke chairs and cried like crazy, appealing: 'Dostoevsky!'"

March 28   In the Hall of Nobility Club in St. Petersburg, D. reads from *Crime and Punishment*: "He was at the literary evening with other writers: Polonsky, Miller and Weinberg; our youth showed a touching and admirable attitude to the literature."

April 10   In an article titled "Ten Great Years," literary critic Pavel Annenkov accuses D. of egotism: "When the first novel *Poor People* appeared in 1848, Dostoevsky addressed the publisher and insisted that he make a special ornament on the margins of the text that had never been done before. Moreover, he asked for a different ornament design decorating each page."

April 27   At a literary evening of the Slavic Charity Society, D. reads the last chapter from *The Brothers Karamazov*. This is his last public appearance at a literary evening before traveling to his summer house in Staraya Russa. Late the same night D. writes a letter about this reading to his publisher Liubimov in Moscow: "I should say that the effect, without exaggeration, was overwhelming."

End of April   In an official letter to the Russian government, D. writes,

"Twenty-five years have passed after my release from prison.... During this time I repeatedly expressed my political and religious views on hundreds of pages ... can I ask you to stop a police surveillance over me."

May   From the memoirs of Anna Dostoevskaya: "A slander of Annenkov about a special ornament on the pages made my husband so furious that he decided not to notice Annenkov whenever he meets him, not to shake hands with him...."
               An article in *The European Herald* reports, "The author of *Literary Memoirs* is abroad now, but we can tell the story.... Dostoevsky in 1846 asked that his first story should be put at the beginning or at the end of the journal and under any pretext not in the middle, between other authors. Besides, every page of his work had to be framed with a special ornament, different for each page...."

May 2   An article in *Time*: "Mr. Annenkov created this anecdote about the ornament on the margins fifty years ago and continues to distribute these dirty rumors."

May 4   At a meeting of the Slavic Charity Society, D. is unanimously elected to represent the society at the opening of the monument to the Russian poet Aleksandr Pushkin in Moscow. Konstantin Romanov, the Great Prince of Russia, sends a note to D.: "Let me impose upon your freedom and ask you to visit us this Thursday at 9 P.M. Your reading was much appreciated by the Princess...." (Several members of the royal family will be present at the meeting: Sergei, son of Alexander II; Helen, daughter of Nikolai I; and Prince Konstantin.

May 8   Great Prince Konstantin: "I asked Dostoevsky to read the confession of monk Zosima.... Helen was crying, tears rolled along her cheeks." Future Tsar Alexander III, who is Grand Prince at the time, is interested in the Russophile movement, and D. is to see him to express his views on Russian and Slavic questions.

May 22   D. leaves his summer house in Staraya Russa for Moscow to participate in the Pushkin Festival. The celebrations are postponed for several days because of the death of the Tsarina, the wife of Alexander II.

May 23   D. arrives in Moscow to participate in the opening of the monument to Aleksandr Pushkin. Several of the best Russian journalists (S. Iuriev, I. Lavrov, N. Aksakov) meet him at the railway station.

May 23   An evening dinner at the Hermitage, featuring six speeches.

May 26	An article about the continuation of *The Brothers Karamazov*: "Alyosha … under the influence of the mental processes in his soul … comes to a conclusion about the assassination of the Tsar."
May 28	In a letter to his wife, D. writes that he wants to work on the final part of *The Brothers Karamazov* but has decided to stay for the opening of the monument to Pushkin.
Late May	The family moves from St. Petersburg to Staraya Russa.
Early June	Amnesty is announced for A. Mikhailov and O. Weimar, the organizers of the assassination attempt on the head of Russian police.
June 5	Reception of the Pushkin Festival delegates at Moscow City Hall. D. meets Maria Pushkina, the daughter of the great poet and prototype of Anna Karenina. There are delegations from the whole of Russia, ranging from the Russian Choir Society, to the Society of Acclimatization of Animals and Plants. At 8 P.M. D. writes to Anna: "Here there is a great conflict … tomorrow there will be a dinner for 500 people with speeches and, maybe, with fights."
June 6	A dinner at Moscow City Hall, with representatives of two political groups in Russian society: the Westernizers (I. Turgenev, M. Kovalevsky) and the Slavophiles (I. Aksakov, D., N. Katkov). From Katkov's speech: "This meeting will help us to find peaceful solutions."
June 7	A meeting at the Moscow Nobility Club. Turgenev speaks at the opening of the Pushkin monument: "There is no doubt that Pushkin … created our literary language and created our Russian literature."
June 8	The second meeting of the Society of Lovers of Russian Literature. D. makes his famous speech about Pushkin as a father of Russian literature; it is met with great success and public admiration. A crowd of admirers follows D. to the Loskutny Hotel in Moscow, where he is staying. Late at night D. writes a letter to his wife: "When at the end I proclaimed about the universal fraternity and brotherhood, the audience went completely mad and hysterical."
June 9	D.'s photograph is made in the Panov Photo Shop. D. is invited to a special breakfast with the leading Moscow literary figures: Ostrovsky, Grigorovich, Suvorin, Maksimov, and Berg.
June 10	Departure to Staraya Russa. D. works very hard on *The Brothers Karamazov*.
June 11	D.'s arrival in Staraya Russia from Moscow. "He was very tired."

June 25	In a letter to Alexander Ostrovsky, Mikhail Saltykov writes, "Looks like clever Turgenev and crazy Dostoevsky have stolen Pushkin's holiday from Pushkin."
End of June	D. writes about fifty pages of *The Brothers Karamazov* in several days.
July 6–10	D. sends the eleventh chapter of *The Brothers Karamazov* to the publisher.
July 15	Ivan Turgenev makes several very critical remarks about D.'s speech at the birthday party of a Russian musical critic, Vladimir Stasov, in Paris. He expresses amazement that "Russian society could accept this sermon about superman."
July 16	D. writes to Stakenshneider, "Yesterday there was the birthday of my son Fedya. The guests came, but I had to sit in the corner finishing my work." During the summer, in a period of about four months, he writes twenty signatures (about 320 pages) of *The Brothers Karamazov* and three signatures of *A Writer's Diary*.
July 17	D. sends to the publisher a new chapter for *A Writer's Diary* titled "My Answer to Gradovsky." "The most conservative part of our society is as shitty as any other part," he writes. "So many villains have joined it: Filonov, Krestovsky and a general, stupid fool...."
August 10	A brief visit to St. Petersburg about the publishing of *A Writer's Diary*. Letter from Pobedonostsev: "Here there are the best pages ever written by you."
August 16	Alexander II closes the Special Executive Commission, declaring that order in the country has been restored. He announces also, "The Third Section of the Secret Police will become a part of regular police at the Ministry of Internal Affairs."
Fall	Many critical reviews of the published portion of *The Brothers Karamazov* appear.
August 26	In a letter to Orest Miller, D. stresses, "We need to revive in the literature the great events from Russian history."
August 28	Letter from D. to I. Aksakov: "I am finishing *The Karamazovs*; consequently, I am summing up a work which I value, because much of me and what is mine has gone into it. I've been working altogether nervously, with torment and concern. When I work hard, I fall ill even physically. What has been thought over, formed, jotted down for three years is now being summed up...."
September 8	Letter from D. to Nikolai Liubimov, his publisher: "I don't

think that I made any technical mistakes in the novel. I have consulted two prosecutors in St. Petersburg."

September 26 Letter from Leo Tolstoy to Nikolai Strakhov: *"The Dead House* by Dostoevsky is the best book from all contemporary Russian literature."

September 30 Letter from D. to Victor Gaevsky: "From June 15 to October 1, I wrote almost 400 pages for the novel and 70 pages for *A Writer's Diary.* ... I have to write artistically."

October 7 The Dostoevsky family returns to St. Petersburg.

October 10 Visit to the Stakenshneider family.

October 15 D. writes in a letter to P. Guseva, "If there is a man working as if in a prison, that is me. My days are coming to an end."

October 19 Literary Fund organizes a reading of Russian writers dedicated to the anniversary of the Tsar's College. From a review in *The New Times*: "The huge hall of St. Petersburg Credit Society was packed. Every movement of our great novelist-psychologist Fyodor Dostoevsky resulted in a thunderstorm of applause. The audience abused its privilege to call the speaker for repeated encores." From a review in *The Shore*: "With his first words Dostoevsky became straight. You could not recognize this curved tired broken man; he changes in seconds into a giant made of steel.... He read his last phrase with an unusual strength, with tears in his throat.... The audience raved from admiration. Dostoevsky became pale; it seemed he was going to faint."

October 26 D. reads Pushkin's works at a meeting of the Literary Fund. A friend wrote, "What a marvel! A small, thin, unhealthy looking man, whispering all the time; but when he starts to read he becomes big and strong.... Great success among the audience!"

October 28 An article appears in the newspaper *Time* about the growing socialist movement in Europe. D. makes critical notes in his notebooks.

Late October D. invites Nikolai Lebedev-Morskoi, a beginning writer and the author of *The Aristocracy of Gostinny Yard*, to visit his home. He sees in Lebedev "the successor of his literary tasks."

October 30 D.'s 59th birthday.

October 31 General Loris-Melikov sends a telegram to the Tsar, cautioning that "The execution of all sixteen convicts will cast a gloomy impression in the capital. I recommend to execute only two persons...."

November 1   D. visits Konstantin Pobedonostsev at the Royal Palace.

November 2   D. writes a letter to Weinberg: "I cannot read for you, I am sorry. I have invitations to five parties and cannot attend all of them at the same time. Besides, I am busy with my work." At the time he is writing the final chapters of *The Brothers Karamazov.*

November 4   The Case of the Sixteen ends with the executions of Kviatkovsky and Presniakov in the St. Peter and Paul Fortress in St. Petersburg.

November 8   D. sends his Moscow publisher the epilogue of *The Brothers Karamazov.* In a letter to Nikolai Liubimov he rejoices, "Finally, the novel is finished! I have worked on it for three years, spent two years publishing it—this is a significant moment for me. I want to publish a separate edition for Christmas.... I intend to live and write for another twenty years."

November 11 At a literary evening hosted by the Stakenshneiders, D. speaks about the negative influence of the French Revolution and the socialist movement on the future of Europe. He also says that he is proud to receive a letter from Leo Tolstoy.

November 21, 30   D. reads his works at literary evenings.

November 28 In a letter to his brother Andrei, D. writes, "I doubt that I'll live long; it's very hard for me, with my emphysema, to get through the St. Petersburg winter.... It would remain only to thank God and rejoice at the children."

November 30 D. reads for the Charity Fund of the poor students of St. Petersburg University in the building of the Russian Credit Society. He reads the epilogue of the newly finished *Brothers Karamazov*: "You could hear the moans and yelling, hatred and Christian confession in the writer's voice; he showed us all psychological states of a human being, everything you can imagine. A noisy storm of applause interrupted him...."

Early December   The first edition of *The Brothers Karamazov* is published in a printing of 3,000 copies, half of which is sold in several days. D. writes, "A dirty wave. Is it me they call a dirty wave? After *The Brothers Karamazov*? And you are a clear shining wave, I guess...." Negative reviews of the novel appeared in the press.

December 4   Letter from G. Filippov, a church historian, to D.: "I just finished reading *The Brothers Karamazov* and I cannot find the proper words of gratitude." D. answers him the same day: "I am so persecuted in the journals. Your opinions, letters of sympathy from my readers, from youth ... raise my spirit."

December 9 Konstantin Pobedonostsev writes to D., "Thank you for your gift, the book *The Brothers Karamazov*. Let me recommend that you present this book to the royal family." An advertisement appears in many Russian newspapers: "A novel *The Brothers Karamazov* is published in book form and can be bought from the author."

December 14 A literary evening and reading with D. and his old friend Dmitry Grigorovich at the Bestuzhev Courses for Women.

December 16 D. visits the Royal Anichkov Palace. His daughter Liubov Fyodorovna is struck that her father, "who was a passionate monarchist at that time, did not want to follow court etiquette."

December 19 Letter to Aleksandr Blagonravov (doctor and writer): "People here are trying with all their might to wipe me off the face of the earth for the fact that I preach God and national roots. For the chapter of *The Karamazovs* (about the hallucination) that you, a doctor, are so satisfied with, they've already tried to call me a reactionary and fanatic.... I thank you, especially as a doctor, for your informing me of the accuracy of that person's mental illness depicted by me. An expert's opinion will support me, and you have to agree that under the given circumstances a person (Ivan Karamazov) could not have had any hallucination other than that one."

December 22 Cultural evening to raise funds for St. Ksenia's Shelter. After the evening D. meets with Maria Fyodorovna, the wife of the royal heir.

December 24 D. writes one of his last letters, to poet A. Pleshcheev: "I still owe you a little bit. But I'll repay you in the nearest future, when I get rich. But for the time being I'm just getting by. Everything is still just starting up for me...."

December 28 D. says about Tolstoy at a meeting with Mikoliukin, "Yes, Tolstoy is powerful. He is a great talent. He did not say all he could."

Year's End A fifteen-year old Dmitry Merezhkovsky, later to become a famous Russian writer, visits D. and receives the following advice: "If you want to write well, you have to suffer, my dear friend, you have to suffer!"

1881

January 1	Notes of Anna Dostoevskaya: "We visited the Sidorkin Theatre and he was in good spirits."
Early January	D. reflects the latest political events in what is to be the last issue of *A Writer's Diary*. He praises the Russian people, Russian military victories, the Orthodox church and Russian monarchy and gives a strong critique of the nihilists and socialists: "The nihilists appeared in Russia because we all are nihilists. This is a story that is washed with blood.... The Tsar is the personification of his people, of their ideas, hopes and beliefs."
January 12	Russian troops capture the city of Geoktepe on the Russian-Iranian border in the war in Middle Asia.
January 16	The contract deadline for *The Brothers Karamazov*.
January 19	A literary evening hosted by the Duchess Sofia Tolstaya, widow of A.K. Tolstoy. D. plays in an amateur drama performance.
January 23	D. tells Anna, "We have to buy an estate close to Moscow ... with a very big forest." In the evening he makes a visit to Duchess Alexandra Tolstaya. She asks D. to read several letters of Leo Tolstoy to his cousin.
January 25	The Dostoevskys have guests: Apollon Maikov, Nikolai Strakhov, and Orest Miller.
Monday, January 26	At 3 A.M., D. suffers an internal hemorrhage. Another massive bleeding occurs in the evening. At 6 P.M. D.'s pastor visits; D. confesses and receives communion.
January 27	Alexei Suvorin, a publisher and close friend, visits. He and D. talk about the latest issue of *A Writer's Diary* and D.'s literary plans.
January 28	At 7 A.M., D. tells his wife that he will probably die today. D. sleeps much of the day but also talks to several close friends and members of the family. At 7 P.M. he calls for his children and gives his copy of the New Testament to his son Fyodor. Around 8:30 P.M. Fyodor Mikhailovich Dostoevsky dies.
January 29	Thousands of visitors go to pay their final respects to D.
January 30	Professors from St. Petersburg University stop their lectures as a sign of mourning. The Tsar issues a special order granting a substantial pension to D.'s widow.
January 31	The funeral procession with D.'s coffin wrapped in golden cloth goes across St. Petersburg. According to the newspapers, this crowd of 50,000 people is the biggest public gathering of its kind in Russia in the nineteenth century.

February 1   D.'s burial ceremony at the Tikhvin Cemetery, close to the tombs of Russian poets Zhukovsky and Nekrasov.

February 2–3   Special meetings of Russian Literary Foundation, Russian Lawyers' Association, and other societies are devoted to D.

February 4   At a musical evening, Russian composer Modest Mussorgsky plays a special composition imitating funeral chimes and dedicated to D.

February 14   A meeting of the Slavic Charity Society is dedicated to the memory of D.

February–   A special commission is created, headed by Anna Dostoev-
March   skaya and consisting of Russian writers, poets and literary critics, for the purpose of preparing the publication of the complete works of Fyodor Dostoevsky. First translations of his late works into English, German, French, Swedish and other European languages appear in western Europe. The First Posthumous Edition of the *Complete Works* in fourteen volumes is published in 1881. Further, enlarged editions follow in 1894–1895, 1904–1906, 1910, 1926–1930, and 1974–1985.

APPENDIX A.
DICTIONARY OF
PERSONS MENTIONED

ABAZA, NIKOLAI SAVICH (1837–1910). The Minister of Press; the censor of the last issue of *A Writer's Diary*.

AKHSHARUMOV, NIKOLAI DMITRIEVICH (1822–1893). Novelist, journalist and literary critic. Worked on *Epoch* in the 1860s and left memoirs about D.

AKSAKOV, IVAN SERGEEVICH (1823–1886). Moscow publisher and journalist, one of the leaders of the Slavophile movement; he highly praised D.'s speech about Pushkin; he and D. shared similar views on the missionary role of the Russian people in the unification of Slavs.

ALCHEVSKAYA, CHRISTINA DANILOVNA (1841–1920). The principal of a Sunday school in Kharkov, a journalist, a teacher and a woman activist; she left memoirs about her visits to D. in 1876.

ALEXANDER II (1818–1881). The Russian Tsar who granted D. amnesty in 1858 and allowed him to move from Siberia to St. Petersburg after D. wrote him two letters in 1858 and 1859; after D. demonstrated complete loyalty to the Russian monarchy, the Tsar invited him to the Royal Palace frequently in 1879–1880 for private talks.

ALEXANDROV, ANATOLY ALEXANDROVICH (1861–1930). A journalist and associate professor of Russian literature at Moscow University; he met with D. in Staraya Russa when he was a student and left memoirs about this meeting.

ALEXANDROV, MIKHAIL ALEXANDROVICH. A publishing house worker who prepared D.'s manuscripts for publication and received many letters from D. He left his memoirs about D.'s amiable relationships with the editors and staff of the publishing houses.

ALEXEEVA, NADYA. A teenage friend of the Ivanovs who was present in Lublino in 1866 when D. wrote *Crime and Punishment*.

ALYONA FROLOVNA (ca. 1780–1850s). D.'s nurse when he was a young boy. D. remembered this kind and simple Russian woman in *A Writer's Diary* and called her "a saint woman." She was the prototype of Liza Tushina's nurse in *The Demons*.

ANNENKOV, PAVEL VASILIEVICH (1812–1887). Literary critic and journalist who worked on *The Contemporary*. He was close to Belinsky, Nekrasov, and Saltykov-Schedrin and therefore wrote very critical articles about D.

ANTONELLI, PYOTR. Police agent in the Petrashevsky case; after his reports to the police D. was arrested and convicted.

ARSENIEV. Professor of mathematics at the Engineering Academy.

AVERKIEV, DMITRY VASILIEVICH (1836–1905). Playwright and journalist; an active Slavophile; worked on the journal *Epoch* edited by D.; contributed to D.'s first biography (1883); continued *A Writer's Diary* in 1885–86.

BABIKOV, KONSTANTIN IVANOVICH (1841–1873). Writer whose works were published in *Time* and *Epoch*. He personally knew D. in 1864–65 and corresponded with him.

BAKUNIN, MIKHAIL ALEXANDROVICH (1814–1876). Russian anarchist and revolutionary activist in exile; participated in the First Congress of Peace, at which D. was present.

BALZAC, HONORE DE (1799–1850). French novelist whom D. greatly admired.

BARANOV, PAVEL TROFIMOVICH (1815–1864). Governor-general of Tver who supported D.'s request to live in St. Petersburg after Siberia; he is the prototype of Von Lembke in *The Demons*.

BAZUNOV, ALEKSANDR FYODOROVICH (1825–1899). Publisher and bookseller who published several of D.'s major novels in book form in the 1860s and 1870s.

BEETHOVEN, LUDWIG VAN (1770–1827). German composer whose works D. often listened to during his stay abroad with his wife in the 1860s and early 1870s.

BEKETOV, ALEXEI NIKOLAEVICH (1823–?). D.'s schoolmate at the Engineering Academy. D. shared an apartment with the Beketov brothers in 1846–47.

BELIKHOV, COLONEL. Commander of the Siberian Seventh Infantry Battalion, in which D. served as a private. He treated D. very nicely and often invited him to his home.

BELINSKAYA, MARIA VASILIEVNA (1812–1890). The wife of Vissarion Belinsky; D. wrote her a letter.

BELINSKY, VISSARION GRIGORIEVICH (1811–1848). Prominent Russian literary critic; he supported D.'s first novel *Poor People* but was very critical of his later works.

BERANGER, PIERRE JEAN DE (1780–1857). French poet and writer of popular songs whose works D. admired.

BEREZHETSKY, IVAN IGNATIEVICH (1820–?). A schoolmate with whom D. discussed his views on literature.

BERG, FYODOR NIKOLAEVICH (184?–1909). Poet and translator who met D. at several literary salons, published his works in *Time* and was present at the Pushkin Festival in 1880.

BLAGONRAVOV, ALEKSANDR FYODOROVICH. A writer and doctor who corresponded with D. in 1880.

BOBORYKIN, PYOTR DMITRIEVICH (1836–1921). Writer and literary critic. He was the editor of *The Library for Reading* and in 1863 invited D. to contribute to this journal.

BOGDANOVICH, ALEXANDRA. The wife of General Bogdanovich, who was one of the senior state officers at the Russian royal court. She published his *Daybook* with detailed memoirs about the Romanov dynasty.

BORISLAVSKY, GENERAL. The Supervisor of the convicts' labor in the Omsk Fortress in 1849.

BRIULLOV, ALEKSANDR PAVLOVICH (1798–1877). Russian architect and painter who invited D. to his house in the 1870s.

BRODNIKOV. Russian actor who was present at D.'s funeral.

BROWN (PANINA, NÉE ELIZAVETA KHLEBNIKOVA), MARFA (OR MARTHA) PETROVNA. A woman who traveled across Europe and planned to publish her memoirs in *Epoch*; D. visited her in the hospital and was on friendly terms with her in 1864.

BULL, OLE (1810–1880). Famous Norwegian virtuoso violinist who toured in Russia and visited St. Petersburg; D. admired his play.

BUSHEN, MASHA. A visitor to the Stakenshneiders' salon.

BUTASHEVICH-PETRASHEVSKY, MIKHAIL VASILIEVICH (1821–1866). The organizer of a secret socialist revolutionary circle which D. joined in the 1840s. After the trial he lived in Siberia. He was the prototype of Pyotr Verkhovensky in *The Demons*.

BUTLEROV, ALEKSANDR MIKHAILOVICH (1928–1886). Russian scholar and professor of chemistry at St. Petersburg University.

BYKOV, PYOTR VASILIEVICH (1843–1930). Poet and literary critic who left memoirs about D. as editor of *Time*.

CATHERINE. A servant in the Dostoevsky house who became the lover of D.'s father.

CHERMAK, LEONTII IVANOVICH (d. 1840s). Director of one of the oldest private high schools in Moscow, where D. and his brother Mikhail studied from 1834 to 1837.

CHERNYSHEVSKY, NIKOLAI GAVRILOVICH (1828–1889). Journalist who promoted socialist ideas in Russia; he knew D. personally in the early 1860s and wrote several critical articles about him.

COOPER, JAMES FENIMORE (1789–1851). An American novelist whose works D. greatly admired.

DANDUKOVA, COUNTESS NADEZHDA MIKHAILOVNA. A guest at the Stakenshneiders' literary salons.

DANILEVSKY, GRIGORY PETROVICH (1829–1890). Russian writer who was published in *Time*.

DANILEVSKY, NIKOLAI JAKOVLEVICH (1822–1885). Philosopher and journalist who was a member of the Petrashevsky Circle; D. was interested in his works on the unity of the Slavic people and met with him in the 1870s.

DANILOV, FOMA. Sergeant of the Russian army whose heroic wartime deed was described in *A Writer's Diary*.

DAVYDOV, VLADIMIR NIKOLAEVICH (1849–1925). One of the best Russian dramatic actors of the 1870s and 1880s. He was well acquainted with all the famous Russian playwrights, poets and writers of the time. He listened to D. at literary readings and wrote a detailed account of these events.

DE GRAVE, ALEKSEI FYODOROVICH (1793–1864). Major-general who served as director of the Omsk Fortress and Prison.

DERZHAVIN, GAVRIIL ROMANOVICH (1743–1816). Russian writer and poet whose works D. admired.

DICKENS, CHARLES (1812–1870). English novelist who was one of D.'s favorite writers.

DOLGORUKOV, GENERAL VASILII ANDREEVICH (1804–1868). A member of the investigatory committee in the Petrashevsky case and the chief of the Third Section of the Secret Police.

DOSTOEVSKAYA, ALEXANDRA (in her first marriage Golenovskaya; in her second marriage Sheviakova; 1835–1889). D.'s sister, with whom he was not very close.

DOSTOEVSKAYA (NÉE SNITKINA), ANNA GRIGORIEVNA (1846–1918). D.'s second wife; she was with him during the last 14 years of his life, his most prolific period when he wrote most of his famous novels. In her memoirs she described her life with D. in great detail. D. wrote her letters practically every day when he was away, as for example during his trips to Germany or to Pushkin celebrations.

DOSTOEVSKAYA, DOMINIKA (1825–1887). D.'s sister-in-law, wife of brother Andrei.

DOSTOEVSKAYA, EMILIA FYODOROVNA (1822–1879). D.'s sister-in-law.

DOSTOEVSKAYA, LIUBOV (1869–1926). D.'s daughter.

DOSTOEVSKAYA, MARIA DMITRIEVNA (née Constant); in her first marriage Isaeva; (1825–1864). D.'s first wife whom he met in 1854 and married in 1857 in Siberia; she died of tuberculosis.

DOSTOEVSKAYA, MARIA FYODOROVNA (née Nechaeva; 1800–1837). D.'s mother, who belonged to a wealthy merchant family; she influenced D. in his love for literature at an early age. She died very young, at the age of 37.

DOSTOEVSKAYA, VARVARA MIKHAILOVNA (née Karepina; 1822–1893). D.'s sister, who after her aunt's death, quarrelled with D. about the inheritance.

DOSTOEVSKAYA, VERA *see* IVANOVA, VERA.

DOSTOEVSKY, ANDREI (1825–1897). D.'s younger brother. A civil engineer and architect, he left detailed memoirs about D.'s childhood.

DOSTOEVSKY, FYODOR FYODOROVICH (1871–1921). D.'s son who became an expert in horse breeding.

DOSTOEVSKY, MIKHAIL ANDREEVICH (1789–1839). D.'s father born in a priest's family; he became a military surgeon. His hobbies were literature and history, and he gave a good home education to his children.

DOSTOEVSKY, MIKHAIL MIKHAILOVICH (1820–1864). D.'s elder brother, a writer, literary critic and journalist.

DOSTOEVSKY, NIKOLAI MIKHAILOVICH (1831–1883). D.'s younger brother, civil engineer who died from alcoholism.

DRUZHININ, ALEKSANDR VASILIEVICH (1824–1864). A writer, editor, literary critic and translator who was one of the organizers of the Literary Fund; he took part in the amateur performances of Russian writers with D.

DUBELT, LEONTY VASILIEVICH (1792–1862). The police general who from 1839 to 1856 was the head of the Third Section of the Secret Police, which investigated the Petrashevsky case.

DUMAS, ALEXANDRE, PÈRE (1802–187). French novelist whose works D. admired.

DUROV, SERGEI FYODOROVICH (1816–1869). Member of the Petrashevsky Circle who spent four years with D. in the same prison, though there was no friendship between them; he was the prototype of Stepan Verkhovensky in *The Demons*.

FEOKTISTOV, EVGENY MIKHAILOVICH (1828–1898). Journalist and expert on literary history; minister of press in the 1870s.

FILIPPOV, PAVEL NIKOLAEVICH (1825–1855). Member of the Petrashevsky Circle, introduced by D. to the Durov Circle; he set up equipment for an underground publishing house. Died during the war in the Caucasus, near Chechnya.

FILIPPOV, TERTII IVANOVICH (1825–1899). A journalist, state official, active Slavophile and specialist in the history of Russian church; D. published his works in *The Citizen*.

FILOSOFOVA, ANNA PAVLONVA (1837–1912). One of the organizers of the women's movement in Russia and of the first women's colleges in the 1870s; she was connected with revolutionary circles and lived abroad in exile from 1879 to 1881.

FON-FOKHT, NIKOLAI. A friend of the Ivanov family who left memoirs about D. in the summer of 1866 in Lublino.

FONVIZINA, NATALIA DMITRIEVNA (1805–1869). The wife of Russian Decembrist M. Fonvisin who met D. briefly in the Tobolsk prison terminal in the winter of 1850 and presented him with the New Testament.

FOURIER, F.M. CHARLES (1772–1837). Social theorist and philosopher whose theories interested D. during his youth.

FREUD, SIGMUND (1856–1939). Founder of psychoanalysis. He wrote a large article on D. and often acknowledged his indebtedness to D.'s works.

GAEVSKY, VICTOR PAVLOVICH (1826–1888). A lawyer, bibliographer, and expert in the history of literature; one of the founders of the Literary Fund. He corresponded with D. in the late 1870s.

GAGARIN, PRINCE PAVEL PAVLOVICH (1789–1872). As one of the senior state officials, he participated in the investigation of the Petrashevsky case and interrogated D.

GARIBALDI, GUISEPPE (1807–1882). Military leader in the Italian movement for independence; D. listened to his speech at the Congress of Peace during his trip abroad in the late 1860s.

GASFORT, GUSTAV CHRISTIANOVICH (1794–1874). Infantry general who commanded the Special Siberian Division in which D. served as a private, a sergeant and ultimately a junior lieutenant. He promoted D. in rank and then supported D.'s request to be dismissed from the army.

GEIDEBUROV, PAVEL ALEXANDROVICH (1841–1893). Journalist and publisher.

GOETHE, JOHANN (1749–1832). German poet and dramatist, whom D. often quoted.

GOFMAN, ERNST T. AMADEI (1776–1822). German writer; influenced early D.

GOGOL, NIKOLAI VASILIEVICH (1809–1852). Russian writer whom D. considered one of his literary teachers.

GONCHAROV, IVAN ALEXANDROVICH (1821–1891). Russian novelist.

GORBUNOV, IVAN FYODOROVICH (1831–1895). Actor and storyteller.

GRADOVSKY, GRIGORY KONSTANTINOVICH (1842–1915). Professor at Moscow University; wrote detailed memoirs about D.

GRIBBE, COLONEL A. The former owner of the house in Staraya Russa which D. bought in 1876 and where he wrote his last novels.

GRIGORIEV, APOLLON ALEXANDROVICH (1822–1864). A poet, journalist and literary critic who highly appreciated D.'s novels and who worked on *Time* and *Epoch*.

GRIGORIEV, NIKOLAI PETROVICH (1822–1886). Junior military officer who was a member of the Petrashevsky Circle.

GRIGOROVICH, DMITRY VASILIEVICH (1822–1899). A writer and journalist who was D.'s schoolmate and close friend for many years.

HEIBOVICH, ARTEMII IVANOVICH (?–1865). Commander of D.'s company in the army in Siberia.

HERZEN, ALEKSANDR IVANOVICH (1812–1870). Journalist and Russian revolutionary in exile with whom D. met during his trips abroad.

HUGO, VICTOR (1802–1885). French writer.

IAKOVLEV, VLADIMIR DMITRIEVICH (1817–1884). Writer and journalist.

IANOVSKY, STEPAN DMITRIEVICH (1817–1897). A doctor who was a close personal friend of D. in the late 1840s.

IASINSKY, I. Russian journalist and writer who met D. at literary gatherings and circles.

IASTRZHEMBSKY, IVAN L'VOVICH (1814–1880). Member of the Petrashevsky Circle.

ISAEV, ALEKSANDR IVANOVICH (?–1855). The first husband of D.'s first wife, Maria Dmitrievna; he died from alcoholism.

ISAEV, PAVEL (1848–1900). D.'s son-in-law.

IURIEV, SERGEI ANDREEVICH (1821–1888). Literary activist, journalist, and chairman of the Society of Lovers of Russian Literature.

IVANCHINA-PISAREVA, MARIA SERGEEVNA. A friend of the Ivanov family.

IVANOV, ALEKSANDR PAVLOVICH (1813–1968). D.'s brother-in-law, the husband of his favorite sister Vera who lived in Moscow and whom D. often visited.

IVANOV, I. A Moscow student who became a member of a socialist circle and was killed by his associates; he became one of the prototypes of D.'s novel *The Demons*.

IVANOV, KONSTANTIN (?–1887). Junior lieutenant in Siberia who helped D.

IVANOVA, ELENA PAVLOVNA. D.'s sister-in-law.

IVANOVA, MARIA ALEXANDROVNA (1848–1929). D.'s niece.

IVANOVA, SOFIA ALEXANDROVNA (1847–1907). D's niece.

IVANOVA, VERA MIKHAILOVNA (1829–1896). D's favorite sister; he often celebrated New Year's Eve with her family. D. wrote major chapters of *Crime and Punishment* in her summer estate in Lublino, one of the suburbs of Moscow, and depicted her family in *The Eternal Husband*.

KALMYKOV. Members of the Petrashevsky Circle.

KAMENETSKAYA, M.V. The daughter of A.P. Filosofova.

KARAMZIN, NIKOLAI MIKHAIKLOVICH (1766–1826). Historian.

KARAZIN, NIKOLAI NIKOLAEVICH (1842–1908). Russian painter and writer who was present at D.'s funeral.

KAREPINA, MARIA PETROVNA (1842–?). D.'s niece.

KASHKIN, NIKOLAI SERGEEVICH (1829–1914). Member of the Petrashevsky Circle.

KATKOV, MIKHAIL NIKIFOROVICH (1818–1887). Editor-in-chief of *The Russian Herald*, which published most of D.'s novels.

KELLER. A patient of Dr. Riesenkampf who supplied D. with material for his first novel, *Poor People*.

KHALTURIN, STEPAN. Tsar Nikolai I's assassin.

KHOTIAINTSEVA, FEDOSIA JAKOVLEVNA. D.'s neighbor who lived close to Darovoe village.

KIREEVSKY, IVAN VASILIEVICH (1806–1856). Slavophile journalist and philosopher.

KOLTSOV, ALEXEI VASILIEVICH (1809–1842). Russian poet.

KONI, ANATOLY FYODOROVICH (1844–1927). Famous Russian lawyer, senator, member of the Russian Supreme Court, and author of numerous memoirs. D. often consulted him on different legal matters when writing his novels, most of which were based on actual crimes.

KORNILOVA, KATERINA. A woman whose act of throwing her six-year-old stepdaughter out a fourth-floor window interested D. to the extent that he devoted an essay in *A Writer's Diary* to her case. His support was probably influential in her ultimate acquittal.

KOROLENKO, VLADIMIR GALAKTIONOVICH (1853–1921). Writer and member of Russian Academy of Sciences; as a student, he listened to D.'s speech at Nekrasov's funeral.

KORVIN-KRUKOVSKAYA, ANNA (ANIUTA) VASILIEVNA (1843–1887). The senior daughter of General Korvin-Krukovsky whom D. asked to marry him in 1864.

KORVIN-KRUKOVSKAYA, SOFIA VASILIEVNA (Kovalevskaya after marriage; 1850–1991). Younger daughter of General Korvin-Krukovsky; she became a mathematician and writer.

KORVIN-KRUKOVSKY, GENERAL VASILY VASILIEVICH (1800–1875). Father of Anna and Sofia Korvin-Krukovsky.

KOSHLIAKOV, DMITRY IVANOVICH (1835–1891). Professor at the Medical Academy.

KOSTOMAROV, KORONAD FILIPPOVICH (1803–1873). D.'s teacher who prepared him for entering the Engineering Academy.

KOVALEVSKY, PAVEL MIKHAILOVICH (1823–1907). Journalist, poet and literary critic. The author of famous memoirs about several Russian writers.

KRAEVSKY, ANDREI ALEKSANDROVICH (1810–1889). Journalist and literary critic.

KRAMSKOI, IVAN (1837–1887). Painter; made several portraits of D.

KRESTOVSKY, VSEVOLOD VLADIMIROVICH (1840–1895). Writer.

KRIVOPISHIN, GENERAL IVAN GRIGORIEVICH (1796–1867). A Distant relative who helped D. to enter the Academy.

KULIKOVA, V. N. (1846–1894). A friend of famous Russian lawyer A. Koni, who introduced him to D.

KUMANIN, ALEKSANDR ALEXEEVICH (1792–1863). Dostoevsky's uncle; husband of A.F. Kumanina.

KUMANINA (NÉE NECHAEVA), ALEKSANDRA FYODOROVNA (1796–1871). The sister of D.'s mother who took care of the younger Dostoevsky children after their parents' deaths and who left D. a considerable inheritance.

LAVROV, IAKOV MIKHAILOVICH (1852–1912). Publisher of *The Russian Thought*; also a journalist and translator.

LEBEDEV-MORSKOI, NIKOLAI KONSTANTINOVICH (1846–1888). A writer.

LEONTIEV, KONSTANTIN NIKOLAEVICH (1831–1891). Writer and literary critic.

LEONTIEV, PAVEL MIKHAILOVICH. A journalist and professor of literature at Moscow University.

LESKOV, NIKOLAI SEMYONOVICH (1831–1895). Russian writer.

LETKOVA, KATERINA PAVLOVNA (1856–1937). A writer, translator, and organizer of the women's movement in Russia. She published two volumes of short stories and wrote memoirs dedicated to D.

LIUBIMOV, DMITRY NIKOLAEVICH (1864–1942). The son of Nikolai Liubimov. He was present for D.'s Pushkin speech on June 8, 1880, in the Hall of Russian Nobility in Moscow. Later he became a senior official, governor-general of Vilno province; in 1919 he emigrated from Russia.

LIUBIMOV, NIKOLAI ALEXEEVICH (1830–1897). Journalist, publisher and professor of physics at Moscow University. He assisted Mikhail Katkov with the publication of *The Brothers Karamazov* and other works of D. in *The Russian Herald* between 1863 and 1882.

LORIS-MELIKOV, GENERAL MIKHAIL TARIELOVICH (1825–1888). Minister of the interior who highly praised D. The survivor of an 1880 assassination attempt.

MAIKOV, APOLLON NIKOLAEVICH (1821–1897). A poet and writer who was D.'s close personal friend.

MAIKOV, VARERIAN NIKOLAEVICH (1823–1847). Literary critic and journalist.

MAKOVSKAYA, JULIA PAVLOVNA. Sister of K. Letkova.

MAKSIMOV, SERGEI VASILIEVICH (1831–1901). Writer.

MARKEVICH, BOLESLAV MARKOVICH (1822–1884). Writer, the author of "anti-nihilistic novels."

MARTIANOV, PYOTR KUZMICH (1827–1899). A writer and journalist popular in the 1880s-90s.

MENDELSSOHN-BARTHOLDY, FELIX (1809–1847). Composer whose music D. liked.

MEREZHKOVSKY, D. S. Russian writer.

MESHCHERSKY, PRINCE VLADIMIR PETROVICH (1839–1914). Journalist and publisher of *The Citizen*; a monarchist.

MIKHAILOVSKY, KONSTANTIN. Professor of Moscow University who was a writer, friend of Turgenev, and one of the leaders of the Westernizers.

MIKHAILOVSKY, NIKOLAI KONSTANTINOVICH (1842–1904). Russian journalist and literary critic.

MILIUKOV, ALEKSANDR PETROVICH (1817–1897). Journalist, writer and historian of literature; D.'s close personal friend.

MILIUTIN, DMITRY ALEXEEVICH (1816–1912). Minister of Defense, state official.

MILLER, OREST FYODOROVICH (1833–1889). Professor of literary history who studied Russian folklore, supported D. in his pro–Slavicism, and was close to D. in the late 1870s. Miller wrote the first biography of D. in 1883.

MOMBELLI, NIKOLAI ALEKSANDROVICH (1823–1902). A member of the Petrashevsky Circle.

MOZART, WOLFGANG AMADEUS (1756–1791). German composer whose works D. liked very much.

MUSSORGSKY, MODEST. Russian composer who dedicated several musical pieces to D. after his funeral.

NABOKOV, GENERAL IVAN ALEXANDROVICH (1787–1852). Director of the St. Peter and Paul Fortress; he interrogated D. after the arrest.

NAVROTSKY, ALEKSANDR ALEXANDROVICH (1839–1914). Writer and lawyer.

NECHAEV, SERGEI (1847–1882). Terrorist and revolutionary who headed the secret terrorist society "The People's Revenge."

NEKRASOV, NIKOLAI ALEKSEEVICH (1821–1887). Russian poet and publisher who introduced D. to the literary world.

NEVROTOVA, ELIZAVETA. A peasant woman with whom D. was in love during his service in the army in Siberia.

NIKOLAI I (1796–1855). Russian Tsar.

OGAREV, NIKOLAI PLATONOVICH (1813–1877). Poet, journalist and revolutionary leader.

OKEL. Doctor of St. Peter and Paul Fortress.

OL'KHIN, PAVEL MATVEEVICH (1830–?). Teacher of stenography who introduced to D. his second wife, Anna Snitkina.

OPOCHININ, EVGENY (1858–1918). Writer, archive expert, and author of historical sketches about the old Russian life. The supervisor of several major Russian archives, libraries and museums, he met D. in 1879.

ORLOV, PRINCE ALEXEI FYODOROVICH (1786–1861). Chief of the Secret Police.

OSTROVSKY, ALEXANDER NIKOLAEVICH (1823–1886). Major Russian playwright in the middle of the nineteenth century; he worked at D.'s journal *Time*. The two writers read their works together at literary evenings in 1880.

PANAEV, IVAN IVANOVICH (1812–1862). Writer, journalist and literary artist.

PANAEVA, AVDOTIA (1820–1893). The wife of Ivan Panaev; she had a literary salon in St. Petersburg frequented by D. in the late 1840s.

PAVLOVNA, ELENA *see* ROMANOVA, HELEN.

PETRASHEVSKY *see* BUTASHEVICH-PETRASHEVSKY, MIKHAIL VASILIEVICH.

PISEMSKY, ALEXEI (1821–1881). Writer.

PLESHCHEEV, ALEXANDER NIKOLAEVICH (1825–1893). Poet.

POBEDONOSTSEV, KONSTANTIN (1827–1907). Senior state official, serving at different times as a government minister and as professor of law at Moscow University. The mentor of the children of the royal family, he taught the future Alexander II and Nikolai II. He was a great admirer of D.'s works and introduced D. to the royal family.

POLETIKA, VASILY APOLLONOVICH (1820–1888). Colonel in Siberia.

POLONSKY, IAKOV (1819–1898). Russian poet who worked with D. on *Time* in the 1860s and often met D. at the Stakenshneiders' literary salon in the late 1870s.

POTEKHIN, ALEXEI ANTIPOVICH (1829–1908). Journalist and playwright.

PUTSYKOVICH, VICTOR FEOFILOVICH (1843–1912?). Writer, journalist, professor of law. He was the editor of *The Citizen* after D. resigned from this position. D. wrote him 14 letters. Between 1903 and 1912 Putsykovich wrote several brief memoirs about D.

RADETSKY, FYODOR FYODOROVICH (1820–1890). D.'s schoolmate and a famous Russian general.

RAPHAEL (1483–1520). D.'s favorite painter.

RIESENKAMPF, ALEKSANDR EGOROVICH (1821–1895). Doctor who shared an apartment with D. in 1843 and wrote detailed memoirs about this period of D.'s life.

ROMANOV, KONSTANTIN KONSTANTINOVICH (1827–1892). The Great Prince of Russia. He was a great admirer of D. and introduced him to other members of the royal family.

ROMANOVA, GRAND PRINCESS HELEN (OR ELENA PAVLOVNA) (1806–1873).

ROSTOVTSEV, GENERAL JAKOV IVANOVICH (1803–1860). A member of the investigatory committee in the Petrashevsky case.

RUBINSTEIN, ANTON GRIGORIEVICH (1829–1894). Russian musician and composer.

RUBINSTEIN, NIKOLAI GRIGORIEVICH (1835–1881). Russian musician.

SALTYKOV, MIKHAIL (pseudonym Shchedrin; 1826–1889). Russian satirical writer and editor of the literary journal *The Fatherland Notes*. At the beginning of D.'s career he was among D.'s friends, but by the 1870s Saltykov had become rather critical of D.

SAVELIEV, ALEKSANDR IVANOVICH (1816–1907). A journalist and historian; he served as an officer at the Military Engineering Academy when D. was a cadet there.

SAVINA, MARIA (1854–1915). Actress who participated in public literary readings with D.

SAZONOV, NIKOLAI FYODOROVICH (1843–1902). Russian actor who was present at D.'s funeral.

SEMENOV TAIN-SHANSKY, COUNT PYOTR PETROVICH (1827–1914). Prominent Russian explorer and geographer.

SHARNHORST, GENERAL VASILII L'VOVICH (1798–1873). Director of the Military Engineering Academy in St. Petersburg.

SHIDLOVSKY, IVAN NIKOLAEVICH (1816–1872). Poet and D's schoolmate.

SHILLER, FRIEDRICH (1759–1805). German poet and dramatist; D. translated some of his works into Russian.

SHUBERT, ALEKSANDRA IVANOVNA (1827–1909). Russian comedy actress; S. Ianovsky's wife.

SLIVITSKY, ALEXEI (1850–1913). Children's writer, teacher, journalist. He assisted Professor Polivanov at the Pushkin Festival in 1880 in Moscow where D. made his famous speech.

SLUCHEVSKY, KONSTANTIN (1837–1904). Writer and poet, visitor to the Stakenshneiders' literary salon.

SMIRNOV, VASILII. The husband of Maria Karepina, D.'s niece whom the writer met in Lublino in 1866.

SNITKIN, IVAN GRIGORIEVICH (1849–1887). D.'s brother-in-law during his second marriage.

SNITKINA, ANNA NIKOLAEVNA (?–1893). D.'s mother-in-law during his second marriage.

SOLLOGUB, VLADIMIR ALEKSANDROVICH (1814–1883). Writer, senior state official and monarchist.

SOLOVIEV, VLADIMIR (1853–1900). Philosopher, poet, literary critic. After the death of D.'s younger son Alexei, he made a pilgrimage with D. to the remote Optina Pustin' Monastery in Northern Russia where D. discussed with him the message and plot of *The Brothers Karamazov*.

SOLOVIEV, VSEVOLOD (1849–1903). Poet, novelist, brother of Russian philosopher Vladimir Soloviev. He worked as a lawyer at the Ministry of Justice and published some of his poems and lengthy historical novels in *The Citizen* while D. was the editor. In 1881 he wrote memoirs about D.

SPESHNEV, NIKOLAI ALEXANDROVICH. Member of the Petrashevsky Circle.

SPIRIDONOV. Governor-general of Semipalatinsk, a city in Siberia where D. served in the army.

STAKENSHNEIDER, ELENA ANDREEVNA (1836–1897). Daughter of the famous Russian architect A.I. Stakenshneider, who built many palaces, mansions and summer cottages for the royal family and for the senior officials. The Stakenshneiders had a literary salon in St. Petersburg in 1860s and 1870s and D. often visited their home.

STELLOVSKY, FYODOR TIMOTEEVICH (?–1875). Publisher and book wholesaler.

STEPANOV. Commander of D.'s company in Semipalatinsk.

STRAKHOV, NIKOLAI NIKOLAEVICH (1828–1896). Literary critic, journalist, and author of *Memoirs About Dostoevsky*. He worked with D. in different literary journals for many years during the 1860s and 1870s.

SUSLOVA, APPOLINARIA (POLINA) PROKOFIEVNA (1839–1918). D.'s secret lover in 1863–64, and the prototype of Poline in *The Gambler*.

SUVORIN, ALEXEI SERGEEVICH (1834–1912). Literary artist, journalist and major Russian publisher. He was close to the royal family and published works of D., Tolstoy, Chekhov and many other outstanding Russian writers.

SUVORINA, ANNA I. (1858–1936). The second wife of Alexei Suvorin; she left brief memoirs about the last period of D.'s life.

TCHAIKOVSKY, PYOTR (1840–1893). Russian composer who wrote his major works at the same time as D., in the 1870s and 1880s. He was greatly impressed by *The Brothers Karamazov* and held D. in high esteem in his letters. He was present at the famous Pushkin speech made by D. in 1880.

TOLSTAYA, SOFIA ANDREEVNA (1844–1892). Wife of writer and poet A.K. Tolstoy. D. often visited her literary salon in St. Petersburg in 1879 and 1880 and supported her after the death of her husband.

TOLSTOY, COUNT ALEXEI KONSTANTINOVICH (1817–1875). Novelist, poet and dramatist.

TOLSTOY, COUNT LEV (OR LEO) NIKOLAEVICH (1828–1910). Russian novelist, greatly admired D. though they never met personally.

TOTLEBEN, EDUARD IVANOVICH (1818–1884). General at the Russian Royal Court who assisted D. in transferring from Siberia to St. Petersburg.

TOYSTAYA, ALEXANDRA ANDREEVNA (1817–1904). Distant aunt of Leo Tolstoy, and the grande dame at the Russian royal court. Leo Tolstoy visited her several times in St. Petersburg in 1878 and wrote her several letters in which he discussed his religious views. She presented these letters to D. in 1880.

TRETIAKOV, PAVEL MIKHAILOVICH (1832–1898). Art collector, the founder of the largest gallery of Russian art in Moscow.

TRUTOVSKY, KONSTANTIN ALEKSANDROVICH (1826–1893). A painter who was D.'s schoolmate during his studies at the Engineering Academy.

TURGENEV, IVAN (1818–1883). Russian writer. D. knew Turgenev for almost 35 years. The friendly relationship they enjoyed from 1849 to 1867 became more tense and sometimes developed into animosity after Turgenev published his novel *The Smoke*. Turgenev was one of the leaders of the Westernizers; D. was among the leaders of the Slavophile movement.

USPENSKY, GLEB IVANOVICH (1843–1902). Russian writer, publisher and journalist. At the Pushkin celebrations in Moscow in 1880 he represented the major Russian literary journal *The Fatherland Notes.*

VALUEV, PYOTR ALEXANDROVICH (1815–1890). Minister of the interior from 1861 through 1868.

VEINBERG, PYOTR ISAEVICH (1831–1908). Poet, translator, literary artist.

VELIKHANOV, CHOKAN CHINGISOVICH. Kasakh historian, educator, traveler and explorer; he met D. in Siberia in 1854 and in St. Petersburg around 1860.

VERGUNOV, NIKOLAI BORISOVICH (1832–?). High school teacher in Kuznetsk, Siberia. D.'s first wife, Maria Isaeva, was in love with him before her marriage to D.

VRANGEL, BARON ALEKSANDR EGOROVICH (1833–?). Russian diplomat and archaeologist who was D.'s close friend from 1854 to 1856 and left detailed memoirs about D.'s stay in Siberia.

VUICH, I. Colonel of the Royal Guard Regiment who was present at D.'s mock execution.

ZAGULIAEV, MIKHAIL ANDREEVICH (1834–1900). A journalist who was a visitor at the Stakenshneiders' literary salon and witnessed D.'s mock execution.

APPENDIX B.
TRANSLATIONS AND
ABBREVIATIONS OF
RUSSIAN PERIODICAL TITLES

Annual Review of Russian Royal The-aters—Ezhegodnik Russkikh Imperatorskikh Teatrov
Art Journal—Khudozhestvennyi Zhur-nal
Art Life—Zhizn' Isskusstva
Beginnings—Nachala
Berlin Newsletter—Berlinskii Listok
Business—Delo
Candle and Diary of a Writer—Svetoch i Dnevnik Pisatelia
Caucasus—Kavkaz
Chains—Zvenia
Church Slavonic Newsletter—Tser-kovno-Slavianskii Vestnik
Contemporary Life—Sovremennaia Zhizn'
Day—Den'
Epoch—Epokha
The Evening—Vecher
Family Evenings—Semeinye Vechera
The Fatherland Notes—Otechestvennye Zapiski
Goodness—Dobro
History Archive—Istoricheskii Arkhiv
The History Herald—Istoricheskii Vest-nik
The Library for Reading—Biblioteka dlia chteniia
The Light—Ogoniok
The Literary Herald—Vestnik Liter-atury
Moscow—Moskva
Moscow Daily—Moskovskii Ezhenedel-nik
Moscow News—Moskovskie Vedomosti

New Moscow—Novaia Moskva
New People—Novyi Liudi
New Times—Novoe Vremia
New World—Novyi Mir
News—Novosti
Observer—Nabliudatel'
The Odessa Herald—Odesskii Vestnik
The Odessa Newsletter—Odesskii Lis-tok
The Order—Poriadok
Past Times—Byloe
The Petersburg Newsletter—Peter-burgskii Listok
Petersburg Newspaper—Peterburgskaia Gazeta
The Polar Star—Poliarnaia Zvezda
Problems of Literature—Voprosy Liter-atury
The Puzzle—Rebus
The Red Field—Krasnaia Niva
The Resurrection—Vozrozhdenie
Review of Russian Theater—Biruch Petrogradskikh Teatrov
Rumors—Molva
Russia—Rus'
Russian Archive—Russkii Arkhiv
The Russian Herald—Russkii Vestnik
The Russian Past—Russkoe Proshloe
Russian Reading—Russkoe Chtenie
The Russian Review—Russkoe Obozre-nie
The Russian Sun—Solntse Rossii
Siberia—Sibir'
Siberian Archives—Sibirskii Arkhiv
The Siberian Light—Sibirskie Ogni
Speech—Rech'

The Star—Zvezda
Stock Exchange News—Birzhevye Vedomosti
The Steppes—Stepnoi Krai
The Tomsk Newsletter—Tomskii Listok

Toys—Igrushechka
Turkestan News—Turkestanskie Vedomosti
Voice from the Past—Golos Minuvshego

SELECTED ANNOTATED BIBLIOGRAPHY

This bibliography lists primarily rare Russian publications used as major source material for this book. It is based on the three major bibliographies on Dostoevsky, by Anna Dostoevskaya (1913), Belov (1964 and 1967) and Leatherbarrow (1981 and 1991), which together include more than 3,000 monographs, articles and essays on Dostoevsky. About 100 of the most revealing memoirs of Dostoevsky's contemporaries have been selected for inclusion here. Less than 10 percent of this material was published in English. About 80 percent was published between 1881 and 1935 in rare publications or ephemeral periodicals.

For further information on sources, see the bibliographic compilation in the section of this book titled "History of the Dostoevsky Archive in Russia" (pp. 33–41), the lists of Works Cited at the end of the Preface (pp. 5–6), and individual citations accompanying extracts throughout the text.

Abeldiaev, V. "Pamiati Dostoevskogo" ("In Memoria of Dostoevsky"), *Moskovskie Vedomosti* (*Moscow News*) January 29, 1891: 1.
  Presents a brief report about the huge procession at D.'s funeral and D.'s importance as the greatest Russian novelist.

Akhsharumov, D.D. *Iz moikh vospominanii* (*From My Memoirs*). St. Petersburg, 1905, pp. 100–113.
  Recollects the literary atmosphere in St. Petersburg in the late 1840s, at the time when D. started his literary career.

Aksakov, I.S. "Pis'mo o moskovskikh prazdnikakh po povodu otkrytiia pamiatnika Pushkinu" ("A Letter About the Festival Dedicated to the Opening of the Pushkin Monument in Moscow"), *Russkii Arkhiv* (*Russian Archive*) 2 (1891): 93–98.
  Reports on the emotional and prophetic speech made by D. at the Pushkin Festival and the significance of this speech in understanding the Russian national identity.

    . "Primechanie k rechi Maikova, prochitannoe O. Millerom na sobranii Slavianskogo Bogotvoritel'nogo obshchestva" ("Some Remarks to the Maikov's Speech Made by O. Miller at the Meeting of the Slavic Charity Society"), *Rus'* (*Russia*) 18, March 14, 1881: 14–15.
  Comments on the meeting of the Russian Charity Society dedicated to D. and discusses D.'s importance as a well-respected social figure who formed Russian public opinion.

348   *Selected Annotated Bibliography*

Alchevskaia, Ch. D. *Peredumannoe i perezhitoe. Dnevniki, pis'ma, vospominaniia* ("The Things That I Have Seen and Experienced: Daybooks, Letters and Memoirs"). Moscow, 1912, pp. 73–81.
    A Russian women's rights activist visited D. in his study in St. Petersburg in the late 1870s. She left recollections about D.'s manner of talking to his visitors, his views on social, literary and women's questions, his appearance and his apartment.

Alexandrov, Anatoly Alexandrovich. "Fyodor Mikhailovich Dostoevsky (stranichka vospominanii)" ["F.M. Dostoevsky: A Page from the Memoirs"]. *Svetoch i dnevnik pisatelia* (*Candle and Diary of a Writer*) 1 (1913): 53–56.
    Alexandrov recollects his brief meeting with D. when as a student he had medical treatment at the water resort in Staraya Russa, where D. used to spend his summers in the late 1870s.

Alexandrov, Mikhail Alexandrovich. "Dostoevsky v vospominaniiakh tipografskogo naborshika" ("Dostoevsky in the Memoirs of a Publishing House Worker"), *Russkaia Starina* (*The Russian Past*) 4 (1892): 117–207; 5 (1892): 293–336.
    The author provides a detailed account of the many years he spent working in close association with D. while preparing his manuscripts for publication. Alexandrov was a technical worker at the several major publishing houses in St. Petersburg which published D.'s novels and *A Writer's Diary*. He describes D.'s attitude concerning his manuscripts and stresses his demanding yet very amicable relationship with all members of the publishing staff.

Annenkov, P. *Literaturnye vospominaniia* (*Literary Memoirs*). Moscow: Goslitizdat, 1960, pp. 282–284.
    Contains an account of D.'s first literary success, when he became famous practically overnight after his friend Grigorovich together with the poet and publisher Nekrasov read the manuscript of his first novel, *Poor People*. The same story was told by D. himself in *A Writer's Diary* and by Grigorovich in his *Memoirs*, but Annenkov reveals many important additional details, for example, the admiration of D.'s work by other writers. Annenkov, a prominent writer of the time, was a close friend of Vissarion Belinsky. He describes one of his visits to Belinsky and the admiration for D. expressed by this major journalist and Russian literary critic.

Arepiev, I. "Iz vospominanii o Fyodore Mikhailoviche Dostoevskom" ("From the Memoirs About Fyodor Mikhailovich Dostoevsky") *Peterburgskii Listok* (*The Petersburg Newsletter*) 22, January 31, 1881.
    Arepiev, in this short journalistic piece written on the day of D.'s funeral, remembers his brief meeting with D. during the last period of D.'s life and stresses his huge popularity among Russian intelligentsia.

Arepiev, N. "Na pokhoronakh Nekrasova" ("At Nekrasov's Funeral") *Vestnik Litaratury* (*Problems of Literature*) 12 (1921): 7.
    Arepiev, in this concise piece from his memoirs, recollects about D.'s speech at Nekrasov's funeral and the great impact he had on the young generation of Russian writers.

Barsukova, A. "Pis'mo o pushkinskoi rechi Dostoevskogo" ("A Letter About the Pushkin Speech by Dostoevsky"), in *Zvenia* (*Chains*), vol. 1. Moscow, 1932, pp. 478–481.
    Supplies an exciting report of the impact that D.'s celebrated Pushkin speech

made on Russian students. D. was already very popular among the monarchists and Slavophiles, but after his glorification of Russian people and praise of Russian youth in this speech, he was received enthusiastically by the younger generation as well.

Belousov, I.A. "Literaturnaia sreda. Vospominaniia" ("Literary Life: Memoirs"), in *Nikitinskie Subbotniki* (*The Nikitin Saturdays*). Moscow, 1928, p. 6

Belousov recollects D.'s huge popularity among Russian writers and the public during the last years of his life.

Bobchev, S.S. "Informatsiia o torzhestvakh po povodu osviashcheniia pamiatnika Pushkinu v Moskve" ("Information About the Opening of the Pushkin Monument in Moscow"), *Godishnik na Sofiiskiia universitet* (*The Annual Proceedings of the Sofia University*) vol. LIV, Sofia, 1961, pp. 813–815.

Bobchev, a Bulgarian scholar and journalist, describes in detail the Pushkin Festival in Moscow in 1880, commenting on the speeches made by D. and Turgenev.

Boborykin, P.D. *Za polveka. Moi vospominaniia* (*Half a Century: My Memoirs*). Moscow: Zemlia i fabrika, 1929, pp. 212, 304–305.

Presents an inside view of the world of Russian journalism and literature. D. was a very good journalist but a bad editor, because he had a difficult character and it was hard for his colleagues to deal with him, working at the same journal. In 1863 Boborykin invited D. to work on the journal which he edited, *The Library for Reading*.

Borozdin, A. "Pamiati F.M. Dostoevskogo. Iz vospominanii" ("To the Memory of F.M. Dostoevsky: From My Memoirs") *Den'* (*Day*) 27, January 28, 1916.

In this short newspaper article Borozdin remembers the feeling of great loss he experienced after D.'s death.

Brailovsky, S.N. "Dostoevsky v Omskoi katorge i poliaki" ("Dostoevsky in the Omsk Prison and the Poles"), *Istoricheskii Vestnik* (*The History Herald*) 4 (1908): 189–198.

Brailovsky describes D.'s encounters with the other political prisoners during his incarceration in Omsk Fortress in Siberia—specifically with a group of Polish officers who were sent to the Russian prison after their fight for Polish independence.

Briullov, B. and P.A. Briullov. "Vstrecha s F.M. Dostoevskim" ("Meetings with F.M. Dostoevsky") *Nachala* (*Beginnings*) 2 (1922): 264–265.

Comments on Dostoevsky's admiration of Italian art, Raphael in particular, and his critical and prejudiced attitude toward the German culture.

Bukva (I.F. Vasilevsky). "Literaturnye znamenitosti na Pushkinskom prazdnike v Moskve v 1880 godu" ("Famous Literary Artists at the Pushkin Festival in Moscow in 1880") *Odesskii Listok* (*The Odessa Newsletter*) 134, May 25, 1899.

Provides a brief account about the celebrities who were present at the Pushkin Festival in Moscow and D.'s famous speech.

Bykov, P.V. "Pamiati proniknovennogo serdtseeda. Iz lichnykh vospominanii" ("To the Memory of the Man Who Broke Many Hearts: From My Memoirs"), *Vestnik Literatury* (*The Literary Herald*) 2 (1921): 4–5.

Bykov highly appreciates D.'s understanding of the human soul, the Russian soul in particular.

_____. *Siluety dalekogo proshlogo* (*Shadows from the Past*). Moscow: Zemlia i fabrika, 1930, pp. 51–59.
        Bykov describes the support D. gave to young writers and his attentive attitude toward other literary works.

Chernyshevsky, N.G. "Moi svidaniia s Dostoevskim" ("My Meetings with Dostoevsky"), in N.G. Chernyshevsky, *Polnoe sobranie sochinenii* [*Complete Works*] Vol. 1. Moscow: Goslitizdat, 1939, pp. 777–779.
        Chernyshevsky, a Russian socialist and journalist, met D. briefly in 1862 when D. visited him with a personal request to stop the organizers of huge fires in St. Petersburg (that is, revolutionary terrorists). Chernyshevsky wrote very ironic memoirs about this visit, in which he almost called D. a madman.

Davydov, V.N. *Rasskaz o proshlom* (*A Story from the Past*). Moscow: Academia, 1931, pp. 379–380.
        Davydov, as a professional actor, did not hold a very high opinion of D.'s literary reading, though he admired him as a person and a great writer. He depicted his attendance at D.'s funeral with actress Maria Savina.

Debu, I.M. "Vospominaniia" ("Memoirs") in O. Miller. *Biografiia, pis'ma i zametki iz zapisnoi knizhki Dostoevskogo* (*Biography, Letters and Notes from the Dostoevsky Notebooks*). St. Petersburg, 1883, pp. 90–91.
        Debu, a member of the secret socialist circle, spoke highly of D.'s behavior during the investigation of the Petrashevsky case.

De Vogue, M. "F.M. Dostoevsky kak psikholog pod sudom frantsuzkoi kritiki" ("F.M. Dostoevsky as a Psychologist: Notes by a French Literary Critic"), *Epokha* (*Epoch*) 2 (1886): 93–96.
        De Vogue reveals D.'s opinions of Russian people and Russian literature from the viewpoint of a West European literary critic who had lengthy conversations with him concerning the unique role of Russian culture in Europe.

De Vollan, Count G. "Ocherki proshlogo. F.M. Dostoevsky" ("Sketches from the Past: F.M. Dostoevsky"), *Golos Minuvshego.* (*The Voice of the Past*) 4 (1914): 123–125.
        Describes in a rather emotional way his brief meeting with D. at a literary salon and comments on D.'s criticism of Western culture and praise of Russia's national roots.

Dmitrieva, V.I. *Tak bylo. Put' moei zhizni* (*It Happened. The Story of My Life*). Moscow, 1930, pp. 183–187.
        Dmitrieva, a professional Russian revolutionary, was rather critical of D.'s support for the monarchy.

Dostoevskaya, A.G. *Dnevnik, 1867 god.* (*Diary, 1867*). Moscow, 1923.
_____. *Vospominaniia* (*Memoirs*). Moscow: Gosizdat, 1925.
        In these two volumes Anna Dostoevskaya describes in detail the fourteen years she spent with D. as his second wife. Major events include the story of her acquaintance with him, his proposal, her work as a stenographer on his novels, their trip abroad and D.'s funeral.

_____. "Pis'mo k Strakhovu ot 21 oktiabria 1883 goda" ("A Letter to Strakhov, Dated October 21, 1883") in L. Grossman, *Zhizn' i trudy F.M. Dostoevskogo*

(*The Chronology of F.M. Dostoevsky's Life and Works*). Moscow: Academia, 1935, p. 352.

D.'s widow supplies a detailed picture of D.'s agony and death.

_____. "Vospominaniia" ("Memoirs"), in A. Izmalov "U A.G. Dostoevskoi" ("A Visit to A.G. Dostoevskaya"), *Birzhevie Vedomosti* (*Stock Exchange News*), January 28, 1916: 15350.

Very personal and emotional memoirs about her late husband.

_____. "Vospominaniia" ("Memoirs"), in Z. Kovrigina, "Poslednie mesiatsy Dostoevskoi" ("The Last Months of A. Dostoevskaya"), collected in A. Dolinin, ed., *F.M. Dostoevsky. Stat'i i materialy* (*F.M. Dostoevsky: Articles and Materials*). Moscow, 1924, Vol. 2, pp. 583–590.

After D.'s death, his widow became a rather wealthy woman from the publication of her husband's works. After the Red revolution in 1917–18, however, she lived in poverty, and died in Yalta, a small resort town in Crimea. She passionately loved D. to the last days of her life.

_____. "Vospominaniia" ("Memoirs"), in O. Miller, "Dom i kabinet Dostoevskogo" ("The House and the Office of Dostoevsky"), *Istoricheskii Vestnik* (*The History Herald*) 3 (1887): 572–574.

D.'s wife recollects his admiration of the *Sistine Madonna* by Raphael, his favorite work of art.

Dostoevskaya, L.F. *Dostoevsky v izobrazhenii ego docheri* (*Dostoevsky in the Reminiscences of His Daughter*). Moscow: Gosizdat, 1922.

D.'s daughter's highly personal account of her father's last years describes the members of the family, their friends and frequent visitors to their home. D. dearly loved his children and spent most of his free time with them.

Dostoevsky, A.M. "Eshche o bolezni F.M. Dosevskogo" *Novoe Vremia* ("Some News About Dostoevsky's Illness"), (*New Times*) March 1, 1881, No. 1798.

D.'s younger brother suggests possible explanations of D.'s illness and death, which he attributes to nervous stress connected with a dispute over his aunt's inheritance.

_____. *Vospominaniia* (*Memoirs*). Leningrad: Izdatelstvo pisatelei v Leningrade, 1930.

Andrei spent his childhood together with Fyodor in the Moscow Shelter for the Poor. His memoirs are the only firsthand sources of information about D.'s childhood. After graduating from the Military Academy, Andrei was arrested by mistake in connection with the Petrashevsky case but was released almost instantly. In this part of his *Memoirs* he vividly describes how the arrest of the Petrashevsky Circle concluded and what happened to the convicts (D. among them) in the first few days after their arrest and during the investigation. He also presents a detailed inside account of Russian prisons.

Feoktistov N. "Propavshie pis'ma Dostoevskogo" ("Several Lost Letters by Dostoevsky"), *Sibirskie ogni* (*The Siberian Light*) 2 (1928): 122–125.

Tells a story about D.'s love for a peasant woman in Siberia during his service in the army.

Filosofova, A.P. "O Dostoevskom" (About Dostoevsky"), in *Sbornik pamiati A.P. Filosofovoi* (*A Collection of Articles Dedicated to A.P. Filosofova*). Vol. 1. St. Petersburg, 1915, pp. 258–259.

Filosofova often invited D. her house in the 1870s to participate in her literary salons. She left memoirs about the huge effect D. produced on his listeners through readings of his literary works.

Firsov, N. "V redaktsii zhurnala *Russkoe slovo*. Iz vospominaniia shestidesiatnika" ("In the Editorial Office of *The Russian Language Journal* from the memoirs of a man from the generation of the sixties"), *Istoricheskii Vestnik* (*The History Herald*) 6 (1914): 897–899.
    Comments about D.'s journalistic activity.

Fon-Fokht, N. "K biografii Dostoevskogo" ("Some Materials for Dostoevsky Biography"), *Istoricheskii Vestnik* (*The History Herald*) 12 (1901): 1023–1033.
    Fon-Fokht was a close friend of Vera Dostoevskaya, D.'s sister, and was educated in her home with her children. He recollects D.'s social activity in the late 1860s, his friendship with the young people, his stays at the Ivanovs' summer cottage and the process of creation of *Crime and Punishment*.

Gaevsky, V.P. "Rech' na sobranii chlenov Literaturnogo Fonda 2 fevralia 1881" ("A Speech Made at the Meeting of the Russian Literary Fund on February 2, 1881"), *Novoe Vremia* (*New Times*) 1773 (February 3, 1881).
    Gaevsky made a speech dedicated to the memory of D. as the greatest Russian writer of his time.

Garshin, E.M. "Vospominaniia o I.S. Turgeneve" ("Memoirs About I.S. Turgenev"), *Istoricheskii Vestnik* (*The History Herald*) 11 (1883): 386–388.
    Garshin meditates on the complicated relationship which existed between D. and Turgenev, two of the best Russian novelists of the nineteenth century.

Gerasimov, B. "F.M. Dostoevsky v Semipalatinske" ("F.M. Dostoevsky in Semipalatinsk"), *Sibirskie Ogni* (*The Siberian Light*) 3 (1926): 135–136; 4 (1924): 143–144.
    Determines several minor details about the exact places of D.'s stay in Semipalatinsk, Siberia, during his service in the army.

_____. "K pebyvaniiu Dostoevskogo v Semipalatinske." ("Dostoevsky's stay in Semipalatinsk"), *Sibirskii Arkhiv* (*Siberian Archives*) 1 (1913): 5.
    Gerasimov found old citizens of Semipalatinsk, a small town in Siberia, who remembered D.'s stay there during his service in the army.

Gnedich, P.P. *Kniga zhisni. Vospominaniia. 1855–1918 gody* (*The Book of My Life: Memoirs, 1855–1918*). Leningrad: Priboi, 1929, pp. 121–122, 130–133.
    Remembers the artistic and literary circles of St. Petersburg in the 1860s and 1870s, providing many names and details, and comments on D.'s active participation in artistic and social life.

Gradovsky, G.K. *Itogi: 1862–1907* (*The Final Results: 1862–1907*). Kiev, 1908, pp. 16–18.
    Gradovsky depicts D.'s participation in the Zasulich case when the famous writer, in his articles, defended a woman terrorist who attempted to assassinate the St. Petersburg chief of police. He claimed that participation in a trial could be a good lesson for the young woman. Due to D.'s passionate articles and his activity as a public figure, Zasulich was found not guilty.

Grigorovich, D.V. *Literaturnye Vospominaniia* (*Literary Memoirs*). Moscow: Goslitizdat, 1961, pp. 46–49, 86–93.

Grigorovich spent several years with D. as a schoolmate at the Engineering Academy. He recollects the early period of D.'s literary career, when he displayed his early interest in literature. Grigorovich published his first literary work, "Sketches of St. Petersburg: The Street Organ-Grinders," several months before D.'s first serious work and was the first person to read D.'s first novel. He subsequently showed it to Nekrasov, his publisher and a famous Russian poet, who immediately recognized the young D.'s talent. In January 1881, Grigorovich was the coordinator of the huge procession of about 50,000 people which accompanied D.'s funeral.

Grossman, L. *The Chronology of F.M. Dostoevsky's Life and Works* (*Zhizn' i trudy F.M. Dostoevskogo*). Moscow: Academia, 1935.

_____. *Dostoevsky: A Biography*. Moscow: Molodaia guardia, 1962.
 One of the best biographies written for a lay reader.

_____. *Seminars on Dostoevsky* (*Seminarii po Dostoevskomu*). Moskow: Gosudarstuennoe izdatelstvo, 1923.
 Contains many documentary materials and a detailed bibliography.

Ianovsky, S.D. "Bolezn' Dostoevskogo" ("Dostoevsky's Illness"), *Novoe Vremia* (*New Times*), February 24, 1881: 1793.
 Ianovsky, as D.'s personal doctor for many years, provides a story about one of D.'s first epileptic seizures, which occurred during a walk through the streets of St. Petersburg.

Ivanova, M.A. "Vospominaniia" ("Memoirs"), in V. Nechaeva "Iz literatury o Dostoevskom. Poezdka v Darovoe" ("From the Literature About Dostoevsky: A Visit to Darovoe Village"), *Novyi Mir* (*New Times*), February 14, 1893: 12.
 Depicts the summer vacations the author spent in Lublino in 1886 at the summer estate of her mother (D.'s sister). D. was very close to his sister, Vera Ivanova, and he often visited this summer estate. It was there that he wrote the major part of *Crime and Punishment*.

Kamenetskaya, M.V. "Vstrechi s Dostoevskim" ("Meetings with Dostoevsky"), in *Sbornik pamiati A.P. Filosofovoi* (*A Collection of Articles Dedicated to A.P. Filosofova*), Vol. 1. St. Petersburg, 1915, pp. 258–266.
 Kamenetskaya, who was a teenage girl when D. frequented the literary salon of her mother, A. Filosofova, comments how he ignored and interrupted other speakers when they did not interest him. At the same time he was a very attentive and caring friend to those people he knew well.

Kashkin, N. "Iz zapisok" ("From the Notebook"), in *Petrashevtsy v vospominanaiiakh sovremennikov* (*The Petrashevsky Society in the Memoirs of the Contemporaries*). Moscow, 1926, pp. 193–198.
 Recollects the most dramatic period in D.'s life, his involvement with the secret socialist circle.

Katarygin, V. "Dostoevsky i muzyka" ("Dostoevsky and Music") *Zhizn' isskusstva* (*The Art Life*) 819 (1921): 3.
 D. passionately loved classical music, and he participated in several musical concerts by reading pieces from his works.

Katz, N.F. "Vospominaniia. Zametka o prebyvanii Dostoevskogo v Semipalatinske" ("Memoirs: Notes About Dostoevsky's Stay in Semipalatinsk"), *Stepnoi Krai* (*The Steppes*), March 17, 1896: 21.

A journalist researched D.'s stay in Siberia and discovered some interesting facts of certain places connected with his stay in this provincial Russian town.

Kaufman, A.K. "Vengerov i ego arkhiv" ("Vengerov and His Archive"), *Solntse Rosii (The Russian Sun)* 351 (1916): 4.
  Professor Vengerov collected the biggest private archive in Russia of D.'s letters and manuscripts.

Khranevich, V. "Dostoevsky po vospominaniiam ssyl'nogo poliaka" ("Dostoevsky in the Reminiscences of a Pole in Exile"), *Russkaia Starina (The Russian Past)* 2 (1910): 367–377, 605–621. Supplements Brailovsky (1908).

Koni, A.F. *Nekrasov i Dostoevsky. Po lichnym vospominaniiam. (Nekrasov and Dostoevsky. My memoirs).* St. Petersburg, 1921.
  Koni left detailed memoirs about the complex relationship existing between D. and Nekrasov. He also recollects his numerous meetings with D. at the Russian Supreme Court.

_____. "Vsterchi s Dostoevskim." ("Meetings with Dostoevsky"), *Vestnik Literatury (The Literary Herald)* 2 (1912): 2–8.
  Koni, as a member of the Supreme Court, was often consulted by D. on different legal matters while D. was working on his novels, which are often based on criminal plots. He provided D. with material on criminal matters, consulted with other experts, and took D. to talk to convicts. The day after D.'s funeral, Koni read his famous speech, "Dostoevsky as a Criminologist," at St. Petersburg University.

Korolenko, V.G. "Pokhorony Nekrasova i rech' Dostoevskogo na ego mogile" ("Nekrasov's Funeral and Dostoevsky's Speech on His Grave"), V.G. Korolenko, *Sobranie sochinenii (Works).* Moscow: Gosizdat, 1953, pp. 197–200.
  Korolenko was greatly influenced by D. when he heard D.'s speech at Nekrasov's funeral at the end of 1877. This article in which he meditates about the social position of the literary artist was inspired by D.'s speech about Russian literature.

Kovalevskaya, S.V. *Vospominaniia i pis'ma (Memoirs and Letters).* Moscow: Academy Press, 1961, pp. 102–121, 122–132.
  Sofia Kovalevskaya describes in her memoirs D.'s proposal to her sister Anna. Anna refused him, being afraid of the significant age difference. This event happened during a very hard period for D., between the death of his first wife and his second marriage.

Kovalevsky, P.M. *Stikhi i vospominaniia (Poems and Memoirs).* St. Petersburg, 1912, pp. 275–278.
  Discloses very interesting details of the relationship between D. and other writers of the time. Being a writer, an organizer of the Russian Literary Fund and a diplomat, Kovalevsky was familiar with everything going on in the Russian literary world. He was very much surprised to find out that Nekrasov, a leading poet and a publisher, refused to publish D.'s novels after his return from Siberia. As a result of this, D. had to start his own literary journal, but his relationships with many other writers remained rather tense.

Letkova-Sultanova, K. "O F.M. Dostoevskom. Iz vospominanii" ("About F.M. Dostoevsky: From My Memoirs"), *Zvenia (Chains),* vol. 1, Moscow: Academia, 1932, pp. 459–477.

Letkova visited a literary salon in St. Petersburg where D. was a regular guest. D. spoke about his literary work and future plans, as well as about recent political issues, such as the Balkan war and the unification of the Slavic people. He was very popular among the Russian student youth, who attended his funeral in large numbers and considered him to be "a writer of genius."

Librovich, S.F. *Na knizhnom postu. Vospominaniia. Zapiski. Dokumenty* ("My Work with Books: Memoirs, Notes, Documents"). St. Petersburg: Wolf, 1916, p. 42.

Librovich shares his recollections about the literary world of St. Petersburg and the famous Wolf Book Store and publishing house, where he worked for many years and where D. used to talk with other writers.

Liubimov, D. "Iz vospominanii. Rech' Dostoevskogo na Pushkinskikh torzhestvakh" ("From the Memoirs: Dostoevsky's Speech at the Pushkin Festival"), *Voprosy Literatury (Problems of Literature)* 7 (1961): 156–166.

Dmitry Liubimov was present at D.'s famous Pushkin speech, calling it "the greatest speech I ever heard in my entire life." Dmitry was Nikolai Liubimov's son, and Nikolai was one of the organizers of the Pushkin celebrations on June 8, 1880, in the Hall of Russian Nobility in Moscow.

Maikov, A.N. "Rech' na torzhestvennom obshchem sobranii St. Petersburgskogo Slavianskogo Bogotvoritelnogo Obshchestva" ("Speech Made at the General Meeting of the St. Petersburg Branch of the Slavic Charity Society"), *Rus' (Russia)* 18 (1881): 14–15.

Maikov, as one of D.'s closest personal friends, made a long speech about their relationship at the meeting of the Russian Charity Society. He also spoke about D.'s religious beliefs, his stay in prison and his explanation of his talent as an act of the Holy Spirit.

Makarov, I. "Vospominaniia" ("Memoirs"), quoted in D. Stonov "Sel'tso Darovoe" ("Village Darovoe"), *Krasnaia Niva (The Red Field)* 16 (1926): 19.

Makarov provides additional detail about the tragic death of D.'s father in Darovoe village. At the time the article was written, in 1926, some witnesses of this crime were still alive.

Markevich, A.I. "Pamiati Dostoevskogo. Rech', proiznesennaia na torzhestvennom zasedanii Odesskogo Slavianskogo Bogotvoritelnogo Obshchestva" ("Speech Made at the Special Meeting of the Odessa Branch of the Slavic Charity Society"), *Rus' (Russia)*, February 10, 1881: 32.

In his speech, made several months after D.'s death, Markevich praised D. as an active social figure and a highly talented national writer.

Markevich, B. "Neskolko slov o konchine Dostoevskogo" ("Several Words About the Death of Dostoevsky"), *Moskovskie Vedomosti (The Moscow News)*, February 1, 1881: 32–33.

In his detailed memoirs, Markevich leaves one of the most terrible depictions of D.'s agony and death. He also describes in detail the grief of D.'s wife and children.

Martianov, P.K. "Na perelome veka" ("At the End of the Century"), P.K. Martianov, *Dela i liudi veka (Major Events and People of the Century)*. St. Petersburg, 1896, pp. 263–270, 276, 281–282.

Martianov describes D.'s life in prison, his alienation from other prisoners and his animosity towards S. Durov, his former friend and fellow member of the Petrashevsky Circle. However, as a famous writer and a member of the Russian nobility, D. received all possible support and understanding from the prison doctor, and sympathy and respect from the prison guard officers.

Merezhkovsky, D.S. "Avtobiograficheskaia zametka" ("Autobiographical notes"), in S.A. Vengerov, ed., *Russkiaia Literatura XX veka* (*Russian Literature, Twentieth Century*), Vol 1. Moscow, 1914, p. 291.
   Merezhkovsky, while a college student, met D. briefly late in the writer's life.

_____. *Tolstoi i Dostoevsky. Zhizn' i tvorchestvo* (*Tolstoy and Dostoevsky: Life and Works*). St. Petersburg, 1909, p. 132.
   A long chapter devoted to D. stresses the importance of D.'s works in the literary process in Russia and gives detailed analyses of D.'s major novels.

Meshchersky, V.P. *Moi vospominaniia* (*My Memoirs*). St. Petersburg, 1898, pp. 175–182.
   Meshchersky, as a senior state official, represented the most conservative wing of the monarchist movement. He considered D. "the most passionate monarchist in Russia." This estimate may be accepted with a certain degree of caution, because Prince Meshchersky could exaggerate D.'s praise of monarchism. Nevertheless, such memoirs are sensational in a way, because they depict new features of the great novelist who ardently supported the existing government in the seventies.

Miliukov, A.P. *Literaturnye vstrechi i znakomstva* (*Literary Meetings and Friends*). St. Petersburg: Suvorin Press, 1890, pp. 168–249.
   Miliukov was a close friend of D. and, together with D.'s brother Mikhail, saw the writer off to Siberia from the prison in St. Petersburg. He was also the only old friend who met D. on his return to the Russian capital ten years later. Miliukov gave in his memoirs a detailed account of D.'s involvement in the Petrashevsky Circle. D. supported a rather moderate position as compared to other members of the circle, his major concern being the abolition of serfdom in Russia. According to Miliukov, D. never supported the idea of overthrowing the existing Russian government and never criticized the institution of monarchy. Miliukov stressed that the Petrashevsky Circle was neither a secret socialist society nor an organization of any kind, but simply a group of young men who discussed literature and topics "of social interest." Besides his unique comments concerning one of the most tragic periods in D.'s life, Miliukov inserts in his memoirs the story of D.'s arrest, presented by D. himself and written down in the album of Miliukov's daughter. In this story D., being the artist that he was, described his own arrest in a humorous, somewhat ironic tone. Miliukov was D.'s very close associate and a personal friend of both Dostoevsky brothers in the late 1850s and early 1860s, when they published their journals *Time* and *Epoch*, and in his memoirs he gives additional details about D.'s personal features as a writer and a personal friend.

Miller, O. *Biografiia....* (*Biography...*). [See Debu, I.M. for complete title of this book] St. Petersburg, 1883, p. 1–74.
   Miller wrote the first biography of D. in 1883, combining his own memoirs with documentary material and unique stories told to him by D.'s friends. He suggests several explanations for D.'s involvement in the Petrashevsky Circle, incorporating detailed excerpts from many rare, ephemeral, and often invaluable sources, such as court documents containing the Tsar's remarks in the margins, etc.

Nikolaevsky, K. "Tovarishchi Dostoevskogo po katorge" ("Dostoevsky's Friends in the Prison"), *Istoricheskii Vestnik (The History Herald)* 1 (1898): 219–224.
Nikolaevsky comments on the other, less famous prisoners who were incarcerated with D. and who were described in his later works.

Opochinin, E.N. "Besedy s Dostoevskim" ("Talking to Dostoevsky"), *Zvenia (Chains)*, vol. 6. Moscow, 1936, pp. 457–484.
Opochinin remembers D. as a colleague and fellow writer. During their meetings, he and D. discussed other writers, including Flaubert, Viazemsky and Turgenev. Being a very religious person, D. enjoyed talking about God and the Holy Spirit.

Pal'm, A.I. "Rech' proiznesennaia na mogile Dostoevskogo" ("The Speech Made at Dostoevsky's Funeral"), *Novoe Vremia (New Times)*, February 2, 1881: 1772.

Panaev, I.I. *Literaturnye vospominaniia (Literary Memoirs)*. Moscow: Goslitizdat, 1950, pp. 308–309.
Ivan Panaev was one of the first literary figures of St. Petersburg, together with Grigorovich, Belinsky and Nekrasov, to read *Poor People*, D.'s first novel. Panaev relates the exciting story of D.'s instant recognition as a great writer.

Panaeva (Golovacheva), A. *Vospominaniia (Memoirs)*. Moscow: Goslitizdat, 1956, pp. 143–146, 175, 177–178.
Panaeva writes that the young D. during his first appearance at literary salons in St. Petersburg in the 1840s, had an overestimated opinion of himself and that he treated his colleagues, other young writers and journalists in a somewhat snobbish manner. Naturally, this attitude engendered antipathy among most regular members of the Panaeva literary salon; consequently they wrote epigrams and anecdotes about D. and started to mock and laugh at him. As a result, D. broke off all relations with this literary circle and, soon afterwards, joined another group of young men, namely the Petrashevsky secret socialist circle. Its politically minded young members discussed questions of censorship, the abolition of serfdom, and the overthrow of the existing government.

Panteleev, L.F. *Vospominaniia (Memoirs)*. Moscow: Goslitizdat, 1958, pp. 225–226.
Recalls D.'s friendly attitude toward the young, beginning authors to whom he gave his unconditional support.

Pavlov, I.P. "Pis'ma k neveste" ("Letters to the Bride"), *(Moscow)* 10 (1959): 175–178.
A Russian Nobel prize winner in physiology and medicine in 1904, Pavlov was present as a student at D.'s funeral in 1881, and described this event in lengthy letters to his bride. He was impressed most by the huge number of people at the funeral, most of them students and Russian intellectuals.

Perov, V. "Pis'ma k Tretiakovu" ("Letters to Tretiakov"), in I. Eiges, *Matrialy iz arkhiva P.M. Tretiakova (Materials from the Tretiakov Archives)*. Iskusstvo, 1929, pp. 46–47.
Perov, a famous Russian painter, created one of the best oil portraits of D. In his letters to the Moscow art collector Tretiakov, he admired D. both as a writer and as a person.

Plekhanov, G.V. "Pokhorony Nekrasova" ("Nekrasov's Funeral"), in G.V. Plekhanov, *Literatura i estetika (Literature and Aesthetics)*. Moscow: Goslitizdat, 1958, pp. 206–209.

Plekhanov adds a social element to his reserved appraisal of Nekrasov and
D.'s speech at his grave dedicated to the greatest Russian writers and poets.

Polivanova, M.A. "Zapis' o poseshchenii F.M. Dostoevskogo" ("Notes About a
Visit to Dostoevsky"), *Golos Minuvshego* (*Voice from the Past*) 3 (1923): 29–38.
In 1880 Maria Polivanova visited D. in his hotel immediately after his famous
Pushkin speech, in which he spoke about the moral values of Russian people, his
admiration of Pushkin and his further literary plans.

Popov, I.I. *Minuvshee i perezhitoe. Iz vospominanii* (*The Things I Have Experienced: From the Memoirs*). Moscow: Academia, 1933, pp. 87–91.
Ivan Popov, among other students, was present at D.'s funeral. He describes
the huge procession after the funeral in which representatives of all social groups of
Russian society were present. D. was admired by all: his writer colleagues, senior
officials, simple Russian people and even the revolutionary youth whom he strongly
criticized in his works.

Posse, V.A. *Perezhitoe i produmannoe. Molodost'. 1864–1894* (*Meditations About
the Past: Youth, 1864–1894*). Leningrad, 1933, pp. 72–82.
Vladimir Posse was present at literary readings by D. When D. read from
his works, he "addressed himself not to the reading audience, but directly to suffering
souls." Posse was greatly moved by the huge procession of people at D.'s funeral.

Pribytkova, V. "Vospominaniia o Dostoevskom" ("Memoirs About Dostoevsky"),
Rebus (*The Puzzle*) 25 (1885): 230–231; 26 (1885): 240–245.
Pribytkova, as an activist of the Russian Society of Spiritualism, tried to con-
vince D. to visit spiritualistic meetings and discussed these questions in her numer-
ous conversations with D. in the late seventies. As a result of his contact with
Pribytkova, D. published an article in *A Writer's Diary* about Russian spiritualists.

Putsykovich, V.F. "O Dostoevskom. Iz vospominaii o nem" ("About Dostoevsky: From My Memoirs About Him"), *Novoe Vremia* (*New Times*) January 16, 1910: 22.
Putsykovich recollects his journalistic work with D. and gives a high estimate of D. as a journalist.

_____. "Predskazaniia Dostoevskogo o konstitutsii i revoliutsii v Rosii. Iz moikh
vospominanii" ("Dostoevsky's Predictions About Russian Revolution and
Constitution: From My Memoirs"), *Berlinskii Listok* (*Berlin Newsletter*) January 25, 1906: 2–3.
_____. "Vospomianiia o Dostoevskom" ("Memoirs About Dostoevsky"),
Moskovskie vedomosti (*Moscow News*), January 28, 1910: 22.
In these two short sections of Putsykovich's memoirs, D. is presented as a
real prophet who predicted in much detail many changes in Russian society, including in particular the Russian Revolution more than thirty years before the actual event
took place.

Riesenkampf, A.E. "Pis'mo k A.M. Dostoevskomu" ("A Letter to A.M. Dostoevsky") *Novoe Vremia* (*New Times*), March 1, 1881: 1798.
_____. "Vospominaniia o Dostoevskom" ("Memoirs About Dostoevsky"),
in: O Miller. *Biografiia, pis'ma i zametki iz zapisnoi knizhki Dostoevskogo*
(*Biography, Letters and Notes from the Dostoevsky Notebook*). St. Petersburg,
1883, pp. 34–35, 48–53.

Aleksandr Riesenkampf shared an apartment with D. from 1843 to 1845 when D. was working on his first novel, *Poor People*. As a young man D. was a very impractical person and could hardly make ends meet, spending most of his time on creative writing. Several of Dr. Riesenkampf's patients provided D. with important material for his literary work, telling him stories about the life of the poorest classes of St. Petersburg.

Saveliev, A.I. "Vospominaniia o Dostoevskom" ("Memoirs About Dostoevsky"), *Russkaia Starina* (*The Russian Past*) 1–2 (1912): 13–20.

Aleksandr Saveliev, who was an officer at the Military Academy, wrote about D. spending many night hours at the Academy reading books or writing his first literary works in a quiet corner of the military barracks. During the intervals between lectures D. liked to discuss literature with a select circle of friends.

Savina, M.G. "Moe znakomstvo s Turgenevym" ("My Friendship with Turgenev") in A. Koni, ed., *Turgenev i Savina* (*Turgenev and Savina*). St. Petersburg, 1918, pp. 68–69.

According to Savina's personal memoirs, Turgenev was jealous of D.'s huge popularity among the St. Petersburg public during literary concerts.

_____. "Vospominaniia" ("Memoirs"), in A. Koni, ed. *Turgenev i Savina* (*Turgenev and Savina*). St. Petersburg, 1918, p. 80.

Savina, a famous theater actress, described D.'s public appearance at literary concerts when he read excerpts from his novels and received a very warm welcome from the audience.

Semenov Tian-Shansky, P.P. *Detstvo i junost'* (*Childhood and Youth*). St. Petersburg: The Author, 1917, pp. 195–214.

The author was present at D.'s mock execution and greatly affected by it.

_____. *Puteshestvie v Tian'-Shan'* (*Traveling to Tian-Shan*). Moscow: Geografizdat, 1958, pp. 76–77, 134–135.

The author met D. during two of his trips to Semipalatinsk. He wrote down a story of D.'s service in the army after four years in prison, and added another unique story, that of D.'s first marriage, as told by D. himself.

Simonova, L. "Iz vospominanii o Dostoevskom" ("From the Memoirs About Dostoevsky"), *Tserkovno-obschestvennyi vestnik* (*Church and Society Messenger*) 16 (1881): 4–5.

Simonova, one of the first female Russian writers, met with D. around 1876 and remembered him as a "very nervous but kind person." Even at the height of his fame, D. lived in a modest two-bedroom apartment in downtown St. Petersburg, and there he shared with her, as well as with his other visitors, his views on religion, the future of mankind, major criminal events of the time, etc.

Slivitsky, A.M. "Iz moikh vospominanii o Polivanove. Pushkinskie dni" ("From My Memoirs About Polivanov: The Days of the Pushkin Festival"), *Mosvkovskii ezhenedelnik* (*Moscow Weekly*) 46 (1908): 41–45.

Slivitsky assisted Professor Polivanov at the Pushkin Festival in 1880 in Moscow, where D. made his famous speech about the unity of the Russian people, Russian intellectuals in particular. He presented a laurel wreath to D. and met with him at dinner the next day. After this important event D. became the most popular writer in Russia.

Soloviev, V. "Vospominaniia o Dostoevskom" ("Memoirs About Dostoevsky"), *Istoricheskii Vestnik* (*The History Herald*) 4 (1981): 839–853.
Vsevolod Soloviev was D.'s close personal friend, though he was almost thirty years younger than the famous writer. In his memoirs he discussed his acquaintance with D. and gave a good description of D.'s study where D. created his novels. D. was a difficult man in everyday life; he was often in a gloomy mood, and even his close friends suffered from this. D. liked to discuss his literary plans and his social views with his friends.

Stakenshneider, E.A. *Dnevnik i zapiski (1854–1886)* ("Diary and Notes: 1854–1886") Moscow-Leningrad: Academia, 1934, pp. 269–270, 281, 456–465.
Stakenshneider had a literary salon in St. Petersburg in the 1860s amd 1870s which D. often visited. She described him as being "like a fairy-tale," a mysterious old man. At these salons D. exhibited a difficult character, and it took him a long time to start new friendships. He became extremely popular with the Russian youth after the publication of his *Diary* and his last novels.

Strakhov, N.N. "Iz vospominanii o Dostoevskom" ("From the Memoirs About Dostoevsky"), *Semeinye Vechera* (*Family Evenings*), February 1881: 235–248.
Strakhov exposes a very interesting side of D.'s literary activity, namely his work as a journalist and an editor of literary journals. D. considered journalism a social activity, and he dedicated many pages of his writing to the praising of Russian patriotism, his Slavophile views and his analysis of world events, thus influencing Russian public opinion.

Suslova, A.P. *Gody blizosti s Dostoevskim. Dnevnik* (*Years of My Intimacy with Dostoevsky: A Diary*). Moscow: Sabashnikov, 1928.
Suslova left lengthy memoirs about her travels in 1864 with D. to France, Italy and Germany. She was D.'s secret lover for several months, and, according to him, turned out to be "a very egoistic woman" who betrayed him with a young Spanish student. Nevertheless, he proposed to marry her, though she refused.

Suvorin, A.S. "Nekrolog. Fyodor Mikhailovich Dostoevsky" ("In Memoriam: F.M. Dostoevsky"), *Khudozhestvennyi Zhurnal* (*Art Journal*) 2 (1881): 118–119.
Provides one of the most impressive reports about D.'s funeral, a magnificent event which gathered a huge procession of several tens of thousands of people and became the largest public gathering in Russia in the nineteenth century.

_____. "Vospominaniia" ("Memoirs"), *Poliarnaia Zvezda* (*The Polar Star*), February 1881: 139–143.
_____. *Dnevnik* (*The Diary*). Moscow–St. Petersburg: Frenkel, 1923, pp. 15–16, 212–213.
Alexei Suvorin, a leading journalist and publisher, visited D. quite often. During one of his meetings, he heard D. express a strong criticism of revolutionary terrorism, as well as his desire to support the existing government and the Tsar.

Teleshov, N. "Pamiatnik Pushkinu" ("A Monument to Pushkin"), in N. Teleshov. *Izbrannye Proizvedeniia* (*Selected Works*). Moscow, 1959, pp. 7–9.
Describes the feeling of pride among Russian students at the Pushkin Festival who heard D.'s speech.

Timofeeva, V. (O. Pochinkovskaia). "God raboty so znamenitym pisatelem. Posviashchaetsia pamiati Dostoevskogo" ("A Year of Work with a Famous

Writer: Dedicated to the Memory of Dostoevsky"), *Istoricheskii Vestnik* (*The History Herald*) 2 (1904): 488–542.

Varvara Timofeeva worked, as a deputy editor, with editor-in-chief D. at *The Citizen* for about a year. She provides important details about D.'s way of life, editorial work and everyday activity as well as on his journalistic and social polemics of the early 1870s. D. was very friendly toward his colleagues, but at the same time was an extremely hard-working and demanding editor.

Tokarzhevskii, Sh. "Dostoevsky v Omskoi katorge. Vospominaniia katorzhanina" ("Dostoevsky in the Omsk prison: Memoirs of a Convict") *Zvenia* (*Chains*), vol 6. Moscow, 1936, pp. 495–512.

Highly personal memoirs about meeting D. in prison in Siberia.

Tolstaya, A.A. *Perepiska grafa L.N. Tolstogo s grafinei A.A. Tolstoi. 1857–1903* ("Correspondence Between Count Leo Tolstoy and Countess A. Tolstaya, 1857–1903") St. Petersburg: Tolstoy Museum Press, 1911, pp. 25–26.

Alexandra Tolstaya was a distant aunt of Leo Tolstoy, who visited her repeatedly in St. Petersburg in 1878 and wrote her several letters in which he discussed his religious views. She presented these letters to D. in 1880 and wrote about this brief meeting with D. who was very critical of Tolstoy's philosophy.

Tretiakova, V.N. "Vospominaniia" ("Memoirs") in A.P. Botkina. *Pavel Mikhailovich Tretiakov v zhizni i iskusstve* ("Pavel Mikhailovich Tretiakov in His Life and His Art"). Moscow: Iskusstvo, 1960, pp. 237–241.

About art collector Tretiakov and his friendship with D.

Trutovsky, K.A. "Vospominaniia o Dostoevskom" ("Memoirs About Dostoevsky"), *Russkoe obozreniie* (*The Russian Review*) 1 (1893): 212–217.

Trutovsky was D.'s schoolmate at the Military Academy and was greatly influenced by him in the development of his artistic talent. D. gave Trutovsky a list of his favorite books and often discussed literature with him. Later, Trutovsky was invited by D. to join the Petrashevsky Circle, but by chance the young man missed their meeting and thus avoided arrest, trial and imprisonment in Siberia.

Uspensky, G.I. "Prazdnik Pushkina" ("Pushkin Festival"), in G.I. Uspensky, *Polnoe sobranie sochinenii* (*Complete Works*). Moscow: Academy Press, 1953, pp. 407–430.

Uspensky represented the major Russian literary journal *The Fatherland Notes* at the Pushkin celebrations in Moscow in 1880, and he gave an exciting account of the Pushkin speech made by D. In spite of his admiration of the great writer, Uspensky, as a representative of the Westernizers, was rather critical of D.'s speech.

Veinberg, P.I. "4-je aprelia 1866 goda. Iz moikh vospominanii." ("The Fourth of April, 1866: From My Memoirs") *Byloe* (*The Past*) 4 (1906): 299–300.

Veinberg comments on D.'s response to the assassination attempt on the Russian Tsar in 1866, when D. displayed himself as an ardent supporter of the monarchy.

_____. "Literaturnye spektakli (Iz moikh vospominanii)" ("Literary Spectacles: From My Memoirs"), in *Ezhegodnik Imperatorskikh Teatrov* (*Annual Review of Russian Royal Theaters*), Vol. 3, 1893–1894, pp. 96–107.

Veinberg describes D.'s passion for theater and his participation in the amateur performances which were very popular in St. Petersburg.

Vengerov, S.A. "Tchetyre vstrechi s Turgenevym" ("Four Meetings with Turgenev"), quoted in V. Rosenberg, "Tchetyre vstrechi s Turgenevym" ("Four Meetings with Turgenev"), *Biriutch Petrogradskikh Teatrov* (*Review of St. Petersburg Theaters*) 2 (1918): 43–44.
    Vengerov, a professor of Russian literature, had one of the best literary archives in Russia. As a student, he met Turgenev and D. at literary readings.

Viatkin, G. "Dostoevsky v Omskoi katorge" ("Dostoevsky in the Omsk Prison"), *Sibirskie Ogni* (*The Siberian Light*) 1 (1925): 179–180.
    Viatkin managed to discover new details about D.'s incarceration in Omsk prison in the 1840s.

Vrangel, A.E. *Vospominaniia o Dostoevskom v Sibiri* ("Memoirs About Dostoevsky in Siberia"). St. Petersburg, 1912.
    Vrangel recounts several years he spent in Siberia as a military prosecutor in Semipalatinsk, where D. served as a private and a junior officer. D. liked to be engaged in physical activities in his spare time—he liked to walk, to ride horses and to work in the garden—but his primary and favorite activity was reading literature. He read all the fiction books he had and created the plots of some of his future novels. Vrangel also tells about D.'s romance and marriage with Maria Isaeva.

Vuich I. "Dnevnik" ("Diary"), *Poriadok* (*The Order*) February 18, 1881: 48.
    In this controversial article Vuich claims that D. and other members of the Petrashevsky Circle were not sentenced to death, and that they supposedly knew beforehand that this sentence was changed by the Tsar to the mock execution at the Semyonovsky Parade Grounds, with different prison terms for the convicts. Colonel Vuich was one of the senior officers of the Royal Guard Regiment and knew only that information which was given to the officers of the execution squad; therefore, his account of the events contains many personal opinions and factual mistakes. Colonel Vuich probably did not know the original verdict of the secret military tribunal, which really existed and which is quoted in the work of Miller (1883), together with other documents. In spite of this misunderstanding of the events, Vuich presents a vivid and detailed account of D.'s near execution.

INDEX